WHAT EVERY VETERAN SHOULD KNOW
75th EDITION
BOOK PRICE - $23.00 – INCLUDES SHIPPING

This is the 75th Edition of the book "WHAT EVERY VETERAN SHOULD KNOW," a service officer's guide since 1937.

Monthly supplements are available from the publisher, which provide updates to the information contained in this book. A one-year subscription to the supplement service is $32.00.

The material herein covers veterans' benefits, rights, privileges, and services over which the Department of Veterans Affairs has jurisdiction. All references to "VA" pertain to the Department of Veterans Affairs. Revised and new laws passed by the 111th Congress as of December 31, 2010, are incorporated in this text.

This guide was prepared solely for convenient reference purposes, and does not have the effect of law. Although diligent effort has been made to ensure its accuracy, in the event of any conflict between this book and any regulation, the latter is, of course, controlling.

Veterans and the dependents of deceased veterans are advised to contact their local veterans organization service officers, or the nearest Veterans Administration Office, for help in completing any valid claim.

VETERANS INFORMATION SERVICE
P.O. Box 111
East Moline, Illinois 61244-0111
Telephone and Fax: (309) 757-7760
Email: help@vetsinfoservice.com
www.vetsinfoservice.com

ASK FOR YOUR **FREE** SAMPLE COPY OF THE
MONTHLY SUPPLEMENT,
DESIGNED TO KEEP THIS BOOK UP-TO-DATE.
ONE-YEAR SUPPLEMENT SERVICE: $32.00

W9-BUC-229

WHAT EVERY VETERAN SHOULD KNOW

VETERANS INFORMATION SERVICE
P.O. Box 111
East Moline, Illinois 61244-0111

Phone and Fax: (309) 757-7760
E-mail: help@vetsinfoservice.com
www.vetsinfoservice.com

═══════════════════════════════

A NOTE TO THE READER:

Revised and new laws passed by the 111th Congress as of December 31, 2010, are incorporated in the text of this book. Chapter 1 of the book contains a brief summary of some of the important legislative changes affecting veterans' benefits during 2010.

You will find a Table of Contents, listing the main subject headings. For your convenience there is also a complete index in the back of the book, as well as an Edge Index on the back cover.

We hope you enjoy this edition of **WHAT EVERY VETERAN SHOULD KNOW**. Any comments or suggestions for future improvements are welcome.

═══════════════════════════════

© 2011
What Every Veteran Should Know
Library of Congress Cataloging in Serials
ISSN 1532-8112
ISBN 0-9820586-2-4

Publisher:

Veterans Information Service
P.O. Box 111
East Moline, IL 61244-0111

TABLE OF CONTENTS

CHAPTER 1

2010 UPDATES

Following is a brief summary of some of the important legislative changes, as well as VA-policy changes, affecting veterans' benefits during 2010.

Veterans Emergency Care Fairness Act
Public Law 111-137
Became law February 1, 2010

Enables the Department of Veterans Affairs to reimburse qualified veterans enrolled in VA health care for the remaining cost of emergency treatment if the veteran has outside insurance that only covers part of the cost. Previously, VA could reimburse veterans or pay outside hospitals directly only if a qualified veteran had no outside health insurance.

In addition to reimbursing veterans for emergency care in the future, the bill allows the Secretary of Veterans Affairs to provide retroactive reimbursements for care received prior to the passage of this bill, and on or after July 19, 2001, if considered appropriate under the circumstances.

Public Law 111-156
Became law April 7, 2010

Expresses appreciation for the efforts of the Blinded Veterans Association in improving rehabilitation services, education, and benefits for blinded veterans. Supports the goals and ideals of Blinded Veterans Day, and calls upon the people of the United States to observe such Day.

TRICARE Affirmation Act
Public Law 111-159
Became law April 26, 2010

This law fixes a flaw in the recently passed healthcare reform law.

The Patient Protection and Affordable Care Act did not clarify that the earned coverage of TRICARE programs for service members and military retirees under age 65 provided minimum acceptable coverage. This law completes the TRICARE package so *all TRICARE plans are now considered, explicitly in law, as minimal acceptable coverage under the new health care law.*

Caregivers and Veterans Omnibus Health Services Act of 2010
Public Law 111-163
Became law May 5, 2010

This landmark bill establishes a permanent program to support the caregivers of wounded warriors, improve health care for veterans in rural areas, help VA adapt to the needs of women veterans, and expand supportive services for homeless veterans.

Providing for Family Caregivers:

- Fulfills VA's obligation to care for the nation's wounded veterans by providing their caregivers with training, counseling, supportive services, and a living stipend.

- Provides health care to the family caregivers of injured veterans under CHAMPVA.

- Requires independent oversight of the caregiver program.

Removing Barriers to Care for the Catastrophically Disabled:

- Eliminates copayments for veterans who are catastrophically disabled.

Expanding Health Care Services for Women Veterans:

- Requires VA to report to Congress on its comprehensive assessment of the barriers in providing health care to women veterans.

- Authorizes VA to provide health care to a newborn child of qualifying women veterans for up to 7 days after the birth of the child.

- Requires VA to train its mental health providers in the treatment of military sexual trauma.

- Mandates that VA implement pilot programs to provide child care to women veterans receiving medical care, and to provide readjustment services to women veterans.

Reaching Out to Rural Veterans:

- Expands VA's authority to provide incentives so that VA can recruit and retain high quality health care providers.

- Increases oversight of care purchased in the community by mandating financial incentives for providers who maintain high quality standards.

- Provides travel reimbursements for veterans receiving treatment at facilities of the Department of Veterans Affairs and grants for veterans service organizations transporting veterans residing in highly rural areas.

- Expands VA's telehealth program, and its ability to collaborate with the Indian Health Service and community organizations to provide medical services, including mental health care, in rural communities.

Improvements to Mental Health Care:

- Establishes and increases eligibility for Operation Enduring Freedom/Operation Iraqi Freedom servicemembers, including National Guard or Reserve, to receive readjustment counseling.

- Requires VA to conduct a study on veteran suicides.

Enhancements to VA Medical Services:

- Allows VA to disclose certain personal information in limited circumstances to an authorized surrogate or third party payer.

- Mandates improved quality controls at the facility, Veterans Integrated Service Network (VISN), and national levels.

- Requires VA to implement pilot programs to provide grants to community organizations assisting veterans in the transition from military service to civilian life.

- Mandates that VA payments to health care providers for CHAMPVA beneficiaries will now constitute full payment, eliminating any liabilities on the part of the beneficiary.

- Requires VA to contract with the Institute of Medicine of the National Academies to conduct an expanded study on the health impact of Project SHAD.

- Authorizes VA to provide care to veterans with traumatic brain injury through contracts with non-VA providers when necessary.

- Requires VA to carry out a pilot program to determine the feasibility and advisability of providing dental insurance to veterans.

Improvements to the VA Department Personnel:

- Gives the Secretary greater discretion in determining compensation for health care workers and executives so that VA can compete effectively with private employers.

- Improves transparency in VA's methods of computing locality pay scales and ensures patient safety by limiting the use of mandatory overtime for nurses.

- Expands loan repayment programs.

Programs to Enhance Services for Homeless Veterans:

- Authorizes the VA to make per-diem payments to more organizations that meet criteria to receive such payments under the Grant and Per Diem Program.

Increased Focus on Research:

- Authorizes the creation of VA multi-medical center nonprofit research and education corporations.

- Enhances the abilities of VA nonprofit research and education corporations to administer and transfer funds to VA.

- Improves VA's ability to oversee VA-affiliated nonprofit research and education corporations.

Construction Projects:

- Authorizes six different construction projects in the states of California, Kentucky, Texas, Missouri, Colorado, and Florida.

- Renames VA medical facilities in Montana, Tennessee, and Minnesota.

Prioritization of Safety on VA Grounds:

- Allows VA police officers to enforce local and Federal laws and conduct investigations into acts occurring on Department property.

Public Law 111-164
Became law May 7, 2010

Designates the Department of Veterans Affairs blind rehabilitation center in Long Beach, CA as the "Major Charles Robert Soltes, Jr., O.D. Department of Veterans Affairs Blind Rehabilitation Center."

Veterans' Compensation Cost-of–Living Adjustment Act of 2010
Public Law 111-247
Became law September 30, 2010

Directs that the cost-of-living adjustments to VA compensation and pension benefits be paid based on the Social Security Administration (SSA) COLA. By statue, compensation COLA may not be more than the SSA COLA; and pension COLA is equal to the SSA COLA.

*This year SSA did not increase COLA, therefore there is **no** COLA for 2011.*

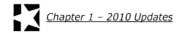

Public Law 111-246
Became law September 30, 2010

Enables State homes to furnish nursing home care to parents whose children died while serving in the Armed Forces.

Veterans' Benefits Act of 2010
Public Law 111-275
Became law October 13, 2010

Employment, Small Business, and Education Matters:

- Extends the authority for work-study as part of the Veterans' Educational Assistance Program (VEAP) provided through the VA thru June 30, 2013. The extension allows for veteran students to complete work study in congressional offices, state veteran agencies, or any position working jointly between the VA and an institution of higher learning.

- Reauthorizes the Veterans' Advisory Committee on Education.

- Requires the Secretary of the VA to verify small business ownership and operate a database of veteran-owned small businesses and service-connected veteran-owned small business in an effort to end contracting with businesses that fraudulently claim to be owned by a veteran.

- Increases job opportunities for veterans by reimbursing energy employers for the cost of providing on-the-job training for veterans in the energy sector. Specifically, the bill would create the pilot "Veterans Energy Related Employment Program" which would award competitive grants to three states that are able to serve a population of eligible veterans, boast a diverse energy industry, and have the ability to carry out such a training program.

Housing and Homelessness Matters:

- Reauthorizes the Homeless Veterans Reintegration Program through fiscal year 2011.

- Authorizes an additional $1 million to provide dedicated services for homeless women veterans and homeless veterans with children. Grants would be made available to provide job training, counseling, placement services, and child care services to expedite the reintegration of veterans into the labor force.

Servicemembers Civil Relief Act Matters:

- Amends the Servicemembers Civil Relief Act (SCRA) to prohibit lessors from charging early termination fees with respect to residential, business, agricultural, or motor vehicle leases entered into by servicemembers who subsequently enter military service or receive orders for a permanent change of station or deployment in support of a military operation.

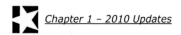

- Allows a servicemember to terminate a contract for cellular or home telephone service at any time after receiving military orders to deploy for at least 90 days to a location that does not support the contract. Requires the return of any advance payments made by a deploying servicemember under such a contract.

- Allows the Attorney General to bring a civil suit against any violator of the SCRA. Also gives servicemembers a "private right of action" to file their own lawsuits against those who violate their legal rights.

Insurance Matters:

- Increases the Supplemental Service-Disabled Life Insurance for totally disabled veterans, effective October 1, 2011 from $20,000 to $30,000.

- Extends, for those separated or released on or after June 15, 2005, the termination of SGLI coverage for totally disabled veterans to two years after their separation or release from active duty or active duty for training of at least 30 days.

- Limits the duration of a dependent's coverage under SGLI to 120 days after the member's separation or release from service or assignment.

- Allows veterans to increase Veterans' Group Life Insurance (VGLI) coverage by $25,000, to a maximum of $400,000, every five years until reaching age 60.

- Eliminates an authorized reduction in the amount of SGLI or VGLI received as an accelerated death benefit by a terminally-ill insured.

- Permits the VA to distinguish, in specifying payments for qualifying SGLI traumatic injury losses, between the severity of a qualifying loss of a dominant hand and a nondominant hand.

- Increases the maximum loan guarantee amount under the Veterans' Mortgage Life Insurance program from $90,000 to $150,000, effective October 1, 2011. The maximum benefit will subsequently increase to $200,000 on January 1, 2012.

- Retroactively expands traumatic injury protection coverage under SGLI (called TSGLI) to include veterans who incurred qualifying traumatic injuries on or after October 7, 2001, but before December 1, 2005, regardless of where the injuries occurred.

Burial and Cemetery Matters:

- Increases burial and funeral benefits and plot allowances for veterans who are eligible for a burial at a national cemetery, or who died in a VA facility from $300 to $700, effective October 1, 2011.

- Allows a parent whose child gave their life in service to our country to be buried in a national cemetery with that child when their veteran child has no living spouse or children.

Compensation and Pension:

- Authorizes higher levels of veterans' disability compensation for certain veterans who experience difficulty using prostheses after the loss of hands, arms, or legs and those in need of regular aid and attendance from residuals of traumatic brain injury.

- Establishes an annual cost-of-living adjustment, based on increases in amounts payable under title II (Old Age, Survivors and Disability Insurance) of the Social Security Act, for the temporary payment of dependency and indemnity compensation (DIC) to a veteran's surviving spouse with one or more children under the age of 18.

- Requires the payment of DIC to the survivors of former prisoners-of-war (POWs) who died on or before September 30, 1999, on the same basis as survivors of former POWs who die after such date.

- Excludes monetary payments from a state or municipality as a veterans' benefit due to injury or disease from consideration as income for purposes of pension benefits paid by the Secretary.

- Requires that, in the case of a veteran who is retired or separated from active duty due to a catastrophic disability, payment of VA disability benefits based on an original claim shall be made on the date the award becomes effective (thereby eliminating certain procedural delays in such payments).

- Makes limitations to pension payable to certain children of veterans of a period of war the same as those applied to a veteran having neither spouse nor child.

- Extends through May 31, 2015, the expiration date for the reduction of VA pensions for certain beneficiaries with no dependents who are covered by Medicaid plans for services furnished by nursing facilities.

Benefit Matters:

- Increases the Automobile and Special Adaptive Equipment Grant effective October 1, 2011, from $11,000 to $18,900. Also requires that this amount be adjusted annually by the percentage increase in the Consumer Price Index.

- Increases from 2,600 to 2,700 per year the number of veterans who may enroll in a VA program of independent living services and assistance.

- Authorizes the VA to provide automobile and adaptive equipment assistance to disabled veterans and veterans with severe burn injuries.

- Requires: (1) the Secretary to enter into an agreement with the Institute of Medicine of the National Academy of Sciences (NAS) to conduct a comprehensive review of best treatments for chronic multisymptom illness

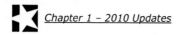

in Persian Gulf War veterans; and (2) the Institute to report review results to the Secretary and the veterans committees.

- Amends the Persian Gulf War Veterans Act of 1998 to: (1) extend until October 1, 2015, an NAS review and evaluation concerning associations between illnesses and exposure of Gulf War veterans to toxic agents, environmental or wartime hazards, or preventive medicines or vaccines; (2) require such review and evaluation to include service in any post-9/11 global theater of operations; and (3) require review and evaluation results to be listed separately for Gulf War service and post-9/11 service. Amends the Veterans Programs Enhancement Act of 1998 to: (1) extend until October 1, 2018, an NAS report on the health effects of such exposure; and (2) make the same service inclusion and separate listing requirements as above.

- Extends through 2011 VA authority to operate a regional office in the Republic of the Philippines. Requires a report from the CG to the veterans committees on office activities, as well as the costs and benefits of maintaining such office there in lieu of the United States.

- Extends through 2014 a report from the Secretary to Congress on cases of equitable relief in the disposition of veterans' benefits necessitated by VA administrative error.

- Amends the Veterans Benefits Act of 2003 to extend through 2012 VA authority for the performance of medical disability evaluations by contract physicians.

Public Law 111-339
Became law December 22, 2010

Directs the Secretary of the Army to submit to the congressional defense, homeland security, and veterans committees an accounting of the gravesites at Arlington National Cemetery, including, among other things, whether such gravesites are correctly identified, labeled, and occupied.

Helping Heroes Keep Their Homes Act of 2010
Public law 111-346
Became law December 29, 2010

Extends enhanced protections for service members relating to mortgages and mortgage foreclosures through December 31, 2012. (These provisions had been set to expire December 31, 2010.)

Veterans Educational Assistance Improvements Act of 2010
Public Law 111-377
Became law January 4, 2011

Effective August 1, 2009, but not payable until October 1, 2011:

- Certain National Guard members mobilized on Title 32 orders on-or-after September 11, 2001 are now eligible for the Post-9/11 GI Bill and any qualifying Title 32 mobilization may be used to increase his or her percentage of eligibility.

Effective March 5, 2011:

- Limits active duty members to the net cost for tuition and fees prorated based on the eligibility tiers (40%-100%) previously established for Veterans. (Same limitations apply to transferee spouses of active duty servicemembers.)

Effective August 1, 2011:

- The Post-9/11 GI Bill will now pay all public school in-state tuition and fees; this includes graduate training, etc.

- For students attending private institutions of higher learning or foreign schools, the tuition and fee reimbursement is capped at the lesser of net out-of-pocket cost or $17,500 annually - however the Yellow Ribbon Program still exists.

- MGIB-AD & MGIB-SR College fund payments will now be paid on a monthly basis instead of a lump-sum at the beginning of the term.

- Reimbursement is now available for multiple Licensing and Certification Tests.

- Reimbursement is now available for fees paid to take national examinations used for admission to an institution of higher learning (e.g. SAT, LSAT, ACT, GMAT, etc).

- Vocational Rehabilitation participants may now elect the higher housing allowance offered by the Post-9/11 GI Bill if otherwise eligible for the Post-9/11 GI Bill.

- If training at greater than ½ time the housing allowance is now prorated according to the training time the individual is enrolled (rounded to the nearest tenth). So, if a student's full housing allowance is $1000, and he or she is attending ¾ time - the housing allowance would be $800 (80% of $1000).

- Break or interval pay is no longer payable under any VA education benefit program unless under an Executive Order of the President or due to an emergency situation such as a natural disaster or strike. Entitlement which

9

previously would have been used for break pay will be available for use during a future enrollment.

This means that if the semester ends December 15, the housing allowance is paid for the first 15 days of December only. Benefits will begin again when the new semester begins (e.g. January 15), and the student will be paid for the remaining days of that month and term.

Students using other VA education programs are included in this change. Monthly benefits will be prorated in the same manner.

- NOAA and PHS personnel are now eligible to transfer their entitlement to eligible dependents

Effective October 1, 2011:

- If a student is training at greater than ½ time, his or her housing allowance is now prorated according to the training time he or she is enrolled. For example, if full housing allowance for is $1000, and the student is attending ¾ time - the housing allowance would be $750 (¾ of $1000)

- Housing allowance is now payable to students enrolled solely in distance learning. The housing allowance is ½ the national average BAH for an E-5 with dependents (the rate would be $673.50 for 2011).

- Non-college degree programs, on-the-job training, and flight training programs are now covered under the Post-9/11 GI Bill.

- The book stipend is now payable to active duty members.

Ike Skelton National Defense Authorization Act for Fiscal Year 2011
Public Law 111-383
Became law January 7, 2011

- Approves a 1.4% military pay raise.

- Extends for 1 year (through September 30, 2011) the prohibition on increasing the premium and copayment for TRICARE Prime, charges for inpatient care in civilian hospitals under TRICARE Standard, and cost sharing requirements for drugs provided through the TRICARE retail pharmacy.

- TRICARE-26, Extends health care eligibility to adult dependent children to age 26, requires premium for their coverage.

- Clarifies that the Secretary of Defense has sole jurisdiction over the administration of military health care/TRICARE — no other department or agency involved.

- Authorizes combat benefits for service members and their survivors of those killed or wounded at Fort Hood shooting.

* Directs DoD to pay retired annuities on the first day of the month, thus eliminating delayed payments when paydays fall on weekends.

New Hotline for Homeless Veterans

In March 2010, VA announced a new hotline for homeless veterans – 1-877-4AID VET (1-877-424-2838).

Well trained expert responders will staff the hotline 24 hours a day, seven days a week. Responders can provide emergency support and resources to homeless veterans, as well as family members, community agencies and non-VA providers.

Medication Copay Increases for Priority Groups 7 and 8

Effective July 1, 2010, the medication copay increased from $8 to $9 for veterans in Priority Groups 7 and 8.

Bronze Medallions Available for Headstones or Markers

VA made available a new medallion to be affixed to an existing privately purchased headstone or marker to signify the deceased's status as a veteran.

If requested, the medallion will be furnished in lieu of a traditional Government headstone or marker for veterans that died on or after November 1, 1990, and whose grave is marked with a privately purchased headstone or marker.

The medallion is currently available in three sizes, 5 inches, 3 inches, and 1 ½ inches. Each medallion will be inscribed with the word VETERAN across the top and the Branch of Service at the bottom. Appropriate affixing adhesive, instructions and hardware will be provided with the medallion.

Important: This benefit is only applicable if the grave is marked with a privately purchased headstone or marker. In these instances, eligible veterans are entitled to either a traditional Government-furnished headstone or marker, or the new medallion, but not both.

VA Simplifies Access To Health Care And Benefits For Veterans With PTSD

In July 2010, VA simplified the process for a veteran to claim service connection for PTSD. VA reduced the evidence needed if the trauma claimed by a veteran is related to "fear of hostile military or terrorist activity," and is consistent with the places, types, and circumstances of the veteran's service.

Previously, unless the veteran was a combat veteran, claims adjudicators were required to corroborate that a non-combat veteran actually experienced a stressor related to hostile military activity.

The new rule will apply to claims:

- Received by VA on or after July 13, 2010;
- Received before July 13, 2010 but not yet decided by a VA regional office;
- Appealed to the Board of Veterans' Appeals on or after July 13, 2010;
- Appealed to the Board before July 13, 2010, but not yet decided by the Board; and
- Pending before VA on or after July 13, 2010, because the Court of Appeals for Veterans Claims vacated a Board decision and remanded for re-adjudication.

VA Issues List of Ships with Agent Orange Exposure

In 2010, the Department of Veterans Affairs Compensation and Pension (C&P) Service initiated a program to collect data on Vietnam naval operations for the purpose of providing regional offices with information to assist with development of claims based on herbicide exposure from Navy Veterans.

To date, the Department of Veterans Affairs (VA) has received verification from various sources showing that a number of offshore "blue water naval vessels conducted operations on the inland "brown water rivers and delta areas of Vietnam. The VA also has identified certain vessel types that operated primarily or exclusively on the inland waterways.

If a Veteran's service aboard one of these ships can be confirmed through military records during the time frames specified, then exposure to herbicide agents can be presumed without further development.

Refer to Chapter 24 for a comprehensive, up-to-date list of the identified vessels.

VA Recognizes "Presumptive" Illnesses In Iraq, Afghanistan

In late 2010, VA the VA established new presumptions of service connection for nine specific infectious diseases associated with military service in Southwest Asia beginning on or after the start of the first Gulf War on August 2, 1990, through the conflict in Iraq and on or after September 19, 2001, in Afghanistan.

The nine disease are:

- Brucellosis,
- Campylobacter jejuni,
- Coxiella burnetii (Q fever),
- Malaria,
- Mycobacterium tuberculosis,
- Nontyphoid Salmonella,
- Shigella,
- Visceral leishmaniasis and
- West Nile virus.

A veteran now only has to show service in Southwest Asia or Afghanistan and that he or she had one of the nine diseases within a certain time after service, and has a current disability as a result of that disease, subject to certain time limits for seven of the diseases.

CHAPTER 2

PERIODS OF WAR

Indian Wars:
The period January 1, 1817 through December 31, 1898. Service must have been rendered with the United States military forces against Indian tribes or nations.

Spanish-American War:
The period April 21, 1898 through July 4, 1902. In the case of a veteran who served with the United States military forces engaged in hostilities in the Moro Province the ending date is July 15, 1903.

Mexican Border Period:
The period May 9, 1916 through April 5, 1917, in the case of a veteran who during such period served in Mexico, on the borders thereof, or in the waters adjacent thereto.

World War I:
The period April 6, 1917, through November 11, 1918. In the case of a veteran who served with the United States military forces in Russia, the ending date is April 1, 1920. Service after November 11, 1918 and before July 2, 1921 is considered World War I for compensation or pension purposes, if the veteran served in the active military, naval, or air service after April 5, 1917 and before November 12, 1918.

World War II:
The period December 7, 1941through December 31, 1946. If the veteran was in service on December 31, 1946, continuous service before July 26, 1947 is considered World War II service.

Korean Conflict:
The period June 27, 1950 through January 31, 1955.

Vietnam Era:
The period August 5, 1964 (February 28, 1961 for Veterans who served "in country" before August 5, 1964), and ending May 7, 1975.

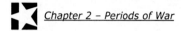

Persian Gulf War:

The period August 2, 1990 through a date to be set by law or Presidential Proclamation.

Future Dates:

The period beginning on the date of any future declaration of war by the Congress, and ending on a date prescribed by Presidential Proclamation or concurrent resolution of the Congress. (Title U.S.C. 101)

CHAPTER 3

DISABILITY COMPENSATION
FOR SERVICE-CONNECTED DISABILITIES
(TITLE 38, CHAPTER 11)

BENEFIT DESCRIPTION

In grateful recognition of their dedication and sacrifice, the United States, through the Veterans Administration has provided its former servicemen and women with compensation and pension programs designed to assist disabled veterans and their dependents. The disability compensation program provides financial assistance to veterans with service-connected disabilities to compensate them for the loss of, or reduction in earning power resulting from comparable injuries and disease in civil life.

Disability compensation payments vary in amount, depending on the impairment of earning capacity suffered by the veteran. The degree is assessed in multiples of 10, from 10 percent to 100 percent, with special statutory rates for such disabilities as blindness and loss of use of limbs.

> *Disability compensation payments vary in amount, depending on the impairment of earning capacity suffered by the veteran. The degree is assessed in multiples of 10, from 10 percent to 100 percent, with special statutory rates for such disabilities as blindness and loss of use of limbs.*

The VA shall adopt and apply a schedule of ratings in reductions in earning capacity from specific injuries or combination of injuries. The rating shall be based, as far as practicable, upon the average impairments of earning capacity resulting from such injuries in civil occupations. The Administrator shall from time to time readjust this schedule or ratings in accordance with experience. The rates of compensation payments are not automatically adjusted for inflation, and they can be increased only if Congress passes specific enabling legislation. However, almost without exception, each Congress has acted to grant an increase equal to the consumer price index or the cost-of-living formula that determines the social security old-age increase.

If a veteran is evaluated as having a service-connected disability of 30 percent or more, the veteran is entitled to additional allowances for his or her dependents. In addition, in cases where a veteran has suffered certain severe disabilities, the veteran may be entitled to *special monthly compensation* (SMC), which can provide compensation payments at a rate much greater than the 100 percent rate. Severely disabled veterans in need of regular aid and attendance, or daily health-care services may be eligible for additional compensation.

WAR TIME DISABILITY COMPENSATION

ELIGIBILITY

A veteran may be entitled to VA disability compensation for any medical condition or injury that was incurred in, or aggravated by his or her military service. The veteran must have been discharged or released under conditions other than dishonorable from the period of service in which the injury or disease was incurred or aggravated.

> *There is no time limit for applying for VA disability compensation. However, veterans are encouraged to apply within one year of release from active duty. If a claim is filed within this period, entitlement may be established retroactively to the date of separation from service. If a claim is filed beyond one year of release from active duty, the effective date of eligibility for benefits will be based upon the date of the claim, not the date of separation.*

No compensation shall be paid if the disability is a result of the person's own willful misconduct or abuse of alcohol or drugs.

There is no time limit for applying for VA disability compensation. However, veterans are encouraged to apply within one year of release from active duty. If a claim is filed within this period, entitlement may be established retroactively to the date of separation from service. If a claim is filed beyond one year of release from active duty, the effective date of eligibility for benefits will be based upon the date of the claim, not the date of separation.

INDIVIDUAL UNEMPLOYABILITY

There is a benefit administered by the U.S. Department of Veterans Affairs (VA) that is payable under certain conditions when a veteran has one or more service connected disabilities rated less than 100% that interfere with his or her ability to secure or retain employment. This benefit is known as Individual Unemployability (I.U.). I.U. must be established on a factual basis.

I.U. establishes entitlement to compensation at the 100% disability rate even though a veteran's combined disabilities are less than a scheduler 100% rating.

To apply for I.U. benefits VA form 21-8940, Application for Increased Compensation Based on Unemployability, must be submitted to the VA with current medical evidence on the extent of the service connected disabilities.

When an application for I.U. benefits is received by the VA, VA must first decide whether the veteran meets the requirements for a scheduler 100% rating before considering I.U.

The scheduler requirements for I.U. benefits are provided in the Code of Federal Regulations (38 CFR 4.16), which states in essence, that total disability ratings for compensation may be assigned when there is one disability rated at 60% or more, or two or more disabilities combined at 70% or more, with at least one of the combined disabilities rated at least 40%.

In addition, for the purpose of one 60% disability, or one 40% disability in the case of combined disabilities, the following will be considered one disability:

- Disabilities of one or both upper or lower extremities, including the bilateral factor if applicable.
- Disabilities resulting from common etiology or a single accident
- Disabilities affecting a single body system, such as, orthopedic, digestive, respiratory, cardiovascular-renal, neuropsychiatric
- Multiple injuries incurred in action
- Multiple disabilities incurred as a Prisoner of War (POW)

When considering I.U., the VA looks at the following evidence:

- Current degree of service connected disability
- Employment status
- Results of VA examination(s)
- Hospital reports and/or outpatient treatment records
- Current physical and mental status
- Nature of employment
- Reason employment was terminated
- Whether disabilities meet scheduler consideration (38 CFR 4.16)
- Whether Extra Scheduler consideration is warranted (38 CFR 3.321(b)(1)

In addition, VA will take in to consideration the veteran's previous type of occupation (such as physical or non physical) and his or her level of formal education.

Factors that may not be taken in to account when considering I.U. are:

- Age
- Non service connected (NSC) disabilities
- Injuries occurring after military service
- Availability of work

In certain situations where a veteran does not meet the percentage standards under 38 CFR 4.16 for scheduler consideration of I.U but the evidence supports that the veteran is unemployable due to his or her service connected conditions, VA rating boards may submit to the Director of Compensation and Pension Service for an Extra Scheduler consideration.

Once an I.U. rating is granted, VA will pay service connected compensation at the 100% rate.

Receipt of I.U. benefits does not mean that a veteran is never allowed to work again; however, if a veteran receiving I.U. benefits obtains substantially gainful employment, I.U. benefits can be terminated.

VA's definition of substantial gainful employment is basically any amount earned above the annual poverty limit for one person set by the U.S. Census Bureau. In 2007 the poverty limit for one person was $10,210.

Amounts earned below the Census Bureau annual poverty limit are considered marginal employment and do not affect receipt of I.U. benefits.

Each year after the U.S. Census Bureau sets the new poverty limit, VA publishes notice in the Federal Register.

Other Benefits or Payments That May Affect VA Disability Compensation

By law, receipt of certain types of military pay may affect an individual's eligibility for VA Disability Compensation. Following are the categories of pay that may affect eligibility:

VA Pension Benefits

Occasionally, a veteran may be entitled to both VA Compensation benefits, and VA Pension benefits. The VA is prohibited from paying both benefits concurrently. In the event a veteran is entitled to both, he or she must elect to receive one benefit or the other. This election prevails, even if the option paying a lower benefit is chosen, and even if the election reduces the benefits payable to his or her dependents.

Selected Reserve and National Guard

Since September 11, 2001, numerous members of the Armed Forces Reserves have been called to active duty. Some of these individuals had already filed claims for VA compensation, based on earlier periods of active service. In September 2004, the VA General Counsel issued a precedent opinion that discussed the effect of a return to active service on a pending disability compensation claim.

In general, a veteran's return to active duty does not affect his or her claim for VA benefits, and does not alter either the veteran's right or the VA's duty to develop and adjudicate the claim. If the veteran is temporarily unable to report for a medical examination, or take some other required action because of his or her return to active duty, the VA must defer processing the claim until the veteran can take the required action. The VA cannot deny a claim because a veteran is temporarily unavailable due to a return to active duty.

A veteran is not entitled to receive both active duty pay and VA disability compensation for the same period of time. However, he or she is permitted to elect the higher benefit. If a veteran with a pending claim dies on active duty before the claim is decided, an eligible survivor may be entitled to any accrued benefits payable.

Military Retired Pay

Historically, veterans were not permitted to receive **full** military retirement pay and VA compensation benefits at the same time. Veterans who were entitled to both had to either elect one of the benefits, or waive the amount of retirement pay which equaled the amount of VA disability compensation to which he or she was entitled. (This issue was commonly known as "concurrent receipt".)

> *Since this type of rule against "concurrent receipt" does not apply to any other group of federal or state retirees, many individuals and service organizations felt this was unfair discrimination against disabled military retirees.*
>
> *This has been a very hot topic for the last several years, and Congress and the President have taken several steps toward eliminating the bar to concurrent receipt of full military retired pay and full disability compensation.*

Because there was often a tax advantage to receive VA disability compensation, which is tax free, rather than military retirement pay, most disabled retirees chose to have a $1 reduction in their retired pay for each $1 of VA disability compensation they received.

Since this type of rule against "concurrent receipt" does not apply to any other group of federal or state retirees, many individuals and service organizations felt this was unfair discrimination against disabled military retirees.

This has been a very hot topic for the last several years, and Congress and the President have taken several steps toward eliminating the bar to concurrent receipt of full military retired pay and full disability compensation.

Following is a summary of the steps taken from 1999 to the present.

Special Compensation for Severely Disabled Length of Service Military Retirees

Section 658 of the National Defense Authorization Act for Fiscal Year 1999, Public Law 106-65, dated October 5, 1999, and (Title 10 U.S.C.1413) provided a "special compensation" for severely disabled length of service retirees of the Uniformed Services. This benefit was administered by the Department of Defense (DoD). The "special compensation" was paid to retirees with at least 20 years of regular service, who incurred VA disability ratings of 60% or higher within 4 years after retiring. (Payments ranged from $50 per month to $325 per month.)

This "special compensation" was repealed as of January 1, 2004, since the first increment of concurrent receipt (described below) is bigger than the "special compensation" for all recipients.

National Defense Authorization Act for Fiscal Year 2003

The National Defense Authorization Act for *Fiscal Year 2003* instituted a program called **Combat-Related Special Compensation (CRSC)**, which became effective with benefits payable June 1, 2003. Under the CRSC program, a new, tax-free, special compensation benefit was made available to the following military retirees:

- Veterans rated at least 10% disabled due to a combat wound for which they received the Purple Heart; or
- Veterans rated at least 60% disabled, and the disability was directly attributed to combat situations, combat-related training, hazardous duty, or instrumentalities of war.

Details Of CRSC Payments

- CRSC payments will be in the amount of the VA disability compensation paid for whatever percentage of the member's disability rating is due to combat-related disabilities, as determined by the parent service.
- Retirees must apply to their parent service for CRSC payments.
- There is no phase-in period for CRSC.
- CRSC is not subject to taxation.
- Individuals must apply for CRSC. For detailed information, individuals should contact the following:

ARMY:
DEPARTMENT OF THE ARMY
U.S. Army Physical Disabilities Agency/
Combat Related Special Compensation (CRSC)
200 Stovall Street
Alexandria, VA 22332-0470
(866) 281-3254

NAVY AND MARINE CORPS:
Department of Navy Naval Council of Personnel Boards
Combat-Related Special Compensation Branch
720 Kennon Street S.E., Suite 309
Washington Navy Yard, DC 20374-5023
(877) 366-2772

AIR FORCE:
United States Air Force Personnel Center Disability Division (CRSC)
550 C Street West, Suite 6
Randolph AFB TX 78150-4708
(866)229-7074

National Defense Authorization Act for Fiscal Year 2004

The National Defense Authorization Act for Fiscal Year 2004 further authorized that:

- Beginning January 1, 2004, all retirees with at least 20 years of service and VA disability ratings of 50% or higher began having their military retired pay offsets phased out over a ten-year period. (This is referred to as **Concurrent Receipt** throughout the remainder of this section.)

- The Combat Related Special Compensation (CRSC) (as outlined above) was expanded to include all combat-or-operations-related disabilities (from 10% to 100% ratings), effective January 1, 2004. In effect, this fully eliminated the offset to retired pay for any combat-or-operations-related disability.

In both of the above cases, Guard and Reserve retirees with 20 qualifying years of service (including those with less than 7,200 retirement points) were considered eligible.

Details Of Concurrent Receipt

For those retirees eligible for concurrent receipt (50% - 100%), there is to be a ten-year phase-out of the disability offset. For 2004, qualifying retirees should have seen their retired pay increase by a flat monthly amount for these ratings:

Disability Rating	Amount Of Monthly Increase
100%	$750
90%	$500
80%	$350
70%	$250
60%	$125
50%	$100

The remaining retired pay offset is then to be phased out over the following nine years:

Year	Remaining Offset To Be Reduced By
2005	10%
2006	20%
2007	30%
2008	40%
2009	50%
2010	60%
2011	70%
2012	80%
2013	90%
2014	100%

By January 2014, disabled retirees with 50% and higher ratings were entitled to full concurrent receipt of military retired pay and VA disability compensation.

Because Concurrent Receipt is the restoration of retired pay, it is thus subject to the same tax provisions as a veteran's retired pay. If an individual's retired pay is taxable, concurrent receipt payments are taxable. If an individual's retired pay is non-taxable, concurrent receipt payments are to be non-taxable.

The changes approved in the 2005 NDAA did not apply to retirees who were rated 100 percent disabled because they are Individually Unemployable (IU) due to a service-connected disability.

However, the 2006 NDAA reduced the phase-in time from 10 years to 5 years for these individuals.

Concurrent Receipt is automatic. If you qualify you will automatically see an increase in your monthly retirement check.

National Defense Authorization Act of 2005:

The National Defense Authorization Act of 2005 eliminated the 9 year phase-in for full concurrent receipt payments to eligible retirees rated at 100% disabled by the VA, as of January 1, 2005. However the 9-year phase-in schedule *is* still in effect for retirees with disabilities rated at 50% to 90%, and, at that time, *was* still in effect for retirees who are rated 100 percent disabled because they are Individually Unemployable (IU) due to a service-connected disability.

National Defense Authorization Act of 2006:

The National Defense Authorization Act of 2006 reduced the phase-in time for full concurrent-receipt payments from 10 years to five years, for retirees who are rated 100 percent disabled because they are Individually Unemployable (IU) due to a service-connected disability.

2008 UPDATE:
The National Defense Authorization Act of 2008 directed that ALL retirees who were rated by the Department of Veterans Affairs (DVA) as unemployable, and are in receipt of DVA disability compensation as a result of IU, will become eligible to receive full concurrent receipt of both their DVA compensation and Retired Pay. This section of the Act is effective October 1, 2008 and is retroactive to January 1, 2005.

2008 UPDATE:
National Defense Authorization act of 2008:
Up to this point, excluded from eligibility were reservists and those who were medically retired under Chapter 61 of Title 10 prior to completing 20 years of service. Section 641 of the National Defense Authorization Act of 2008 expanded CRSC eligibility to include all service members eligible for retired pay, to include those retired under Chapter 61 and almost all reserve retirees. It excludes reservists who retire under a special provision (10 USC 12731b), which allows reservists with a physical disability not incurred in the line of duty to retire with between 15 and 19 creditable years of reserve service.

What If A Retiree Is Eligible For Both The CRSC And Concurrent Receipt Programs?

Retirees eligible for both programs will be able to make an election between the two programs, depending on which one is more advantageous.

Because the CRSC program provides full payment immediately, versus the 10—year phase in for concurrent receipt, the election can be changed each year. (This recognizes that a retiree who is 100% disabled, but only 60% of that is due to combat-related conditions, may find it advantageous to elect full CRSC payments for a few years until the concurrent receipt payment rises to a level that exceeds the CRSC payment. Because CRSC payments are tax-free, and non-disability retired pay is not, this could also figure into a retiree's election decision.)

BENEFIT RATES FOR SERVICE-CONNECTED DISABILITY COMPENSATION

VA compensation and pension benefits cost of living allowance (COLA) is paid based on the Social Security Administration (SSA) COLA. By statue, compensation COLA may not be more than the SSA COLA; and pension COLA is equal to the SSA COLA.

This year SSA did not increase COLA. Therefore, there will be no COLA for 2011.

Basic Rates of Disability Compensation – Rates Effective December 1, 2008:		
Title 38, USC 1114 subsection:	**Disability Rating**	**Monthly Benefit**
(a)	10 percent	$ 123.00
(b)	20 percent	243.00
(c)	30 percent	376.00
(d)	40 percent	541.00
(e)	50 percent	770.00
(f)	60 percent	974.00
(g)	70 percent	1228.00
(h)	80 percent	1427.00
(i)	90 percent	1604.00
(j)	100 percent	2673.00

Detailed Rates of Disability Compensation – Rates Effective December 1, 2008:										
DEPEN-DENT STATUS	**DISABILITY RATING**									
	10%	20%	30%	40%	50%	60%	70%	80%	90%	100%
Veteran Alone	$123	$230	$376	$541	$770	$974	$1228	$1427	$1604	$2673
Veteran & Spouse	123	230	421	601	845	1064	1333	1547	1739	2823
Veteran & Spouse & 1 Child	123	230	453	644	899	1129	1409	1634	1837	2932
Veteran & No Spouse & 1 Child	123	230	406	581	820	1034	1298	1507	1694	2774

Detailed Rates of Disability Compensation –
(Continued from previous page)
Rates Effective December 1, 2008

DEPEN-DENT STATUS	DISABILITY RATING									
	10%	20%	30%	40%	50%	60%	70%	80%	90%	100%
Veteran & Spouse & No Children & 1 Parent	123	243	457	649	905	1136	1417	1643	1847	2943
Veteran & Spouse & 1 Child & 1 Parent	123	243	489	692	959	1201	1493	1730	1945	3052
Veteran & Spouse & No Children & 2 Parents	123	243	493	697	965	1208	1501	1739	1955	3063
Veteran & Spouse & 1 Child & 2 Parents	123	243	525	740	1019	1273	1577	1826	2053	3172
Veteran & No Spouse & No Children & 1 Parent	123	243	412	589	830	1046	1312	1523	1712	2793
Veteran & No Spouse & 1 Child & 1 Parent	123	243	442	629	880	1106	1382	1603	1802	2894
Veteran & No Spouse & No Children & 2 Parents	123	243	448	637	890	1118	1396	1619	1820	2913
Veteran & No Spouse & 1 Child & 2 Parents	123	243	478	677	940	1178	1466	1699	1910	3014

Additional Amount Payable For Spouse
Requiring Aid & Attendance
(Rates Effective December 1, 2008)

Disability Rating	30%	40%	50%	60%	70%	80%	90%	100%
Monthly Benefit	$40	$54	$68	$81	$95	$108	$122	$136

Additional Amount Payable For Each Additional Child Under Age 18 (Rates Effective December 1, 2008)								
Disability Rating	30%	40%	50%	60%	70%	80%	90%	100%
Monthly Benefit	$22	$30	$37	$45	$52	$60	$67	$75

Additional Amount Payable For Each Additional Child Over Age 18 Attending School (Rates Effective December 1, 2008)								
Disability Rating	30%	40%	50%	60%	70%	80%	90%	100%
Monthly Benefit	$72	$96	$120	$144	$168	$192	$216	$240

Notes:
Rates for Children over age 18 attending school are shown separately in the above chart. All other entries in the above charts reflect rates for children under age 18, or helpless.

All references in the preceding charts to parents refer to parents who have been determined to be dependent by the Secretary of Veterans Affairs.

Higher Statutory Awards for Certain Multiple Disabilities

Title 38, USC 1114 subsection (k)
If a veteran, as the result of a service-connected disability, has suffered the anatomical loss or loss of use of one or more creative organs, or one foot, or one hand, or both buttocks, or 25 percent or more tissue from a single breast or from both breasts in combination (loss by mastectomy or partial mastectomy or following radiation treatment), or blindness of one eye, having only light perception, or has suffered complete organic aphonia with constant inability to communicate by speech, or deafness of both ears, having absence of air and bone conduction, the rate of compensation shall be **$96** per month for each such loss or loss of use.

This additional amount is independent of any other disability compensation provided in subsections (a) through (j) of the above table, or subsection (s) described below; however, in no event may the total amount exceed **$3,327** per month.

In the event the veteran has suffered one or more of the disabilities previously specified in this subsection, in addition to the requirement for any of the rates specified in subsections (l) through (n), described below, the rate of compensation shall be increased by **$96** per month for each such loss or loss of use, but in no event may exceed **$4,667** per month.

Title 38, USC 1114 subsection (l)

If the veteran, as the result of a service-connected disability, has suffered the anatomical loss or loss of use of both feet, or of one hand and one foot, or is blind in both eyes, with 5/200 visual acuity or less, or is permanently bedridden or so helpless as to be in need of regular aid and attendance, the monthly compensation shall be **$3,327**.

Title 38, USC 1114 subsection (m)

If the veteran, as the result of a service-connected disability, has suffered the anatomical loss or loss of use of both hands, or of both legs at a level, or with complications, preventing natural knee action with prostheses in place, or of one arm and one leg at levels, or with complications, preventing natural elbow and knee action with prostheses in place, or has suffered blindness in both eyes, having only light perception, or has suffered blindness in both eyes, rendering such veteran so helpless as to be in need of regular aid and attendance, the monthly compensation shall be **$3,671**.

Title 38, USC 1114 subsection (n)

If the veteran, as the result of a service-connected disability, has suffered the anatomical loss or loss of use of both arms at levels, or with complications, preventing natural elbow action with prostheses in place, has suffered the anatomical loss of both legs so near the hip as to prevent the use of prosthetic appliances, or has suffered the anatomical loss of one arm and one leg so near the shoulder and hip as to prevent the use of prosthetic appliances, or has suffered the anatomical loss of both eyes, or has suffered blindness without light perception in both eyes, the monthly compensation shall be **$4,176**.

Title 38, USC 1114 subsection (o)

If the veteran, as the result of a service-connected disability, has suffered disability under conditions which would entitle such veteran to two or more of the rates provided in one or more subsections (l) through (n) of this section, no condition being considered twice in the determination, or if the veteran has suffered bilateral deafness (and the hearing impairment in either one or both ears is service connected) rated at 60% or more disabling, and the veteran has also suffered service-connected total blindness with 5/200 visual acuity or less, or if the veteran has suffered service-connected total deafness in one ear or bilateral deafness (and the hearing impairment in either one or both ears is service connected) rated at 40% or more disabling, and the veteran has also suffered service-connected blindness having only light perception or less, or if the veterans has suffered the anatomical loss of both arms so near the shoulder as to prevent the use of prosthetic appliances, the monthly compensation shall be **$4,667**.

Title 38, USC 1114 subsection (p)

In the event a veteran's service-connected disabilities exceed the requirements for any of the rates previously prescribed in this section, the Secretary of Veterans Affairs may allow the next higher rate, or an intermediate rate, but in no event in excess of **$4,667**.

In the event a veteran has suffered service-connected blindness with 5/200 visual acuity or less, and (1) has also suffered bilateral deafness (and the hearing impairment in either one or both ears is service connected) rated at no less than 30% disabling, the Secretary of Veterans Affairs shall allow the next higher rate, or (2) has also suffered service-connected total deafness in one ear or service-connected anatomical loss or loss of use of one hand or one foot, the

Secretary shall allow the next intermediate rate, but in no event in excess of **$4,667**.

In the event a veteran has suffered service-connected blindness, having only light perception or less, and has also suffered bilateral deafness (and the hearing impairment in either one or both ears is service-connected) rated at 10 or 20% disabling, the Secretary shall allow the next intermediate rate, but in no event in excess of **$4,667**.

In the event a veteran has suffered the anatomical loss or loss of use, or a combination of anatomical loss and loss of use, of three extremities, the Secretary shall allow the next higher rate or intermediate rate, but in no event in excess of **$4,667**.

Any intermediate rate under this subsection shall be established at the arithmetic mean, rounded down to the nearest dollar, between the two rates concerned.

Title 38, USC 1114 subsection (q)
This subsection was repealed by Public Law 90-493.

Title 38, USC 1114 subsection (r)
If a veteran is entitled to compensation under (o) of this section, at the maximum rate authorized under (p) of this section, or at the intermediate rate authorized between the rates authorized under subsections (n) and (o) of this section and at the rate authorized under subsection (k) of this section, is in need of regular aid and attendance, then, in addition to such compensation:

- The veteran shall be paid a monthly aid and attendance allowance at the rate of **$2,002**; or

- If the veteran, in addition to such need for regular aid and attendance, is in need of a higher level of care, such veteran shall be paid a monthly aid and attendance allowance at the rate of **$2,983**, in lieu of the allowance authorized in the previous paragraph. (Need for a higher level of care shall be considered to be need for personal health-care services provided on a daily basis in the veteran's home by a person who is licensed to provide such services or who provides such services under the regular supervision of a licensed health-care professional. The existence of the need for such care shall be determined by a physician employed by the VA, or in areas where no such physician is available, by a physician carrying out such function under contract or fee arrangement based on an examination by such physician).

Title 38, USC 1114 subsection (s)
If a veteran has a service-connected disability rated as total, and:

- Has additional service-connected disability or disabilities independently ratable at 60% or more; or

- By reason of such veteran's service-connected disability or disabilities, is permanently housebound, and then the monthly compensation shall be **$2,993**.

For the purposes of this subsection, the requirement of "permanently housebound" will be considered to have been met when the veteran is substantially confined to such veteran's house (ward or clinical areas, if institutionalized) or immediate premised due to a service-connected disability or disabilities which it is reasonable certain will remain throughout such veteran's lifetime.

Title 38, USC 1114 subsection (t)
This subsection was repealed by Public Law 99-576.

Additional Compensation For Dependents (38 USC 1115)

Any veteran entitled to compensation under 38 USC 1114, and whose disability is rated not less than 30%, shall be entitled to additional compensation for dependents in the following monthly amounts:

If and while the veteran is rated totally disabled and:

1.	Has a spouse but no child living:	$150.00
2.	Has a spouse and one child living:	259.00
	(plus for each additional living child under age 18):	75.00
3.	Has no spouse, but one child living:	101.00
	(plus for each additional living child under age 18):	75.00
4.	Has a mother or father, either or both dependent upon him for support - for each parent so dependent:	120.00
5.	For a spouse who is a patient in a nursing home, or who is so helpless or blind as to require the regular aid and attendance of another person:	136.00 for a totally disabled veteran, and proportionate amounts for partially disabled veterans.
6.	For each child who is between the ages of 18-23, and who is pursuing a course of instruction at an approved educational institution:	240.00 for a totally disabled veteran, and proportionate amounts for partially disabled veterans.

Adjustment To Individual VA Awards

There will be no adjustment of VA awards. Special Compensation paid under 10 USC 1413 is provided under chapter 71, title 10, USC, "Computation of Retired Pay." However, it is NOT RETIRED PAY. It is to be paid from funds appropriated for pay and allowances of the recipient member's branch of service. Eligible retirees in receipt of VA disability compensation may receive this special compensation in addition to their VA disability compensation.

PRESUMPTIONS

Presumption Of Sound Condition

Every veteran will be assumed to have been in sound medical condition when examined, accepted, and enrolled for service, except any defects, infirmities, or disorders noted at the time of the examination, acceptance, and enrollment, or if there is clear and unmistakable evidence showing that the injury or disease did exist before acceptance and enrollment, and the injury or disease was not aggravated by such service.

Presumptions Of Service-Connection Relating To Certain Chronic Diseases And Disabilities

In the case of any veteran who served for 90 days or more during a period of war, any of the following shall be considered to have been incurred in, or aggravated by such service, notwithstanding there is no record of evidence of such disease during the period of service:

- A chronic disease (detailed below), becoming manifest to a degree of 10% or more within one year from the date of separation from such service.

- A tropical disease (detailed below), and the resultant disorders or disease originating because of therapy, administered in connection with such diseases, or as a preventative thereof, becoming manifest to a degree of 10% or more within one year from the date of separation from such service. Additionally, if it is shown to exist at a time when standard and accepted treatises indicate that the incubation period thereof commenced during active service, it shall be deemed to have incurred during such service.

- Active tuberculosis disease developing a 10% degree of disability or more within 3 years from the date of separation from such service.

- Multiple sclerosis developing a 10% degree of disability or more within seven years from the date of separation from such service.

- Hansen's disease developing a 10% degree of disability or more within three years from the date of separation from such service.

Chronic Diseases:

- Amyotrophic lateral sclerosis (ALS)
- Anemia, primary
- Arteriosclerosis
- Arthritis
- Atrophy, progressive muscular
- Brain hemorrhage
- Brain thrombosis
- Bronchiectasis
- Calculi of the kidney, bladder, or gallbladder
- Cardiovascular-renal disease, including hypertension
- Cirrhosis of the liver
- Coccidiodomycosis
- Diabetes mellitus
- Encephalitis lethargica residuals
- Endocarditis
- Endocrinopathies
- Epilepsies
- Hansen's disease
- Hodgkin's disease
- Leukemia
- Lupus erythematosus, systemic
- Myasthenia gravis
- Myelitis
- Myocarditis
- Nephritis
- Organic diseases of the nervous system
- Osteitis deformans (Paget's disease)
- Osteomalacia
- Palsy, bulbar
- Paralysis agitans
- Psychoses
- Purpura idiopathic, hemorrhagic
- Raynaud's disease
- Sarcoidosis
- Scleroderma
- Sclerosis, amyotrohpic lateral
- Sclerosis, multiple
- Syringomyelia
- Thromboangiitis obilterans (Buerger's disease)
- Tuberculosis, active
- Tumors, malignant, or of the brain or spinal cord or peripheral nerves
- Ulcers, peptil (gastric or duodenal)
- Other chronic diseases the Secretary of Veterans Affairs may add to this list.

Tropical Diseases:

- Amebiasis
- Blackwater fever
- Cholera
- Dracontiasis
- Dysentery

- Filiariasis
- Hansen's disease
- Leishmaniasis, including kala-azar
- Loiasis
- Malaria
- Onchocerciasis
- Oroya fever
- Pinta
- Plague
- Schistosomiasis
- Yaws
- Yellow fever
- Other tropical diseases the Secretary of Veterans Affairs may add to this list.

Presumptions Of Service-Connection Relating To Certain Diseases And Disabilities For Former Prisoners Of War

In the case of any veteran who is a former prisoner of war, and who was detained or interned for not less than thirty days, any of the following which became manifest to a degree of 10% or more after active military, naval or air service, shall be considered to have been incurred in or aggravated by such service, notwithstanding that there is no record of such disease during the period of service:

Starting October 7, 2005, VA expanded benefits to all former POWs with strokes and common heart diseases. Affected veterans will automatically be eligible for disability compensation for those common ailments, and their spouses and dependents will be eligible for service-connected survivors' benefits if these diseases contribute to the death of a former POW.

Public Law 108-183, The Veterans Benefits Act of 2003, eliminated the requirement that a veteran was a POW for at least 30 days for certain conditions. Therefore, there are now two categories of presumptive conditions – those that include the 30-day requirement, and those that do not.

In the case of any veteran who is a former prisoner of war, and **who was detained or interned for not less than thirty days,** any of the following which became manifest to a degree of 10% or more after active military, naval or air service, shall be considered to have been incurred in or aggravated by such service, notwithstanding that there is no record of such disease during the period of service:

- Avitaminosis

- Beriberi (including beriberi heart disease, which includes Ischemic Heart Disease-coronary artery disease-for former POWs who suffered during captivity from edema-swelling of the legs or feet- also known as "wet" beriberi)

- Chronic dysentery

- Helminthiasis

- Malnutrition (including optic atrophy associated with malnutrition)

- Pellagra

- Any other nutritional deficiency

- Peripheral neuropathy, except where directly related to infectious causes

- Irritable bowel syndrome

- Peptic ulcer disease

- Cirrhosis of the liver (This condition was added as part of Public Law 108-183, The Veterans Benefit Act of 2003.)

- Atherosclerotic heart disease or hypertensive vascular disease (including hypertensive heart disease) and their complications (including myocardial infarction, congestive heart failure and arrhythmia) (These conditions were added as part of Public Law 109-233.)

- Stroke and its complications (This condition was added as part of Public Law 109-233.)

- 2008 UPDATE:

- The Veterans Benefits Improvement Act, which became law on 10/10/08, added osteoporosis to the list of disabilities presumed to be service-connected (and therefore compensable through VA disability compensation) in the case of veterans who are former prisoners of war, if the Secretary determines that such veteran has post-traumatic stress disorder (PTSD).

In the case of any veteran who is a former prisoner of war, and **who was detained or interned for any period of time,** any of the following which became manifest to a degree of 10% or more after active military, naval or air service, shall be considered to have been incurred in or aggravated by such service, notwithstanding that there is no record of such disease during the period of service:

- Psychosis

- Any of the anxiety states

- Dysthymic disorder (or depressive neurosis)

- Organic residuals of frostbite, if the VA determines the veteran was interned in climatic conditions consistent with the occurrence of frostbite

- Post-traumatic osteoarthritis

Update:
Starting October 7, 2005, VA expanded benefits to all former POWs with strokes and common heart diseases. Affected veterans will be automatically eligible for disability compensation for those common ailments, and their spouses and dependents will be eligible for service-connected survivors' benefits if these diseases contribute to the death of a former POW.

Presumptions Relating To Certain Diseases Associated With Exposure To Radiation

VA may pay compensation for radiogenic diseases under two programs specific to radiation-exposed veterans and their survivors:

Statutory List

- Veterans who participated in nuclear tests by the U.S. or its allies, who served with the U.S. occupation forces in Hiroshima or Nagasaki, Japan, between August 1945 and July 1946, or who were similarly exposed to ionizing radiation while a prisoner of war in Japan, are eligible for compensation for cancers specified in legislation.

- The definition of radiation-risk activities was expanded in March 2002 to include service at Amchitka Island, Alaska, prior to January 1, 1974, if a veteran was exposed while performing duties related to certain underground nuclear tests.

- The new definition also included service at gaseous diffusion plants located in Paducah, Ky., Portsmouth, Ohio and an area known as K25 at Oak Ridge, Tenn.

The types of cancer covered by these laws are:

- All forms of leukemia except chronic lymphocytic leukemia;
- Cancer of the thyroid,
- Cancer of the breast,
- Cancer of the pharynx,
- Cancer of the esophagus,
- Cancer of the stomach,
- Cancer of the small intestine,
- Cancer of the pancreas,
- Cancer of the bile ducts,
- Cancer of the gall bladder,
- Cancer of the salivary gland,
- Cancer of the urinary tract,
- Lymphomas (except Hodgkin's disease),
- Multiple myeloma,
- Primary liver cancer.

In March 2002, VA announced the addition of five new cancers to the list of diseases presumed to be connected to the exposure of veterans to radiation during their military service:

- Bone Cancer
- Brain Cancer
- Colon Cancer
- Lung Cancer
- Ovary Cancer

The new rules apply to those veterans who participated in "radiation-risk activities" while on active duty, during active duty for training or inactive duty training as a member of a reserve component.

Regulatory List

Disability compensation claims of veterans who were exposed to radiation in service and who develop a disease within specified time periods not specified in the statutory list are governed by regulation. Under the regulations, various additional factors must be considered in determining service-connection, including amount of radiation exposure, duration of exposure, and elapsed time between exposure and onset of the disease. VA regulations identify all cancers as potentially radiogenic, as well as certain other non-malignant conditions: posterior subcapsular cataracts; non-malignant thyroid nodular disease; parathyroid adenoma; and tumors of the brain and central nervous system.

A final rule that expanded the regulatory list from more than a dozen specific cancers to add "any other cancer" (any malignancy) was published Sept. 24, 1998. The rulemaking began following a 1995 review of the radiogenicity of cancer generally by the Veterans Advisory Committee on Environmental Hazards. It concluded that, on the basis of current scientific knowledge, exposure to ionizing radiation can be a contributing factor in the development of any malignancy. VA also will consider evidence that diseases other than those specified in regulation may be caused by radiation exposure.

Presumptions Of Service-Connection For Diseases Associated With Exposure To Certain Herbicide Agents

A disease specified below, becoming manifest in a veteran, who, during active military, naval, or air service, served in the Republic of Vietnam during the period beginning on January 9, 1962, and ending on May 7, 1975 shall be considered to have been incurred in or aggravated by such service, notwithstanding that there is no record of evidence of such disease during the period of such service.

The diseases referred to above are:

- **Acute and Subacute Peripheral Neuropathy**

  A nervous system condition that causes numbness, tingling, and motor weakness. Under VA's rating regulations, it must be at least 10% disabling within 1 year of exposure to Agent Orange and resolve within 2 years after the date it began.

- **AL Amyloidosis**

  A rare disease caused when an abnormal protein, amyloid, enters tissues or organs.

- **B Cell Leukemias**

  Cancers which affect B cells, such as hairy cell leukemia.

- **Chloracne (or Similar Acneform Disease)**

  A skin condition that occurs soon after dioxin exposure and looks like common forms of acne seen in teenagers. Under VA's rating regulations, chloracne (or other acneform disease similar to chloracne) must be at least 10% disabling within 1 year of exposure to Agent Orange.

- **Chronic Lymphocytic Leukemia**

  A disease that progresses slowly with increasing production of excessive numbers of white blood cells.

- **Diabetes Mellitus (Type 2)**

  A disease characterized by high blood sugar levels resulting from the body's inability to respond properly to the hormone insulin.

- **Hodgkin's Disease**

  A malignant lymphoma (cancer) characterized by progressive enlargement of the lymph nodes, liver, and spleen, and by progressive anemia.

- **Ischemic Heart Disease**

  A disease characterized by a reduced supply of blood to the heart.

- **Multiple Myeloma**

  A cancer of specific bone marrow cells that is characterized by bone marrow tumors in various bones of the body.

- **Non-Hodgkin's Lymphoma**

  A group of cancers that affect the lymph glands and other lymphatic tissue.

- **Parkinson's Disease**

  A motor system condition with symptoms that include trembling of the limbs and face and impaired balance.

- **Porphyria Cutanea Tarda**

  A disorder characterized by liver dysfunction and by thinning and blistering of the skin in sun-exposed areas. Under VA's rating regulations, it must be at least 10% disabling within 1 year of exposure to Agent Orange.

- **Prostate Cancer**

  Cancer of the prostate; one of the most common cancers among men.

- **Respiratory Cancers**

  Cancers of the lung, larynx, trachea, and bronchus.

- **Soft Tissue Sarcoma (other than Osteosarcoma, Chondrosarcoma, Kaposi's sarcoma, or Mesothelioma)**

  A group of different types of cancers in body tissues such as muscle, fat, blood and lymph vessels, and connective tissues.

- Each additional disease (if any) that the Secretary of the VA determines warrants a presumption of service-connection by reason of having positive association with exposure to an herbicide agent, becomes manifest within the period (if any) prescribed in such regulations in a veteran who, during active military, naval, or air service, served in the Republic of Vietnam during the period beginning on January 9, 1962 and ending on May 7, 1975, and while so serving was exposed to that herbicide agent.

Veterans having a disease referred to above, shall be presumed to have been exposed during such service to an herbicide agent containing dioxin or 2,4-dichlorophenoxyacetic acid, and may be presumed to have been exposed during such service to any other chemical compound in an herbicide agent, unless there is affirmative evidence to establish that the veteran was not exposed to any such agent during that service.

If the Secretary of the VA later determines that a previously established presumption of service-connection for one of the above diseases is no longer warranted, all veterans currently awarded compensation on the basis of the presumption shall continue to be entitled to receive compensation. Additionally, all survivors of any such veterans who were awarded dependency and indemnity compensation shall continue to be entitled to receive dependency and indemnity compensation on that basis.

Presumptions Of Service-Connection For Illnesses Associated With Service In The Persian Gulf During The Persian Gulf War

Like all other veterans, veterans of the Persian Gulf War can receive service-connected compensation for mental and physical disabilities that were incurred during, or aggravated by their service in the armed forces.

Recent legislation also authorized disability compensation for Persian Gulf veterans with chronic, **undiagnosed** illness resulting in a permanent disability that developed after they left the Persian Gulf.

Congress created this legislation after many Persian Gulf War veterans reported they were suffering from multi-symptom disabilities that are poorly understood by the medical profession, and may be classified as "undiagnosed" by one physician, or referred to as "chronic fatigue syndrome" by another physician.

Public Law 107-103, signed by then-President Bush on December 27, 2001, extended the presumptive period for disabilities associated with Persian Gulf War service until December 31, 2011, or such later date as prescribed by VA.

To be entitled to disability compensation due to an undiagnosed illness, the claimant must meet the following requirements:

1. The veteran must qualify as a Persian Gulf War veteran.

    VA considers an individual to be a Persian Gulf War veteran if he or she served on active military, naval, or air service in the Southwest Asia theater of operations during the Persian Gulf War. This includes service in Iraq, Kuwait, Saudi Arabia, the neutral zone between Iraq and Saudi Arabia, Bahrain, Qatar, the United Arab Emirates, Oman, the Gulf of Aden, the Gulf of Oman, the Persian Gulf, the Arabian Sea, the Red Sea, and the airspace above these locations.

    The veteran's period of service must have included service in the designated area after August 2, 1990. Since members of the armed services are still serving in the area of operations, they qualify as Persian Gulf veterans because the end date for the Persian Gulf War has not been set.

2. The veteran must suffer from a "qualifying chronic disability."

    A "qualifying chronic disability" can be any of the following (or combination of the following):

    a. An undiagnosed illnesses;
    b. A medically unexplained chronic multi-symptom illness (such as chronic fatigue syndrome, fibromyalgia, or irritable bowel syndrome) that is defined by a cluster of signs or symptoms;
    c. Any diagnosed illness that the VA Secretary determines warrants a presumption of service connection.

    (VA considers disabilities to be chronic if they have existed for 6 months or more, or if they have exhibited intermittent episodes of improvement and worsening over a 6-month period. The 6-month period is measured from the earliest date that the signs or symptoms manifested.)

3. The "qualifying chronic disability" must have appeared either during active duty in the Southwest Asia Theater of Operations during the Gulf War or it must have manifested to a degree of at least 10 percent during the presumptive period.

The following symptoms may be manifestations of an undiagnosed illness:

*   Fatigue

*   Skin disorders

*   Headaches

*   Muscle pain

*   Joint pain

*   Neurological symptoms

*   Neuropsychological symptoms

- Symptoms involving the respiratory system

- Sleep disturbances

- Gastrointestinal symptoms

- Cardiovascular symptoms

- Abnormal weight loss

- Menstrual disorders

- Any poorly defined chronic multi-symptom illness of unknown etiology characterized by 2 or more of the above symptoms.

Rates of compensation depend upon the degree of disability, and follow a payment schedule that is adjusted annually and applies to all veterans. Please refer to the charts detailed earlier in this chapter for the current rates payable.

2010 Update:

VA Recognizes "Presumptive" Illnesses In Iraq, Afghanistan

In late 2010, VA the VA established new presumptions of service connection for nine specific infectious diseases associated with military service in Southwest Asia beginning on or after the start of the first Gulf War on August 2, 1990, through the conflict in Iraq and on or after September 19, 2001, in Afghanistan.

The nine disease are:

- Brucellosis,

- Campylobacter jejuni,

- Coxiella burnetii (Q fever),

- Malaria,

- Mycobacterium tuberculosis,

- Nontyphoid Salmonella,

- Shigella,

- Visceral leishmaniasis and

- West Nile virus.

A veterans now only has to show service in Southwest Asia or Afghanistan and that he or she had one of the nine diseases within a certain time after service, and has a current disability as a result of that disease, subject to certain time limits for seven of the diseases.

LOU GEHRIG'S DISEASE
AMYOTROPHIC LATERAL SCLEROSIS (ALS)

> *VA has evidence that veterans who deployed to the Gulf War are nearly twice as likely as their non-deployed counterparts to develop Lou Gehrig's Disease, technically known as amyotrohpic lateral sclerosis, or ALS.*

Based on new research, VA now has evidence that veterans who deployed to the Gulf War are nearly twice as likely as their non-deployed counterparts to develop Lou Gehrig's Disease, technically known as amyotrohpic lateral sclerosis, or ALS.

On December 10, 2001, VA reported that veterans who served in the Gulf during the period from August 2, 1990 through July 31, 1991, and who subsequently developed Lou Gehrig's Disease will be compensated.

Anyone seeking more information should contact the VA Gulf War Helpline at (800) 749-8387.

VA has established a national ALS registry to identify veterans with the disease – regardless of when they served – and track their health status. Veterans with ALS who enroll will complete an initial telephone interview covering their health and military service, and will be interviewed twice yearly thereafter.

For more information about VA's ALS registry, call toll free (877) 342-5257.

Presumptions Rebuttable

If there is affirmative evidence to the contrary, or evidence to establish that an intercurrent injury or disease which is a recognized cause of any of the diseases or disabilities mentioned in the above sections, has been suffered between the date of separation from service and the onset of any such diseases or disabilities, or if the disability is due to the veteran's own willful misconduct, payment of compensation shall not be made.

Special Provisions Relating To Claims Based Upon Effects Of Tobacco Products

Effective June 10, 1998, a veteran's death or disability will not be considered to have resulted from personal injury suffered, or disease contracted in the line of duty if the injury or disease is attributable to the use of tobacco products by the veteran during the veteran's service.

PEACETIME DISABILITY COMPENSATION

Basic Entitlement

A veteran may be entitled to VA disability compensation for any medical condition or injury that was incurred in, or aggravated by his or her military service, during any period other than a period of war. The veteran must have been discharged or released under conditions other than dishonorable from the period of service in which the injury or disease was incurred or aggravated.

No compensation shall be paid if the disability is a result of the person's own willful misconduct or abuse of alcohol or drugs.

Presumption of Sound Condition

Every person employed in the active military, naval, or air service during any period other than a period of war, for 6 months or more, will be assumed to have been in sound medical condition when examined, accepted, and enrolled for service, except any defects, infirmities, or disorders noted at the time of the examination, acceptance, and enrollment, or if there is clear and unmistakable evidence showing that the injury or disease did exist before acceptance and enrollment, and the injury or disease was not aggravated by such service.

Presumptions Relating to Certain Diseases

If a veteran who served in the active military, naval, or air service after December 31, 1946, during any period other than a period of war, for 6 months or more, contracts any of the following, it shall be considered to have been incurred in, or aggravated by such service, notwithstanding there is no record of evidence of such disease during the period of service:

- A chronic disease, becoming manifest to a degree of 10% or more within one year from the date of separation from such service.

- A tropical disease, and the resultant disorders or disease originating because of therapy, administered in connection with such diseases, or as a preventative thereof, becoming manifest to a degree of 10% or more within one year from the date of separation from such service. Additionally, if it is shown to exist at a time when standard and accepted treatises indicate that the incubation period thereof commenced during active service, it shall be deemed to have incurred during such service.

- Active tuberculosis disease developing a 10% degree of disability or more within 3 years from the date of separation from such service.

- Multiple sclerosis developing a 10% degree of disability or more within seven years from the date of separation from such service.

- Hansen's disease developing a 10% degree of disability or more within three years from the date of separation from such service.

In the case of any veteran who served for 90 days or more during a period of war, service-connection will not be granted in any case where the disease or disorder is shown by clear and unmistakable evidence to have had its inception before or after active military, naval, or air service.

Presumptions Rebuttable

If there is affirmative evidence to the contrary, or evidence to establish that an intercurrent injury or disease which is a recognized cause of any of the diseases or disabilities mentioned in the above sections, has been suffered between the date of separation from service and the onset of any such diseases or disabilities, or if the disability is due to the veteran's own willful misconduct, payment of compensation shall not be made.

Rates Of Peacetime Disability Compensation

The compensation payable shall be the same as the compensation payable for Wartime Disability Compensation. Please refer to the charts presented earlier in this chapter.

Additional Compensation For Dependents

Any veteran entitled to peacetime disability compensation, and whose disability is rated as 30% or greater, will be entitled to additional monthly compensation for dependents in the same amounts payable for Wartime Disability Compensation. Please refer to the charts presented earlier in this chapter.

GENERAL DISABILITY COMPENSATION PROVISIONS

How To Apply For Disability Compensation Benefits

In order to apply for disability compensation benefits from the VA, Form 21-526, Veteran's Application for Compensation or Pension, must be completed and returned to the VA Regional Office serving the veteran's area (refer to Chapter 36 for a listing of regional offices). In addition to the application, the following documents must be submitted:

- Service Medical Records: In order to expedite processing of the claim, if an applicant has his or her service medical records, they should be submitted with the application. If not included with the application, VA will contact the veteran's service department to obtain them.

- Other Medical Records: Any medical records from private doctors or hospitals pertaining to the claim should be submitted along with the application.

- Dependency Documents: Copies of pertinent birth, marriage, death and divorce certificates should be submitted along with the application.

- Military Discharge / DD Form 214-Copy 4-Member Copy: In order to expedite processing of the claim, if an applicant has a copy of his or her DD-214, it should be submitted with the application. If not included with the application, VA will attempt to obtain verification from the veteran's service department.

- Copies of missing DD Forms 214 may be obtained from the National Personnel Records Center – 9700 Page Blvd. – St. Louis, MO – 63132-5100.

If any of the pertinent supporting evidence is not immediately available, the applicant should send in the application anyway. The date VA receives the application is important! If VA approves the claim, benefit payments usually begin from the date the application is received, regardless of when the claim is approved.

Adjudication

Adjudication means a judicial decision made by the Veterans Administration in claims filed within their jurisdiction. There is an Adjudication Division in each regional office, under the direction of an adjudication officer, who is responsible for the preparation of claims.

Upon the receipt of an original application in the Adjudication Division, it will be referred to the Authorization Unit for review and development in accordance with established procedures. All reasonable assistance will be extended a claimant in the prosecution of his or her claim, and all sources from which information may be elicited will be thoroughly developed prior to the submission of the case to the rating board. Every legitimate assistance will be rendered a claimant in obtaining any benefit to which he or she is entitled, and the veteran will be given every opportunity to substantiate his or her claim. Information and advice to claimants will be complete, and will be given in words that the average person can understand.

VA personnel must at all times give to claimants and other properly interested and recognized individuals courteous and satisfactory service which is essential to good public relations. It is incumbent upon the claimant to establish his or her case in accordance with the law. This rule, however, should not be highly technical and rigid in its application. The general policy is to give the claimant every opportunity to substantiate the claim, to extend all reasonable assistance in its prosecution, and to develop all sources from which information may be obtained. Information and advice to claimants will be complete and expressed, so far as possible, in plain language, which can be easily read and understood by persons not familiar with the subject matter.

Benefits For Persons Disabled By Treatment Or Vocational Rehabilitation

Compensation shall be awarded for a qualifying additional disability or a qualifying death of a veteran in the same manner as if such additional disability or death were service-connected, provided:

- The disability or death was caused by hospital care, medical or surgical treatment, or examination was furnished under any law administered by the VA, either by a VA employee, or in a VA facility, and the proximate cause of the disability or death was:

- Carelessness, negligence, lack of proper skill, error in judgment, or similar instance of fault on the part of the VA in furnishing the hospital care, medical treatment, surgical treatment, or examination; or

- An event not reasonably foreseeable.

- The disability or death was proximately caused by the provision of training and rehabilitation services by the VA (including a service-provider used by the VA) as part of an approved rehabilitation program.

Effective December 1, 1962, if an individual is awarded a judgment against the United States in a civil action brought pursuant to Section 1346(b) of Title 28, or enters into a settlement or compromise under Section 2672 or 2677 of Title 28 by reason of a disability or death treated pursuant to this section as if it were service-connected, then no benefits shall be paid to such individual for any month beginning after the date such judgment, settlement, or compromise on account of such disability or death becomes final until the aggregate amount of benefits which would be paid out for this subsection equals the total amount included in such judgment, settlement, or compromise.

Person Heretofore Having A Compensable Status

The death and disability benefits outlined in this chapter, shall, notwithstanding the service requirements thereof, be granted to persons heretofore recognized by law as having a compensable status, including persons whose claims are based on war or peacetime service rendered before April 21, 1898.

Aggravation

A preexisting injury or disease will be considered to have been aggravated by active military, naval, or air service, if there is an increase in disability during such service, unless there is a specific finding that the increase in disability is due to the natural progress of the disease.

Consideration To Be Accorded Time, Place And Circumstances Of Service

Consideration shall be given to the places, types, and circumstances of each veteran's service. The VA will consider the veteran's service record, the official history of each organization in which such veteran served, such veteran's medical records, and all pertinent medical and lay evidence. The provisions of Public Law 98-542 – *Section 5 of the Veterans' Dioxin and Radiation Exposure Compensation Standards Act* shall also be applied.

In the case of any veteran who engaged in combat with the enemy in active service with a military, naval, or air organization of the United States during a period of war, campaign, or expedition, the Secretary shall accept as sufficient proof of service-connection of any disease or injury alleged to have been incurred in or aggravated by such service, if consistent with the circumstances, conditions, or hardships of such service. This provision will apply even if there is no official record of such incurrence or aggravation in such service. Every reasonable doubt in such instance will be resolved in favor of the veteran.

Service-connection of such injury or disease may be rebutted only by clear and convincing evidence to the contrary. The reasons for granting or denying service-connection in each case shall be recorded in full.

Disappearance

If a veteran who is receiving disability compensation disappears, the VA may pay the compensation otherwise payable to the veteran to such veteran's spouse, children, and parents. Payments made to such spouse, child, or parent shall not exceed the amounts payable to each if the veteran had died from a service-connected disability.

Combination Of Certain Ratings

The VA shall provide for the combination of ratings and pay compensation at the rates prescribed previously in this chapter to those veterans who served during a period of war and during any other time, who have suffered disability in the line of duty in each period of service.

Combined ratings can be figured out by the following formula:

1. Subtract the highest rating, for the major disability, from 100%
2. Multiply the rating for the next lower disability by the sum remaining after the first subtraction.
3. Add the product to the major rating to arrive at the combined rating for two disabilities.

If there are three rated service-connected disabilities, then, after the combined rating for the two larger ratings has been calculated, subtract such combined rating from 100% and multiply the rating for the third disability times the remainder, and add the resulting product to the combined rating of the first two disabilities to arrive at the combined rating for the three disabilities.

Thus, if a veteran has a 60% disability, a 40% disability, and a 20% disability, the following calculation would be done to arrive at the combined rating of 81%:

1. $100 - 60 = 40$
2. $40 \times .40 = 16$
3. $16 + 60 = 76$
4. $100 - 76 = 24$
5. $24 \times .20 = 4.8$ (round up to 5)
6. $76 + 5 = 81\%$

Tax Exemption

Compensation and pension may not be assigned to anyone, and are exempt from taxation (including income tax). No one can attach, levy, or seize a compensation or pension check either before or after receipt. Property purchased with money received from the government is not protected.

Protection Of Service Connection

Service connection for any disability or death granted under this title which has been in force for ten or more years shall not be severed on or after January 1, 1962, unless it is shown that the original grant of service connection was based on fraud, or it is clearly shown from military records that the person concerned did not have the requisite service or character of discharge. The mentioned period shall be computed from the date determined by the VA as the date on which the status commenced for rating purposes.

Preservation of Ratings

Public Law 88-445, approved August 19, 1964, effective the same date, amends Section 110, Title 38, U.S. Code as follows:

The law provides that a disability which has been continuously rated at or above a given percentage for 20 years or longer for the purpose of service connection compensation under laws administered by the VA shall not thereafter be rated at any lesser percentage except upon showing that the rating was based on fraud.

Special Consideration For Certain Cases Of Loss Of Paired Organs Or Extremities

If a veteran has suffered any of the following, the VA shall assign and pay to the veteran the applicable rate of compensation, as if the combination of disabilities were the result of a service-connected disability:

- Blindness in one eye as a result of a service-connected disability, and blindness in the other eye as a result of a non-service-connected disability not the result of the veteran's own willful misconduct; or

- The loss or loss of use of one kidney as a result of a service-connected disability, and involvement of the other kidney as a result of a non-service connected disability not the result of the veteran's own willful misconduct; or

- Total deafness in one ear as a result of a service-connected disability, and total deafness in the other ear as the result of non-service-connected disability not the result of the veteran's own willful misconduct; or

- The loss or loss of use of one hand or one foot as a result of a service-connected disability and the loss or loss of use of the other hand or foot as a result of non-service-connected disability not the result of the veteran's own willful misconduct; or

- Permanent service-connected disability of one lung, rated 50% or more disabling, in combination with a non-service-connected disability of the other lung that is not the result of the veteran's own willful misconduct.

If a veteran described above receives any money or property of value pursuant to an award in a judicial proceeding based upon, or a settlement or compromise of, any cause of action for damages for the non-service-connected disability, the increase in the rate of compensation otherwise payable shall not be paid for any month following a month in which any such money or property is received until such time as the total of the amount of such increase that would otherwise have been payable equals the total of the amount of any such money received, and the fair market value of any such property received.

Payment Of Disability Compensation In Disability Severance Cases

The deduction of disability severance pay from disability compensation, as required by Section 1212(c) of Title 10, shall be made at a monthly rate not in excess of the rate of compensation to which the former member would be entitled based on the degree of such former member's disability, as determined on the initial Department rating.

Trial Work Periods And Vocational Rehabilitation For Certain Veterans With Total Disability Ratings

The disability rating of a qualified veteran who begins to engage in a substantially gainful occupation after January 31, 1985, may not be reduced on the basis of the veteran having secured and followed a substantially gainful occupation unless the veteran maintains such an occupation for a period of 12 consecutive months.

("Qualified Veteran" means a veteran who has a service-connected disability or disabilities, not rated as total, but who has been awarded a rating of total of disability by reason of inability to secure or follow a substantially gainful occupation as a result of such disability or disabilities.)

Counseling services, placement, and post placement services shall be available to each qualified veteran, whether or not the veteran is participating in a vocational rehabilitation program.

CHAPTER 4

MISCELLANEOUS BENEFITS

(AUTOMOBILES, ADAPTIVE EQUIPMENT, HOUSING GRANTS, CLOTHING ALLOWANCE AND MEDAL OF HONOR PENSION)

AUTOMOBILE ASSISTANCE PROGRAM

The VA offers an automobile assistance program for eligible veterans, or eligible members of the Armed Forces serving on active duty who are suffering from a disability as described below, if such disability is the result of an injury incurred or disease contracted in or aggravated in the line of duty in the active military, naval, or air service. Following are highlights of the VA program:

Financial Assistance

Qualified veterans may receive a **one-time** payment from VA of up to $11,000 to be used toward the purchase of an automobile or other conveyance. (This grant was increased from $9,000 to $11,000 as part of Public Law 108-183, the Veterans Benefits Act of 2003, which became law December 16, 2003.)

UPDATE:

- *The Veterans Benefits Act of 2010 contains a provision increasing the Automobile and Special Adaptive Equipment Grant effective October 1, 2011, from $11,000 to $18,900. The law also requires that this amount be adjusted annually by the percentage increase in the Consumer Price Index.*

Eligibility Requirements For Receipt Of One-Time Payment:

Veterans or service members who are entitled to Disability Compensation under Chapter 11 of Title 38 due to one of the following service-connected losses:

- The loss or permanent loss of use of one or both feet; or
- The loss or permanent loss of use of one or both hands; or
- The permanent impairment of vision of both eyes of the following status:

- Central visual acuity of 20/200 or less in the better eye, with corrective glasses, or central visual acuity of more than 20/200 if there is a field defect in which the peripheral field has contracted to such an extent that the widest diameter of visual field subtends an angular distance no greater than twenty degrees in the better eye.

ADAPTIVE EQUIPMENT

In addition to the one-time payment described above, VA will also pay for installation of adaptive equipment deemed necessary to insure that the eligible veteran will be able to safely operate the vehicle, and to satisfy the applicable State standards of licensure.

VA will also repair, replace, or reinstall adaptive equipment determined necessary for the operation of a vehicle acquired under this program, or for the operation of a vehicle an eligible veteran may previously or subsequently have acquired.

Eligibility Requirements For Receipt Of Adaptive Equipment:

- The loss or permanent loss of use of one or both feet; or

- The loss or permanent loss of use of one or both hands; or

- The permanent impairment of vision of both eyes of the following status:

- Central visual acuity of 20/200 or less in the better eye, with corrective glasses, or central visual acuity of more than 20/200 if there is a field defect in which the peripheral field has contracted to such an extent that the widest diameter of visual field subtends an angular distance no greater than twenty degrees in the better eye; or

- Ankylosis (immobility) of one or both knees; or

- Ankylosis (immobility) of one or both hips.

Adaptive Equipment Available for Installation

The term adaptive equipment, means generally, any equipment which must be part of or added to a vehicle manufactured for sale to the general public in order to make it safe for use by the claimant, and to assist him or her in meeting the applicable standards of licensure of the proper licensing authority.

Following is a partial list of adaptive equipment available under this program:

- Power steering;
- Power brakes;
- Power window lifts;
- Power seats;
- Special equipment necessary to assist the eligible person into and out of the automobile or other conveyance;
- Air-conditioning equipment, if such equipment is necessary to the health and safety of the veteran and to the safety of others, regardless of whether the automobile or other conveyance is to be operated by the eligible person or is to operated for such person by another person;
- Any modification of the size of the interior space of the automobile or other conveyance if necessary for the disabled person to enter or operate the vehicle;
- Other equipment, not described above, if determined necessary by the Chief Medical Director or designee in an individual case.

Eligible veterans are not entitled to adaptive equipment for more than 2 vehicles at any one time during any four-year period. (In the event an adapted vehicle is no longer available for use by the eligible veteran due to circumstances beyond his or her control, i.e. loss due to fire, theft, accident, etc., an exception to this four-year provision may be approved.)

SPECIALLY ADAPTED HOUSING GRANTS

There are three types of grants that may be payable:

- Specially Adapted Housing Grants (SAH)
- Special Housing Adaptations Grants (SHA)
- Temporary Residence Adaptation Grants (TRA)

SPECIALLY ADAPTED HOUSING GRANT (SAH)

The VA may approve a grant of not more than 50% of the cost of building, buying, or remodeling adapted homes, or paying indebtedness on homes previously acquired, up to a maximum of **$63,780.**

UPDATE: Public law 110-289 directed that the maximum grant amount will be adjusted annually, starting October 1, 2009 based on a cost-of-construction index. The amount will either increase or stay the same each year – it cannot decrease. **For Fiscal Year 2010, the aggregate amount of assistance available for the Paraplegic Housing (PH) grant increased from $60,000 to $63,780**.

To qualify for this grant, veterans must be entitled to compensation for permanent and total service-connected disability due to:

- Loss or loss of use of both lower extremities, which prevents movement without the aid of braces, crutches, canes, or a wheelchair; or

- Disability which includes:

- Blindness in both eyes, having only light perception; **with**

- Loss or loss of use of one lower extremity; or

- Loss or loss of use of one lower extremity together with:

- Residuals of organic disease or injury; **or**

- The loss or loss of use of one upper extremity, which so affects the functions of balance or propulsion as to preclude locomotion without using braces, canes, crutches, or a wheelchair.

- Loss of, or loss of use, of both upper extremities such as to preclude use of the arms at or above the elbows. (This disability was added as part of the Veterans Benefits Act of 2005.)

- A severe burn injury (as so determined.) (This disability was added as part of Public Law 110-289, The Economic and Housing Recovery Act of 2008, dated July 30, 2008.)

Eligibility For Active Duty Members

Public Law 108-183, The Veterans Benefits Act of 2003, which became law on December 16, 2003, extended eligibility for the $63,780
grant to members of the Armed Forces serving on *active duty* who are suffering from a disability as described above, if such disability is the result of an injury incurred or disease contracted in or aggravated in the line of duty in the active military, naval, or air service.

Public Law 110-289, The Economic and Housing Recovery Act of 2008, dated July 30, 2008, extended eligibility for active duty servicemembers to the same extent, and subject to the same limitations, as veterans.

> **IMPORTANT UPDATE:**
>
> On June 15, 2006, the President signed Public Law 109-233, the Veterans Housing Opportunity and Benefits Act of 2006. One section of the law made several significant changes to the Specially Adapted housing (SAH) benefits.
>
> **Benefit Changes**
>
> - An eligible veteran or active duty service member can now use his or her benefit up to **three times**, as long as the aggregate amount of assistance does not exceed the maximum amounts allowable. (Prior to this law, grant recipients could only receive their SAH benefit from VA one time, regardless of the grant amount.)
>
> - This benefit extends to previous grant recipients, however, they cannot obtain a subsequent grant(s) to pay for adaptations made prior to June 15, 2006, or to reduce an existing mortgage principal balance for properties acquired prior to June 15, 2006.

SPECIAL HOUSING ADAPTATIONS GRANT (SHA)

VA may approve a grant for the actual cost, up to a maximum of $12,756, for adaptations to a veteran's residence that are determined by VA to be reasonable necessary.

UPDATE: Public law 110-289 directed that the maximum grant amount will be adjusted annually, starting October 1, 2009 based on a cost-of-construction index. The amount will either increase or stay the same each year – it cannot decrease. Effective October 1, 2009, the aggregate amount of assistance available for the Adaptive Housing (AH) grant increased from $12,000 to $12,756.

The grant may also be used to assist veterans in acquiring a residence that already has been adapted with special features for the veteran's disability.

To qualify for this grant, veterans must be entitled to compensation for permanent and total service-connected disability due to:

- Blindness in both eyes, with 5/200 visual acuity or less; or
- Anatomical loss or loss of use of both hands.

TEMPORARY RESIDENCE ADAPTIONS GRANT (TRA)

Eligible veterans and servicemembers who are temporarily residing in a home owned by a family member may also receive a Temporary Residence Adaptation (TRA) grant to help the veteran or servicemember adapt the family member's home to meet his or her special needs. While the SAH and SHA grants require ownership and title to a house, in creating the TRA, Congress recognized the need to allow veterans and active duty members who may not yet own homes to have access to the adaptive housing grant program.

- VA may provide a **TEMPORARY RESIDENCE ADAPTATION GRANT** of up to $14,000 (for those eligible for the $60,000 grant) to assist a veteran in adapting a family member's home to meet the veteran's special needs.

- VA may provide a **TEMPORARY RESIDENCE ADAPTATION GRANT** of up to $2,000 (for those eligible for the $12,000 grant) to assist a veteran in adapting a family member's home to meet the veteran's special needs.

Note: The Temporary Residence Adaptation Grant does not apply to active duty personnel, and the Temporary Adaptation Grant is scheduled to expire after June 15, 2011.

Supplemental Financing – Loan Guaranty

Veterans who have available loan guaranty entitlement may also obtain a guaranteed loan or possibly a direct loan from VA to supplement the grant to acquire a specially adapted home. Please refer to Chapter 22 of this book for specific information on VA Loan Guaranties.

CLOTHING ALLOWANCE

The VA shall pay a clothing allowance of $716.00 per year (rate effective December 1, 2008 but not payable until August 1, 2009) to each veteran who:

- Because of a service-connected disability, wears or uses a prosthetic or orthopedic appliance (including a wheelchair) which the VA determines tends to wear out or tear the clothing of the veteran; or

- Uses medication prescribed by a physician for a skin condition that is due to a service-connected disability, and which the VA determines causes irreparable damage to the veteran's outer garments.

MEDAL OF HONOR PENSION

VA administers pensions to holders of the Medal of Honor. In December 1998, Congress set the monthly pension at $600. Public Law 107-330 (signed by then-President Bush on December 6, 2002) increased this monthly amount to $1,000, effective September 1, 2003.

As of December 1, 2008, the Medal of Honor pension is $1,194 per month.

Public Law 107-330 also directed the VA to increase the amount of the monthly Medal of Honor Pension December 1 of each year by the same percentage as the percentage by which benefit amounts payable under Title II of the Social Security Act are increased. As of December 1, 2007, the Medal of Honor pension is $1,129 per month.

The Law further states that VA shall pay, in a lump sum, to each person who is in receipt of the Medal of Honor Pension, an amount equal to the total amount of special pension that the person would have received during the period beginning on the 1st day of the 1st month beginning after the date of the act for which the person was awarded the Medal of Honor, and ending on the last day of the month preceding the month in which the person's special pension commenced.

For each month of a period referred to in the previous paragraph, the amount of special pension payable shall be determined using the rate of special pension that was in effect for such month.

The Secretary of the Department of the Army, the Department of the Navy, the Department of the Air Force, or the Department of Transportation will determine the eligibility of applicants to be entered on the Medal of Honor Roll and will deliver to the Secretary of the Department of Veterans Affairs a certified copy of each certificate issued in which the right of the person named in the certificate to the special pension is set forth. The special pension will be authorized on the basis of such certification.

The special pension will be paid in addition to all other payments under laws of the United States. However, a person awarded more than one Medal of Honor may not receive more than one special pension.

CHAPTER 5

NON-SERVICE CONNECTED DISABILITY PENSION

BENEFIT DESCRIPTION

Non-Service Connected Disability Pension is a Department of Veterans Affairs benefits program that provides financial support to wartime veterans having limited income. The amount payable under this program depends on the type and amount of income the veteran and family members receive from other sources. Monthly payments are made to bring a veteran's total annual income (including other retirement and Social Security income) to an established support level. (Unreimbursed medical expenses may reduce countable income.)

DEFINITIONS

The following definitions apply only to CHAPTER 6 – NON-SERVICE CONNECTED DISABILITY PENSION:

Indian Wars: means the campaigns, engagements, and expeditions of the United States military forces against Indian tribes or nations, service in which has been recognized heretofore as pensionable service.

World War I: means the period April 6, 1917, through November 11, 1918. In the case of a veteran who served with the United States military forces in Russia, the ending date is April 1, 1920. Service after November 11, 1918 and before July 2, 1921 is considered World War I for compensation or pension purposes, if the veteran served in the active military, naval, or air service after April 5, 1917 and before November 12, 1918.

Civil War Veteran: includes a person who served in the military or naval forces of the Confederate States of America during the Civil War, and the term "active military or naval service" includes active service in those forces.

Period of War: means the Mexican border period, World War I, World War II, the Korean conflict, the Vietnam era, the Persian Gulf War, and the period beginning on the date of any future declaration of war by the Congress and ending on the date prescribed by Presidential proclamation or concurrent resolution of the Congress.

Permanently and Totally Disabled: for the purposes of this chapter, a person shall be considered to be permanently and totally disabled if such person is unemployable as a result of a disability reasonably certain to continue throughout the life of the disabled person, or:

- Suffering from any disability which is sufficient to render it impossible for the average person to follow a substantially gainful occupation, but only if it is reasonably certain that such disability will continue throughout the life of the disabled person; or

- Suffering from any disease or disorder determined by the VA Secretary to be of such a nature or extent as to justify a determination that persons suffering are permanently and totally disabled; or

- Is a patient in a nursing home for long-term care because of disability; or

- Is disabled, as determined by the Social Security Administration (SSA) for purpose of benefits administered by the SSA; or

- Is unemployable, as a result of suffering from any disability which is sufficient to render it impossible for the average person to follow a substantially gainful occupation, but only if it is reasonable certain that such disability will continue throughout the life of the person, or otherwise justifying a determination of permanent and total disability.

Regular Aid and Attendance: for the purposes of this chapter, a person shall be considered to be in need of regular aid and attendance if such person is:
- A patient in a nursing home; or

- Helpless or blind, or so nearly helpless or blind as to need or require the aid and attendance of another person.

Permanently Housebound: for the purposes of this chapter, the requirement of "permanently housebound" will be considered to have been met when the veteran is substantially confined to such veteran's house (ward or clinical areas, if institutionalized) or immediate premises due to a disability or disabilities, which it is reasonably certain will remain throughout such veteran's lifetime.

Annual Income: In determining annual income under this chapter, all payments of any kind or from any source (including salary, retirement or annuity payments, or similar income, which has been waived, irrespective of whether the waiver was made pursuant to statue, contract, or otherwise) shall be included except:

- Donations from public or private relief or welfare organizations;

- Payments under this chapter;

- Amounts equal to amounts paid by a spouse of a veteran for the expenses of such veteran's last illness, and by a surviving spouse or child of a deceased veteran for:

- Such veteran's just debts;

- The expenses of such veteran's last illness; and

- The expenses of such veteran's burial to the extent such expenses are not reimbursed through Chapter 23 of Title 38, United States Code (Burial Benefits);

- Amounts equal to amounts paid:

- By a veteran for the last illness and burial of such veteran's deceased spouse or child; or

- By the spouse of a living veteran or the surviving spouse of a deceased veteran for the last illness and burial of a child of such veteran;

- Reimbursements of any kind for any casualty loss, but the amount excluded under this clause may not exceed the greater of the fair market value or reasonable replacement value of the property involved at the time immediately preceding the loss;

- Profit realized from the disposition of real or personal property other than in the course of a business;

- Amounts in joint accounts in banks and similar institutions acquired by reason of death of other joint owner;

- Amounts equal to amounts paid by a veteran, veteran's spouse, or surviving spouse, or by or on behalf of a veteran's child for unreimbursed medical expenses, to the extent that such amounts exceed 5% of the maximum annual rate of pension (including any amount of increased pension payable on account of family members but not including any amount of pension payable because a person is in need of regular aid and attendance, or because a person is permanently housebound) payable to such veteran surviving spouse, or child.

- In the case of a veteran or surviving spouse pursuing a course of education or vocational rehabilitation or training, amounts equal to amounts paid by such veteran or surviving spouse for such course of education or vocational rehabilitation or training, including:

- Amounts paid for tuition, fees, books, and materials; and

- In the case of such a veteran or surviving spouse in need of regular aid and attendance, unreimbursed amounts paid for unusual transpiration expenses in connection with the pursuit of such course of education or vocational rehabilitation or training, to the extent that such amounts exceed the reasonable expenses which would have been incurred by a nondisabled person using an appropriate means of transportation (public transportation, if reasonably available); and

- In the case of a child, or any current-work income received during the year, to the extent that the total amount of such income does not exceed an amount equal to the sum of:

- The lowest amount of gross income for which an income tax return is required under section 6012(a) of the Internal Revenue Code of 1986, to be filed by an individual who is not married, is not a surviving spouse, and is not a head of household; and

- If the child is pursuing a course of postsecondary education or vocational rehabilitation or training, the amount paid by such child for such course of education or vocational rehabilitation or training, including the amount paid for tuition, fees, books, and materials.

Note: Where a fraction of a dollar is involved, annual income shall be fixed at the next lower dollar.

ELIGIBILITY

- Veteran was discharged from service under other than dishonorable conditions; and
- Veteran served 90 days or more of active duty with at least 1 day during a period of war time. However, 38 CFR 3.12a requires that anyone who enlisted after 9/7/80 generally has to serve at least 24 months or the full period for which a person was called or ordered to active duty in order to receive any benefits based on that period of service; and
- Veteran is permanently and totally disabled, or is age 65 or older; and
- Veteran's countable family income is below a yearly limit set by law.

AMOUNT OF VA PAYMENTS

If eligible, VA pays the difference between a recipient's countable family income and the annual income limit set by law (see following charts) for his or her status. This difference is generally paid in 12 equal monthly installments.

Family Income Limits

Improved Pension Annual Rates (PL-95-588) Effective December 1, 2008	
STATUS OF VETERAN:	**ANNUAL INCOME LIMITATION:**
Permanently & totally disabled veterans:	
Veteran alone	*$11,830.00*
Veteran with one dependent	*15,492.00*
Each additional dependent child	*2,020.00*
Veteran – Aid and Attendance:	
Veteran alone	*19,736.00*
Veteran with one dependent	*23,396.00*
Each additional dependent child	*2,020.00*
Veteran – Housebound:	
Veteran alone	*14,457.00*
Veteran with one dependent	*18,120.00*
Each additional dependent child	*2,020.00*
Two veterans married to one another:	*15,493.00*
Each additional dependent child	*2,020.00*
Add for Mexican Border Period or World War I Veterans:	*2,686.00*
Child Earned Income Exclusion effective 1-1-2009 –	
$9,350.00	

Maximum Annual Income Limitations For Protected Pensions - (Effective December 1, 2008)

Pensioners entitled to benefits as of December 31, 1978, who do not elect to receive a pension under the Improved Pension Program, may continue to receive pension benefits at the rates they were entitled to receive on December 31, 1978 or June 30, 1960, as long as they remain permanently and totally disabled, do not lose a dependent, and their income does not exceed the income limitation, adjusted annually. Under the Old Law Disability Pensions, all veterans whose income was under the annual limitation received the same monthly amount. These monthly amounts are also listed below, following the annual income limitation charts.

Pension Law in Effect on December 31, 1978 (Section 306): The rate entitled to on December 31, 1978 may be continued if the recipient's IVAP for 2008 is below the following limits:	
STATUS OF RECIPIENT:	**ANNUAL INCOME LIMITATION:**
Veteran / widow with no dependents	$ 13,456.00
Veteran / widow with one or more dependent	18,087.00
Child (no entitled veteran or surviving spouse)	11,001.00
Veteran with no dependents in receipt of A&A	13,956.00
Veteran with one dependent in receipt of A&A	18,587.00
Surviving spouse's income exclusion	4,295.00
Pension Law in Effect on June 30, 1960 (Old Law): The rate entitled to on June 30, 1960 may be continued if the recipient's IVAP for 2008 is below the following limits:	
STATUS OF RECIPIENT:	**ANNUAL INCOME LIMITATION:**
Veteran / widow with no dependents	$ 11,780.00
Veteran / widow with one or more dependents	16,982.00
Child (no entitled veteran or surviving spouse)	11,780.00
Monthly Benefit Payable To Eligible Veterans Receiving Disability Pension Under Laws In Effect June 30, 1960 Or December 31, 1978	
VETERAN'S ENTITLEMENT:	**RATE PAYABLE:**
Basic Rates	$ 66.15
10 Years or Age 65	78.75
If Entitled To Aid & Attendance	135.45
If Entitled To Housebound	100.00

APPLYING FOR BENEFITS

Veterans can apply for a Disability Pension by completing VA Form 21-526, Veteran's Application for Compensation or Pension. If available, the applicant should attach copies of dependency records (marriage and children's birth certificates) and current medical evidence (doctor and hospital reports). The completed form should be sent to the veteran's VA Regional Office. (Refer to Chapter 36 for a listing of all VA regional offices.)

If any of the pertinent supporting evidence is not immediately available, the applicant should send in the application anyway. The date VA receives the application is important! If VA approves the claim, benefit payments usually begin from the date the application is received, regardless of when the claim is approved.

NET WORTH LIMITATION

The VA shall deny or discontinue the payment of pension to a veteran under this chapter when the corpus of the estate of the veteran, or, if the veteran has a spouse, the corpus of the estates of the veteran and of the veteran's spouse is such that under all the circumstances, including consideration of the annual income of the veteran, the veteran's spouse, and the veteran's children, it is reasonable that some part of the corpus of such estates be consumed for the veteran's maintenance.

The VA shall deny or discontinue the payment of increased pension under this chapter on account of a child when the corpus of such child's estate is such that under all the circumstances, including consideration of the veteran's and spouse's income, and the income of the veteran's children, it is reasonable that some part of the corpus of such child's estate be consumed for the child's maintenance. During the period such denial or discontinuance remains in effect, such child shall not be considered as the veteran's child for purposes of this chapter.

PROOF OF INCOME AND OVERPAYMENT ADJUSTMENTS

As a condition of granting, or continuing payment of a Disability Pension for a Non-Service-Connected Disability, the VA:

- May require from any person who is an applicant or recipient, such information, proof, and evidence the VA determines to be necessary in order to determine the annual income and the value of the corpus of the estate of such person, and of any spouse or child for whom the person is receiving, or is to receive increased pension, and in the case of a child applying for or in receipt of benefits, of any person with whom such child is residing who is legally responsible for such child's support.

- May require that any such applicant or recipient file for a calendar year with the VA, a report showing:

- The annual income which such applicant or recipient (and any spouse or dependent child) received during the preceding year, the corpus of the estate of such applicant or recipient (and of any such spouse or dependent child) at the end of such year, and in the case of a surviving child, the income and corpus of the estate of any person with whom such child is residing who is legally responsible for such child's support.

- Such applicant's or recipient's estimate for the current year of the annual income such applicant or recipient (and any such spouse or dependent child) expects to receive, and of any expected increase in the value of the corpus of the estate of such applicant or recipient (and for any such spouse or dependent child); and

- In the case of a surviving child, an estimate of the annual income of any person with whom such child is residing who is legally responsible for such child's support, and of any expected increase in the value of the corpus of the estate of such person;

- Shall require that any such applicant or recipient promptly notify the VA whenever there is a material change in the annual income of such applicant or recipient (or of any such spouse or dependent child) or a material change in the value of the corpus of the estate of such applicant or recipient (or of any such spouse or dependent child), and in the case of a surviving child, a material change in the annual income or value of the corpus of the estate of any person with whom such child is residing who is legally responsible for such child's support; and

- Shall require that any such applicant or recipient applying for or in receipt of increased pension on account of a person who is a spouse or child of such applicant or recipient promptly notify the VA if such person ceases to meet the applicable definition of spouse or child.

COMBINATION OF RATINGS

The VA shall provide that, for the purpose of determining whether or not a veteran is permanently and totally disabled, ratings for service-connected disabilities may be combined with ratings for non-service-connected disabilities.

Where a veteran is found to be entitled to a Non-Service-Connected Disability Pension, and is also entitled to Service-Connected Disability Compensation, the VA shall pay the veteran the greater benefit.

VOCATIONAL TRAINING FOR CERTAIN PENSION RECIPIENTS

In the case of a veteran who is awarded a Non-Service-Connected Disability Pension, the VA shall, based on information on file with the VA, make a preliminary finding whether such veteran, with the assistance of a vocational training program, has a good potential for achieving employment. If such potential is found to exist, the VA shall solicit from the veteran an application for vocational training. If the veteran thereafter applies for such training, the VA shall provide the veteran with an evaluation, which may include a personal interview, to determine whether the achievement of a vocational goal is reasonably feasible.

If the VA, based on the evaluation, determines that the achievement of a vocational goal by a veteran is reasonably feasible, the veteran shall be offered, and may elect to pursue a vocational training program.

If the veteran elects to pursue such a program, the program shall be designed in consultation with the veteran in order to meet the veteran's individual needs, and shall be set forth in an individualized written plan of vocational rehabilitation.

A vocational training program under this section:

- May not exceed 24 months unless, based on a determination by the VA that an extension is necessary in order for the veteran to achieve a vocational goal identified in the written plan formulated for the veteran, the VA grants an extension for a period not to exceed 24 months.

- May not include the provision of any loan or subsistence allowance, or any automobile adaptive equipment.

- May include a program of education at an institution of higher learning, only in a case in which the Secretary of the VA determines that the program involved is predominantly vocational in content.

When a veteran completes a vocational training program, the VA may provide the veteran with counseling, placement and post-placement services for a period not to exceed 18 months.

A veteran may not begin pursuit of a vocational training program under this chapter after the later of:

- December 31, 1995; or

- The end of a reasonable period of time, as determined by the VA, following either the evaluation of the veteran or the award of pension to the veteran.

In the case of a veteran who has been determined to have a permanent and total non-service-connected disability and who, not later than one year after the date the veteran's eligibility for counseling under this chapter expires, secures employment within the scope of a vocational goal identified in the veteran's individualized written plan of vocational rehabilitation (or in a related field which requires reasonably developed skills, and the use of some or all of the training or services furnished the veteran under such plan), the evaluation of the veteran as having a permanent and total disability may not be terminated be reason of the veteran's capacity to engage in such employment until the veteran first maintains such employment for a period of not less than 12 consecutive months.

PROTECTION OF HEALTH-CARE ELIGIBILITY

In the case of a veteran whose entitlement to pension is terminated after January 31, 1985, by reason of income from work or training, the veteran shall retain for a period of three years, beginning on the date of such termination, all eligibility for care and services that the veteran would have had if the veteran's entitlement to pension had not been terminated.

DISAPPEARANCE

When a veteran receiving a non-service-connected disability pension from the VA disappears, the VA may pay the pension otherwise payable to such veteran's spouse and children. Payments made to a spouse or child shall not exceed the amount to which each would be entitled if the veteran died of a non-service-connected disability.

CHAPTER 6

DEPENDENCY AND INDEMNITY COMPENSATION FOR SERVICE-CONNECTED DEATHS

Dependency and Indemnity Compensation (DIC) payments may be available for:

- Surviving spouses who have not remarried (please refer to boxes on bottom of this page for important additional information regarding remarriage);

- Surviving spouses who remarry after attaining age 57 (see following "Important Update.")

- Unmarried Children under 18;

- Helpless children;

- Children between 18 and 23, if attending a VA-approved school; and

- Low-income parents of deceased servicemembers or veterans.

IMPORTANT: *Public Law 108-183, The Veterans Benefits Act of 2003, restores DIC eligibility, effective January 1, 2004, for surviving spouses who remarry after age 57.*	*Qualifying spouses who remarried at age 57 or older prior to enactment of this bill had until December 16, 2004 to apply for reinstatement of these benefits. No retroactive benefits will be paid for any period prior to January 1, 2004.*

Public Law 108-183 also provided that, for surviving spouses who remarry after attaining age 57, DIC be paid with no reduction of certain other Federal benefits to which a surviving spouse might be entitled. This provision, in essence eliminates the requirement for DIC to offset military SBP annuities, as was required under prior law. In other words, concurrent receipt of DIC and SBP without an offset of either is now allowed for surviving spouses who remarry after attaining age 57.

DEFINITIONS

The following definitions apply only to CHAPTER 6 – DEPENDENCY AND INDEMNITY COMPENSATION FOR SERVICE-CONNECTED DEATHS:

Veteran: in this chapter, the term includes a person who died in the active military, naval, or air service.

Social Security Increase: in this chapter, the term means the percentage by which benefit amounts payable under Title II of the Social Security Act (42 U.S.C. 401 et seq.) are increased for any fiscal year as a result of a determination under section 215(i) of such Act (42 U.S.C. 415(i)).

Permanently Housebound: for the purposes of this chapter, the requirement of "permanently housebound" will be considered to have been met when the individual is substantially confined to such individual's house (ward or clinical areas, if institutionalized) or immediate premises due to a disability or disabilities, which it is reasonably certain will remain throughout such individual's lifetime.

ELIGIBILITY

To receive Dependency and Indemnity Compensation (DIC), an individual must be an eligible survivor of a veteran who died from:

- A disease or injury incurred or aggravated while on active duty or active duty for training; or

- An injury incurred or aggravated in the line of duty while on inactive duty training; or

- A disability compensable by VA.

- The death cannot be a result of the veteran's willful misconduct.

DIC also may be authorized for survivors of veterans who at the time of death, were determined to be totally disabled as a result of military service, even though their service-connected disabilities did not cause their deaths. The survivor qualifies if:

- The veteran was continuously rated totally disabled for a period of 10 or more years immediately preceding death; or

- The veteran was so rated for a period of at least five years from the date of military discharge; or

- The veteran was a former prisoner of war who died after Sept. 30, 1999, and who was continuously rated totally disabled for a period of at least one year immediately preceding death.

To qualify as an eligible survivor, an individual must have proof of the following:

- Proof that he or she was married to the veteran for at least 1 year (Note: If a child was born, there is no time requirement); AND

- Proof that the marriage was VALID; AND

- Proof that he or she lived with the veteran continuously until his/her death or, if separated, the surviving spouse wasn't at fault; AND

- Proof that he or she did not remarry. (Note: The remarriage of the surviving spouse of a veteran shall not bar the furnishing of DIC if the remarriage is terminated by death, divorce, or annulment, unless the VA determines that the divorce or annulment was secured through fraud or collusion.)

OR

- The individual is an unmarried child of a deceased veteran; AND

- The individual is under age 18, or between the ages of 18 and 23 and attending school.

IMPORTANT UPDATE: Public Law 108-183, The Veterans Benefits Act of 2003, restores DIC eligibility, effective January 1, 2004, for surviving spouses who remarry after age 57. Qualifying spouses who remarried at age 57 or older prior to enactment of this bill had until December 16, 2004 to apply for reinstatement of these benefits. No retroactive benefits will be paid for any period prior to January 1, 2004.

Note: Certain helpless adult children and some parents of deceased veterans are entitled to DIC. Call VA at (800) 827-1000 for the eligibility requirements for these survivors.

AMOUNT OF DIC PAYMENTS TO SURVIVING SPOUSES

-

- Surviving spouses of veterans who died after January 1, 1993, receive a basic monthly rate of **$1,154 (effective December 1, 2008.)**

- Surviving spouses entitled to DIC based on the veteran's death prior to January 1, 1993, receive the greater of:

- The basic monthly rate of **$1,154, or**

- An amount based on the veteran's pay grade. (See following sections for Pay Grade tables and Determination of Pay Grade.)

There are additional DIC payments for dependent children. (Refer to the following charts.)

Additional Allowances For Surviving Spouses

- Add **$246.00** to the basic monthly rate if, at the time of the veteran's death, the veteran was in receipt of, or entitled to receive compensation for a service-connected disability rated totally disabling (including a rating based on individual unemployability) for a continuous period of at least 8 years immediately preceding death AND the surviving spouse was married to the veteran for those same 8 years.

- Add **$286.00** per child to the basic monthly rate for each dependent child under age 18.

- If the surviving spouse is entitled to Aid & Attendance, add **$286.00** to the basic monthly rate.

- If the surviving spouse is Permanently Housebound, add **$135.00** to the basic monthly rate.

SURVIVING SPOUSE DIC RATES IF VETERAN'S DEATH WAS PRIOR TO JANUARY 1, 1993

Rates Effective December 1, 2008

Pay Grade	Monthly Rate	Pay Grade	Monthly Rate
E-1*:	$1154	W-4**:	$1380
E-2*:	$1154	O-1**:	$1219
E-3* (see footnote #1):	$1154	O-2**:	$1260
E-4*:	$1154	O-3**:	$1347
E-5*:	$1154	O-4:	$1427
E-6*:	$1154	O-5:	$1571
E-7**:	$1194	O-6:	$1771
E-8**:	$1260	O-7:	$1912
E-9** (see footnote #2):	$1314 or $1419	O-8:	$2100
W-1**:	$1219	O-9:	$2246
W-2**:	$1267	O-10 (see footnote #3):	$2463 or $2643
W-3**:	$1305		

Footnotes to Table:
*   Add $246 if veteran rated totally disabled 8 continuous years prior to death,   and surviving spouse was married to veteran those same 8 years.
** Base rate is $1400 if veteran rated totally disabled 8 continuous years prior to death, and surviving spouse was married to vet those same 8 years.
1. A surviving spouse of an Aviation Cadet or other service not covered by this table is paid the DIC rate for enlisted E-3 under 34.
2. $1419 is for a veteran who served as Sergeant Major of the Army or Marine Corps, Senior Enlisted Advisor of the Navy, Chief Master Sergeant of the Air Force, or Master Chief Petty Officer of the Coast Guard.
3. $2643 is for a veteran who served as Chairman of the Joint Chiefs of Staff, Chief of Staff of the Army or Air Force, Chief of Naval Operations, or Commandant of the Marine Corps.

Determination Of Pay Grade

With respect to a veteran who died in the active military, naval, or air service, such veteran's pay grade shall be determined as of the date of such veteran's death, or as of the date of a promotion after death, while in a missing status.

With respect to a veteran who did not die in the active military, naval, or air service, such veteran's pay grade shall be determined as of:
- The time of such veteran's last discharge or release from active duty under conditions other than dishonorable; or

- The time of such veteran's discharge or release from any period of active duty for training or inactive duty training, if such veteran's death results from service-connected disability incurred during such period, and if such veteran was not thereafter discharged or released under conditions other than dishonorable from active duty.

If a veteran has satisfactorily served on active duty for a period of six months or more in a pay grade higher than that specified in the previous paragraphs of this section, and any subsequent discharge or release from active duty was under conditions other than dishonorable, the higher pay grade shall be used if it will result in greater monthly payments to such veteran's surviving spouse under this chapter. The determination as to whether an individual has served satisfactorily for the required period in a higher pay grade shall be made by the Secretary of the department in which such higher pay grade was held.

The pay grade of any person not otherwise described in this section, but who had a compensable status on the date of such person's death under laws administered by the Secretary, shall be determined by the head of the department under which such person performed the services by which such person obtained such status.

DIC PAYMENTS TO CHILDREN

Whenever there is no surviving spouse of a deceased veteran entitled to DIC, DIC shall be paid in equal shares to the children of the deceased veteran at the following monthly rates (effective December 1, 2008):

Number of Children	Total Payable (to be divided in equal shares):
1	$488
2	$701
3	$915
4	$1089
5	$1263
6	$1437

- If DIC is payable monthly to a person as a surviving spouse, and there is a child (of such person's deceased spouse) who has attained the age of 18, and who, while under such age, became permanently incapable of self-support, DIC shall be paid monthly to each such child, concurrently with the payment of DIC to the surviving spouse, in the amount of **$488**.

- If DIC is payable monthly to a person as a surviving spouse, and there is a child (of such person's deceased spouse) who has attained the age of 18 and who, while under the age of 23, is pursuing a course of instruction at a VA-approved educational institution, DIC shall be paid monthly to each such child, concurrently with the payment of DIC to the surviving spouse, in the amount of **$243**.

DIC PAYMENTS FOR PARENTS

Parents whose child died in-service or from a service-connected disability may be entitled to DIC if they are in financial need. Parents may be biological, step, adopted, or *in loco parentis*.

The monthly payment for parents of deceased veterans depends upon their income. The following 3 charts outline the monthly rates payable, **effective December 1, 2008,** under various conditions.

Chart #1
Sole Surviving Parent Unremarried or
Remarried Living With Spouse

Income Not Over:	Monthly Rate:	Income Not Over:	Monthly Rate:
$ 800	$ 569	$ 2,500	$ 433
900	561	2,600	425
1,000	553	2,700	417
1,100	545	2,800	409
1,200	537	2,900	401
1,300	529	3,000	393
1,400	521	3,100	385
1,500	513	3,200	377
1,600	505	3,300	369
1,700	497	3,400	361
1,800	489	3,500	353
1,900	481	3,600	345
2,000	473	3,700	337
2,100	465	3,800	329
2,200	457	3,900	321
2,300	449	4,000	313
2,400	441	4,100	305

Chart #1 Continued -			
Income Not Over:	**Monthly Rate:**	**Income Not Over:**	**Monthly Rate:**
$4,200	$297	$6,300	$129
4,300	289	6,400	121
4,400	281	6,500	113
4,500	273	6,600	105
4,600	265	6,700	97
4,700	257	6,800	89
4,800	249	6,900	81
4,900	241	7,000	73
5,000	233	7,100	65
5,100	225	7,200	57
5,200	217	7,300	49
5,300	209	7,400	41
5,400	201	7,500	33
5,500	193	7,600	25
5,600	185	7,700	17
5,700	177	7,800	5.08
5,800	169	7,850	5.00
5,900	161		
6,000	153	If A&A add:	308
6,100	145	If living w/ spouse:	18,087
6,200	137	**If not living w/ spouse: 13,456	

Chart #2 - One of Two Parents Not Living With Spouse

Income Not Over:	Monthly Rate:	Income Not Over:	Monthly Rate:
$ 800	$ 412	$ 3,600	$ 192
900	406	3,700	184
1,000	399	3,800	176
1,100	395	3,900	168
1,200	384	4,000	160
1,300	376	4,100	152
1,400	368	4,200	144
1,500	360	4,300	136
1,600	352	4,400	128
1,700	344	4,500	120
1,800	336	4,600	112
1,900	328	4,700	104
2,000	320	4,800	96
2,100	312	4,900	88
2,200	304	5,000	80
2,300	296	5,100	72
2,400	288	5,200	64
2,500	280	5,300	56
2,600	272	5,400	48
2,700	264	5,500	40
2,800	256	5,600	32
2,900	248	5,700	24
3,000	240	5,800	16
3,100	232	5,900	8
3,200	224	5,937	5.04
3,300	216	5,938 to 13,456	5
3,400	208		
3,500	200	If A&A add: $308	

Chart #3
1 of 2 Parents Living with Spouse or Other Parent

Income Not Over:	Monthly Rate:	Income Not Over:	Monthly Rate:
$1,000	$387	$4,000	$216
1,100	384	4,100	208
1,200	381	4,200	200
1,300	378	4,300	192
1,400	375	4,400	184
1,500	372	4,500	176
1,600	368	4,600	168
1,700	364	4,700	160
1,800	360	4,800	152
1,900	356	4,900	144
2,000	351	5,000	136
2,100	346	5,100	128
2,200	341	5,200	120
2,300	336	5,300	112
2,400	331	5,400	104
2,500	325	5,500	96
2,600	319	5,600	88
2,700	313	5,700	80
2,800	307	5,800	72
2,900	301	5,900	64
3,000	294	6,000	56
3,100	287	6,100	48
3,200	280	6,200	40
3,300	272	6,300	32
3,400	264	6,400	24
3,500	256	6,500	16
3,600	248	6,600	8
3,700	240	6,637	5.04
3,800	232	6,638 to 18,087	5
3,900	224	If A&A add:	308

Miscellaneous Information Regarding Income Limitations For Parents

The VA may require, as a condition of granting or continuing DIC to a parent that such parent, other than one who has attained 72 years of age, and has been paid DIC during 2 consecutive calendar years, file for a calendar year with the VA, a report showing the total income which such parent expects to receive in that year, and the total income which such parent received in the preceding year. The parent or parents shall notify the VA whenever there is a material change in annual income.

In determining income under this section, all payments of any kind, or from any source shall be included except:

- Payments of a death gratuity;
- Donations from public or private relief or welfare organizations;
- Payments under this chapter (DIC), Chapter 11 of Title 38, United States Code (Disability Compensation), and Chapter 15 of Title 38, United States Code (Non-Service Connected Disability/Death Pension);
- Payments under policies of servicemembers group life insurance, United States Government life insurance, or national service life insurance, and payments of servicemen's indemnity;
- 10% of the amount of payments to an individual under public or private retirement, annuity, endowment, or similar plans or programs;
- Amounts equal to amounts paid by a parent of a deceased veteran for:
- A deceased spouse's just debts;
- The expenses of the spouse's last illness, to the extent such expenses are not reimbursed under Chapter 51 of Title 38 of the United States Code;
- The expenses of the spouse's burial to the extent that such expenses are not reimbursed under Chapter 23 or Chapter 51 of Title 38 of the United States Code;
- Reimbursements of any kind for any casualty loss (as defined in regulations which the VA shall prescribe), but the amount excluded under this clause may not exceed the greater of the fair market value or the reasonable replacement value of the property involved at the time immediately preceding the loss;
- Amounts equal to amounts paid by a parent of a deceased veteran for:
- The expenses of the veteran's last illness, and
- The expenses of such veteran's burial, to the extent that such expenses are not reimbursed under Chapter 23 of Title 38 of the United States Code;
- Profit realized from the disposition of real or personal property other than in the course of a business;
- Payments received for discharge of jury duty or obligatory civic duties;
- Payments of annuities elected under Subchapter I of Chapter 73 of Title 10.

Where a fraction of a dollar is involved, annual income shall be fixed at the next lower dollar.

The VA may provide by regulation for the exclusion from income under this section of amounts paid by a parent for unusual medical expenses.

SPECIAL PROVISIONS RELATING TO SURVIVING SPOUSES

No Dependency and Indemnity Compensation shall be paid to the surviving spouse of a veteran dying after December 31, 1956, unless such surviving spouse was married to such veteran:

- Before the expiration of 15 years after the termination of the period of service in which the injury or disease causing the death of the veteran was incurred or aggravated; or

- For one year or more; or

- For any period of time if a child was born of the marriage, or was born to them before the marriage.

APPLYING FOR DEPENDENCY AND INDEMNITY COMPENSATION

Eligible surviving spouses and dependent children can apply for DIC by completing VA Form 21-534, *Application for Dependency and Indemnity Compensation or Death Pension by Surviving Spouse or Child.* If available, copies of dependency records (marriage records, divorce records, & children's birth certificates) should be attached to the application. A copy of the veteran's DD Form 214 and a copy of the veteran's death certificate should also be included with the completed application.

The completed form should be sent to the applicable VA Regional Office (refer to Chapter 36 for a listing of all VA regional offices.)

> ### Note:
> *If any of the pertinent supporting evidence is not immediately available, the applicant should send in the application anyway. The date VA receives the application is important! If VA approves the claim, benefit payments usually begin from the date the application is received, regardless of when the claim is approved.*

CHAPTER 7

DEATH PENSIONS TO SURVIVING SPOUSES AND CHILDREN

A Death Pension is a benefit paid to eligible dependents of deceased wartime veterans.

DEFINITIONS

The following definitions apply only to CHAPTER 7 – DEATH PENSIONS TO SURVIVING SPOUSES AND CHILDREN:

Veteran: as used in this chapter, includes a person who has completed at least 2 years of honorable active military, naval, or air service, as certified by the appropriate authority, but whose death in such service was not in line of duty.

Indian Wars: means the campaigns, engagements, and expeditions of the United States military forces against Indian tribes or nations, service in which has been recognized heretofore as pensionable service.

World War I: means the period April 6, 1917, through November 11, 1918. In the case of a veteran who served with the United States military forces in Russia, the ending date is April 1, 1920. Service after November 11, 1918 and before July 2, 1921 is considered World War I for compensation or pension purposes, if the veteran served in the active military, naval, or air service after April 5, 1917 and before November 12, 1918.

Civil War Veteran: includes a person who served in the military or naval forces of the Confederate States of America during the Civil War, and the term "active military or naval service" includes active service in those forces.

Period of War: means the Mexican border period, World War I, World War II, the Korean conflict, the Vietnam era, the Persian Gulf War, and the period beginning on the date of any future declaration of war by the Congress and ending on the date prescribed by Presidential proclamation or concurrent resolution of the Congress.

Regular Aid and Attendance: for the purposes of this chapter, a person shall be considered to be in need of regular aid and attendance if such person is:

- A patient in a nursing home; or

- Helpless or blind, or so nearly helpless or blind as to need or require the aid and attendance of another person.

Permanently Housebound: for the purposes of this chapter, the requirement of "permanently housebound" will be considered to have been met when the surviving spouse is substantially confined to such surviving spouse's house (ward or clinical areas, if institutionalized) or immediate premises due to a disability or disabilities, which it is reasonably certain will remain throughout such surviving spouse's lifetime.

ELIGIBILITY REQUIREMENTS

Eligible dependents may qualify for a Death Pension if:

- The deceased veteran was discharged from service under other than dishonorable conditions; **AND**

- He or she served 90 days or more of active duty with at least 1 day during a war, or must have had a service-connected disability justifying discharge for disability. If the veteran died in service but not in the line of duty, pension may be payable if the veteran had completed at least two years of honorable service; **AND**

- The dependent is the surviving spouse (spouse must not have remarried), or the unmarried child of the deceased veteran (children must be under age 18, or under age 23 if attending a VA-approved school); **AND**

- The dependent's countable income is below an annual limit set by law (See below for 2005 annual income limitations.)

(Children who become incapable of self-support because of a disability before age 18 may be eligible for a pension as long as the condition exists, unless the child marries or the child's income exceeds the applicable limit.)

ADDITIONAL REQUIREMENTS

No Death Pension shall be paid under this chapter to a surviving spouse of a veteran unless the spouse was married to the veteran:

Before:

- December 14, 1944, in the case of a surviving spouse of a Mexican Border period or World War I veteran; or

- January 1, 1957 in the case of a surviving spouse of a World War II veteran; or

- February 1, 1965, in the case of a surviving spouse of a Korean conflict veteran; or

- May 8, 1985, in the case of a surviving spouse of a Vietnam era veteran, or

- January 1, 2001, in the case of a surviving spouse of a veteran of the Persian Gulf War;

- For one year or more; or
- For any period of time if a child was born of the marriage, or was born to them before the marriage.

ANNUAL INCOME LIMITATIONS

DEATH PENSION RATE TABLE FOR SURVIVING SPOUSES & CHILDREN

RATES EFFECTIVE DECEMBER 1, 2008

Maximum Annual Pension Rate (MAPR) Category	Annual Income Must Be Less Than:
Surviving Spouse Alone (No Dependent Child):	$7,933
Surviving Spouse With One Dependent Child:	10,385
Child Alone:	2,020
Housebound Spouse Without Dependents:	9,696
Housebound Spouse With One Dependent:	12,144
Surviving Spouse In Need Of Aid And Attendance (No Dependent Child):	12,681
Surviving Spouse In Need Of Aid And Attendance With One Dependent Child:	15,128
For Each Additional Child:	2,020
Child Earned Income Exclusion Effective 1/1/2008:	9,350

MAXIMUM ANNUAL INCOME LIMITATIONS FOR PROTECTED PENSIONS (EFFECTIVE DECEMBER 1, 2008)

(Pensioners entitled to benefits as of December 31, 1978, who do not elect to receive a pension under the Improved Pension Program, may continue to receive pension benefits at the rates they were entitled to receive on December 31, 1978 or June 30, 1960, as long as they remain permanently and totally disabled, do not lose a dependent, and their income does not exceed the income limitation, adjusted annually.)

Pension Law in Effect on December 31, 1978 (Section 306):

The rate entitled to on December 31, 1978 may be continued if the recipient's IVAP for 2008 is below the following limits:

STATUS OF RECIPIENT:		ANNUAL INCOME LIMITATION:
Surviving spouse with no dependents	$	13,456.00
Surviving spouse with one or more dependents		18,087.00
Child (no entitled veteran or surviving spouse)		11,001.00

Pension Law in Effect on June 30, 1960 (Old Law):

The rate entitled to on June 30, 1960 may be continued if the recipient's IVAP for 2008 is below the following limits:

STATUS OF RECIPIENT:	ANNUAL INCOME LIMITATION:
Surviving spouse with no dependents	11,780.00
Surviving spouse with one or more dependents	16,982.00
Child only (no entitled veteran or surviving spouse)	11,780.00

Note: Some income is not counted toward the yearly limit (for example, welfare benefits, some wages earned by dependent children, and Supplemental Security Income).

In determining the annual income of a surviving spouse, if there is a child of the veteran in the custody of the surviving spouse, that portion of the annual income of the child that is reasonably available to or for the surviving spouse shall be considered to be income of the surviving spouse, unless in the judgment of the VA, to do so would work a hardship on the surviving spouse.

AMOUNT PAID BY VA

VA pays eligible spouses and dependents the difference between his or her countable income and the annual income limit outlined in the above table. The difference is generally paid in 12 equal monthly payments rounded down to the nearest dollar.

NET WORTH LIMITATION

The VA shall deny or discontinue payment of pension to a surviving spouse when the corpus of the estate of the surviving spouse is such that under all the circumstances, including consideration of the income of the surviving spouse and the income of any child from whom the surviving spouse is receiving increased pension, it is reasonable that some part of the corpus of such estate be consumed for the surviving spouse's maintenance.

The VA shall deny or discontinue the payment of increased pension on account of a child when the corpus of such child's estate is such that under all the circumstances, including consideration of the income of the surviving spouse and such child and the income of any other child for whom the surviving spouse is receiving increased pension, it is reasonable that some part of the corpus of the child's estate be consumed for the child's maintenance. During the period such denial or discontinuance remains in effect, such child shall not be considered as the surviving spouse's child for purposes of this chapter.

The VA shall deny or discontinue payment of pension to a child when the corpus of the state of the child is such that under all the circumstances, including consideration of the income of the child, the income of any person with whom such child is residing who is legally responsible for such child's support, and the corpus of the estate of such person, it is reasonable that some part of the corpus of such estate be consumed for the child's maintenance.

APPLYING FOR DEATH PENSION BENEFITS

Eligible surviving spouses and dependent children can apply for Death Pension benefits by completing VA Form 21-534, *Application for Dependency and Indemnity Compensation or Death Pension by Surviving Spouse or Child.* If available, copies of dependency records (marriage & children's birth certificates) should be attached to the application. A copy of the veteran's DD Form 214 and a copy of the veteran's death certificate should also be included with the completed application.

The completed forms should be sent to the applicable VA Regional Office. (Refer to Chapter 36 for a listing of all VA regional offices.)

Special Note: If any of the pertinent supporting evidence is not immediately available, the applicant should send in the application anyway. The date VA receives the application is important! If VA approves the claim, benefit payments usually begin from the date the application is received, regardless of when the claim is approved.

CHAPTER 8

MISCELLANEOUS BENEFITS FOR SURVIVING SPOUSES AND CHILDREN

SURVIVOR BENEFIT PLAN (SBP)

The Survivor Benefit Plan (SBP) was established by Congress effective September 21, 1972 (Public Law 92-425) to provide a monthly income to survivors of retired military personnel upon the member's death when retired pay stops. Survivors of members who die while on active duty, and survivors of members recalled to active duty from retirement who die while on active duty may also be protected by the SBP.

The SBP is free for active duty service members with 20 years of qualifying service. The SBP for retirees is paid for by premium payments from a retiree's paycheck. There is a tax break for the retiree in that the amount of the SBP premium is not included in the taxable portion of his or her retired pay.

If you elect to participate in the SBP you will be required to pay a monthly premium. SBP Premiums and benefits are based on the "base amount" or benefit level that you elect.

At retirement, full basic SBP for spouse and children will take effect *automatically* if you make no other valid election. You may not reduce or decline spouse coverage without your spouse's written consent. This means you will have to have your spouse's input in the decision and his or her signature is required. You may choose coverage for a former spouse or, if you have no spouse or children, you may be able to cover an "insurable interest" (such as, a business partner or parent).

If you elect to participate in the SBP you will be required to pay a monthly premium. SBP Premiums and benefits are based on the "base amount" or benefit level that you elect.

Your base amount can be any amount from full coverage down to as little as $300 a month. Full coverage is based on your full retired pay meaning your spouse will receive **55 percent** of your retirement pay. If you select lesser coverage then your spouse will receive 55 percent of your elected "base amount."

Note: A surviving spouse's SBP annuity is reduced when they reach age 62 and become eligible for Social Security. This is called the Social Security offset. In the past the offset reduced the SBP annuity to 35 percent of the base amount. The offset created a need for members to purchase a Supplemental Survivor Benefit Plan (SSBP) policy. Fortunately the National Defense Authorization Act of

2005 established a phase out of the offset by 2008. Thus eliminating the need for the SSBP. Details of the National Defense Authorization Act of 2005 are described below.

PHASED-IN INCREASE IN BASIC ANNUITY

One major provision of the Ronald W. Reagan FY2005 National Defense Authorization Act included an increase in the minimum SBP annuity for survivors age 62 and older from 35% to 55% over a 3-year period.

The FY 2005 Defense Authorization Act included provisions to eliminate the social security offset under SBP by increasing the annuities paid to survivors of military retirees who are 62 or older from 35 percent of retired pay to the percentages indicated below:

- For months after September 2005 and before April 2006:   40 percent
- For months after March 2006 and before April 2007:   45 percent
- For months after March 2007 and before April 2008:   50 percent
- For months after March 2008:
  55 percent

In addition, a one-year open-enrollment period began on October 1, 2005, allowing retirees not enrolled in SBP to participate, provided they make a lump-sum payment covering all back premiums, plus interest, since their retirement.

Note: Public Law 108-183, The Veterans Benefits Act of 2003 provided that, for surviving spouses who remarry after attaining age 57, Dependency and Indemnity Compensation (DIC) be paid with no reduction of certain other Federal benefits to which a surviving spouse might be entitled. This provision, in essence eliminates the requirement for DIC to offset military SBP annuities, as was required under prior law. In other words, concurrent receipt of DIC and SBP without an offset of either is now allowed for surviving spouses who remarry after attaining age 57.

SPECIAL SURVIVOR INDEMNITY ALLOWANCE (SSIA)

Section 644 of the National Defense Authorization Act (NDAA) for Fiscal Year 2008 created the Special Survivor Indemnity Allowance (SSIA). This allowance is payable to all Survivor Benefit Plan (SBP) annuitants whose annuity has been offset for receipt of Dependency and Indemnity Compensation (DIC) from the Department of Veterans Affairs (DVA). This allowance becomes payable for the month of October 2008 in the monthly amount of $50. This amount will be increased as per the following schedule:

October 2008	**$50**
October 2009	**$60**

October 2010	**$70**
October 2011	**$80**
October 2012	**$90**
October 2013	**$100**

The payment remains at $100 from October 2013, until March 1, 2016, when this allowance is currently scheduled to terminate.

The initial payment will be made on Nov. 3, 2008 representing entitlement for the month of October 2008. This allowance is taxable. Your DIC payment address will be used for your SSIA payment. If you are currently receiving your DIC payment from the DVA at your home address, your SSIA payment will also be sent there. If your DIC payment is paid via electronic funds transfer (EFT) by the DVA, your DIC electronic payment address will be used for the SSIA payment.

If you have any questions concerning this allowance you may contact the Cleveland Center at 1-800-321-1080, between 7 a.m. and 7:30 p.m., Eastern Time, Monday through Friday, or write to Defense Finance and Accounting Service, U.S. Military Annuitant Pay, P.O. Box 7131, London, KY 40742-7131.

SURVIVOR BENEFIT PLAN – MINIMUM INCOME ANNUITY

Eligible surviving spouses of military retirees who did not participate in the plan, and who died prior to September 21, 1973 are eligible for SBP-MIW (Survivor Benefit Plan – Minimum Income Annuity). To be eligible the surviving spouse must not be remarried, must be eligible for VA death pension, and must have income for VA purposes, excluding any SBP annuity, of less than the MIW-SBP annuity limitation. Effective December 1, 2008, the SBP-MIW annuity limitation is $7,933.

> *Effective December 1, 2008, the SBP-MIW annuity limitation is $7,933.*

BENEFITS FOR CHILDREN OF WOMEN VIETNAM VETERANS BORN WITH CERTAIN BIRTH DEFECTS

Section 401 of P.L. 106-416, which became law on November 1, 2000 directed the Secretary of VA to identify birth defects of children of female Vietnam veterans that: (1) are associated with service during the Vietnam era; and (2) result in the permanent physical or mental disability of such children. The law excludes from such defects familial or birth-related defects or injuries. The law further directs the Secretary to provide to such children necessary health care to address the defect and any associated disability. It authorizes the Secretary to provide vocational training to such a child if the achievement of a vocational goal is reasonably feasible.

The law also directs the Secretary to pay a monthly allowance to such a child, the amount to be determined through a schedule rating the various defects and disabilities and their degrees. The receipt of such allowance shall not infringe upon the right to receive any other benefit to which the individual is entitled. Such allowance shall not be considered income for purposes of other veterans' benefits for which income limitations exist. In the case of an eligible child whose only covered birth defect is spina bifida, a monetary allowance shall be paid under these provisions only. An eligible individual shall be provided only one program of vocational training.

The monthly allowance is set at four levels, depending upon the degree of disability suffered by the child.

Children of Women Vietnam Veterans Born With Certain Birth Defects (P.L 106-419)

(Rates Effective 12-01-2008)

Disability Level	Monthly Allowance
Level I	$131.00
Level II	$286.00
Level III	$984.00
Level IV	$1,678.00

CHAPTER 9

BURIAL BENEFITS

REIMBURSEMENT OF BURIAL EXPENSES

The Veterans Benefits Administration administers a burial benefits program designed to assist claimants in meeting the funeral and burial costs of a deceased veteran. The type and amount of benefits payable depends on the veteran's individual service record and cause of death.

Service-Connected Death

If a veteran's death is service-connected, the VA will pay a burial allowance of up to $2,000 (for deaths on or after 9-11-2001 - prior to 9-11-2001, the burial allowance was $1,500). If the veteran is buried in a VA national cemetery, some or all of the cost of moving the deceased to the national cemetery nearest the veteran's home may also be reimbursed. There is no time limit for applying for a service-connected burial allowance. The person who bore the veteran's burial expense may claim reimbursement from any VA regional office.

Non-Service Connected Death

If a veteran's death is not service-connected, there are two types of payments the VA may make:

Burial and Funeral Expense Allowance

The VA will pay a burial and funeral allowance of $300 *(effective 10/1/11 the amount will increase to $700)*, provided the veteran was discharged under conditions other than dishonorable; and:

- The veteran was in receipt of VA pension or compensation at the time of death; or

- The veteran was, at the time of death, receiving military retired pay in lieu of compensation; or

- The veteran, at the time of death, had an original or reopened claim pending, and had been found entitled to compensation or pension from a date prior to the date of death; or

- The veteran's death occurred in a VA facility; or

- The veteran died while traveling, under proper authorization and at VA expense, to or from a specified place for the purpose of examination, treatment, or care; or

- The veteran died on or after October 9, 1996, while a patient at an approved State nursing home or while residing in a VA-approved State nursing home, is transferred to a non-VA facility for acute medical care, and then dies at that location. (Contact a VA regional office for a complete listing of approved State nursing homes.); or

- The veteran's remains are being held by a State or political subdivision of a State, there is no next of kin or other person claiming the body and the veteran's estate does not have enough resources to cover the cost of the funeral and burial, and the veteran served during wartime or was released from active service for a disability incurred or aggravated in the line of duty.

Payment may be made to:

- The creditor who provided services or furnished merchandise in connection with burial, funeral, transportation, plot or interment; or

- The person or persons whose personal funds were used to pay such expenses; or

- The representative of the estate of the deceased veteran or claimant when the estate funds were used to pay the expenses or the veteran or claimant prepaid them.

Plot Allowance

If a veteran is not buried in a cemetery that is under U.S. government jurisdiction, the VA may also pay a plot allowance of $300 (for deaths on or after 12-1-2001 - prior to 12-1-2001, the plot allowance was $150; effective 10/1/11 it will increase to $700), provided that the veteran was discharged under conditions other than dishonorable; and:

- The veteran was discharged from active duty because of a disability incurred or aggravated in the line of duty; or

- The veteran was receiving VA pension or compensation at the time of death, or would have been entitled to receive VA pension or compensation, but for receipt of military retirement or disability pay; or

- The veteran died in a VA facility.

The plot allowance may be paid to the state if a veteran is buried without charge for the cost of a plot or interment in a state-owned cemetery reserved solely for veteran burials. Burial expenses paid by the deceased veteran's employer or a state agency will not be reimbursed.

Reimbursement Of Transportation Costs

The costs of transporting a veteran's body to the place of burial may be authorized if a veteran's death occurs while:

- Enroute for a VA authorized examination, treatment or care; or

- The veteran is properly hospitalized at an approved medical center domiciliary; or

- The veteran is in a nursing home under the direct jurisdiction of the VA; or if the veteran's death occurred on or after October 9, 1996, while a patient at an approved State nursing home; or

- The costs of transporting the veteran's body to the place of burial may also be authorized if the veteran is buried in a national cemetery, and died of a service-connected condition. If burial is not in the national cemetery nearest the veteran's last place of residence, the total reimbursement will not be more than the amount which would have been payable for burial in the nearest national cemetery.

Filing Claim for Reimbursement of Expenses

Reimbursement of burial expenses may be applied for by submitting VA Form 21-530, Application for Burial Allowance. A certified copy of the death certificate, proof of the veteran's military service (Form DD-214), and itemized bills of the funeral and burial expenses must be submitted by the person(s) filing the claim(s).

The itemized bills must clearly show the name of the veteran for whom services were performed, the nature and cost of the service rendered, all credits, and the name(s) of the person or persons by whom payment in whole or in part was made.

If the undertaker's bill is not paid, he is entitled to file claim for reimbursement.

If more than one person is entitled to reimbursement, each claimant must submit a separate VA Form 21-530 containing the signature of the person who authorized services or the responsible official. Any burial allowance awarded will be apportioned according to the proportionate share paid by each, unless a waiver is executed in favor of one of such person by the other person or persons. However, in no case will there be allowed the person in whose favor payment is waived a sum greater than that which was paid by him/her toward the burial, funeral, and transportation expenses. If two or more persons have paid such expenses from their personal funds, and one or more of such persons dies before filing claim, no consideration will be given to the amount paid by the deceased person(s).

> *The itemized bills must clearly show the name of the veteran for whom services were performed, the nature and cost of the service rendered, all credits, and the name(s) of the person or persons by whom payment in whole or in part was made.*

If applying for reimbursement of transportation expenses, a statement of account identifying the charges for transporting the body is required.

Unpaid Balance Due Persons who Performed Services

If there is an unpaid balance due the person who performed burial, funeral, and transportation services, such claim as a creditor for the statutory burial allowance will be given priority over any claim for reimbursement based on use of personal funds, unless there is executed by such creditor a waiver in favor of the person or persons whose personal funds were used in making the partial payment of the account.

No reimbursement may be made to a State, County, or other governmental subdivision.

Veteran's Estate

The representative of a deceased person's estate may file a claim for reimbursement, if estate funds were used to pay the expenses of the veteran's burial, funeral, and transportation. Accordingly, if otherwise in order, reimbursement may be made to the estate, regardless of whether such person pre-deceased the veteran or was deceased at the time the expenses were incurred or paid, or burial of the veteran actually occurred.

Death of Active Duty Personnel

The VA does not pay a burial or plot interment allowance if a veteran dies while on active military duty. However, such veteran is entitled to certain benefits from the military. Information should be obtained from the branch of the armed forces in which the person served at time of death.

Burial of Unclaimed Bodies

If the body of an eligible deceased veteran is unclaimed by relatives or friends, the Director of any regional VA office or any VA medical center is authorized to arrange for burial in either a national cemetery or in a cemetery or section of a cemetery, owned by a state, a state agency, or political subdivision of a state, and used solely for the interment of persons eligible for burial in a national cemetery.

If an organization provides a burial or furnishes a burial plot as a humanitarian measure, and not pursuant to a legal obligation, it may be reimbursed for its actual cost. Reimbursement to such organization cannot exceed the maximum benefits payable based on the veteran's eligibility.

Correction of Discharge to Honorable Conditions

Public Law 88-3 (H.R. 212) provides that where burial allowance was not payable at the time of a veteran's death because of the nature of his discharge from service, but after death his discharge is corrected by competent authority so as to reflect a discharge under conditions other than dishonorable, claim may be filed within two years from the date of correction of the discharge.

Legal Execution

The execution of a veteran as a lawful punishment for a crime does not of itself preclude a payment of the statutory burial allowances.

State Burial Allowance

There are some burial allowances allowed by states or counties for the burial of needy veterans, and in some instances, of their dependents. Check with the veteran's state or county of residence for specific information.

Assistance to Claimants

It is incumbent upon the claimant to establish his case in accordance with the law. This rule, however, will not be highly technical or rigid in its application. The general policy of the VA is to give the claimant every opportunity to substantiate his claim, to extend all reasonable assistance in its prosecution, and develop all sources from which information may be obtained. Assistance may also be secured from post, state, and national service officers or veterans' organizations.

Miscellaneous

If the deceased veteran is entitled to payment in full of burial expenses by the Employees' Compensation Commission, Workman's Compensation, or employer, the Veterans Administration will make no payment.

Appeal

An appeal may be made within one year from the date of denial of a claim. The appeal must be sent to the regional VA office that denied the claim. (For specific information regarding Appeals Procedures, refer to Chapter 36 of this book.)

BURIAL FLAGS

The VA shall furnish a United States flag, at no cost, for burial or memorial purposes in connection with the death of an eligible veteran who served honorably in the U.S. Armed Forces.

Public Law 105-261, added eligibility for former member of the Selected Reserve who:

- Completed at least one enlistment as a member of the Selected Reserve or, in the case of an officer, completed the period of initial obligated service as a member of the Selected Reserve; or
- Was discharged before completion of the person's initial enlistment as a member of the Selected Reserve or, in the case of an officer, period of initial obligated service as a member of the Selected Reserve, for a disability incurred or aggravated in line of duty; or
- Who died while a member of the Selected Reserve.

Burial flags may not be furnished on behalf of deceased veterans who committed capital crimes.

After the burial of the veteran, the flag shall be given to his next of kin. If no claim is made for the flag by the next of kin, it may be given, upon request, to a close friend or associate of the deceased veteran. If a flag is given to a close friend or associate of the deceased veteran, no flag shall be given to any other person on account of the death of such veteran.

When burial is in a national, state or post cemetery, a burial flag will automatically be provided. When burial is in a private cemetery, an American flag may be obtained by a service officer, an undertaker or other interested person from the nearest Veterans Administration office or most U.S. Post Offices. VA Form 2008, Application for United States Flag for Burial Purposes, must be completed and submitted along with a copy of the veteran's discharge papers. Generally, the funeral director will help the next of kin with this process.

The proper way to display the flag depends upon whether the casket is open or closed. VA Form 2008 provides the proper method for displaying and folding the flag. The burial flag is not suitable for outside display, because of its size and fabric.

After burial of a veteran, the flag should be folded in military style and presented to the next of kin at the cemetery. Local veteran organizations, when presenting the flag, usually say something like this:

> "In the name of the United States government and *name of veterans organization,* (such as A.L., D.A.V., V.F.W., and American Veterans of World War II, etc.) we present you this flag, in loving memory of our departed comrade."

Presenting of the flag is sometimes a difficult task when there is a disagreement in the family. However, the Veterans Administration gives the following order of preference to be followed:

1. Widow or widower (even if separated but not divorced)
2. Children according to age (minor child may be issued flag on application signed by guardian)
3. Father, including adopted, step and foster father
4. Mother, including adopted, step and foster mother
5. Brothers or sisters, including brothers and sisters of half blood.
6. Uncles or aunts
7. Nephews or nieces
8. Cousins, grandparents, etc. (but not in-laws)

(If two relatives have equal rights, the flag will be presented to the elder one.)

Following a veteran's burial, the United States flag received by the next of kin may be donated to the VA, for use on national holidays at VA national cemeteries. If the next of kin chooses to make such a donation, it should be given or mailed to the Director of any national cemetery selected by the donor with a written request that the flag be flown at that location. If the flag is brought into a Veterans Service Division, it will be accepted and forwarded to the cemetery chosen by the donor. A Certificate of Appreciation is presented to the donor for providing their loved ones' burial flag to a national cemetery.

Please note that VA cannot provide flag holders for placement on private headstones or markers. These flag holders may be purchased from private manufacturing companies.

The law allows the VA to issue one flag for a veteran's funeral. The VA cannot replace it if it is lost, destroyed, or stolen. However, if this occurs, a local veteran's organization or other community group may be able to assist you in obtaining another flag.

HEADSTONES AND MARKERS IN PRIVATE CEMETERIES

On December 27, 2001, then-President Bush signed Public Law 107-103, The Veterans Education and Benefits Expansion Act of 2001.

This law included a provision that allows the VA to furnish an appropriate headstone or marker for the graves of eligible veterans buried in private cemeteries, whose deaths occur on or after December 27, 2001, regardless of whether the grave is already marked with a non-government marker. (Headstones or markers may not be furnished on behalf of deceased veterans who committed capital crimes.)

On December 6, 2002, the law was further amended by Public Law 107-330, which changed the effective date to deaths occurring on or after September 11, 2001.

For all deaths occurring prior to September 11, 2001, the VA may provide a headstone or marker only for graves that are not marked with a private headstone.

Spouses and dependents buried in a private cemetery are not eligible for a Government-provided headstone or marker.

Flat markers in granite, marble, and bronze; and upright headstones in granite and marble are available. The style chosen must be consistent with existing monuments at the place of burial. Niche markers are also available to mark columbaria used for cremated remains.

Government-furnished headstones and markers must be inscribed with the name of the deceased, branch of service, and the year of birth and death, in this order. Headstones and markers also may be inscribed with other items, including an authorized emblem of believe and, space permitting, additional text including military grade, rate or rank, war service such as "World War II", complete dates of birth and death, military awards, military organizations, and civilian or veteran affiliations. To apply, and to obtain specific information on available styles, contact the cemetery where the headstone or marker is to be placed.

When burial occurs in a private cemetery, an application for a government-furnished headstone or marker must be made to VA. The government will ship the headstone or marker free of charge, but will not pay for its placement. To apply, complete VA Form 40-1330, Application for Standard Government Headstone or Marker for Installation in a Private or State Veterans' Cemetery, and forward it along with a *copy* of the veteran's military discharge documents (do not send original discharge documents, as they will not be returned) to:

Director
Memorial Programs Service (403)
Department of Veterans Affairs
810 Vermont Avenue, NW
Washington, DC 20420-0001

2010 Update: Bronze Medallions

VA made available a new medallion to be affixed to an existing privately purchased headstone or marker to signify the deceased's status as a veteran.

If requested, the medallion will be furnished in lieu of a traditional Government headstone or marker for veterans that died on or after November 1, 1990, and whose grave is marked with a privately purchased headstone or marker.

The medallion is currently available in three sizes, 5 inches, 3 inches, and 1 ½ inches. Each medallion will be inscribed with the word VETERAN across the top and the Branch of Service at the bottom. Appropriate affixing adhesive, instructions and hardware will be provided with the medallion.

Important: This benefit is only applicable if the grave is marked with a privately purchased headstone or marker. In these instances, eligible veterans are entitled to <u>either</u> a traditional Government-furnished headstone or marker, or the new medallion, but not both.

Eligibility Rules For A Government Headstone Or Marker In a Private Cemetery

1. **Veterans and Members of the Armed Forces (Army, Navy, Air Force, Marine Corps, Coast Guard):**

    a. Any veterans or members of The Armed Forces who dies while on active duty.

    b. Any veteran who was discharged under conditions other than dishonorable. With certain exceptions, service beginning after September 7, 1980, as an enlisted person, and service after October 16, 1981, as an officer, must be for a minimum of 24 months or the full period for which the person was called to active duty. (Examples include those serving less than 24 months in the Gulf War or Reservists that were federalized by Presidential Act.)

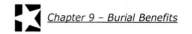

Undesirable, bad conduct, and any other type of discharge other than honorable may or may not qualify the individual for veterans benefits, depending upon a determination made by a VA Regional Office. Cases presenting multiple discharges of varying character are also referred for adjudication to a VA Regional Office.

2. Members of Reserve Components and Reserve Officers' Training Corps:

    a.   Reservists and National Guard members who, at time of death, were entitled to retired pay under Chapter 1223, Title 10, United States Code, or would have been entitled, but for being under the age of 60.

    b.   Members of reserve components who die while hospitalized or undergoing treatment at the expense of the United States for injury or disease contracted or incurred under honorable conditions while performing active duty for training or inactive duty training, or undergoing such hospitalization or treatment.

    c.   Members of the Reserve Officers' Training Corps of the Army, Navy, or Air Force who die under honorable conditions while attending an authorized training camp or on an authorized cruise, while performing authorized travel to or from that camp or cruise, or while hospitalized or undergoing treatment at the expense of the United States for injury or disease contracted or incurred under honorable conditions while engaged in one of those activities.

    d.   Members of reserve components who, during a period of active duty for training, were disabled or died from a disease or injury incurred or aggravated in the line of duty or, during a period of inactive duty training, were disabled or died from an injury incurred or aggravated in the line of duty.

3. Commissioned Officers, National Oceanic and Atmospheric Administration:

    a.   A commissioned Officer of the National Oceanic and Atmospheric Administration (formerly titled the Coast and Geodetic Survey and the Environmental Science Services Administration) with full-time duty on or after July 29, 1945.

    b.   A commissioned Officer who served before July 29, 1945, and:

        i.   Was assigned to an area of immediate military hazard while in time of war, or of a Presidentially declared national emergency as determined by the Secretary of Defense; or

        ii.   Served in the Philippine Islands on December 7, 1941, and continuously in such islands thereafter; or

    iii.   Transferred to the Department of the Army or the Department of the Navy under the provisions of the Act of May 22, 1917.

4. Public Health Service:

a. A Commissioned A Commissioned Officer of the Regular or Reserve Corps of the Public Health Service who served on full-time duty on or after July 29, 1945. If the service of the particular Public Health Service Officer falls within the meaning of active duty for training, as defined in section 101(22), title 38, United States Code, he or she must have been disabled or died from a disease or injury incurred or aggravated in the line of duty.

b. A Commissioned Officer of the Regular or Reserve Corps of the Public Health Service who performed full-time duty prior to July 29, 1945:

    i.   In time of war;

    ii.   On detail for duty with the Army, Navy, Air Force, Marine Corps, or Coast Guard; or,

    iii.   While the Service was part of the military forces of the United States pursuant to Executive Order of the President.

c. A Commissioned Officer serving on inactive duty training as defined in section 101(23), title 38, United States Code, whose death resulted from an injury incurred or aggravated in the line of duty.

5. World War II Merchant Mariners

a. United States Merchant Mariners with oceangoing service during the period of armed conflict, December 7, 1941, to December 31, 1946. Prior to the enactment of Public Law 105-368, United States Merchant Mariners with oceangoing service during the period of armed conflict of December 7, 1941, to August 15, 1945, were eligible. With enactment of Public Law 105-368, the service period is extended to December 31, 1946, for those dying on or after November 11, 1998. A DD-214 documenting this service may be obtained by submitting an application to Commandant (G-MVP-6), United States Coast Guard, 2100 2nd Street, SW, Washington, DC 20593. Notwithstanding, the Mariner's death must have occurred after the enactment of Public Law 105-368 and the interment not violate the applicable restrictions while meeting the requirements held therein.

b. United States Merchant Mariners who served on blockships in support of Operation Mulberry during World War II.

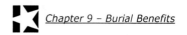

Persons NOT Eligible for a Headstone or Marker

1. **Disqualifying Characters of Discharge**

    A person whose only separation from the Armed Forces was under dishonorable conditions or whose character of service results in a bar to veterans benefits.

2. **Discharge from Draft**

    A person who was ordered to report to an induction station, but was not actually inducted into military service.

3. **Person Found Guilty of a Capital Crime**

    Eligibility for a headstone or marker is prohibited if a person is convicted of a Federal capital crime and sentenced to death or life imprisonment, or is convicted of a State capital crime, and sentenced to death or life imprisonment without parole. Federal officials are authorized to deny requests for headstones or markers to persons who are shown by clear and convincing evidence to have committed a Federal or State capital crime but were not convicted of such crime because of flight to avoid prosecution or by death prior to trial.

4. **Subversive Activities**

    Any person convicted of subversive activities after September 1, 1959, shall have no right to burial in a national cemetery from and after the date of commission of such offense, based on periods of active military service commencing before the date of the commission of such offense, nor shall another person be entitled to burial on account of such an individual. Eligibility will be reinstated if the President of the United States grants a pardon.

5. **Active or Inactive Duty for Training**

    A person whose only service is active duty for training or inactive duty training in the National Guard or Reserve Component, unless the individual meets the following criteria.

    a. Reservists and National Guard members who, at time of death, were entitled to retired pay under Chapter 1223, title 10, United States Code, or would have been entitled, but for being under the age of 60. Specific categories of individuals eligible for retired pay are delineated in section 12731 of Chapter 1223, title 10, United States Code.

    b. Members of reserve components who die while hospitalized or undergoing treatment at the expense of the United States for injury or disease contracted or incurred under honorable conditions while performing active duty for training or inactive duty training, or undergoing such hospitalization or treatment.

    c. Members of the Reserve Officers' Training Corps of the Army, Navy, or Air Force who die under honorable conditions while attending an authorized training camp or on an authorized cruise, while performing authorized travel to or from that camp or cruise, or while hospitalized or undergoing treatment at the expense of the United States for injury or disease contracted or incurred under honorable conditions while engaged in one of those activities.

d.   Members of reserve components who, during a period of active duty for training, were disabled or died from a disease or injury incurred or aggravated in line of duty or, during a period of inactive duty training, were disabled or died from an injury incurred or aggravated in line of duty.

6.   Other Groups

Members of groups whose service has been determined by the Secretary of the Air Force under the provisions of Public Law 95-202 as not warranting entitlement to benefits administered by the Secretary of Veterans Affairs.

BURIAL IN NATIONAL CEMETERIES

The National Cemetery Administration honors Veterans with a final resting place and lasting memorials that commemorate their service to our nation.

Veterans and service members who meet the eligibility requirements, and their eligible dependents may be buried in one of the VA's national cemeteries. The National Cemetery Administration currently includes 122 national cemeteries. The Department of the Army administers 2 national cemeteries, and the Department of the Interior administers 14 national cemeteries. There are also numerous state cemeteries for veterans throughout the U.S. For a listing of all national cemeteries as well as state veterans cemeteries refer to the listing at the end of this chapter.

Respect for America's Fallen Heroes Act
(Became Public Law 109-228 on May 29, 2006)

On May 29, 2006, then-President Bush signed the *"Respect For America's Fallen Heroes Act"* into law. This law does the following:

- Prohibits a demonstration on the property of a cemetery under the control of the National Cemetery Administration or on the property of Arlington National Cemetery unless the demonstration has been approved by the cemetery superintendent or the director of the property on which the cemetery is located.

> The Respect For America's Fallen Heroes Act prohibits certain demonstrations at cemeteries under the control of the National Cemetery Administration and at Arlington National Cemetery.

- Prohibits, with respect to the above cemeteries, a demonstration during the period beginning 60 minutes before and ending 60 minutes after a funeral, memorial service, or ceremony is held, which:

- o   Takes place within 150 feet of a road, pathway, or other route of ingress to or egress from such cemetery property; or
- o   Is within 300 feet of such cemetery and impedes access to or egress from such cemetery.

- The term "Demonstration" includes the following:

  - o   Any picketing or similar conduct.
  - o   Any oration, speech, use of sound amplification equipment or device, or similar conduct that is not part of a funeral, memorial service, or ceremony.
  - o   The display of any placard, banner, flag, or similar device, unless the display is part of a funeral, memorial service, or ceremony.
  - o   The distribution of any handbill, pamphlet, leaflet, or other written or printed matter other than what is distributed as part of a funeral, memorial service, or ceremony.

- Amends the federal criminal code to provide criminal penalties for violations of such prohibitions.

- Express the sense of Congress that each state should enact similar legislation to restrict demonstrations near any military funeral.

Eligibility

The VA national cemetery directors have the primary responsibility for verifying eligibility for burial in VA national cemeteries. A dependent's eligibility for burial is based upon the eligibility of the veteran. To establish a veteran's eligibility, a copy of the official military discharge document bearing an official seal or a DD 214 is usually sufficient. The document must show that release from service was under conditions other than dishonorable. A determination of eligibility is usually made in response to a request for burial in a VA national cemetery.

The cemeteries administered by the National Cemetery Administration and the Department of the Interior use the eligibility requirements that follow. The Department of the Interior can be contacted at:

U.S. Department of the Interior
National Park Service
1849 C Street, N.W.
Washington, D.C. 20240
(202) 208-4621

The Department of the Army should be contacted directly for inquiries concerning eligibility for interment in either of the two cemeteries under its jurisdiction (call 703-695-3250).

Eligibility requirements for burial in state veterans cemeteries are the same, or similar, to the eligibility requirements that follow. However, some states also have residency and other more restrictive requirements. Please contact the specific state cemetery for its eligibility requirements.

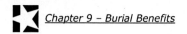

The following veterans and members of the Armed Forces (Army, Navy, Air Force, Marine Corps, Coast Guard) are eligible for burial in a VA national cemetery:

Veterans and Members of the Armed Forces

- Any member of the Armed Forces of the U.S. who dies on active duty.

- Any citizen of the U.S. who, during any war in which the U.S. has been engaged, served in the Armed Forces of any U.S. ally during that war, whose last active service terminated honorably by death or otherwise, and who was a citizen of the U.S. at the time of entry into such service and at the time of death.

- Any veteran discharged under conditions other than dishonorable, and who has completed the required period of service. With certain exceptions, service beginning after September 7, 1980, as an enlisted person, and service after October 16, 1981, as an officer, must be for a minimum of 24 months or the full period for which the person was called to active duty.

Members of Reserve Components and Reserve Officers' Training Corps

- Reservists and National Guard members with 20 years of qualifying service, who are entitled to retired pay, or would be entitled, if at least 60 years of age.

- Members of reserve components who die under honorable conditions while hospitalized or undergoing treatment at the expense of the U.S. for injury or disease contracted or incurred under honorable conditions, while performing active duty for training, or inactive duty training, or undergoing such hospitalization or treatment.

- Members of the Reserve Officers' Training Corps of the Army, Navy, or Air Force who die under honorable conditions while attending an authorized training camp or cruise, or while traveling to or from that camp or cruise, or while hospitalized or undergoing treatment at the expense of the U.S. for injury or disease contracted or incurred under honorable conditions while engaged in one of those activities.

- Members of reserve components who, during a period of active duty for training, were disabled or died from a disease or injury incurred or aggravated in the line of duty, or, during a period of inactive duty training, were disabled or died from an injury incurred or aggravated in the line of duty.

Commissioned Officers, National Oceanic and Atmospheric Administration

- A Commissioned Officer of the National Oceanic and Atmospheric Administration with full-time duty on or after July 29, 1945.

- A Commissioned Officer of the National Oceanic and Atmospheric Administration who served before July 29, 1945, and:

- Was assigned to an area of immediate hazard described in the Act of December 3, 1942 (56 Stat. 1038; 33 U.S.C. 855a), as amended;

- Served in the Philippine Islands on December 7, 1941, and continuously in such islands thereafter.

Public Health Service

- A Commissioned Officer of the Regular or Reserve Corps of the Public Health Service who served on full-time duty on or after July 29, 1945. If the service of such Officer falls within the meaning of active duty for training, he must have been disabled or died from a disease or injury incurred or aggravated in the line of duty.

- A Commissioned Officer of the Regular or Reserve Corps of the Public Health Service who performed full-time duty prior to July 29, 1945:

  a. In time of war; or

  b. On detail for duty with the Army, Navy, Air Force, Marine Corps, or Coast Guard; or

  c. While the service was part of the military forces of the U.S. pursuant to Executive Order of the President.

- A Commissioned Officer of the Regular or Reserve Corps of the Public Health Service serving on inactive duty training as defined in Section 101 (23), title 39, U.S. Code, whose death resulted from an injury incurred or aggravated in the line of duty.

World War II Merchant Mariners

- U.S. Merchant Mariners with oceangoing service during the period of armed conflict, December 7, 1941 to December 31, 1946. Prior to the enactment of Public Law 105-368, United States Merchant Mariners with oceangoing service during the period of armed conflict of December 7, 1941, to August 15, 1945, were eligible. With enactment of Public Law 105-368, the service period is extended to December 31, 1946, for those dying on or after November 11, 1998.

- U.S. Merchant Mariners who served on blockships in support of Operation Mulberry during WWII.

The Philippine Armed Forces

- Any Philippine veteran who was a citizen of the United States or an alien lawfully admitted for permanent residence in the United States at the time of their death; and resided in the United States at the time of their death; and:

- Was a person who served before July 1, 1946, in the organized military forces of the Government of the Commonwealth of the Philippines, while such forces were in the service of the Armed Forces of the United States pursuant to the military order of the President dated July 26, 1941, including organized guerilla forces under commanders appointed, designated, or subsequently recognized by the Commander in Chief,

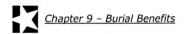

Southwest Pacific Area, or other competent authority in the Army of the United States who dies on or after November 1, 2000; or

- Was a person who enlisted between October 6, 1945, and June 30, 1947, with the Armed Forces of the United States with the consent of the Philippine government, pursuant to Section 14 of the Armed Forces Voluntary Recruitment Act of 1945, and who died on or after December 16, 2003.

Spouses and Dependents

- The spouse or surviving spouse of an eligible veteran is eligible for interment in a national cemetery even if that veteran is not buried or memorialized in a national cemetery. In addition, the spouse or surviving spouse of a member of the Armed Forces of the United States whose remains are unavailable for burial is also eligible for burial.

- The surviving spouse of an eligible veteran who had a subsequent remarriage to a non-veteran and whose death occurred on or after January 1, 2000, is eligible for burial in a national cemetery, based on his or her marriage to the eligible veteran.

- The minor children of an eligible veteran. For the purpose of burial in a national cemetery, a minor child is a child who is unmarried and:

- Under 21 years of age; or

- Under 23 years of age and pursuing a full-time course of instruction at an approved educational institution.

- An unmarried adult child of an eligible veteran if the child became permanently physically or mentally disabled and incapable of self-support before reaching 21 years of age, or before reaching 23 years of age if pursuing a full-time course of instruction at an approved educational institution.

- Any other persons or classes of persons as designated by the Secretary of Veterans Affairs or the Secretary of the Air Force.

2010 Update:

(The Veterans' Benefits Act of 2010 contains a provision which allows a parent whose child gave their life in service to our country to be buried in a national cemetery with that child when their veteran child has no living spouse or children.)

The following are not eligible for burial in a VA national cemetery:

- A former spouse of an eligible individual whose marriage to that individual has been terminated by annulment or divorce, if not otherwise eligible.

- Family members other than those specifically described above.

- A person whose only separation from the Armed Forces was under dishonorable conditions, or whose character of service results in a bar to veterans benefits.

- A person ordered to report to an induction station, but not actually inducted into military service.

- Any person found guilty of a capital crime. Interment or memorialization in a VA cemetery or in Arlington National Cemetery is prohibited if a person is convicted of a Federal capital crime and sentenced to death or life imprisonment, or is convicted of a State capital crime, and sentenced to death or life imprisonment without parole. Federal officials are authorized to deny burial in veterans cemeteries to persons who are shown by clear and convincing evidence to have committed a Federal or State capital crime but were not convicted of such crime because of flight to avoid prosecution or by death prior to trial. The Secretary is authorized to provide aid to States for the establishment, expansion and/or improvement of veterans cemeteries on the condition that the State is willing to prohibit interment or memorialization in such cemeteries of individuals convicted of Federal or State capital crimes, or found by clear and convincing evidence to have committed such crimes, without having been convicted of the crimes due to flight to avoid prosecution or death prior to trial.

- Any person convicted of subversive activities after September 1, 1959, shall have no right to burial in a national cemetery from and after the date of commission of such offense, based on periods of active military service commencing before the date of the commission of such offense, nor shall another person be entitled to burial on account of such an individual. Eligibility will be reinstated if the President of the United States grants a pardon.

Requests for Gravesites in National Cemeteries

An eligible veteran or family member may be buried in the VA national cemetery of his choice, provided space is available. A veteran may not reserve a gravesite in his name prior to his death. However, any reservations made under previous programs will be honored. The funeral director or loved one making the burial arrangements must apply for a gravesite at the time of death. No special forms are required when requesting burial in a VA national cemetery. The person making burial arrangement should contact the national cemetery in which burial is desired at the time of need.

If possible, the following information concerning the deceased should be provided when the cemetery is first contacted:

- Full name and military rank;

- Branch of service;

- Social security number;

- VA claim number, if applicable;

- Date and place of birth;

- Date and place of death;

- Date of retirement or last separation from active duty; and

- Copy of any military separation documents (such as DD-214)

When a death occurs and eligibility for interment in a national cemetery is determined, grave space is assigned by the cemetery director in the name of the veteran or family member.

One gravesite is permitted for the interment of all eligible family members, unless soil conditions or the number of family decedents necessitate more than one grave.

There is no charge for burial in a national cemetery.

One gravesite is permitted for the interment of all eligible family members, unless soil conditions or the number of family decedents necessitate more than one grave.

There is no charge for burial in a national cemetery.

The availability of grave space varies among each National Cemetery. In many cases, if a national cemetery does not have space for a full-casket burial, it may still inter cremated remains. Full-casket gravesites occasionally become available in such cemeteries due to disinterment or cancellation of prior reservations. The cemetery director can answer such questions at the time of need.

Most national cemeteries do not typically conduct burials on weekends. However, weekend callers trying to make burial arrangements for the following week will be provided with the phone number of one of three strategically located VA cemetery offices that remains open during weekends.

Burial at Sea

The National Cemetery Administration cannot provide burial at sea. For information, contact the United States Navy Mortuary Affairs office toll-free at (888) 647-6676, and select option 4.

Furnishing and Placement of Headstones and Markers

In addition to the gravesite, burial in a VA national cemetery also includes furnishing and placement of the headstone or marker, opening and closing of the grave, and perpetual care. Many national cemeteries also have columbaria or gravesites for cremated remains. (Some State Veterans' cemeteries may charge a nominal fee for placing a Government-provided headstone or marker.)

SPECIAL NOTES:

- For person's with 20-years service in the National Guard or Reserves, entitlement to retired pay must be subsequent to October 27, 1992 in order to qualify for a Government-provided headstone or marker. A copy of the Reserve Retirement Eligibility Benefits Letter must accompany the application. Active duty service while in the National Guard or Reserves also establishes eligibility.

- Service prior to World War I requires detailed documentation to prove eligibility such as muster rolls, extracts from State files, military or State organizations where served, pension or land warrants, etc.

Flat bronze, granite, or marble grave markers and upright marble or granite headstones are available to mark graves in the style consistent with existing monuments in the national cemetery. Niche markers are also available for identifying cremated remains in columbaria. The following is a brief description of each type:

- *Upright Marble and Upright Granite:* 42 inches long, 13 inches wide, 4 inches thick, approximately 230 pounds.

- *Flat Bronze:* 24 inches long, 12 inches wide, ¾ inch rise, approximately 18 pounds. Anchor bolts, nuts and washers for fastening to base are supplied with marker. The government does not provide the base.

- *Flat Granite and Flat Marble:* 24 inches long, 12 inches wide, 4 inches thick, approximately 130 pounds.

- *Bronze Niche:* 8 ½ inches long, 5 ½ inches wide, 7/16 inch rise, approximately 3 pounds. Mounting bolts and washers are supplied with marker.

- There are also two special styles of upright marble headstones and flat markers available - one for those who served with the Union Forces during the Civil War or the Spanish-American War; and one for those who served with the Confederate Forces during the Civil War.

Inscriptions

Headstones and markers are inscribed with the name of the deceased, branch of service, year of birth, and year of death.

The word "Korea" may be included on Government headstones and markers for the graves of those members and former members of the United States Armed Forces who served within the areas of military operations in the Korean Theater between June 27, 1950 and July 27, 1954; and for headstones and markers for active duty decedents who lost their lives in Korea or adjacent waters as a result of hostile action subsequent to the 1953 Armistice.

The word "Vietnam" may be included on Government headstones and markers for the graves of those members and former members of the United States Armed Forces who died in Vietnam or whose death was attributable to service in Vietnam, and on the headstones and markers of all decedents who were on active duty on or after August 5, 1964.

The words "Lebanon" or "Grenada" may be included on Government headstones and markers for those killed as a result of those military actions.

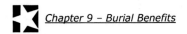

The words "Panama" and "Persian Gulf" may be included on Government headstones and markers for those killed as a result of those military actions.

If desired, the following inscriptions can also be made (space permitting):

- Military grade

- Military rank

- Military rate

- Identification of war service

- Months and days of birth and death

- An authorized emblem of religious belief (see following list of available emblems)

- Military awards (documentation of award must be provided)

- Military organizations

- Civilian or veteran affiliations

With the VA's approval, terms of endearment that meet acceptable standards of good taste may also be added. Most optional inscriptions are placed as the last lines of the inscription. No other graphics are permitted on Government-provided headstones and markers, and inscriptions will be in English text only. Civilian titles such as "Doctor or Reverend" are not permitted on the name line of government-provided headstones and markers.

Available Emblems of Belief for Placement on Government Headstones and Markers:

- Christian Cross

- Buddhist (Wheel of Righteousness)

- Hebrew (Star of David)

- Presbyterian Cross

- Russian Orthodox Cross

- Lutheran Cross

- Episcopal Cross

- Unitarian Church (Flaming Chalice)

- United Methodist Church

- Aaronic Order Church

- Mormon (Angel Moroni)

- Native American Church of North America

- Serbian Orthodox

- Greek Cross

- Bahai (9 Pointed Star)
- Atheist
- Muslim (Crescent and Star)
- Hindu
- Konko-Kyo Faith
- Community of Christ
- Sufism Reoriented
- Tenrikyo Church
- Seicho-No-Ie
- Church of World Messianity (Izunome)
- United Church of Religious Science
- Christian Reformed Church
- United Moravian Church
- Eckankar
- Christian Church
- United Church of Christ
- Christian & Missionary Alliance
- Humanist Emblem Of Spirit
- Presbyterian Church (USA)
- Izumo Taishakyo Mission Of Hawaii
- Soka Gakkai International - USA
- Sikh (Khanda)
- Christian Scientist (Cross and Crown)
- Muslim (Islamic 5 Pointed Star)

Ordering a Headstone or Marker

For burial of a veteran in a national, state veteran, or military post cemetery, the cemetery will order the headstone or marker, and can give loved ones information on style, inscription, and shipment. Shipment and placement of the headstone or marker is provided at no cost.

When burial is in a private cemetery, VA Form 40-1330, *Application for Standard Government Headstone or Marker* must be submitted by the next of kin or a representative, such as funeral director, cemetery official or veterans' counselor, along with the veteran's military discharge documents, to request a Government-provided headstone or marker. Do not send original documents, as they will not be returned.

Headstones and Markers for Spouses and Children

The VA will issue a headstone or marker for an eligible spouse or child buried in a national, state veteran or military post cemetery. However, the VA cannot issue a headstone or marker for a spouse or child buried in a private cemetery.

> *The VA will issue a headstone or marker for an eligible spouse or child buried in a national, state veteran or military post cemetery. However, the VA cannot issue a headstone or marker for a spouse or child buried in a private cemetery.*

The applicant can, however, request to reserve inscription space below the veteran's inscription, so that the non-veteran's commemorative information can be inscribed locally, at private expense, when the non-veteran is buried. The applicant may also choose to have his/her name and date of birth added at Government expense, when the headstone or marker is ordered. The date of death may then be added, at private expense, at the time of his/her death.

Commemoration of Unidentified Remains

Many national cemeteries have areas suitable to commemorate veterans whose remains were not recovered or identified, were buried at sea, or are otherwise unavailable for interment. In such instances, the VA will provide a memorial headstone or marker to be placed in that section of the cemetery. The words *"In Memory of"* must precede the authorized inscription.

Checking Order Status

To check the status of a previously ordered headstone or marker for placement in a private cemetery, applicants may call the VA's Applicant Assistance Line at 1-800-697-6947. The line is open weekdays, from 8:00 A.M. to 5:00 P.M., Eastern Standard Time.

Replacement of Headstones and Markers

> *For guidance on obtaining a replacement headstone or marker, call (800)-697-6947.*

The Government will replace a previously furnished headstone or marker if it: becomes badly damaged, is vandalized, is stolen, becomes badly deteriorated, the inscription becomes illegible, is different from that ordered by the applicant, becomes damaged in transit, or the inscription is incorrect.

Government headstones or markers in private cemeteries damaged by cemetery personnel will not be replaced at Government expense.

If a marble or granite headstone or marker is permanently removed from a grave, it must be destroyed. Bronze markers must be returned to the contractor.

MILITARY HONORS

The rendering of Military Funeral Honors is a way to show the Nation's deep gratitude to those who have faithfully defended our country in times of war and peace. It is the final demonstration a grateful Nation can provide to the veterans' families.

The following service members are eligible for Military Funeral Honors:

- Military members on active duty or in the Selected Reserve at time of death;

- Former military members who served on active duty and departed under conditions other than dishonorable;

- Former military members who completed at least one term of enlistment or period of initial obligated service in the Selected Reserve, and departed under conditions other than dishonorable;

- Former military members discharged from the Selected Reserve due to a disability incurred or aggravated in the line of duty.

Military Funeral Honors have always been provided whenever possible. However, effective October 5, 1999, the law, under P.L. 105-261, Section 578, mandates that all eligible veterans receive basic Military Funeral Honors, if requested by the deceased veteran's family. As provided by law, an honor guard detail for the burial of an eligible veteran shall consist of not less than two members of the Armed Forces. One member of the detail shall be a representative of the parent Service of the deceased veteran. The honor detail will, at a minimum, perform a ceremony that includes the folding and presenting of the American flag to the next of kin, and the playing of Taps. Taps will be played by a bugler, if available, or by electronic recording.

In 2003, the Department of Defense announced its approval of the use of a ceremonial bugle as an alternative to the recorded version of Taps played on stereo at military funerals.

The ceremonial bugle consists of a small cone-shaped device inserted deep into the bell of a bugle that plays an exceptionally high-quality rendition of Taps that is virtually indistinguishable from a live bugler.

The ceremonial bugle will be offered to families as an alternative to the pre-recorded Taps played on a stereo, but will not be used as a substitute for a live bugler when one is available. Live buglers will continue to play at veterans' funerals whenever available.

Funeral Directors have the responsibility of assisting loved ones in requesting military honors. A toll-free telephone number has been established for funeral directors requesting military honors.

The Department of Defense (DOD) has provided registered funeral home directors with a military funeral honors kit and information on how to contact the appropriate military organization to perform the honors ceremony.
Questions about the Military Funeral Honors program should be sent to:

Department of Defense
Directorate for Public Inquiry and Analysis
Room 3A750, The Pentagon
Washington, DC 20301-1400

PREPARATIONS WHICH CAN BE MADE PRIOR TO DEATH

It is suggested that veterans and their families prepare in advance by discussing cemetery options, collecting the veteran's military information (including discharge papers), and by contacting the cemetery where the veteran wishes to be buried. If burial will be in a private cemetery and a Government headstone or marker will be requested, VA Form 40-1330 can be completed in advance and placed with the veteran's military discharge papers for use at the time of need.

BURIAL LOCATION ASSISTANCE

The VA National Cemetery Administration can provide limited burial location assistance to family members and close friends of decedents thought to be buried in a VA national cemetery.

The National Cemetery Administration will research its records to determine if the decedent is buried in one of VA's national cemeteries. A request can include a maximum of ten specific names to locate.

The National Cemetery Administration does not have information on persons buried in cemeteries other than its national cemeteries. Its records do not contain any personal, military or family information – only information regarding whether or not an individual is buried in a VA national cemetery, and if so, where, can be provided.

The "Gravesite Locator" tool is available online at the VA's website.

If the online tool is not available or helpful, you may submit a written request. No form is required to request this information, and no fee is charged. The following information should be provided:

- Full name, including any alternate spellings, of decedent;
- Date and place of birth;
- Date and place of death;
- State from which the individual entered active duty;
- Military service branch;

- Mailing address and phone number of individual requesting the information.

Allow approximately 4 weeks for a reply.

Requests should be sent to:

> U.S. Department of Veterans Affairs
> National Cemetery Administration (41C1)
> Burial Location Request
> 810 Vermont Avenue, N.W.
> Washington, D.C. 20420

U.S. MILITARY CEMETERIES AND MONUMENTS OVERSEAS

The *American Battle Monuments Commission (ABMC)* a small, independent agency of the U.S. government's executive branch, maintains 24 American military cemeteries, and 27 memorials, monuments, or markers. (The VA is not responsible for maintaining cemeteries and monuments honoring deceased veterans buried on foreign soil.)

ABMC Cemeteries

- Aisne Marne - South of Belleau, France

- Ardennes – Neupre (Neuville-enCondroz), Belgium

- Brittany – Southeast of St. James (Marche), France

- Brookwood – Brookwood, Surrey, England

- Cambridge – Cambridge, England

- Corozal – North of Panama City, Republic of Panama

- Epinal – Southeast of Epinal (Vosges), France

- Flanders Field – Waregem, Belgium

- Florence – South of Florence, Italy

- Henri-Chapelle – Northeast of Henri-Chapelle, Belgium

- Lorraine – North of St. Avold (Moselle), France

- Luxembourg – Luxembourg City, Luxembourg

- Manila – Southeast of Manila, Republic of Philippines

- Meuse Argonne – East of Romagne –sous-Montfaucon (Meuse), France

- Mexico City – Mexico City, Mexico

- Netherlands – Margraten, Netherlands

- Normandy – Colleville-sur Mer, France

- North Africa – near Carthage
- Oise-Aisne – East of Fere-en-Tardenois (Aisne), France
- Rhone – Draguignan (Var), France
- Sicily-Rome – Nettuno, Italy
- Somme – Southwest of Bony (Aisne), France
- St. Mihil – Thiaacourt, France
- Surresnes – West of Paris, France

ABMC Monuments

- Audenaude Monument – Oudenaarde (Audenarde), Belgium
- Belleau Wood Monument
- Bellicourt Monument – North of St. Quentin (Aisne), France
- Cabanatuan Memorial - Philippines
- Cantigny Monument – Cantigny (Somme), France
- Chateau-Thierry Monument – West of Chateay-Thierry, France
- Chaumont Marker – Chaumont, France
- East Coast Memorial – Battery Park, New York City
- Guadalcanal Memorial – Honiara, Guadalcanal, Solomon Islands
- Honolulu Memorial – Honolulu, Hawaii
- Kemmel Monument – South of Ieper (Ypres), Belgium
- Montfaucan Monument – Northwest of Verdun, France
- Montsec Monument – Montsec (Thiaucourt), France
- Naval Brest Monument – Brest, France
- Naval Gibraltar Monument – Straights of Gibraltar
- Pointe-du-Hoc Monument – Overlooks Omaha Beach, France
- Papua Marker – Papua, New Guinea
- Saipan Memorial – Saipan, Commonwealth of the Mariana Islands
- Santiago Surrender Tree
- Sommepy Monument – Northwest of Sommepy – Tahure (Marne), France
- Souilly Marker – Souilly, France
- Tours Monument – Tours, France
- Utah Beach Monument – Sainte-Marie-du-Mont (Manche), France

- West Coast Memorial – San Francisco, California
- Western Task Force Marker – Casablanca, Morocco

ABMC Services

The ABMC can provide interested parties with:

- Name, location, and information on cemeteries and memorials.
- Plot, row and grave number or memorialization location of Honored War Dead.
- Best in-country routes and modes of travel to cemeteries or memorials.
- Information on accommodations near cemeteries or memorials.
- Escort service for relatives to grave and memorial sites within the cemeteries.
- Letters authorizing fee-free passports for members of the immediate family traveling overseas to visit a grave or memorialization site.
- Black and white photographs of headstones and Tablets of the Missing on which the names of dead or missing are engraved.
- Arrangements for floral decorations placed at graves and memorialization sites.
- An Honor Roll Certificate containing data on a Korean War casualty suitable for framing.
- Polaroid color photographs of donated floral decorations in place.

The Andrews Project

The commission also provides friends and relatives of those interred in its cemeteries or memorialized on its Tablets of the Missing with color lithographs of the cemetery or memorial on which is mounted a photograph of the headstone or commemorative inscription. The Andrews Project, named in honor of its sponsor, the late Congressman George W. Andrews, is ABMC's most popular service.

For further information, contact the ABMC at:

American Battle Monuments Commission
Arlington Court House Plaza II
2300 Clarendon Blvd., Suite 500
Arlington, VA 22201
(703) 696-6897

Passports to Visit Overseas Cemeteries

Family members who wish to visit overseas graves and memorial sites of World War I and World War II veterans are eligible for "no-fee" passports. Family members eligible for the "no-fee" passports include surviving spouses, parents, children, sisters, brothers and guardians of the deceased veteran buried or commemorated in American military cemeteries on foreign soil. For further

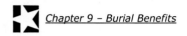

information contact the American Battle Monuments Commission at the address and phone number indicated in the previous section.

PRESIDENTIAL MEMORIAL CERTIFICATES

A Presidential Memorial Certificate is an engraved paper certificate that has been signed by the current president, honoring the memory of any honorably discharged deceased veteran.

Presidential Memorial Certificates may be distributed to a deceased veteran's next of kin and loved ones. More than one certificate can be provided per family, and there is no time limit for applying for the certificate.

Presidential Memorial Certificates may not be furnished on behalf of deceased veterans who committed capital crimes.

Requests for a Presidential Memorial Certificate can be made in person at any VA regional office, by faxing the request and all supporting documents (copy of discharge and death certificate) to (202) 565-8054, or by U.S. Mail.

There is no form to use when requesting a certificate. A copy of the veteran's discharge documents and a return mailing address should be included with any request. Written requests should be sent to:

Presidential Memorial Certificates (41A1C)
Department of Veterans Affairs
5109 Russell Road
Quantico, VA 22134-3903

LISTS OF NATIONAL CEMETERIES

Some national cemeteries can bury only cremated remains or casketed remains of eligible family members of those already buried. Contact the cemetery director for information on the availability of space

Department Of Veterans Affairs National Cemeteries

Alabama

Alabama National Cemetery
3133 Highway 119
Montevallo, AL 35115
(866) 547-5078

Fort Mitchell National Cemetery
553 Highway 165
Seale, AL 36875
(334) 855-4731

Mobile National Cemetery
1202 Virginia Street
Mobile, AL 36604
For information please contact:
Barrancas National Cemetery
(850) 453-4846

Alaska

Fort Richardson National Cemetery
Building #997, Davis Highway
P. O. Box 5-498
Fort Richardson, AK 99505
(907) 384-7075

Sitka National Cemetery
803 Sawmill Creek Road
Sitka, AK 99835
For information please contact:
Fort Richardson National Cemetery
(907) 384-7075

Arizona

National Memorial Cemetery of
Arizona
23029 North Cave Creek Road
Phoenix, AZ 85024
(480) 513-3600

Prescott National Cemetery
500 Highway 89 North
Prescott, AZ 86301
For information please contact
National Memorial Cemetery of
Arizona (480) 513-3600

Arkansas

Fayetteville National Cemetery
700 Government Avenue
Fayetteville, AR 72701
(479) 444-5051

Fort Smith National Cemetery
522 Garland Avenue
Fort Smith, AR 72901
(479) 783-5345

Little Rock National Cemetery
2523 Confederate Boulevard
Little Rock, AR 72206
(501) 324-6401

California

Fort Rosecrans National Cemetery
P. O. Box 6237 Point Loma
San Diego, CA 92106
(619) 553-2084

Golden Gate National Cemetery
1300 Sneath Lane
San Bruno, CA 94066
(650) 761-7737

Los Angeles National Cemetery
950 South Sepulveda Boulevard
Los Angeles, CA 90049
(310) 268-4675

Riverside National Cemetery
22495 Van Buren Boulevard
Riverside, CA 92518
(909) 653-8417

Sacramento Valley National Cemetery
5810 Midway Road
Dixon, CA 95620
(707) 693-2460

San Francisco National Cemetery
P. O. Box 29012
Presidio of San Francisco
San Francisco, CA 94129
For information please contact
Golden Gate National Cemetery
(650) 761-1646

San Joaquin Valley National
Cemetery
32053 West McCabe Road
Gustine, CA 95322
(209) 854-1040

Colorado

Fort Logan National Cemetery
3698 South Sheridan Boulevard
Denver, CO 80235
(303) 761-0117

Fort Lyon National Cemetery
VA Medical Center
Fort Lyon, CO 81038
For information please contact Fort
Logan National Cemetery
(303) 761-0117

Florida

Barrancas National Cemetery
Naval Air Station
80 Hovey Road
Pensacola, FL 32508-1099
(850) 453-4108

Bay Pines National Cemetery
P. O. Box 477
Bay Pines, FL 33504-0477
(727) 398-9426

Florida National Cemetery
6502 SW 102nd Avenue
Bushnell, FL 33513
(352) 793-7740 or 1074
Jacksonville National Cemetery
4083 Lannie Road
Jacksonville, FL 32218-1247
(904) 358-3510

Sarasota National Cemetery
9810 State Hwy 72
Sarasota, FL 34241
(941) 861-9840

South Florida National Cemetery
6501 S. State Road 7
Lake Worth, FL 33467
Phone: (561) 649-6489

St. Augustine National Cemetery
104 Marine Street
St. Augustine, FL 32084
For information please contact
Florida National Cemetery
(352) 793-7740

Georgia

Georgia National Cemetery
2025 Mount Carmel Church Lane
Canton, GA 30114
(866) 236-8159

Marietta National Cemetery
500 Washington Avenue
Marietta, GA 30060
(866) 236-8159

Hawaii

National Memorial Cemetery of the
Pacific
2177 Puowaina Drive
Honolulu, HI 96813-1729
(808) 523-3720

Illinois

Abraham Lincoln National
Cemetery
27034 South Diagonal Road
Elwood, IL 60421
(815) 423-9958

Alton National Cemetery
600 Pearl Street
Alton, IL 62003
For information please contact
Jefferson Barracks National
Cemetery (314) 260-8691

Camp Butler National Cemetery
5063 Camp Butler Road; RR #1
Springfield, IL 62707
(217) 492-4070

Danville National Cemetery
1900 East Main Street
Danville, IL 61832
(217) 554-4550

Mound City National Cemetery
P. O. Box 128
Mound City, IL 62963
For information please contact
Jefferson Barracks National
Cemetery
(314) 260-8691

Quincy National Cemetery
36th and Maine Street
Quincy, IL 62301
For information please contact
Rock Island National Cemetery
(309) 782-2094

Rock Island National Cemetery
Rock Island Arsenal
P. O. Box 737
Moline, IL 61265
Rock Island, IL 61299-7090
(309) 782-2094

Indiana

Crown Hill National Cemetery
700 West 38th Street
Indianapolis, IN 46208
For information please contact
Marion National Cemetery
(765) 674-0284

Marion National Cemetery
VA Medical Center
1700 East 38th Street
Marion, IN 46952
(765) 674-0284

New Albany National Cemetery
1943 Ekin Avenue
New Albany, IN 47150
For information please contact
Zachary Taylor National Cemetery
(812) 948-5234

Iowa

Keokuk National Cemetery
1701 J Street
Keokuk, IA 52632
For information please contact
Rock Island National Cemetery
(309) 782-2094

Kansas

Fort Leavenworth Natl Cemetery
Fort Leavenworth, KS 66027
For information please contact
Leavenworth National Cemetery
(913) 758-4105

Fort Scott National Cemetery
P. O. Box 917
Fort Scott, KS 66701
(620) 223-2840

Leavenworth National Cemetery
P. O. Box 1694
Leavenworth, KS 66048
(913) 758-4105

Kentucky

Camp Nelson National Cemetery
6980 Danville Road
Nicholasville, KY 40356
(859) 885-5727

Cave Hill National Cemetery
701 Baxter Avenue
Louisville, KY 40204
For information please contact
Zachary Taylor National Cemetery
(502) 893-3852

Danville National Cemetery
277 North First Street
Danville, KY 40442
For information please contact
Camp Nelson National Cemetery
(859) 885-5727

Lebanon National Cemetery
20 Highway 208
Lebanon, KY 40033
(502) 893-3852

Lexington National Cemetery
833 West Main Street
Lexington, KY 40508
For information please contact
Camp Nelson National Cemetery
(859) 885-5727

Mill Springs National Cemetery
Nancy, KY 42544
For information please contact
Camp Nelson National Cemetery
(859) 885-5727

Zachary Taylor National Cemetery
4701 Brownsboro Road
Louisville, KY 40207
(502) 893-3852

Louisiana

Alexandria National Cemetery
209 East Shamrock Street
Pineville, LA 71360
For information please contact
Natchez National Cemetery
(318) 449-1793

Baton Rouge National Cemetery
220 North 19th Street
Baton Rouge, LA 70806
For information please contact
Port Hudson National Cemetery
(225) 654-3767

Port Hudson National Cemetery
20978 Port Hickey Road
Zachary, LA 70791
(225) 654-3767

Maine

Togus National Cemetery
VA Medical and Regional Office
Center
Togus, ME 04330
For information please contact
Massachusetts National Cemetery
(508) 563-7113

Maryland

Annapolis National Cemetery
800 West Street
Annapolis, MD 21401
For information please contact
Baltimore National Cemetery
(410) 644-9696

Baltimore National Cemetery
5501 Frederick Avenue
Baltimore, MD 21228
(410) 644-9696

Loudon Park National Cemetery
3445 Frederick Avenue
Baltimore, MD 21228
For information please contact
Baltimore National Cemetery
(410) 644-9696

Massachusetts

Massachusetts National Cemetery
Bourne, MA 02532
(508) 563-7113

Michigan

Fort Custer National Cemetery
15501 Dickman Road
Augusta, MI 49012
(269) 731-4164

Great Lakes National
Cemetery
4200 Belford Road
Holly, MI 48842
(866) 348-8603

Minnesota

Fort Snelling National Cemetery
7601 34th Avenue, South
Minneapolis, MN 55450-1199
(612) 726-1127

Mississippi

Biloxi National Cemetery
P. O. Box 4968
Biloxi, MS 39535-4968
(601) 388-6668

Corinth National Cemetery
1551 Horton Street
Corinth, MS 38834
For information please contact
Memphis National Cemetery
(901) 386-8311

Natchez National Cemetery
41 Cemetery Road
Natchez, MS 39120
(601) 445-4981

Missouri

Jefferson Barracks National
Cemetery
2900 Sheridan Road
St. Louis, MO 63125
(314) 260-8691

Jefferson City National Cemetery
1024 East McCarty Street
Jefferson City, MO 65101
For information please contact
Jefferson Barracks National
Cemetery
(314) 260-8691

Springfield National Cemetery
1702 East Seminole Street
Springfield, MO 65804
(417) 881-9499

Nebraska

Fort McPherson National Cemetery
HCO1, Box 67
Maxwell, NE 69151
(308) 582-4433

New Jersey

Beverly National Cemetery
R.D. #1, Bridgeboro Road
Beverly, NJ 08010
(609) 877-5460

Finn's Point National Cemetery
RFD # 3, Fort Mott Road, Box 542
Salem, NJ 08079
For information please contact
Beverly National Cemetery
(609) 877-5460

New Mexico

Fort Bayard National Cemetery
P. O. Box 189
Fort Bayard, NM 88036
For information please contact
Fort Bliss National Cemetery
(915) 564-0201

Santa Fe National Cemetery
501 North Guadalupe Street
Santa Fe, NM 87501
(505) 988-6400

New York

Bath National Cemetery
VA Medical Center
Bath, NY 14810
(607) 664-4853

Calverton National Cemetery
210 Princeton Boulevard
Calverton, NY 11933-1031
(631) 727-5410 or 5770

Cypress Hills National Cemetery
625 Jamaica Avenue
Brooklyn, NY 11208
For information please contact
Long Island National Cemetery
(631) 454-4949

Long Island National Cemetery
2040 Wellwood Avenue
Farmingdale, NY 11735-1211
(631) 454-4949

Saratoga National Cemetery
200 Duell Road
Schuylerville, NY 12871-1721
(518) 581-9128

Woodlawn National Cemetery
1825 Davis Street
Elmira, NY 14901
(607) 732-5411

North Carolina

New Bern National Cemetery
1711 National Avenue
New Bern, NC 28560
(252) 637-2912

Raleigh National Cemetery
501 Rock Quarry Road
Raleigh, NC 27610
(252) 637-2912

Salisbury National Cemetery
202 Government Road
Salisbury, NC 28144
(704) 636-2661

Wilmington National Cemetery
2011 Market Street
Wilmington, NC 28403
For information please contact New
Bern National Cemetery
(252) 637-2912

Ohio

Dayton National Cemetery
VA Medical Center
4100 West Third Street
Dayton, OH 45428-1008
(937) 262-2115

Ohio Western Reserve National
Cemetery
P.O. Box 8
10175 Rawiga Road
Rittman, OH 44270
(330) 335-3069

Oklahoma

Fort Gibson National Cemetery
1423 Cemetery Road
Fort Gibson, OK 74434
(918) 478-2334

Fort Sill National Cemetery
24665 N-S Road 260
Elgin, OK 73538
(580) 492-3200

Oregon

Eagle Point National Cemetery
2763 Riley Road
Eagle Point, OR 97524
(541) 826-2511

Roseburg National Cemetery
VA Medical Center
Roseburg, OR 97470
(541) 826-2511

Willamette National Cemetery
11800 S.E. Mt. Scott Boulevard
Portland, OR 97266-6937
(503) 273-5250

Pennsylvania

Indiantown Gap National Cemetery
R. R. #2, P. O. Box 484
Annville, PA 17003-9618
(717) 865-5254

National Cemetery of the
Alleghenies
1158 Morgan Road
Bridgeville, PA 15017
(724) 746-4363

Philadelphia National Cemetery
Haines Street and Limekiln Pike
Philadelphia, PA 19138
For information please contact
Beverly National Cemetery
(609) 877-5460

Puerto Rico

Puerto Rico National Cemetery
Avenue Cementario Nacional #50
Bayamon, PR 00960
(787) 798-8400

South Carolina

Beaufort National Cemetery
601 Boundary Street
Beaufort, SC 29902
(843) 524-3925

Florence National Cemetery
803 East National Cemetery Road
Florence, SC 29501
(843) 669-8783

Fort Jackson National Cemetery
4170 Percival Rd
Columbia, SC 29229
(866) 577-5248

South Dakota

Black Hills National Cemetery
P. O. Box 640
Sturgis, SD 57785
(605) 347-3830

Fort Meade National Cemetery
Old Stone Road
Sturgis, SD 57785
For information please contact
Black Hills National Cemetery
(605) 347-3830

Hot Springs National Cemetery
VA Medical Center
Hot Springs, SD 57747
For information please contact
Black Hills National Cemetery
(605) 347-3830

Tennessee

Chattanooga National Cemetery
1200 Bailey Avenue
Chattanooga, TN 37404
(423) 855-6590

Knoxville National Cemetery
939 Tyson Street, N.W.
Knoxville, TN 37917
(423) 855-6590

Memphis National Cemetery
3568 Townes Avenue
Memphis, TN 38122
(901) 386-8311

Mountain Home National Cemetery
P. O. Box 8
Mountain Home, TN 37684
(423) 979-3535

Nashville National Cemetery
1420 Gallatin Road, South
Madison, TN 37115-4619
(615) 860-0086

Texas

Dallas-Fort Worth
National Cemetery
2191 Mountain Creek Parkway
Dallas, TX 75211
(214) 467-3374

Fort Bliss National Cemetery
5200 Fred Wilson Road
P. O. Box 6342
Fort Bliss, TX 79906
(915) 564-0201

Fort Sam Houston National
Cemetery
1520 Harry Wurzbach Road
San Antonio, TX 78209
(210) 820-3891

Houston National Cemetery
10410 Veterans Memorial Drive
Houston, TX 77038
(281) 447-8686

Kerrville National Cemetery
VA Medical Center
3600 Memorial Boulevard
Kerrville, TX 78028
For information please contact
Fort Sam Houston National
Cemetery
(210) 820-3891

San Antonio National Cemetery
517 Paso Hondo Street
San Antonio, TX 78202
For information please contact
Fort Sam Houston National
Cemetery
(210) 820-3891

Virginia

Alexandria National Cemetery
1450 Wilkes Street
Alexandria, VA 22314
For information please contact
Quantico National Cemetery
(703) 221-2183

Balls Bluff National Cemetery
Route 7
Leesburg, VA 22075
For information please contact
Culpeper National Cemetery
(540) 825-0027

City Point National Cemetery
10th Avenue and Davis Street
Hopewell, VA 23860
For information please contact
Fort Harrison National Cemetery
(804) 795-2031

Cold Harbor National Cemetery
Route 156 North
Mechanicsville, VA 23111
For information please contact
Fort Harrison National Cemetery
(804) 795-2031

Culpeper National Cemetery
305 U.S. Avenue
Culpeper, VA 22701
(540) 825-0027

Danville National Cemetery
721 Lee Street
Danville, VA 24541
For information please contact
Salisbury National Cemetery
(704) 636-2661

Fort Harrison National Cemetery
8620 Varina Road
Richmond, VA 23231
(804) 795-2031

Glendale National Cemetery
8301 Willis Church Road
Richmond, VA 23231
For information please contact
Fort Harrison National Cemetery
(804) 795-2031

Hampton National Cemetery
Cemetery Road at Marshall Avenue
Hampton, VA 23667
(757) 723-7104

Hampton National Cemetery
VA Medical Center
Emancipation Drive
Hampton, VA 23667
(757) 723-7104

Quantico National Cemetery
P. O. Box 10
18424 Joplin Road (Route 619)
Triangle, VA 22172
(703) 221-2183 (local)

Richmond National Cemetery
1701 Williamsburg Road
Richmond, VA 23231
For information please contact
Fort Harrison National Cemetery
(804) 795-2031

Seven Pines National Cemetery
400 East Williamsburg Road
Sandston, VA 23150
For information please contact
Fort Harrison National Cemetery
(804) 795-2031

Staunton National Cemetery
901 Richmond Avenue
Staunton, VA 24401
(540) 825-0027

Winchester National Cemetery
401 National Avenue
Winchester, VA 22601
For information please contact
Culpeper National Cemetery
(540) 825-0027

Washington

Tahoma National Cemetery
18600 Southeast 240th Street
Kent, WA 98042-4868
(425) 413-9614

West Virginia

Grafton National Cemetery
431 Walnut Street
Grafton, WV 26354
For information please contact
West Virginia National Cemetery
(304) 265-2044

West Virginia National Cemetery
Route 2, Box 127
Grafton, WV 26354
(304) 265-2044

Wisconsin

Wood National Cemetery
5000 W National Ave,
Bldg 1301
Milwaukee, WI 53295-4000
(414) 382-5300

Department Of The Interior National Cemeteries

District Of Columbia

Battleground National Cemetery
C/O Superintendent, Rock Creek Park
3545 Williamsburg Lane, NW
Washington, DC 20008
(202) 282-1063

Georgia

Andersonville National Historic Site
Route 1, Box 800
Andersonville, GA 31711
(912) 924-0343

Louisiana

Chalmette National Cemetery
C/O Jean Lafitte National
Historical Park and Preserve
365 Canal Street, Suite 2400
New Orleans, LA 70130
(504) 589-3882
(504) 589-4430

Maryland

Antietam National Battlefield
Box 158
301) 432-5124
Sharpsburg, MD 21782-0158
(301) 432-5124

Mississippi

Vicksburg National Military Park
3201 Clay Street
Vicksburg, MS 39180
(601) 636-0583

Montana

Little Bighorn Battle
National Monument
Custer National Cemetery
P. O. Box 39
Crow Agency, MT 59022
(406) 638-2621

Pennsylvania

Gettysburg National Military Park
97 Taneytown Road
Gettysburg, PA 17325-2804
(717) 334-1124

Tennessee

Andrew Johnson National
Historic Site
P. O. Box 1088
Greeneville, TN 37744
(423) 638-3551

Fort Donelson National Battlefield
P. O. Box 434
Dover, TN 37058
(615) 232-5348

Shiloh National Military Park
Route 1, Box 9
Shiloh, TN 38376-9704
(901) 689-5275

Stones River National Battlefield
3501 Old Nashville Highway
Murfreesboro, TN 37129
(615) 893-9501

Virginia

Fredericksburg and Spotsylvania
County Battlefields Memorial
National Military Park
120 Chatham Lane
Fredericksburg, VA 22405
(540) 371-0802

Poplar Grove National Cemetery
Petersburg National Battlefield
1539 Hickory Hill Road
Petersburg, VA 23803
(804) 732-3531

Yorktown Battlefield Cemetery
Colonial National Historical Park
P. O. Box 210
Yorktown, VA 23690
(757) 898-3400

Department Of The Army National Cemeteries

United States Soldiers' & Airmen's
Home National Cemetery
21 Harewood Road, NW
Washington, DC 20011
(202) 829-1829

Arlington National Cemetery
Interment Services Branch
Arlington, VA 22211
(703) 695-3250 or 3255

STATE VETERANS CEMETERIES

Arizona

Southern Arizona Veterans
Memorial
1300 Buffalo Soldier Trail
Sierra Vista, AZ 85635
(520) 458-7144

Arkansas

Arkansas Veterans Cemetery
1501 W Maryland Avenue
North Little Rock, AR 72120
(501) 683-2259

California

Veterans Memorial Grove Cemetery
Veterans Home of California
Yountville, CA 94599
(707) 944-4600

Northern California Veterans Cemetery
P.O. Box 76
11800 Gas Point Road
Igo, CA 96047
(866) 777-4533

Colorado

Colorado State Veterans Cemetery
At Homelake
3749 Sherman Avenue
Monte Vista, CO 81144
(719) 852-5118

Veterans Memorial Cemetery Of
Western Colorado
2830 D Road
Grand Junction, CO 81505
(970) 263-8986

Connecticut

Colonel Raymond F. Gates
Memorial Cemetery
Veterans Home and Hospital
287 West Street
Rocky Hill, CT 06067
(860) 721-5838

Spring Grove Veterans Cemetery
Darien, CT
C/O Veterans Home and Hospital
287 West Street
Rocky Hill, CT 06067
(860) 721-5838

Middletown Veterans Cemetery
C/O Veterans Home and Hospital
287 West Street
Rocky Hill, CT 06067
(860) 721-5838

Delaware

Delaware Veterans Memorial
Cemetery
2465 Chesapeake City Road
Bear, DE 19701
(302) 834-8046

Delaware Veterans Memorial
Cemetery-Sussex County
RD 5 Box 100
Millsboro, DE 19966
(302) 934-5653

Georgia

Georgia Veterans Memorial
Cemetery
2617 Vinson Highway
Milledgeville, Georgia 31061
(478) 445-3363

Georgia Veterans Memorial
Cemetery
8819 U.S. Highway 301
Glennville, Georgia 30427
912-654-5398

Hawaii

Director, Office of Veterans
Services
459 Patterson Road
E-Wing, Room 1-A103
Honolulu, HI 96189
(808) 433-0420

Hawaii State Veterans Cemetery
45-349 Kamehameha Highway
Kaneohe, HI 96744
(808) 233-3630

East Hawaii Veterans
Cemetery - No. I
County of Hawaii
25 Aupuni Street
Hilo, HI 96720
(Island of Hawaii)
(808) 961-8311

East Hawaii Veterans
Cemetery - No. II
County of Hawaii
25 Aupuni Street
Hilo, HI 96720
(Island of Hawaii)
(808) 961-8311

Kauai Veterans Cemetery
County of Kauai Public Works
3021 Umi Street
Lihue, HI 96766
(Island of Kauai)
(808) 241-6670

Maui Veterans Cemetery
1295 Makawao Avenue, Box 117
Makawao, HI 96768
(Island of Maui)
(808) 572-7272

Hoolehua Veterans Cemetery
(Molokai)
P. O. Box 526
Kauna Kakai, HI 96748
(Island of Molokai)
(808) 553-3204

West Hawaii State
Veterans Cemetery
(Currently under construction –
located on the Island of Hawaii
near town of Kona)
(808) 961-8311

Lanai Veterans Cemetery
(Currently under construction –
located on the Island of Lanai)
(808) 565-6979

Idaho

Idaho Veterans Cemetery
10101 North Horseshoe Bend Road
Boise, ID 83714
(208) 334-4796

Illinois

Sunset Cemetery
Illinois Veterans Home
1707 North 12th Street
Quincy, IL 62301
(217) 222-8641

Indiana

Indiana State Soldiers Home
Cemetery
3851 North River Road
West Lafayette, IN 47906-3765
(765) 463-1502

Indiana Veterans Memorial
Cemetery
1415 North Gate Road
Madison, IN 47250
(812) 273-9220

Iowa

Iowa Veterans Home and Cemetery
13th & Summit Streets
Marshalltown, IA 50158
(641) 753-4309

Iowa Veterans Cemetery
34024 Veterans Memorial Drive
Adel, Iowa 50003-3300
(515) 996-9048

Kansas

Kansas Veterans Cemetery
At Fort Dodge
714 Sheridan, Unit #66
Fort Dodge, KS 67801
(620) 338-8775

Kansas Veterans Cemetery
At Wakeeney
P.O. Box 185
4035 13th Street
Wakeeney, KS 67672
(785) 743-5685

Kansas Veterans Cemetery
At Winfield
1208 North College
Winfield, KS 67156
(620) 229-2287

Kentucky

Kentucky Veterans Cemetery-
Central
1111 Louisville Road
Frankfort, Kentucky
(502) 564-9281

Kentucky Veterans Cemetery-
North
205 Eibeck Lane
P.O. Box 467
Williamstown, Kentucky 41097
859-823-0720

Kentucky Veteran's Cemetery-West
5817 Fort Campbell Boulevard
Hopkinsville, Kentucky 42240
(270) 707-9653

Louisiana

Northwest Louisiana Veterans Cemetery
7970 Mike Clark Road
Keithville, Louisiana 71047
(318) 925-0612

Maine

Maine Veterans Memorial Cemetery
(Closed)
Civic Center Drive
Augusta, Maine

Maine Veterans Memorial
Cemetery--Mt. Vernon Rd.
163 Mt. Vernon Road
Augusta, ME 04330
(207) 287-3481

Northern Maine Veterans
Cemetery-Caribou
37 Lombard Road
Caribou, ME 04736
(207)-492-1173

Maryland

Maryland State
Veterans Cemeteries
Federal Building-31 Hopkins Plaza
Baltimore, MD 21201
(410) 962-4700

Cheltenham Veterans Cemetery
11301 Crain Highway
P. O. Box 10
Cheltenham, MD 20623
(301) 372-6398

Crownsville Veterans Cemetery
1080 Sunrise Beach Road
Crownsville, MD 21032
(410) 987-6320 or
(301) 962-4700

Eastern Shore Veterans Cemetery
6827 East New Market
Ellwood Road
Hurlock, MD 21643
(410) 943-3420

Garrison Forest Veterans Cemetery
11501 Garrison Forest Road
Owings Mills, MD 21117
(410) 363-6090

Rocky Gap Veterans Cemetery
14205 Pleasant Valley Road, NE
Flintstone, MD 21530
(301) 777-2185

Massachusetts

Massachusetts State Veterans
Cemetery (Agawam & Winchendon)
1390 Main Street
Agawam, MA 01001
(413) 821-9500

Winchendon Veterans Cemetery
111 Glenallen Street
Winchendon, MA 01475
(978) 297-9501

Michigan

Grand Rapids Home for Veterans
Cemetery
3000 Monroe, NW
Grand Rapids, MI 49505
(616) 364-5400

Minnesota

MN State Veterans Cemetery
15550 HWY 15
Little Falls, MN 56345
(320) 616-2527

Missouri

St. James Missouri Veterans Home
Cemetery
620 North Jefferson
St. James, MO 65559
(573) 265-3271

Missouri Veterans Cemetery -
Higgensville, MO
20109 Bus. Hwy. 13
Higgensville, MO 64037
(660) 584-5252

Missouri Veterans Cemetery –
Springfield. MO
5201 South Southwood Road
Springfield, MO 65804
(417) 823-3944

Missouri State Veterans Cemetery
–Bloomfield
17357 Stars and Strips Way
Bloomfield, Missouri 63825
(573) 568-3871

Missouri State Veterans Cemetery -
Jacksonville
1479 County Road 1675
Jacksonville, Missouri 65260
(660) 295-4237

Montana

State Veterans Cemetery
Fort William H. Harrison
Box 5715
Helena, MT 59604
(406) 324-3740

State Veterans Cemetery
Miles City
Highway 59
Miles City, MT 59301
(406) 324-3740

Montana Veterans Home Cemetery
P. O. Box 250
Columbia Falls, MT 59912
(406) 892-3256

Nebraska

Nebraska Veterans
Home Cemetery
Burkett Station
Grand Island, NE 68803
(308) 385-6252, Ext. 230

Nevada

Commissioner of Veterans Affairs
1201 Terminal Way, Room 108
Reno, NV 89520
(775) 688-1155

Northern Nevada Veterans
Memorial Cemetery
14 Veterans Way
Fernley, NV 89408
(775) 575-4441

Southern Nevada Veterans
Memorial Cemetery
1900 Buchanan Boulevard
Boulder City, NV 89005
(702) 486-5920

New Hampshire

NH State Veterans Cemetery
110 Daniel Webster Hwy, Route 3
Boscawen, NH 03303
(603) 796-2026

New Jersey

Brigadier General William C. Doyle
Veterans Memorial Cemetery
350 Provenceline Road, Route #2
Wrightstown, NJ 08562
(609) 758-7250

New Jersey Memorial Home
Cemetery (Closed)
524 N.W. Boulevard
Vineland, NJ 08360
(609) 696-6350

North Carolina

Western Carolina State Veterans
Cemetery
962 Old Highway 70, West
Black Mountain, NC 28711
(828) 669-0684
Coastal Carolina State Veterans
Cemetery
P. O. Box 1486
Jacksonville, NC 28541
(910) 347-4550 or 3570

Sandhills State Veterans Cemetery
P. O. Box 39
400 Murchison Road
Spring Lake, NC 28390
(910) 436-5630 or 5635

North Dakota

North Dakota Veterans Cemetery
1825 46th Street
Mandan, ND 58554
(701) 667-1418

Ohio

Ohio Veterans Home Cemetery
3416 Columbus Avenue
Sandusky, OH 44870
(419) 625-2454, Ext. 200

Oklahoma

Oklahoma Veterans Cemetery
Military Department (OKFAC)
3501 Military Circle N.E.
Oklahoma City, OK 73111-4398
(405) 228-5334

Pennsylvania

Pennsylvania Soldiers and
Sailors Home Cemetery
P. O. Box 6239
560 East Third Street
Erie, PA 16512-6239
(814) 871-4531

Rhode Island

Rhode Island Veterans Cemetery
301 South County Trail
Exeter, RI 02822-9712
(401) 268-3088

South Carolina

M.J. "Dolly" Cooper Veterans
Cemetery
140 Inway Drive
Anderson, SC 29621
(864) 332-8022

South Dakota

SD Veterans Home Cemetery
2500 Minnekahta Avenue
Hot Springs, SD 57747
(605) 745-5127

Tennessee

East Tennessee State
Veterans Cemetery
5901 Lyons View Pike
Knoxville, TN 37919
(865) 594-6776

Middle Tennessee
Veterans Cemetery
7931 McCrory Lane
Nashville, TN 37221
(615) 532-2238

West Tennessee
Veterans Cemetery
4000 Forest Hill/Irene Road
Memphis, TN 38125
(901) 543-7005

Texas

Central Texas State Veterans
Cemetery
11463 South Highway 195
Killeen, Texas 76542
(512) 463-5977

Rio Grande Valley
State Veterans Cemetery
2520 South Inspiration Road
Mission, TX 78572
(956) 583-7227

Utah

Utah State Veterans Cemetery
Utah Parks and Recreation
17111 South Camp Williams Road
Bluffdale, UT 84065
(801) 254-9036

Vermont

Vermont Veterans Home War
Memorial Cemetery
325 North Street
Bennington, VT 05201
(802) 442-6353

Vermont Veterans Memorial
Cemetery
120 State Street
Montpelier, VT 05602-4401
(802) 828-3379

Virginia

Virginia Veterans Cemetery
10300 Pridesville Road
Amelia, VA 23002
(804) 561-1475

Albert G. Horton, Jr. Memorial
Veterans Cemetery
5310 Milner's Road
Suffolk, Virginia 23434
(757) 334-4731

Washington

Washington Soldiers Home
Colony and Cemetery
1301 Orting-Kapowsin Highway
Orting, WA 98360
(360) 893-4500

Washington Veterans Home
Cemetery
P. O. Box 698
Retsil, WA 98378
(360) 895-4700

Wisconsin

Northern Wisconsin Veterans
Memorial Cemetery
N4063 Wildcat Road QQ
Spooner, WI 54801
(715) 635-5360

Wisconsin Veterans Memorial
Cemetery
Wisconsin Veterans Home
N2665 Highway QQ
King, WI 54946
(715) 258-5586

Southern Wisconsin
Veterans Memorial Cemetery
21731 Spring Street
Union Grove, WI 53182
(262) 878-5660

Wyoming

Oregon Trail Veterans Cemetery
89 Cemetery Road, Box 669
Evansville, WY 82636
(307) 235-6673

Territories

Guam Veterans Cemetery
490 Chalan Palayso
Agatna Heights, Guam 96910
(671) 475-4225

SAIPAN
CNMI Veterans Cemetery
Military/Veterans Affairs
P.O. Box 503416
Saipan, MP 96950
(670) 664-2650
NOTE:

All State cemeteries (except
Nevada, Pennsylvania, Wyoming
and Utah) restrict burials to State
residents.

CHAPTER 10

HEALTHCARE BENEFITS

In October 1996, Congress passed Public Law 104-262, the Veterans' Healthcare Eligibility Reform Act of 1996. This legislation paved the way for the creation of a Uniform Benefits Package - a standard enhanced health benefits plan available to all enrolled veterans. The Law also simplified the process by which veterans can receive services.

Public Law 104-262 was enacted to simplify the rules for providing healthcare to veterans and to introduce improvements in the quality and timeliness of the care veterans receive.

Note: Individuals are encouraged to contact the nearest VA benefits or healthcare facility to obtain the latest information regarding healthcare benefits. Legislation often changes the specific regulations regarding healthcare and nursing home care.

VETERAN HEALTH REGISTRIES

Certain veterans can participate in a VA health registry and receive free medical examinations, including laboratory and other diagnostic tests, when determined necessary by an examining clinician.

Gulf War Registry:
For veterans who served in the Gulf War and Operation Iraqi Freedom

Depleted Uranium Registries:
VA maintains two registries for veterans possible exposed to depleted uranium. The first is for veterans who served in the Gulf War, including Operation Iraqi Freedom. The second is for veterans who served elsewhere, including Bosnia and Afghanistan.

Agent Orange Registry:
For veterans possible exposed to dioxin or other toxic substances in herbicides used during the Vietnam War, while serving in Korea in 1968 or 1969, or as a result of testing, transporting, or spraying herbicides for military purposes.

Ionizing Radiation Registry:
For veterans possibly exposed to atomic radiation during the following activities:

- Atmospheric detonation of a nuclear device;

- Occupation of Hiroshima or Nagasaki from August 6, 1945 through July 1, 1946;

- Internment as a prisoner of war in Japan during WW II

- Serving in official military duties at the gaseous diffusion plants at Paducah, KY; Portsmouth, OH; or the K-25 area at Oak Ridge, TN for at least 250 days before February 1, 1992, or in Longshot, Milrow or Cannikin underground nuclear tests at Amchitka Island, Alaska, before January 1, 1974; or

- Treatment with nasopharyngeal (NP) radium during military service.

ELIGIBILITY

The primary factor in determining a veteran's eligibility to receive VA health care benefits is "veteran status." "Veteran status" is established by active duty service in the military, naval, or air service and a discharge or release from active military service under other than dishonorable conditions.

The veteran's length of service may also matter. It depends on when he or she served. There is no length of service requirement for:

- Former enlisted persons who started active duty before September 8, 1980; or

- Former officers who first entered active duty before October 17, 1981.

All other veterans must have 24 months of continuous active duty military service or meet one of the exceptions described below.

Exceptions to the 24-month Active Duty Rule

The 24 continuous months of active duty service requirement does not apply to:

- Reservists who were called to Active Duty and who completed the term for which they were called, and who were granted an "other than dishonorable" discharge; or

- National Guard members who were called to Active Duty by federal executive order, and who completed the term for which they were called, and who were granted an "other than dishonorable" discharge; or

- Veterans requesting a benefit for, or in connection with, a service-connected condition or disability; or

- Veterans who were discharged or released from active duty under section 1171 or 1173 of title 10; or

- Veterans who were discharged or released from active duty for a disability incurred or aggravated in line of duty; or

- Veterans who have been determined by VA to have compensable service-connected conditions; or

- Veterans requesting treatment for and/or counseling of sexual trauma that occurred while on active military service, for treatment of conditions related to ionizing radiation or for head or neck cancer related to nose or throat radium treatment while in the military.

ENROLLMENT

In order to qualify for VA healthcare, a veteran must first become enrolled. Veterans must answer a few questions, and are then are then assigned by VA to one of the priority groups discussed later in this chapter.

As part of the enrollment process, a veteran may select any VA health care facility to serve as his or her primary treatment facility.

All veterans seeking VA healthcare are required to be enrolled unless they are in one of the following categories:

- VA rated the individual as having a service-connected disability of 50% or more;

- It has been less than one year since the veteran was discharged from military service for a disability that the military determined was incurred or aggravated in the line of duty, and has not yet been rated by VA;

- Veteran is seeking care from VA for a service-connected disability only.

As part of the enrollment process, a veteran may select any VA health care facility to serve as his or her primary treatment facility.

Veterans may apply for enrollment anytime during the year by completing an *Application for Benefits, VA Form 10-10 EZ*. This form may be obtained by contacting the local VA healthcare facility, County Veteran Service Office (VSO), or Veteran Service Organization.

The completed and signed form should be forwarded to the nearest VA healthcare facility. The application will be processed and forwarded to the VA Health Eligibility Center in Atlanta, GA. The Health Eligibility Center will notify the veteran of his or her status.

Once enrolled, most veterans will remain enrolled from year to year without further action on their part. However, certain veterans are required to provide income information to determine their priority level. These veterans will be mailed a *VA Form 10-10 EZ* for completion for re-enrollment on an annual basis.

A veteran may choose not to be re-enrolled, or changes in VA funding may reduce the number of priority groups VA can enroll in a given fiscal year. If VA cannot renew enrollment for another year, the veteran will be notified in writing before their enrollment period expires.

Priority Groups

The number of veterans who can be enrolled in the health care program is determined by the amount of money Congress gives VA each year. Since funds are limited, VA set up priority groups to make sure that certain groups of veterans are able to be enrolled before others.

Once a veteran applies for enrollment, his or her eligibility will be verified. Based on the individual's specific eligibility status, he or she will be assigned a priority group.

The priority groups range from 1-8 with 1 being the highest priority for enrollment. Some veterans may have to agree to pay copay to be placed in certain priority groups.

A veteran may be eligible for more than one Enrollment Priority Group. In that case, VA will always place him or her in the highest priority group that he or she is eligible for. Under the Medical Benefits Package, the same services are generally available to all enrolled veterans.

> *Once a veteran applies for enrollment, his or her eligibility will be verified. Based on the individual's specific eligibility status, he or she will be assigned a priority group.*

The priority groups are complicated and some reference financial thresholds.

As of January 17, 2003, VA is not accepting new Priority Group 8 veterans for enrollment (veterans falling into Priority Groups 8e and 8g.).

Priority Group 1

- Veterans with service-connected disabilities rated 50% or more disabling; or

- Veterans determined by VA to be unemployable due to service-connected conditions.

Priority Group 2

- Veterans with service-connected disabilities rated 30% or 40% disabling.

Priority Group 3

- Veterans who are former POWs;

- Veterans whose discharge was for a disability that was incurred or aggravated in the line of duty;

- Veterans with service-connected disabilities rated 10% or 20% disabling;

- Veterans who are Purple Heart recipients (unless eligible for a higher Priority Group);

- Veterans awarded special eligibility classification under Title 38, U.S.C., Section 1151, "benefits for individuals disabled by treatment or vocational rehabilitation".

Priority Group 4

- Veterans who are receiving aid and attendance or housebound benefits from VA;

- Veterans who have been determined by VA to be catastrophically disabled.

Priority Group 5

- Nonservice-connected veterans and service-connected veterans rated 0% disabled whose annual income and net worth are below the established dollar threshold. (Veterans in this priority group must provide VA with information on their annual income and net worth in order to determine whether they are below the "means test" threshold; or agree to co-payment requirements. The threshold is adjusted annually, and announced in January. In making the assessment, the veteran's household income is considered.);

- Veterans receiving VA pension benefits;

- Veterans eligible for Medicaid benefits.

Priority Group 6

- Veterans with 0% service-connected conditions, but receiving VA compensation benefits

- Veterans seeking care only for disorders relating to:

- Ionizing Radiation during atmospheric testing or during the occupation of Hiroshima and Nagasaki;

- Project 112/SHAD;

- Agent Orange Exposure during service in Vietnam;

- Environmental Contaminants / Gulf War Illness during service in the Persian Gulf;

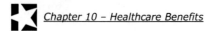

- Veterans of World War I or the Mexican Border War;

- Veterans who served in combat in a war after the Gulf War or during a period of hostility after November 11, 1998 for 2 years following discharge or release from the military.

Priority Group 7

- Veterans who agree to pay specified copayments with income and/or net worth above the VA Means Test threshold and income below the HUD geographic index.

- **Sub-priority a:** Noncompensable 0% service-connected veterans who were enrolled in the VA Health Care System on a specified date and who have remained enrolled since that date.

- **Sub-priority c:** Nonservice-connected veterans who were enrolled in the VA Health Care System on a specified date and who have remained enrolled since that date.

- **Sub-priority e**: Noncompensable 0% service-connected veterans not included in Sub-priority a above.

- **Sub-priority g:** Nonservice-connected veterans not included in Sub-priority c above.

Priority Group 8

Veterans with income and/or net worth above the VA National Income Thresholds and the VA National Geographic Income Thresholds who agree to pay copays.

2009 UPDATE:

Effective January 17, 2003, VA stopped enrolling new veterans in Priority Group 8. However, on June 15, 2009, VA amended its regulations to expand enrollment of certain Veterans with higher income.

Under the new provision, a Veteran who applies for enrollment, who does not qualify for a higher priority group and whose previous year's income does not exceed VA's national and geographically-adjusted income thresholds by 10% or less will be eligible for enrollment into Priority Group 8b (if the Veteran is noncompensable 0% service-connected) or 8d (if the Veteran is nonservice-connected).

- **Sub-priority a:** Noncompensable 0% service-connected veterans enrolled as of January 16, 2003 and who have remained enrolled since that date and/or placed in this subpriority due to changed eligibility status.

- **Sub-priority b: :** Noncompensable 0% service-connected veterans who enrolled on or after June 15, 2009 whose income exceeds the current VA National Income Threshholds or VA National Geographic Income Threshholds by 10% or less.

- **Sub-priority c:** Nonservice-connected veterans enrolled as of January 16, 2003 and who have remained enrolled since that date and/or placed in this subpriority due to changed eligibility status.

- **Sub-priority d:** Nonservice-connected veterans who enrolled on or after June 15, 2009 whose income exceeds the current VA National Income Threshholds or VA National Geographic Income Threshholds by 10% or less.

- **Sub-priority e:** Veterans not meeting the criteria above, Noncompensable 0% service-connected

- **Sub-priority g:** Veterans not meeting the criteria above, Nonservice-connected

-

As of June 15, 2009, Veterans in Priority Group 8, Sub-priority a, b, c, and d are eligible for enrollment.

-

Special Access to Care

Service Disabled Veterans:
Veterans who are 50 percent or more disabled from service-connected conditions, unemployable due to service-connected conditions, or receiving care for a service-connected disability receive priority in scheduling of hospital or outpatient medical appointments.

ENHANCED VA HEALTH CARE BENEFITS
FOR COMBAT VETERANS

Most veterans including National Guard and Reservists, who served in a theater of combat operations after November 11, 1998, are eligible to receive cost-free VA health care for combat-related conditions and enhanced enrollment priority for 5 years after separation from active duty. Combat veterans not previously enrolled who separated from active duty prior to January 28, 2003, are eligible for the enhanced benefits until January 27, 2011.

We encourage veterans to enroll with VA during this enhanced eligibility period to take advantage of these special benefits.

MEANS TEST

As described in the above priority groups, certain nonservice-connected veterans are required to fill out the financial worksheet, referred to as a "Means Test." This is the way the VA gathers financial information to determine a veteran's priority group for enrollment, and whether or not he or she is required to make copayments for services received. The means test is based on prior year income and net worth.

> *New veterans who apply for enrollment after January 16, 2003, and who decline to provide income information are not eligible for enrollment.*

If a veterans declines to complete the financial worksheet, he or she must agree to pay the applicable co-payment, unless otherwise eligible for VA care.

New veterans who apply for enrollment after January 16, 2003, and who decline to provide income information are not eligible for enrollment.

Veterans who are required to provide their financial information generally must do so on an annual basis. To simplify this annual reporting requirement, VA recently introduced *VA Form 10-10EZR*, a new, shorter version of its application form. This new, shorter form is only to be used by previously enrolled veterans to update their previously reported information. The form can be requested toll-free from VA's Health Benefits Service Center at (877) 222-8387.

TRAVEL BENEFITS

Once enrolled in the VA health system, health care benefits become completely portable throughout the entire VA system. Enrolled veterans who are traveling or who spend time away from their primary treatment facility may obtain care at any VA health care facility across the country, without having to reapply.

EXISTING HEALTHCARE COVERAGE

Since VA health care depends primarily on annual congressional appropriations, veterans are allowed to keep their current healthcare coverage and are encouraged to do so. Veterans with private insurance or other coverage such as DoD, Medicare, or Medicaid may find these coverages to be a supplement to their VA enrollment. The use of other available healthcare coverage does not affect a veteran's enrollment status. VA does not charge the veteran for insurance company co-payments and deductibles.

When applying for medical care, all veterans will be asked to provide information pertaining to health insurance coverage, including policies held by spouses. VA is obligated to submit claims to insurance carriers for the recovery of costs for medical care provided to nonservice-connected veterans and service-connected veterans for nonservice-connected conditions.

COPAYMENT REQUIREMENTS

While some veterans qualify for cost-free health care services based on a compensable service-connected condition or other qualifying factor, most veterans are required to complete an annual financial assessment or Means Test to determine if they qualify for cost-free services.

Veterans whose income and net worth exceed the established Means Test threshold, as well as those who choose not to complete the financial assessment must agree to pay required copayments to become eligible for VA health care services. (As stated above please remember that new veterans who apply for enrollment after January 16, 2003 and who decline to provide income information are not eligible for enrollment.)

Along with their enrollment confirmation and priority group assignment, enrollees will receive information regarding their copayment requirements, if applicable.

Veterans may qualify for cost-free health care and/or medications based on:

- Receiving a Purple Heart Medal, or

- Former Prisoner of War Status, or

- Compensable service-connected disabilities, or

- Low income, or

- Other qualifying factors including treatment related to their military service experience. (Some veterans are not charged a copay for health care or medications furnished for treatment of conditions related to their military service experience. This includes exposure to Agent Orange, Ionizing Radiation, Environmental Contaminants during the Gulf War, Project 112/SHAD, Nose and Throat Radium treatment, or Sexual Trauma while in the military, or care of combat-related conditions for 2 years following discharge from active duty.

Copayment Rates – Effective January 1, 2009

OUTPATIENT SERVICES	
Basic Services – Services provided by a primary care clinician	$15/visit
Specialty Care Services – services provided by a clinical specialist such as surgeon, radiologist, audiologist, optometrist, cardiologist, and specialty tests such as magnetic resonance imagery (MRI), computerized axial tomography (CAT) scan, and nuclear medicine studies	$50 /visit
Footnotes for outpatient services: • Copayment amount is limited to a single charge per visit regardless of the number of health care providers seen in a single day. The copayment amount is based on the highest level of service received. There is no copayment requirement for preventive services such as screenings and immunizations.)	
MEDICATIONS	
Veterans in Priority Groups 2-6, for each 30-day supply of medication for treatment of nonservice-connected conditions	$8/prescription
(The total amount paid annually by veterans in Priority Groups 2 through 6 is limited to $960.)	
Effective July 1, 2010, Veterans in Priority Groups 7-8, , for each 30-day supply of medication for treatment of nonservice-connected conditions	$9/prescription
(Veterans in Priority Groups 7-8 do not qualify for medication copay annual cap.)	
(Veterans in Priority Group 1 do not pay for medications.)	
INPATIENT SERVICES	
Inpatient Copayment for the first 90 days of care during a 365-day period	$1,068
Inpatient copayment for each additional 90 days of care during a 365 day period	$534
Per Diem Charge	$10/day
Footnote for inpatient services: Lower income veterans who live in high-cost areas may qualify for a reduction of inpatient copay charges.	
Long-Term Care	
Nursing Home Care / Inpatient Respite Care / Geriatric Evaluation	Maximum of $97/day Adult
Day Health Care / Outpatient Geriatric Evaluation / Outpatient Respite Care	Maximum of $15/day
Domiciliary Care	Maximum of $5/day
Footnote for inpatient services: Copays for Long-Term Care services start on the 22nd day of care during any 12-month period—there is no copay requirement for the first 21 days. Actual copay charges will vary from veteran to veteran depending upon financial information submitted on VA Form 10-10EC.	

HARDSHIP DETERMINATION

A Hardship Determination is a process by which a veteran may request to be placed in a different priority group based on a change in his or her financial situation from the previous year. Circumstances that may warrant hardship consideration would be the loss of employment, business bankruptcy, or out-of-pocket medical expenses.

INFORMATION FOR VETERANS ABOUT THE NEW MEDICARE PRESCRIPTION DRUG BENEFITS

Beginning January 1, 2006, Medicare prescription drug coverage (Medicare Part D) became available to everyone with Medicare Part A or B coverage. The Medicare prescription drug coverage is wholly voluntary on the part of the participant. Each individual must decide whether to participate based on his or her own circumstances.

How This Affects Veterans:

- Each veteran must decide whether to enroll in a Medicare Part D plan based on his or her own situation.

- An individual's VA prescription drug coverage will not change based on his or her decision to participate in Medicare Part D.

- VA prescription drug coverage is considered by Medicare to be at least as good as Medicare Part D coverage. (Therefore, it is considered to be **creditable coverage**. Refer to following section for more information regarding creditable coverage.)

- If an individual's spouse is covered by Medicare, he or she must decide whether to enroll in a Medicare Part D plan regardless of the veteran's decision to participate.

Creditable Coverage

Most entities that currently provide prescription drug coverage to Medicare beneficiaries, including VA, must disclose whether the entity's coverage is "creditable prescription drug coverage."

- Enrollment in the VA health care system is creditable coverage. This means that VA prescription drug coverage is at least as good as the Medicare Part D coverage.

- Because they have creditable coverage, veterans enrolled in the VA health care program who choose not to enroll in a Medicare Part D plan before May 15, 2006 will not have to pay a higher premium on a permanent basis ("late enrollment penalty") if they enroll in a Medicare drug plan during a later enrollment period.

- However, if an individual disenrolls in VA health care or if he or she loses his or her enrollment status through no fault of his/her own (such as an enrollment decision by VA that would further restrict access to certain Priority Groups), he or she may be subject to the late enrollment penalty unless he or she enrolls in a Medicare Part D plan within 62 days of losing VA coverage.

- If a veteran becomes a patient or inmate in an institution of another government agency (for example, a state veterans home, a state institution, a jail, or a corrections facility), he or she may not have creditable coverage from VA while in that institution. For further information, individuals should contact the institution where the veteran resides, the VA Health Benefits Service Center at (877) 222-VETS, or the local VA medical facility.

COVERED SERVICES – STANDARD BENEFITS

VA's medical benefits package provides the following health care services to all enrolled veterans:

Preventive Care Services

- Immunizations
- Physical Examinations (including eye and hearing examinations)
- Health Care Assessments
- Screening Tests
- Health Education Programs

Ambulatory (Outpatient) Diagnostic and Treatment Services

- Emergency outpatient care in VA facilities
- Medical
- Surgical (including reconstructive/plastic surgery as a result of disease or trauma)
- Chiropractic Care
- Bereavement Counseling
- Mental Health
- Substance Abuse

Hospital (Inpatient) Diagnostic and Treatment

- Emergency inpatient care in VA facilities
- Medical
- Surgical (including reconstructive/plastic surgery as a result of disease or trauma)
- Mental Health

- Substance Abuse

Medications and Supplies (when prescribed by a VA physician)

Limited Benefits

The following is a partial listing of acute care services which may have limitations and special eligibility criteria:

- Ambulance Services
- Dental Care (refer to Chapter 11 of this book for additional details.)
- Durable Medical Equipment
- Eyeglasses (see footnote below)
- Hearing Aids (see footnote below)
- Home Health Care
- Homeless Programs
- Maternity and Parturition Services—usually provided in non-VA contracted hospitals at VA expense, care is limited to the mother (costs associated with the care of newborn are not covered)
- Non-VA Health Care Services
- Orthopedic, Prosthetic, and Rehabilitative Devices
- Rehabilitative Services
- Readjustment Counseling
- Sexual Trauma Counseling

Footnote: To qualify for hearing aids or eyeglasses, the individual must have a VA service-connected disability rating of 10% or more. An individual may also qualify if he or she is a former prisoner of war, Purple Heart recipient, require this benefit for treatment of a 0% service-connected condition, or are receiving increased pension based on the need for regular aid and attendance or being permanently housebound.

General Exclusions

The following is a partial listing of general exclusions:

- Abortions and abortion counseling
- Cosmetic surgery except where determined by VA to be medically necessary for reconstructive or psychiatric care
- Gender alteration
- Health club or spa membership, even for rehabilitation
- In-vitro fertilization

- Drugs, biological, and medical devices not approved by the Food and Drug Administration unless part of formal clinical trial under an approved research program or when prescribed under a compassionate use exemption.

- Medical care for a veteran who is either a patient or inmate in an institution of another government agency if that agency has a duty to provide the care or services.

- Services not ordered and provided by licensed/accredited professional staff

- Special private duty nursing

Non-VA Emergency Care

Veterans are eligible for emergency care at non-VA facilities only if:

- It is determined that VA health care facilities were not feasibly available; that a delay in medical attention would have endangered his or her life or health; and the veteran is personally liable for the cost of services; AND

- The care is for a service-connected condition; OR

- If enrolled, the veteran has been provided care by a VA clinician or provider within the past 24 months.

> **2011 UPDATE:** The Veterans' Emergency Care Fairness Act became law on February 1, 2010. This law enables the VA to reimburse veterans enrolled in VA health care for the remaining cost of emergency treatment if the veteran has outside insurance that only covers part of the cost. Previously, VA could reimburse veterans or pay outside hospitals directly only if a veteran had NO OUTSIDE HEALTH INSURANCE.
>
> The bill also allows the Secretary of Veterans Affairs to provide retroactive reimbursements for care received prior to the passage of this bill, and on or after July 19, 2001, if considered appropriate under the circumstances.

If non-VA emergency care is received, notification to the nearest VA health care facility must be made within 48 hours if hospitalization is required. VA payment is limited up to the point that the veteran's condition is stable for transportation to a VA facility.

Travel Benefits

Veterans may qualify for beneficiary travel payments if they fall into one of the following categories:

- Have a service-connected rating of 30 percent or more;

- Are traveling for treatment of a service-connected condition;

- Receive a VA pension;

- Are traveling for a scheduled compensation or pension examination;

- Income does not exceed the maximum annual VA pension rate;

- If the medical condition requires an ambulance or a specially equipped van, the individual is unable to defray the cost, and the travel is pre-authorized.

LONG-TERM CARE BENEFITS

Standard Benefits

The following long-term care services are available to all enrolled veterans:

- Geriatric Evaluation

- A geriatric evaluation is the comprehensive assessment of a veteran's ability to care for him/herself, his/her physical health, and social environment, which leads to a plan of care. The plan could include treatment, rehabilitation, health promotion, and social services. These evaluations are performed by inpatient Geriatric Evaluation and Management (GEM) Units, GEM clinics, geriatric primary care clinics, and other outpatient settings.

- Adult Day Health Care

- The adult day health care (ADHC) program is a therapeutic day care program, providing medical and rehabilitation services to disabled veterans in a combined setting.

- Respite Care

- Respite care provides supportive care to veterans on a short-term basis to give the caregiver a planned period of relief from the physical and emotional demands associated with providing care. Respite care can be provided in the home or other noninstitutional settings.

- Home Care

- Skilled home care is provided by VA and contract agencies to veterans that are homebound with chronic diseases and includes nursing, physical/occupational therapy, and social services.

- Hospice/Palliative Care

- Hospice/palliative care programs offer pain management, symptom control, and other medical services to terminally ill veterans or veterans in the late stages of the chronic disease process. Services also include respite care as well as bereavement counseling to family members.

Financial Assessment for Long-Term Care Services

For veterans who are not automatically exempt from making copayments for long-term care services, a separate financial assessment must be completed to determine whether they qualify for cost-free services or to what extent they are required to make long term care copayments. For those veterans who do not qualify for cost-free services, the financial assessment for long term care

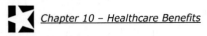

services is used to determine the copayment requirement. Unlike copayments for other VA health care services, which are based on fixed charges for all, long-term care copayment charges are individually adjusted based on each veteran's financial status.

Limited Benefits

Nursing Home Care

While some veterans qualify for indefinite nursing home care services, other veterans may qualify for a limited period of time. Among those that automatically qualify for indefinite nursing home care are veterans whose service-connected condition is clinically determined to require nursing home care and veterans with a service-connected rating of 70% or more. Other veterans—with priority given to those with service-connected conditions—may be provided short-term nursing home care if space and resources are available.

Domiciliary Care

Domiciliary care provides rehabilitative and long-term, health maintenance care for veterans who require some medical care, but who do not require all the services provided in nursing homes. Domiciliary care emphasizes rehabilitation and return to the community. VA may provide domiciliary care to veterans whose annual income does not exceed the maximum annual rate of VA pension or to veterans who have no adequate means of support.

SERVICES AND AIDS FOR BLIND VETERANS

On January 8, 1944, President Franklin D. Roosevelt made an extraordinary commitment to our nation's war-blinded servicemen, when he signed an executive order declaring:

"No blinded servicemen from World War II would be returned to their homes without adequate training to meet the problems of necessity imposed upon them by their blindness."

Meeting the demands of this obligation has resulted in various programs that have evolved throughout the years.

Veterans with corrected central vision of 20/200 or less in both eyes, or field loss to 20 degrees or less in both eyes are considered to be blind.

Blind veterans may be eligible for many of the benefits detailed throughout this book, including, but not limited to: Disability Compensation, Health Insurance, Adaptive Equipment, and Training & Rehabilitation. In addition to these benefits, there are a number of miscellaneous benefits due veterans of all wars who were blinded as the result of their war service. Many individual states offer special programs and benefits for the blind.

Services are available at all VA medical facilities through Visual Impairment Services Team (VIST) coordinators.

The VIST Coordinator is a case manager who has major responsibility for the coordination of all services for legally blind veterans and their families. Duties include providing and/or arranging for appropriate treatment, identifying new cases of blindness, providing professional counseling, resolving problems, arranging annual healthcare reviews, and conducting education programs relating to blindness.

Blind veterans may be eligible for services at a VA medical center, or for admission to a VA blind rehabilitation center or clinic. In addition, blind veterans entitled to receive disability compensation may receive VA aids for the blind, which may include:

- A total health and benefits review by a VA Visual Impairment Services team;

- Adjustment to blindness training;

- Home Improvements and Structural Alterations to homes (HISA Program);

- Specially adapted housing and adaptations;

- Low-vision aids and training in their use;

- Electronic and mechanical aids for the blind, including adaptive computers and computer-assisted devices;

- Guide dogs, including the expense of training the veteran to use the dog, and the cost of the dog's medical care;

- Talking books, tapes, and Braille literature, provided from the Library of Congress.

GUIDE DOGS / SERVICE DOGS

As previously mentioned, VA may provide guide dogs to blind veterans. Additionally, Public Law 107-135 (signed by then-President Bush January 23, 2002) states that VA may provide:

- Service dogs trained for the aid of the hearing impaired to veterans who are hearing impaired, and are enrolled under Section 1705 of Title 38; and

- Service dogs trained for the aid of persons with spinal cord injury or dysfunction or other chronic impairment that substantially limits mobility to veterans with such injury, dysfunction, or impairment who are enrolled under section 1705 of Title 38.

VA may also pay travel and incidental expenses for the veteran to travel to and from the veteran's home while becoming adjusted to the dog.

The VA operates 9 blind rehabilitation centers in the United States and Puerto Rico. Rehabilitation centers offer comprehensive programs to guide individuals through a process that eventually leads to maximum adjustment to the disability, reorganization of the person's life, and return to a contributing place in the family and community. To achieve these goals, the rehabilitation centers offer a variety of skill courses to veterans, which are designed to help achieve a realistic level of independence. Services offered at rehabilitation centers include:

- Orientation and mobility;
- Living skills;
- Communication skills;
- Activities of daily living;
- Independent daily living program;
- Manual skills;
- Visual skills;
- Computer Access Training Section;
- Physical conditioning;
- Recreation;
- Adjustment to blindness;
- Group meetings.

The VA also employs Blind Rehabilitation Outpatient Specialists (BROS) in several areas, including:

- Albuquerque, NM
- Ann Arbor, MI
- Bay Pines / St. Petersburg, FL
- Baltimore, MD
- Boston, MA
- Cleveland, OH
- Dallas, TX
- Gainesville, FL
- Los Angeles, CA
- Phoenix, AZ
- Portland, OR
- San Antonio, TX
- San Juan, PR
- Seattle, WA
- West Haven, CT

Blind Rehabilitation Outpatient Specialists are multi-skilled, experienced, blind instructors who teach skills in the veteran's home environment, and/or local VA facility.

SPECIAL CATEGORIES FOR MEDICAL CARE

Individual chapters of this book discuss the following special categories of veterans who may qualify for medical care, as well as other benefits:

- Gulf War Veterans (See Chapter 33)

- Veterans exposed to Agent Orange during the Vietnam War (See Chapter 24)

- Veterans exposed to atomic radiation, (See Chapter 24)

- Merchant Marine Seamen (See Chapter 29)

- Allied Veterans (See Chapter 29)

HOME IMPROVEMENTS AND STRUCTURAL ALTERATIONS (HISA)

The HISA program provides funding for disabled veterans to make home improvements necessary for the continuation of treatment or for disability access to the home, essential lavatory and sanitary facilities.

Disabled veterans may be eligible for HISA when it is determined medically necessary or appropriate for the effective and economical treatment of the service-connected disability.

Lifetime home improvement benefits may not exceed $4,100.00 (U.S.). Any costs that exceed $4,100.00 (U.S.) will be the veteran's responsibility.

To apply, veterans must submit the following documentation:

- A letter from describing the physical disability and a description of the request home improvement and/or structural alteration;

- A statement from the attending physician or therapist. This statement should describe the physical condition/disability, why the home modification(s) are medically necessary or appropriate for the effective and economical treatment of the service-connected disabling condition;

- A drawing of the work to be undertaken. This drawing can be hand sketched. It should include the height, width and length dimensions. It does not have to be a formal blueprint or architectural drawing;

- A completed, signed home ownership or a rental lease form with a letter from the landlord agreeing with the modifications if required;

- A completed and signed VA Form 10-0103, Veterans Application for Assistance;

- Documentation verifying that the provider/contractor is licensed/bonded;

- An itemized cost estimate of the proposed improvement and/or structural alteration from the provider/contractor.

Preauthorization must be obtained before beginning any alterations, otherwise, HISA benefits will be denied.

LISTING OF VA HEALTHCARE FACILITIES

Alabama
Medical Centers
Birmingham
Montgomery
Tuscaloosa
Tuskegee

Clinics
Dothan
Gadsden
Huntsville
Jasper
Madison
Mobile
Oxford
Shoals Area

Alaska
Medical Center
Anchorage

Clinics
Fairbanks
Kenai

Arizona
Medical Centers
Phoenix
Prescott
Tucson

Clinics
Anthem
Bellemont
Buckeye
Casa Grande
Cottonwood
Fort Huachuca
Green Valley
Kingman
Lake Havasu
Mesa
Payson
Safford
Show Low
Sun City
Yuma

Arkansas
Medical Centers
Fayetteville
Little Rock
North Little Rock

Clinic
Paragould

California
Medical Centers
Fresno
Livermore
Loma Linda
Long Beach
Los Angeles
Menlo Park
Palo Alto
Sacramento
San Diego
San Francisco

Clinics
Anaheim
Atwater
Auburn
Bakersfield
Brawley
Capitola
Chico
Commerce
Chula Vista
Corona
Escondido
Eureka
Fairfield
French Camp
Gardena
Lancaster
Lompoc
Los Angeles
Martinez
Modesto
Oakland
Oxnard
Palm Desert
Redding
Sacramento
San Diego
San Jose
San Luis Obispo
Santa Ana
Santa Barbara

Santa Rosa
Seaside
Sepulveda
Sonora
Sun City
Tulare
Upland
Vallejo
Victorville
Vista

Colorado
Medical Centers
Denver
Grand Junction

Clinics
Alamosa
Aurora
Colorado Springs
Durango
Fort Collins
Greeley
La Junta
Lakewood
Lamar
Montrose
Pueblo

Connecticut
Medical Centers
Newington
West Haven

Clinics
Danbury
New London
Stamford
Waterbury
Willimantic
Winsted

Delaware
Medical Center
Wilmington

District of Columbia
Medical Center
Washington D.C.

Florida
Medical Centers
Bay Pines
Gainesville
Lake City
Miami
Tampa
West Palm Beach

Clinics
Avon Park
Boca Raton
Brooksville
Coral Springs
Daytona Beach
Deerfield Beach
Delray Beach
Dunedin
Ellenton
Fort Myers
Fort Pierce
Hollywood
Jacksonville
Key Largo
Key West
Kissimmee
Lakeland
Lecanto
Leesburg
Miami
Naples
New Port Richey
Oakland Park
Ocala
Okeechobee
Orlando
Panama City Beach
Pensacola
Port Charlotte
St. Augustine
St. Petersburg
Sanford
Sarasota
Sebring
Stuart
Tallahassee
The Villages
Vero Beach
Viera
Zephyrhillis

Georgia
Medical Centers
Atlanta
Augusta
Dublin

Clinics
Albany
Atlanta
Columbus
East Point
Lawrenceville
Macon
Midtown Atlanta
Oakwood
Savannah
Smyrna
Valdosta

Guam
Agana Heights

Hawaii
Medical Office
Honolulu

Idaho
Medical Center
Boise

Clinics
Pocatello
Twin Falls

Illinois
Medical Centers
Chicago
Danville
Hines
Marion
North Chicago

Clinics
Aurora
Belleville
Chicago
Chicago Heights
Decatur
Effingham
Elgin
Evanston
Freeport
Galesburg
Joliet
LaSalle

Manteno
McHenry
Mount Vernon
Oak Lawn
Oak Park
Peoria
Quincy
Rockford
Springfield

Indiana
Medical Centers
Fort Wayne
Indianapolis
Marion

Clinics
Bloomington
Crown Point
Evansville
Hagerstown
Lawrenceburg
Muncie
Richmond
South Bend
Terre Haute
West Lafayette

Iowa
Medical Centers
Des Moines
Iowa City
Knoxville

Clinics
Bettendorf
Dubuque
Fort Dodge
Mason City
Sioux City
Waterloo

Kansas
Medical Centers
Leavenworth
Topeka
Wichita

Clinics
Ft. Dodge
Ft. Scott
Hays
Kansas City
Liberal
Paola
Parsons
Salina

Kentucky
Medical Centers
Lexington
Louisville

Clinics
Bellevue
Hanson
Paducah

Louisiana
Medical Centers
Alexandria
New Orleans
Shreveport
Slidell

Clinics
Baton Rouge
Hammond
Jennings
Lafayette
LaPlace

Maine
Medical Center
Augusta

Clinics
Bangor
Calais
Caribou
Rumford
Saco

Maryland
Medical Centers
Baltimore
Perry Point

Clinics
Baltimore
Cambridge
Charlotte Hall
Cumberland

Fort Howard
Glen Burnie
Greenbelt
Hagerstown
Perry Point
Pocomoke

Massachusetts
Medical Centers
Bedford
Boston
Brockton
Leeds
West Roxbury

Clinics
Boston
Dorchester
Fitchburg
Framingham
Gloucester
Greenfield
Haverhill
Hyannis
Lowell
Lynn
Martha's Vineyard
Nantucket
New Bedford
Pittsfield
Quincy
Springfield
Worcester

Michigan
Medical Centers
Ann Arbor
Battle Creek
Detroit
Iron Mountain
Saginaw

Clinics
Benton Harbor
East Lansing
Flint
Gaylord
Grand Rapids
Hancock
Ironwood
Jackson
Lansing
Marquette
Menominee
Muskegon

Oscoda
Pontiac
Sault Ste. Marie
Traverse City
Yale

Minnesota
Medical Centers
Minneapolis
St. Cloud

Clinics
Arlington
Blue Earth
Brainerd
Bricelyn
Chisholm
Elmore
Fergus Falls
Gaylord
Hibbing
Janesville
Lake Crystal
Madelia
Maplewood
Montevideo
Mountain Iron
Nashwauk
Rochester
Springfield
St. James
Trimont
Waseca
Waterville
Winnebago
Winthrop

Mississippi
Medical Centers
Biloxi
Jackson

Missouri
Medical Centers
Columbia
Kansas City
Poplar Bluff
St. Louis

Clinics
Belton
Camdenton
Cameron
Cape Girardeau
Farmington

Ft. Leonard Wood
Kirksville
Mexico
Mt. Vernon
Nevada
Salem
St. Charles
St. James
St. Joseph
St. Louis
Warrensburg
West Plains

Montana
Medical Centers
Fort Harrison

Clinics
Anaconda
Ashland
Billings
Bozeman
Glasgow
Great Falls
Kalispell
Miles City
Missoula
Sidney

Nebraska
Medical Centers
Grand Island
Omaha

Clinics
Alliance
Lincoln
Norfolk
North Platte
Rushville
Sidney

Nevada
Medical Center
Las Vegas
Reno

Clinics
Ely
Henderson
Las Vegas
Pahrump

New Hampshire
Medical Center
Manchester

Clinics
Conway
Littleton
Portsmouth
Tilton

New Jersey
Medical Centers
East Orange
Lyons

Clinics
Brick
Cape May
Elizabeth
Ft. Dix
Ft. Monmouth
Hackensack
Jersey
Morristown
New Burnswick
Newark
Peterson
Sewell
Trenton
Ventnor
Vineland

New Mexico
Medical Center
Albuquerque

Clinics
Alamogordo
Artesia
Clovis
Espanola
Farmington
Gallup
Hobbs
Las Cruces
Las Vegas
Raton
Santa Fe
Silver City
Truth or Consequences

New York
Medical Centers
Albany
Batavia
Bath
Bronx
Brooklyn
Buffalo
Canandaigua
Castle Point
Montrose
New York City
Northport
Syracuse

Clinics
Auburn
Bainbridge
Binghamton
Bronx
Brooklyn
Carmel
Carthage
Catskill
Clifton Park
Cortland
Dunkirk
Elizabethtown
Elmira
Fonda
Glens Falls
Goshen
Ithaca
Jamestown
Kingston
Lackawanna
Lockport
Malone
Massena
Monticello
New City
New York
Niagara Falls
Olean
Oswego
Patchogue
Pine Plains
Plainview
Plattsburgh
Port Jervis
Poughkeepsie
Rochester
Rome
Schenectady
St. Albans

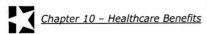

Staten Island
Sunnyside
Troy
Warsaw
Wellsville
Westhampton
White Plains
Yonkers

North Carolina
Medical Centers
Asheville
Durham
Fayetteville
Salisbury

Clinics
Winton-Salem

North Dakota
Medical Center
Fargo

Clinics
Bismarck
Grafton
Minot

Ohio
Medical Centers
Chillicothe
Cincinnati
Cleveland
Dayton

Clinics
Akron
Ashtabula
Athens
Canton
Cincinnati
Cleveland
Columbus
East Liverpool
Grove City
Lancaster
Lima
Lorain
Mansfiled
Marietta
Marion
Middletown
Painesville
Portsmouth
St. Clairsville

Sandusky
Springfield
Toledo
Warren
Youngstown
Zanesville

Oklahoma
Medical Centers
Muskogee
Oklahoma City

Oregon
Medical Centers
Portland
Roseburg

Clinics
Bandon
Bend
Brookings
Eugene
Klamath Falls
Salem
Warrenton

Pennsylvania
Medical Centers
Altoona
Butler
Coatesville
Erie
Lebanon
Philadelphia
Pittsburgh
Wilkes-Barre

Clinics
Aliquippa
Allentown
Bangor
Berwick
Brookville
Camp Hill
DuBois
Ellwood City
Farrell
Frackville
Greensburg
Horsham
Johnstown
Kittanning
Knox
Lancaster
Meadville

Philadelphia
Pottsville
Pottsville
Reading
Reading
Sayre
Schuylkill
Smethport
Spring City
Springfield
State College
Tobyhanna
Washington
Wilkes-Barre
Williamsport
York

Philippines
Outpatient Clinic
Pasay City

Puerto Rico
Medical Center
San Juan

Clinics
Arecibo
Guayama
Mayaguez
Ponce

Rhode Island
Medical Center
Providence

Clinics
Middletown

South Carolina
Medical Centers
Charleston
Columbia

Clinics
Anderson
Beaufort
Florence
Greenville
Myrtle Beach
Orangeburg
Rock Hill
Sumter

South Dakota
Medical Centers
Fort Meade
Hot Springs
Sioux Falls

Clinics
Aberdeen
Eagle Butte
McLaughlin
Mission
Pierre
Pine Ridge
Rapid City
Winner

Tennessee
Medical Centers
Memphis
Mountain Home
Murfreesboro
Nashville

Clinics
Chattanooga
Cookville
Knoxville

Texas
Medical Centers
Amarillo
Big Spring
Bonham
Dallas
El Paso
Houston
Kerrville
San Antonio
Temple
Waco

Clinics
Abilene
Austin
Beaumont
Brownwood
Cedar Park
Childress
College Station
Corpus Christi
Fort Worth
Fort Stockton
Harlingen
Laredo
Lubbock

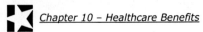

Lufkin
McAllen
Marlin
Odessa
Palestine
San Angelo
San Antonio
Stamford
Stratford
Victoria

Utah
Medical Center
Salt Lake City

Clinics
Fountain Green
Nephi
Ogden
Orem
Roosevelt
St. George

Vermont
Medical Centers
White River Junction

Clinics
Bennington
Colchester
Rutland

Virginia
Medical Centers
Hampton
Richmond
Salem

Clinics
Alexandria
Harrisonburg
Stephens City

Virgin Islands
Clinics
Kings Hill
St. Thomas

Washington
Medical Centers
Seattle
Spokane
Walla Walla

Clinics
Bremerton
Longview
Richland
Seattle
Yakima

West Virginia
Medical Centers
Beckley
Clarksburg
Huntington
Martinsburg

Clinics
Franklin
Gassaway
Parkersburg
Parsons
Petersburg

Wisconsin
Medical Centers
Madison
Milwaukee
Tomah

Clinics
Appleton
Baraboo
Beaver Dam
Chippewa Falls
Cleveland
Green Bay
Janesville
Kenosha
LaCrosse
Loyal
Rhinelander
Superior
Union Grove
Wausau
Wisconsin Rapids

Wyoming
Medical Centers
Cheyenne
Sheridan

Clinics

Casper

Gillette

Green River

New Castle

Powell

Riverton

Rock Springs

CHAPTER 11

DENTAL BENEFITS

VA OUTPATIENT DENTAL BENEFITS

Outpatient dental benefits are provided by the Department of Veterans Affairs according to law. In some instances, the dental care may be extensive, while in other cases treatment may be limited.

Eligibility

Veterans are eligible for outpatient dental treatment if they are determined by VA to meet one of the following criteria:

- Those having a service-connected compensable dental disability or condition are eligible for any needed dental care.

- Those who were prisoners of war are eligible for any needed dental care.

    (Public Law 108-170, which became law December 6, 2003, eliminated the requirement that a prisoner of war have been detained or interned for a period of 90 days or more.)

- Those who have a service-connected disability rated 100% disabling, or are unemployable and paid at the 100% rate due to service-connected conditions are eligible for any needed dental care.

- Please note that veterans paid at the 100% rate based on a temporary rating, such as extended hospitalization for a service-connected disability, convalescence or pre-stabilization are not eligible for comprehensive outpatient dental services based on this temporary rating.)

- Those who are participating in a VA rehabilitation program are eligible for dental care necessary to complete their program.

- **Effective January 28, 2008,** recently discharged veterans with a service-connected noncompensable dental condition or disability who served on active duty 90 days or more and who apply for VA dental care **within 180 days** of separation from active duty, may receive one time treatment for dental conditions if the dental condition is shown to have existed at the time of discharge or release and the veteran's certificate of discharge does not indicate that the veteran received necessary dental care within a 90-day period prior to discharge or release. This includes veterans who reentered active military, naval, or air service within 90 days after the date of a prior discharge and; veterans whose disqualifying discharge or release has been corrected by competent authority.

- Those having a service-connected noncompensable dental condition or disability resulting from combat wounds or service trauma are eligible for repeat care for the service-connected condition(s).

- Those having a dental condition clinically determined by VA to be currently aggravating a service-connected medical condition are eligible for dental care to resolve the problem.

- Those with nonservice-connected dental conditions or disabilities for which treatment was begun while in a VA medical center, when it is clinically determined to be necessary to complete such dental treatment on an outpatient basis.

- Those receiving outpatient care or scheduled for inpatient care may receive dental care if the dental condition is clinically determined to be complicating a medical condition currently under treatment

- Certain veterans enrolled in a VA Homeless Program for 60 consecutive days or more may receive certain medically necessary outpatient dental services.

ENHANCED TRICARE RETIREE DENTAL PROGRAM

The TRICARE Retiree Dental Program (TRDP) was established February 1, 1998. It provides dental care for Uniformed Service retirees, unremarried surviving spouses, and certain other family members. Enrollment in TRDP is voluntary. The TRDP is funded solely by enrollees, and receives **no** government subsidy.

The basic Tricare Retiree Dental Program (TRDP) is available only to those who were enrolled in the TDRP program prior to September 1, 2000, and who chose to remain enrolled in the basic program.

Effective September 1, 2000, the Enhanced Tricare Retiree Dental Program took effect, and new enrollments in the basic program were discontinued.

The TRICARE Retiree Dental Program is administered by the Federal Services division of Delta Dental Plan of California. The TRICARE Retiree Dental Program is designed to provide Uniformed Services retirees and their families with optimum dental coverage at an affordable cost.

Eligibility Requirements:

Eligibility requirements for enrollment in the TRDP are set forth by the federal government in the law that established the program. Applicants may be required to submit additional information if it is needed by Delta to verify eligibility. To enroll in the enhanced program, an individual must be one of the following:

- A member of the Uniformed Services who is entitled to Uniformed Services retired pay, even if you are 65 or older;

- A current spouse of an enrolled member;

- A member of the retired Reserve/Guard, including a "gray-area" reservist, who is entitled to retired pay but does not actually begin receiving it until age 60;

- A child of an enrolled member, up to age 21 (to age 23 if a full-time student, or older if disabled before losing eligibility);

- An unremarried surviving spouse or eligible child of a deceased member who died on retired status or while on active duty;

- A Congressional Medal of Honor recipient and eligible family members, or an unremarried surviving spouse/eligible family members of a deceased recipient;

- A current spouse and/or eligible child of a non-enrolled member with documented proof the member is:
  - Eligible to receive ongoing, comprehensive dental care from the Department of Veterans Affairs;
  - Enrolled in a dental plan through employment and the plan is not available to family members; or
  - Unable to obtain benefits through the TRDP due to a current and enduring medical or dental condition.

Those who are not eligible for this program are:

- Former spouses of eligible members;
- Remarried surviving spouses of deceased members;
- Family members of non-enrolled retirees who do not meet one of the three special circumstances noted above.

Premiums

Premium rates for the enhanced TRICARE Retiree Dental Program vary depending on the retiree's location.

Coverage

This chart provides an overview of coverage under the *enhanced* TRICARE Retiree Dental Program for patients who visit a **participating network dentist**.

Benefits available during the first 12 months of enrollment:	*Delta Pays:
Diagnostic services (such as exams)	100%
Preventive services (such as cleanings)	100%
Basic Restorative services (such as fillings)	80%
Endodontics (such as root canals)	60%
Periodontics (such as gum treatment)	60%
Oral Surgery (such as extractions)	60%
Emergency (such as treatment for minor pain)	80%
Dental Accident Coverage	100%

Additional services available after 12 months of continuous enrollment:	
Cast Crowns, Onlays & Bridges	50%
Partial/Full Dentures	50%
Dental Implants **(effective 10-1-2008)**	50%
Orthodontics	50%
Deductibles & Maximums	
Annual Deductible (per person, limit $150 per family, per benefit year)	$50
Annual Maximum (per person, per benefit year)	$1200
Orthodontic Maximum (per person, per lifetime)	$1500
Dental Accident Maximum (per person, per benefit year)	$1000
Benefit Year: May 1- April 30	

*The percentage paid by Delta is based on the allowed amount for each procedure. Out-of-pocket costs may be higher if care is received from a non-participating provider.

Update For National Guard and Reserve Personnel

National Guard and Reserve personnel who elect to enroll in the TRICARE Retiree Dental Program (TRDP) within 120 days after retirement are now eligible to skip the 12-month waiting period normally required for certain TRDP

Effective February 1, 2005, officials authorized a waiver from requiring retired National Guard/Reserve men and women who meet the criteria to be enrolled in the TRDP for 12 months prior to gaining the maximum allowed benefits for cast crowns, cast restorations, bridges, dentures and orthodontics for both adults and children.

Additionally, this new waiver can be applied retroactively to February 1, 2004 for any Guard and Reserve enrollees who can document their enrollment in the TRDP within 120 days after their retirement effective date.

All new enrollees seeking to obtain the waiver should submit a copy of their retirement orders together with their application.

Contact Information

Covered benefits are subject to certain limitations. For more information on all covered services and detailed information on benefit levels, limitations, exclusions, program policies and payments for non-participating providers, please contact:

Delta Dental of California
Federal Services
P.O. Box 537008
Sacramento, CA 95853-7008
(888) 838-8737

BASIC TRICARE RETIREE DENTAL PROGRAM

The basic program is available **only** to those who were enrolled in the TRDP *prior to September 1, 2000*, when the enhanced program took effect, **and** who wish to remain enrolled in the basic program rather than upgrade their enrollment to the enhanced program. **Effective September 1, 2000 the basic program is no longer accepting new enrollments.**

Retirees who are enrolled in the basic program and have questions about their coverage should contact:

Delta Dental of California
Federal Services
P.O. Box 537008
Sacramento, CA 95853-7008
(888) 838-8737

TRICARE SELECTED RESERVE DENTAL PROGRAM BENEFITS

Individuals with at least one year of service commitment remaining who are serving in the Army Reserve, Naval Reserve, Air Force Reserve, Marine Corps Reserve, Coast Guard Reserve, Army National Guard or Air National Guard, may be eligible to enroll in the Tricare Selected Reserve Dental Program (TSRDP).

The Department of Defense works in conjunction with Humana Military Healthcare Services to offer and administer the TRICARE Selected Reserve Dental Program.

Coverage remains available as long as an individual maintains his or her Reserve status, and is shown as eligible on the DEERS record.

The information provided in this section is intended only as a brief overview. Humana Military Healthcare Services has a staff of trained Beneficiary Services Representatives who are available to answer your questions. They can be reached at (800) 866-8499.

CHAPTER 12

CHAMPVA

> *Under CHAMPVA, VA shares the cost of covered healthcare services and supplies with eligible beneficiaries.*

Although similar, CHAMPVA and TRICARE are completely separate programs, with totally different beneficiary populations. While the benefits provided are similar, the programs are administered separately, with significant differences in claim filing procedures and preauthorization requirements.

Under CHAMPVA, VA shares the cost of covered healthcare services and supplies with eligible beneficiaries.

The administration of CHAMPVA is centralized to the Health Administration Center in Denver, Colorado.

Eligibility Requirements

To be eligible for CHAMPVA, you cannot be eligible for TRICARE/CHAMPUS and you must be in one of these categories:

- The spouse or child of a veteran who has been rated permanently and totally disabled for a service-connected disability by a VA regional office; or
- The surviving spouse or child of a veteran who died from a VA-rated service connected disability; or
- The surviving spouse or child of a veteran who was at the time death rated permanently and totally disabled from a service connected disability; or
- The surviving spouse or child of a military member who died in the line of duty, not due to misconduct (in most of these cases, these family members are eligible for TRICARE, not CHAMPVA).

Update: An eligible CHAMPVA sponsor may be entitled to receive medical care through the VA health care system based on his or her own veteran status. Additionally, as the result of a recent policy change, if the eligible CHAMPVA sponsor is the spouse of another eligible CHAMPVA sponsor, both may now be eligible for CHAMPVA benefits. In each instance where the eligible spouse requires medical attention, he or she may choose the VA health care system or coverage under CHAMPVA for his/her health care needs. If you have been previously denied CHAMPVA benefits and you believe you would now be qualified, please call (800) 733-8387.

Benefits

In general, CHAMPVA covers most healthcare services and supplies that are medically and psychologically necessary.   Upon confirmation of eligibility, applicants will receive program material that specifically addresses covered and noncovered services and supplies.

CHAMPVA General Exclusions

* Services determined by VA to be medically unnecessary;

* Care as part of a grant, study, or research program;

* Care considered experimental or investigational;

* Care for persons eligible for benefits under other government agency programs, except Medicaid and State Victims of Crime Compensation programs;

* Care for which the beneficiary is not obligated to pay, such as services obtained at a health fair;

* Care provided outside the scope of the provider's license or certification;

* Custodial, domiciliary, or rest cures;

* Dental care (except treatment related to certain covered medical conditions);

* Medications that do not require a prescription (except insulin);

* Personal comfort and convenience items;

* Services rendered by providers suspended or sanctioned by other Federal entities.

Important Update Regarding Retention Of CHAMPVA For Surviving Spouses Remarrying After Age 55

Eligibility for CHAMPVA ends at midnight on the date of your remarriage if you remarry prior to age 55.   However, Public Law 107-330 (signed by then-President Bush on December 6, 2002) contained a provision stating that:

"For marriages occurring on or after February 4, 2003, the remarriage after age 55 of the surviving spouse of a veteran shall not bar the furnishing of benefits under CHAMPVA to such person as the surviving spouse of the veteran".

(Such surviving spouses do, however, continue to lose eligibility for DIC.)

The law also contained a provision allowing those widows who remarried prior to February 4, 2003, and were over the age of 55 and lost their CHAMPVA benefits, to apply to have their medical benefits reinstated.   ***However, such widows***

had to apply for reinstatement of benefits by February 4, 2004. (The deadline was later extended to December 16, 2004.)

Termination of Remarriage: If a widow(er) of a qualifying sponsor remarries, and the remarriage is later terminated by death, divorce, or annulment he or she may reestablish CHAMPVA eligibility. The beginning date of re-eligibility is the first day of the month after termination of the remarriage or December 1, 1999, whichever date is later. To reestablish CHAMPVA eligibility, copies of the marriage certificate and death, divorce, or annulment documents (as appropriate) must be provided.

Applying for CHAMPVA And Filing Claims

Generally, applicants can expect to receive written notification from the Health Administration Center within 45 days from the mailing of the application.

Prospective applicants should contact the Health Administration Center at (800) 733-8387.

Applications may also be requested by FAX at (303) 331-7804

For general questions, information on payments, or to reprocess a denied claim, please send you request to:

VA Health Administration Center
CHAMPVA
PO Box 469063
Denver CO 80246-9063

For submitting new health care claims only, please use:

VA Health Administration Center
CHAMPVA Claims
PO Box 469064
Denver CO 80246-9064

To streamline the process, applicants are encouraged to complete the *Application for CHAMPVA Benefits, (VA 10D)* in its entirety and to attach all required documents. As further explained on the application, required documents include a copy of each applicant's Medicare card (if Medicare eligible) and a school certification for all applicant children between the ages of 18 and 23.

Generally, applicants can expect to receive written notification from the Health Administration Center within 45 days from the mailing of the application.

CHAMPVA as Secondary Payer

CHAMPVA is intended to serve as a safety net in the event other coverage is not available—rather than being the primary carrier. While families with other health insurance are not disqualified from CHAMPVA benefits, CHAMPVA's safety net protection only kicks in after the application of all other policies—including benefits available from the enrollment in a health maintenance organization (HMO).

(Exceptions to CHAMPVA's secondary payer status are supplemental CHAMPVA policies, Medicaid, and State Victims Compensation Programs—CHAMPVA assumes primary payer in these cases.)

Beneficiaries enrolled in an HMO cannot elect to waive the HMO benefits without forfeiting their CHAMPVA benefits. CHAMPVA benefits, however, do apply to covered services that are not covered by the HMO.

Healthcare Services at VA Facilities

Under the CHAMPVA In-house Treatment Initiative (CITI for short), CHAMPVA beneficiaries may receive cost-free healthcare services at participating VA facilities.

Although some VA facilities are not CITI participants due to the volume of veterans they are responsible for serving, most are. **The CITI program is not available to beneficiaries with Medicare or with an HMO insurance plan**

Medicare Impact

> *CHAMPVA is always the secondary payer to Medicare.*

If a person is eligible for CHAMPVA, under age 65 and enrolled in both Medicare Parts A & B, SSA documentation of enrollment in both Parts A&B is required.

CHAMPVA is always the secondary payer to Medicare.

For benefits to be extended past age 65, the individual must meet the following conditions:

- If he or she turned 65 before June 5, 2001, and only has Medicare Part A, he or she will be eligible for CHAMPVA without having to have Medicare Part B coverage.

- If he or she turned 65 on/or before June 5, 2001, and has Medicare Parts A and B, he or she must keep both Parts to be eligible.

- If he or she turned 65 on or after June 5, 2001, he or she must be enrolled in Medicare Parts A and B to be eligible.

CHAPTER 13

TRICARE AND TRICARE FOR LIFE

TRICARE is the Department of Defense's worldwide health care program for active duty and retired uniformed services members and their families. TRICARE offers several health plan options to meet your specific needs.

- TRICARE For Life
- TRICARE Global Remote Overseas
- TRICARE Prime
- TRICARE Prime Overseas
- TRICARE Prime Remote
- TRICARE Reserve Select
- TRICARE Standard and Extra
- TRICARE Standard Overseas
- U.S. Family Health Plan

Please note that the Ike Skelton National Defense Authorization Act for Fiscal Year 2011 was signed into law on January 7, 2011.

The law includes a provision called "TRICARE 26" which extends health care eligibility to adult dependent children to age 26. A premium will be required for their coverage. As more information becomes available, we will post it in our monthly newsletter.

TRICARE FOR LIFE

TRICARE For Life (TFL) is TRICARE's Medicare-wraparound coverage available to *all* Medicare-eligible TRICARE beneficiaries, regardless of age, provided they have Medicare Parts A and B.

While Medicare is your primary insurance, TRICARE acts as your secondary payer minimizing your out-of-pocket expenses. TRICARE benefits include covering Medicare's coinsurance and deductible.

Key features of TRICARE For Life include:

- Minimal **out-of-pocket costs** (aside from Medicare part B premium).

- No enrollment fees for TFL. But, you must purchase Medicare Part B and pay monthly premiums to be eligible for TFL.

- Coordination of benefits between Medicare and TRICARE

- TRICARE is the secondary payer for all services covered by both TRICARE and Medicare.

- TRICARE is the primary payer for those services covered only by TRICARE.

- Additional steps may be required in order to coordinate benefits if you have other health insurance in addition to TRICARE and Medicare.

- Freedom to manage your own health care

- No assigned primary care manager.

- Visit any Medicare provider.

- Receive care at a military treatment facility on a space-available basis.

- No claims to file (in most cases).

- Your provider files your claim with Medicare

- Medicare processes the claims

- Medicare forwards it electronically to TRICARE.

- TRICARE pays similarly to TRICARE Standard in those overseas locations where Medicare is not available.

Eligibility

TFL is available to all Medicare-eligible TRICARE beneficiaries, regardless of age, including retired members of the National Guard and Reserve who are in receipt of retired pay, family members, widows and widowers and certain former spouses. Dependent parents and parents-in-law are not eligible for TFL.

Note: *If you're under age 65, have Medicare Part B, and live in a TRICARE Prime service area, you have the option to enroll in* **TRICARE Prime***; TRICARE waives your TRICARE Prime enrollment fee.*

You should confirm that your Medicare status is current in the **Defense Enrollment Eligibility Reporting System** (DEERS). Your uniformed services ID card and your Medicare card, which must reflect enrollment in Medicare Part B, are evidence of your TFL eligibility.

TRICARE GLOBAL REMOTE OVERSEAS

TRICARE Global Remote Overseas (TGRO) is a TRICARE Prime option offered in designated remote overseas locations for active duty service members and their families. TRICARE has partnered with International SOS to identify the best local providers and facilities and develop a network of licensed, qualified physicians in remote overseas areas. The TGRO contractor's careful selection of providers is the first step in ensuring quality care.

Only physicians who are licensed and who have graduated from an accredited medical school are included in the core network. To access a list of TGRO providers please visit the TGRO Provider Directory. The TGRO network is updated daily.

Key features of TGRO include:

- Enrollment is required, but there are no enrollment fees.
- Fewer out-of-pocket costs than TRICARE Standard Overseas.
- You receive most care from your primary care manager (PCM).
- Your PCM or TGRO Call Center refers you to specialists when necessary and will tell you when you need to go to another city, country or the U.S. for quality care.
- No claims to file (in most cases).

Eligibility

In general, TGRO is available to the following beneficiaries:

- Permanently-assigned active duty service members living in designated remote locations.
- Command-sponsored active duty family members living with their active duty sponsors in designated remote locations
- Activated National Guard and Reserve members living in designated remote locations when their orders are for more than 30 consecutive days.
- Command-sponsored family members of activated National Guard and Reserve living with their sponsors in designated remote locations

TRICARE PRIME

TRICARE Prime is a managed care option offering the most affordable and comprehensive coverage. TRICARE Prime is available in Prime Service Areas in each TRICARE Region. To find out if you live in a Prime Service Area, contact your regional contractor. If you don't, you may be eligible for TRICARE Prime Remote, or you may use TRICARE Standard and Extra.

Key features include:

- Enrollment is required.
- Fewer out-of-pocket costs than other TRICARE options.
- Enhanced vision and preventive coverage.
- Priority access for care at military treatment facilities.
- Receive most care from an assigned primary care manager (PCM).
- Your PCM refers you to specialists when necessary.
- No claims to file (in most cases).
- Easy to transfer enrollment when you move.

- Time and distance access standards for care, including wait times for urgent, routine and specialty care.

Eligibility

You may enroll in TRICARE Prime as long as you are not entitled to Medicare based on age (65). (At age 65, you become eligible for **TRICARE For Life** as long as you have Medicare Parts A and B). The following beneficiaries who live in a Prime Service area may enroll in TRICARE Prime:

- Active duty service members* and their families.

- Retired service members and their families.

- Surviving family members (widowed spouses, children)

- Eligible former spouses.

- Activated National Guard/Reserve members* and their families.

- Retired National Guard and Reserve members and their families (upon reaching age 60)

- Medal of Honor recipients and their families.

*Active duty service members and activated National Guard/Reserve members must enroll in one of the TRICARE Prime options (includes TRICARE Prime, TRICARE Prime Remote, TRICARE Prime Overseas and TRICARE Global Remote Overseas)

TRICARE PRIME OVERSEAS

TRICARE Prime Overseas is a managed care plan for active duty service members and their eligible family members residing together in overseas locations in which TRICARE Prime Overseas is available. Retirees and retiree family members are not eligible for TRICARE Prime Overseas.

Key features of TRICARE Prime Overseas include:

- Enrollment required, but no enrollment fees.

- Fewer out-of-pocket costs than TRICARE Standard Overseas.

- Enhanced coverage for vision and clinical preventive services.

- You receive most care from your primary care manager (PCM).

- Your PCM refers you to specialists when necessary.

- No claims to file (in most cases).

- Easy to transfers from one overseas area to another or back to the United States.

- Time and distance access standards for care, including wait times for urgent, routine and specialty care.

- Point of service option available (in certain circumstances) to receive care without requesting a referral from your PCM (resulting in higher out-of-pocket costs)

Eligibility

In general, TRICARE Prime Overseas is available to the following beneficiaries:

- Active duty service members residing in overseas areas in which Prime is offered.

-

- Active duty family members who:

    o Accompany their sponsor;

    o Are command-sponsored on their permanent change of station orders or relocate on service sponsored/funded orders;

    o Are eligible in the Defense Enrollment Eligibility Reporting System; and

    o Enroll through the nearest TRICARE Service Center.

TRICARE PRIME REMOTE

TRICARE Prime Remote (TPR) is a managed care option similar to TRICARE Prime for active duty service members and their eligible family members while they are assigned to remote duty stations in the United States.

Remote locations are those that are 50 miles or an hour drive time from a military treatment facility and the ZIP code areas are pre-determined.

Note: TRICARE Global Remote Overseas is a similar program available in remote locations outside of the United States

Key features of TRICARE Prime Remote include:

- Enrollment required to participate

    o Active duty service members must enroll

    o Active duty family members have the option to enroll or use TRICARE Standard and Extra

- Flexible enrollment options:

    o Online via the Beneficiary Web Enrollment Web Site

    o Submit a *TRICARE Prime Enrollment and PCM Change Form* through the mail

- Receive most care from an assigned network primary care manager (PCM) who will provide referrals for specialty care.

    o If a network PCM is not available, care is received from any TRICARE-authorized provider.

- Fewer out-of-pocket costs.

- Eligible for travel reimbursement if referred for medically necessary care far from home.

- Enhanced coverage for vision and clinical preventive services.

- Time and distance access standards for care.

- No claims to file (in most cases).

- Easy to transfer enrollment when moving to another location in your TRICARE region or to a new TRICARE region.

TRICARE RESERVE SELECT

TRICARE Reserve Select (TRS) is a premium-based health plan that qualified National Guard and Reserve members may purchase. TRS, which requires a monthly premium, offers coverage similar to TRICARE Standard and Extra.

Key features of TRS include:

- Available worldwide to most Selected Reserve members (and families) when not on active duty orders or covered under the Transitional Assistance Management Program.

- Must qualify for and purchase TRS to participate.

- Must pay monthly premiums. Failure to pay monthly premiums on time may result in disenrollment and an enrollment lockout.

- Freedom to manage your own health care; no assigned primary care manager.

    o Visit any TRICARE-authorized provider or qualified host nation provider (if located overseas).

    o Pay fewer out-of-pocket costs when choosing a provider in the TRICARE network.

    o Network providers not available overseas.

- No referrals are required, but some care may require prior authorization.

- May have to pay for services when they are received and then seek reimbursement.

- May have to submit health care claims.

- May receive care in a military treatment facility (MTF) on a space-available basis only.

- Offers comprehensive health care coverage including TRICARE's prescription drug coverage.

TRICARE STANDARD AND EXTRA

TRICARE Standard is a fee-for-service option. When you use TRICARE Standard, you have more choice in providers as you can seek care from any TRICARE-authorized provider (network or non-network), but you'll pay higher out-of-pocket costs.

To reduce your out-of-pocket costs, use the TRICARE Extra option by seeking care TRICARE network providers. Using TRICARE Extra is like using a Preferred Provider Option (PPO).

Key features include:

- Freedom to choose any TRICARE-authorized provider.

- Referrals not required, but some care may require prior authorization.

- Highest out-of-pocket costs.

- You may have to submit health care claims.

- Save time and money with the TRICARE Extra option:

  o Visit a TRICARE network provider.

  o Pay fewer out-of-pocket costs.

  o Network providers will file claims for you.

  o Receive care in a military treatment facility on a space-available basis only.

- TRICARE Standard is available worldwide, but Extra option is not available overseas.

- Enrollment NOT required

Eligibility

In general, the following are eligible for TRICARE Standard and Extra:

- Active duty family members.

- Retirees and their family members

- Surviving family members (widowed spouses, children)

- Eligible former spouses

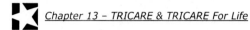

- Family members of activated National Guard or Reserve members

- Retired National Guard and Reserve members and their families (upon reaching age 60)

- Medal of Honor recipients and their families

TRICARE STANDARD OVERSEAS

TRICARE Standard Overseas is a fee-for-service option. TRICARE Standard Overseas gives you more choices in the providers you can see for care, but costs you more in out-of-pocket costs. TRICARE Extra is not available in overseas locations.

Key features of TRICARE Standard Overseas includes:

- Higher out-of-pocket costs than TRICARE Prime Overseas.

- Freedom to choose from any qualified host nation provider.

- Referrals not required, but some care may require prior authorization.

- You may have to pay for services when they are received and then seek reimbursement.

- You may have to submit health care claims.

- There is no assigned primary care manager.

- No enrollment process, which means no enrollment forms to fill out and no annual enrollment fees for retirees and others.

- Receive care in a military treatment facility on a space-available basis only.

Eligibility

In general, TRICARE Standard Overseas is available to the following beneficiaries:

- Active duty family members living overseas with their sponsors and those who have relocated with service sponsored/funded orders.

- Non-command sponsored active duty family members who reside overseas.

- Retirees and their family members who reside overseas.

- Survivors who reside overseas.

- Eligible former spouses who reside overseas.

- National Guard or Reserve family members who are living overseas while their sponsor is on active duty for more than 30 consecutive days.

U.S. FAMILY HEALTH PLAN

The US Family Health Plan is an additional TRICARE Prime option available through networks of community-based, not-for-profit health care systems in six areas of the United States. You must be enrolled in the Defense Eligibility Reporting System (DEERS) and reside in the one of the designated US Family Health Plan service areas.

Key features of the US Family Health Plan include:

- The only TRICARE Prime program that offers benefits to beneficiaries age 65 and over, regardless of whether or not you participate in Medicare Part B. (See "Should I get Medicare Part B" below.)

- Few out-of-pocket costs (similar to TRICARE Prime).

- You do not access Medicare providers, military treatment facilities (MTFs) or TRICARE network providers, but instead receive your care from a primary care physician that you select from a network of private physicians affiliated with one of the not-for-profit health care systems offering the plan. Your primary care physician assists you in getting appointments with specialists in the area and coordinates your care.

- You will benefit from the same level of prescription coverage as that available under the TRICARE program and at the same costs. However, you may only use your US Family Health Plan's list of retail or on-site pharmacies and the US Family Health Plan mail order service instead of TRICARE retail, mail-order or MTF pharmacies.

- If you move or disenroll from the US Family Health Plan, you may choose any TRICARE program that you are eligible for and that is available in your area.

- Each US Family Health Plan site offers enhanced benefits and services such as discounts for eyeglasses, hearing aids and dental care. These enhancements will vary by US Family Health Plan site.

- There are no claims to file when plan-approved providers are used.

- Enrollment is required. You may enroll at anytime throughout the year and enrollment is automatically renewed each year unless you take action to disenroll. Enrollment fees, if applicable, may transfer to another US Family Health Plan location or to TRICARE Prime.

- You are encouraged to enroll in the US Family Health Plan as a complete family unit, but you may enroll on an individual basis. When you enroll in the US Family Health Plan, you are committing to the plan for one year unless moving out of the area or disenrolling for another qualified reason.

Eligibility

Eligible beneficiaries include:

- Active duty family members.

- Retirees and their eligible family members.

- Survivors.

- Former spouses.

- Medal of Honor recipients and their families.

- Family members of activated National Guard or Reserve Members.

Should I Get Medicare Part B?

You do not need to have Medicare Part B to enroll in the US Family Health Plan. However, if you do not enroll in Medicare Part B when first eligible, and subsequently choose to do so, you will pay (in addition to the normal Medicare Part B monthly premium) an annual 10% penalty for each year you were eligible to enroll in Medicare Part B and did not.

In addition, you will only be able to in Medicare Part B enroll during the general enrollment period, January 1-March 31, of each year, and your Part B benefits will not be effective until July 1 of that year. You are encouraged to enroll in Medicare Part B when first eligible.

If you are entitled to Medicare Part A and decide to disenroll from the US Family Health Plan, you will then be able to use the TRICARE For Life benefit, but only if you also are enrolled in Medicare Part B. Additionally, if you subscribe to Medicare Part B, you pay only copayments for prescription drugs and your annual enrollment fee is waived. Medicare Part B also adds coverage for End Stage Renal Disease, a condition that usually involves kidney failure. Medicare Part B is not required for the US Family Health Plan, but you should carefully consider whether or not it is in your best interest to enroll.

TRANSITIONAL ASSISTANCE MANAGEMENT PROGRAM

The Transitional Assistance Management Program (TAMP) provides 180 days of transitional health care benefits upon separation from active duty service. Service members who meet the criteria below are eligible for TRICARE benefits for themselves and their family members.

- A member who is involuntarily separated from active duty.

- A member of a reserve component who is separated from active duty to which called or ordered in support of a contingency operation if the active duty is for a period of more than 30 days.

- A member who is separated from active duty for which the member is involuntarily retained under Section 12305 (also referred to as "stop loss") of Title 10, U.S.C., in support of a contingency operation.

- A member who is separated from active duty served pursuant to a voluntary agreement of the member to remain on active duty for a period of less than one year in support of a contingency operation.

For those who qualify, the 180-day TAMP period begins upon the sponsor's separation. During TAMP, sponsors and family members are eligible to use one of the following health plan options:

- TRICARE Prime (enrollment required)
- TRICARE Standard and Extra
- TRICARE Prime Overseas (enrollment required)
- TRICARE Standard Overseas

CONTINUED HEALTH CARE BENEFIT PROGRAM (CHCBP)

The Continued Health Care Benefit Program (CHCBP) is a premium-based health care program administered by Humana Military Health Care Services, Inc. (Humana Military). CHCBP offers temporary transitional health coverage (18-36 months) after TRICARE eligibility ends. If you qualify, you can purchase CHCBP within 60 days of loss of eligibility for either regular TRICARE or Transitional Assistance Management Program (TAMP) coverage.

CHCBP acts as a bridge between military health benefits and your new civilian health plan. CHCBP benefits are comparable to TRICARE Standard with the same benefits, providers and program rules. The main difference is that you pay premiums to participate.

Who is eligible?

Under certain circumstances, the following beneficiaries may be eligible:

- Former active duty service members released from active duty (under other than adverse conditions) and their eligible family members. *Coverage is limited to 18 months.*

- Unremarried former spouses who were eligible for TRICARE on the day before the date of the final decree of divorce, dissolution or annulment. *Coverage is usually limited to 36 months however some unremarried former spouses may continue coverage beyond 36 months if they meet certain criteria. Contact Humana Military for details.*

- Children who cease to meet the requirements to be an eligible family member and were eligible for TRICARE on the day before ceasing to meet those requirements. *Coverage is limited to 36 months.*

- Certain unmarried children by adoption or legal custody. *Coverage is limited to 36 months.*

For more information about CHCBP, call 1-800-444-5445. Contact your regional contractor or a Beneficiary Counseling and Assistance Coordinator (BCAC) to discuss your eligibility for this program.

EXTENDED CARE HEALTH OPTION

The TRICARE Extended Care Health Option (ECHO) provides financial assistance to eligible beneficiaries who qualify based on specific mental or physical disabilities and offers an integrated set of services and supplies not available through the basic TRICARE program. TRICARE ECHO doesn't replace basic TRICARE programs; it supplements the benefits of the TRICARE program option that eligible beneficiaries use.

ECHO benefits are only available to qualified active duty family members (including family members of activated National Guard or Reserve members). Active duty family members must qualify for ECHO through ECHO case managers in each TRICARE region.

Eligibility

The TRICARE Extended Care Health Option (ECHO) is available **only to active duty family members** who have a qualifying condition.

Qualifying conditions include:

- Moderate or severe mental retardation

- A serious physical disability

- An extraordinary physical or psychological condition of such complexity that the beneficiary is homebound

- A diagnosis of a neuromuscular developmental condition or other condition in an infant or toddler that is expected to precede a diagnosis of moderate or severe mental retardation or a serious physical disability

- Multiple disabilities, which may qualify if there are two or more disabilities affecting separate body systems

If you or your provider believes a qualifying condition exists, talk to a case manager or with your regional contractor or TRICARE Area Office (if stationed overseas) to determine eligibility for TRICARE ECHO benefits.

To begin using TRICARE ECHO, qualifying family members must be enrolled in the *Exceptional Family Member Program* and must be registered for TRICARE ECHO with their regional contractor or TRICARE Area Office. There is no enrollment fee for TRICARE ECHO.

PRE-ACTIVATION BENEFIT FOR NATIONAL GUARD AND RESERVE

National Guard and Reserve members who are issued delayed-effective-date active duty orders for more than 30 days in support of a contingency operation may qualify for "early eligibility for TRICARE" beginning on the later of:

(a) the date their orders were issued; or
(b) 90 days before they report to active duty.

National Guard and Reserve members who qualify for the pre-activation benefit are covered as "active duty service members" and receive active duty medical and dental benefits.

Additionally, when National Guard or Reserve members qualify for pre-activation benefits, family members who are registered in the Defense Enrollment Eligibility Reporting System are also covered under TRICARE up to 90 days before the sponsor's active duty service begins. Family members become covered by TRICARE as "active duty family members during the pre-activation period and while the sponsor is activated.

The member's Service personnel office will tell members if they are eligible for pre-activation benefits when they receive their delayed-effective-date active duty orders.

PHARMACY BENEFITS

TRICARE prescription drug coverage is available to all TRICARE-eligible beneficiaries who are enrolled in the Defense Enrollment Eligibility Reporting System (DEERS). Prescription drug coverage is the same regardless of which health plan option you are using and it is available worldwide.

Eligible beneficiaries include:

- Active duty service members and their families
- Activated National Guard and Reserve Members and their families (on Title 10 or Title 32 [federal] orders)
- Retired service members and their families
- Retired National Guard and Reserve Members and their families (age 60 and above and receiving retired pay)
- Survivors, widows/widowers and certain former spouses
- Medal of Honor recipients and their families
- Beneficiaries enrolled in TRICARE Reserve Select or the Continued Health Care Benefit Program
- Other beneficiaries listed in DEERS as eligible for TRICARE, including foreign force members and their families

CHIROPRACTIC CARE

In 2001, the National Defense Authorization Act established the Chiropractic Health Care Program. The program is currently available to active duty service members (including activated National Guard and Reserve members) at designated military treatment facilities (MTFs) throughout the United States.

Eligibility

- Active duty service members and activated National Guard or Reserve members must obtain chiropractic care at a designated MTF and must receive a referral from their primary care manager (PCM).

- Family members, retirees and their family members, unremarried former spouses and survivors **are not eligible** for this program. They may be referred to non-chiropractic health care services in the Military Health System (e.g., physical therapy or orthopedics) or may seek chiropractic care in the local community at their own expense.

Access to Chiropractic Care

During the course of treatment, the service member's PCM will determine if specialty care (traditional or chiropractic care) is required. If chiropractic care is considered an option, the service member will undergo a screening process to rule out any medical conditions that would prohibit chiropractic care. If appropriate, the PCM will refer the service member to a chiropractic provider for treatment.

While receiving chiropractic care, the service member will continue to see his or her PCM and the duration/frequency of the chiropractic services will be determined by the PCM and follow the usual referral process.

Chiropractic care received outside of the designated locations is not covered under the Chiropractic Health Care Program.

TRICARE CATASTROPHIC CAP

The TRICARE catastrophic cap limits the amount of out-of-pocket expenses a family will have to pay for TRICARE-covered medical services. The cap applies to the allowable charges for covered services—annual deductibles, Prime enrollment fees, pharmacy co-pays, and other cost shares based on TRICARE-allowable charges. Out-of-pocket expenses paid under the TRICARE Prime point-of-service (POS) option (deductibles and cost-shares) are not applied to the annual enrollment year catastrophic cap. Additionally, any POS charges incurred after the catastrophic cap has been met are the beneficiary's financial responsibility.

The catastrophic cap amount depends on an individual's profile, and should be obtained from TRICARE directly.

TRICARE REGIONS

North

TRICARE's North region includes Connecticut, Delaware, the District of Columbia, Illinois, Indiana, Kentucky, Maine, Maryland, Massachusetts, Michigan, New Hampshire, New Jersey, New York, North Carolina, Ohio, Pennsylvania, Rhode Island, Vermont, Virginia, West Virginia, and Wisconsin (and some zip code areas in Iowa, Missouri, and Tennessee). Health Net Federal Services, Inc. is the new regional contractor providing health care services and network-provider support in the TRICARE North region.

Health Net's customer service representatives are available Monday – Friday, 8 a.m. to 7 p.m. in all North region time zones, at 1-877-TRICARE (1-877-874-2273).

South

TRICARE's South region includes Alabama, Arkansas, Florida, Georgia, Louisiana, Mississippi Oklahoma, South Carolina, and Tennessee (excluding 35 Tennessee zip codes in the Fort Campbell, KY area), and Texas (excluding, only, the extreme southwestern El Paso-area). Humana-Military is the regional contractor providing health care services and network provider support in the TRICARE South region.

Humana's customer service representatives are available Monday – Friday, 8 a.m. to 6 p.m. in all South region time zones, at 1-800-444-5445.

West

TRICARE's West region includes Alaska, Arizona, California, Colorado, Hawaii, Idaho, Iowa (except 82 Iowa zip codes that are in the Rock Island, Illinois area), Kansas, Minnesota, Missouri (except the St. Louis area), Montana, Nebraska, Nevada, New Mexico, North Dakota, Oregon, South Dakota, Texas (the southwestern corner, including El Paso, only) Utah, Washington, and Wyoming. TriWest Healthcare Alliance is the regional contractor providing health care services and network-provider support in the TRICARE West region.

TriWest's customer service representatives are available Monday – Friday, 8 a.m. to 6 p.m. in the West Region time zone in which you reside, at 1-888-TRIWEST (1-888-874-9378).

Europe Area

The TRICARE Europe area is managed by the TAO Europe located at Sembach Air Base in Germany, and includes Europe, Africa and the Middle East.

Customer service representatives can be reached at 1-888-777-8343.

Latin America and Canada Area

The TRICARE Latin America and Canada (TLAC) area is managed by the TAO TLAC located at Fort Gordon, Georgia and includes Central and South America, the Caribbean Basin, Canada, Puerto Rico and the Virgin Islands.

Customer service representatives can be reached at 1-888-777-8343.

Pacific Area

The TRICARE Pacific area is managed by the TAO Pacific located at Camp Lester in Okinawa, Japan, and includes Guam, Japan, Korea, Asia, New Zealand, India and Western Pacific remote countries.

Customer service representatives can be reached at 1-888-777-8343.

CHAPTER 14

VOCATIONAL REHABILITATION AND EMPLOYMENT SERVICES FOR VETERANS WITH SERVICE-CONNECTED DISABILITIES

OVERVIEW

Vocational Rehabilitation is a program which helps eligible disabled veterans get and keep lasting, suitable jobs. It also helps seriously disabled veterans achieve independence in daily living.

The program offers a number of services to help each eligible disabled veteran reach his or her rehabilitation goal. These services include:

- Vocational and personal counseling;

- Evaluation of abilities, skill and interests;

- Assistance finding and keeping a suitable job, including special employer incentives;

- If needed, education and training such as certificate, two, or four year college programs;

- Financial aid;

- If needed, training such as on-the-job and non-paid work experiences;

- Supportive rehabilitation services and additional counseling;

- Medical and dental treatment, if needed;

- Education and training benefits for dependent children with the birth defect spina bifida, caused by a veteran-parent's service in the Vietnam theater.

- Vocational and educational guidance and counseling to certain veteran's dependents eligible for one of VA's educational benefit programs.

> *If entitled to Vocational Rehabilitation, the law provides for a maximum of 48 months of services. These limitations may be extended in certain circumstances.*

ELIGIBILITY

Usually, a veteran must first be awarded a monthly VA Disability Compensation payment. In some cases, veterans may be eligible if they are not getting VA compensation (for example, if they are awaiting discharge from the service because of a disability, OR they are entitled to VA compensation but have decided not to reduce their military retirement or disability pay).

Eligibility is also based on meeting the following conditions:

- The veteran served on or after September 16, 1940; and

- The veteran's discharge or release from active duty was under was under other than dishonorable conditions; and

- The veteran's service-connected disabilities are rated at least 20% disabling by VA (**NOTE:** Effective October 1, 1993, a veteran may be eligible for Vocational Rehabilitation if he or she is rated 10% disabled, and has a serious employment handicap.); and

- The veteran needs Vocational Rehabilitation to overcome an employment handicap; and

- It has been less than 12 years since VA notified the veteran of his or her eligibility. (A veteran may have longer than 12 years to use this benefit if certain conditions prevented him or her from training.)

AMOUNT OF VA PAYMENTS

If a veteran needs training, VA will pay his or her training costs, such as:

- Tuition and fees;

- Books;

- Supplies;

- Equipment; and

- Special services (such as prosthetic devices, lip-reading training, or signing for the deaf), if needed

While a veteran is in training, VA will also pay him or her a monthly benefit to help with living expenses, called a subsistence allowance. Details are provided in the next section of this chapter.

SUBSISTENCE ALLOWANCE (CHAPTER 31)

In some cases, a veteran requires additional education or training in order to become employable. A Subsistence Allowance may then be paid each month, and is based on the rate of attendance (full-time or part-time) and the number of dependents. The charts on the following page reflect the rates as of October 1, 2010.

The following Subsistence Allowance rates are paid for training in an Institution of Higher Learning:

Number Of Dependents	Full Time	Three Quarter Time	One Half Time
No Dependents	$554.22	$416.43	$278.64
One Dependent	$687.47	$516.35	$345.23
Two Dependents	$810.13	$605.69	$405.81
Each Additional Dependent	$59.05	$45.41	$30.30

Subsistence Allowance is paid for full time training only, in the following training programs:
Nonpay or nominal pay on-job training in a federal, state, local, or federally recognized Indian tribe agency; training in the home; vocational course in a rehabilitation facility or sheltered workshop; institutional non-farm cooperative.

Number Of Dependents	Full Time
No Dependents	$554.22
One Dependent	$687.47
Two Dependents	$810.13
Each Additional Dependent	$59.05

The following rates are paid for Work Experience programs:
Nonpay or nominal pay work experience in a federal, state, local or federally recognized Indian tribe agency.

Number Of Dependents	Full Time	Three Quarter Time	One Half Time
No Dependents	$554.22	$416.43	$278.64
One Dependent	$687.47	$516.35	$345.23
Two Dependents	$810.13	$605.69	$405.81
Each Additional Dependent	$59.05	$45.41	$30.30

Subsistence Allowance is paid for full time training only in the following training programs:
Farm cooperative, apprenticeship, or other on-job training.

Number of Dependents	Full Time
No Dependents	$484.57
One Dependent	$585.99
Two Dependents	$675.36
Each Additional Dependent	$43.93

Subsistence Allowance is paid at the following rates for combined training programs:
Combination of Institutional and On-Job Training (Full Time Rate Only).

Number Of Dependents	Institutional Greater than one half	On-The-Job Greater than one half
No Dependents	$554.22	$484.57
One Dependent	$687.47	$585.99
Two Dependents	$810.13	$675.36
Each Additional Dependent	$59.05	$43.93

Subsistence Allowance is paid at the following rates for Non-farm Cooperative Training:
Non-farm Cooperative Institutional Training and Non-farm Cooperative On-Job Training - Full Time Rate Only.

Number Of Dependents	FT Non-farm Coop/Institutional	FT Non-farm Coop/On-The-Job
No Dependents	$554.22	$484.57
One Dependent	$687.47	$585.99
Two Dependents	$810.13	$675.36
Each Additional Dependent	$59.05	$43.93

Subsistence Allowance is paid at the following rates for Independent Living programs:

A subsistence allowance is paid each month during the period of enrollment in a rehabilitation facility when a veteran is pursuing an approved Independent Living Program plan. Subsistence allowance paid during a period of Independent Living Services is based on rate of pursuit and number of dependents.

Number Of Dependents	Full Time	Three Quarter Time	One Half Time
No Dependents	$554.22	$416.43	$278.64
One Dependent	$687.47	$516.35	$345.23
Two Dependents	$810.13	$605.69	$405.81
Each Additional Dependent	$59.05	$45.41	$30.30

Subsistence Allowance is paid at the following rates for Extended Evaluation programs:

A subsistence allowance is paid each month during the period of enrollment in a rehabilitation facility when a veteran requires this service for the purpose of extended evaluation. Subsistence allowance during a period of extended evaluation is paid based on the rate of attendance and the number of dependents.

Number of Dependents	Full Time	Three Quarter Time	One Half Time	One Quarter Time
No Dependents	$554.22	$416.43	$278.64	$139.30
One Dependent	$687.47	$516.35	$345.23	$172.63
Two Dependents	$810.13	$605.69	$405.81	$202.90
Each Additional Dependent	$59.05	$45.41	$30.30	$15.11

PROGRAM FOR UNEMPLOYABLE VETERANS

Veterans awarded 100% disability compensation based upon unemployability may still request an evaluation, and, if found eligible, may participate in a vocational rehabilitation program and receive help in getting a job. A veteran who secures employment under the special program will continue to receive 100% disability compensation until the veteran has worked continuously for at least 12 months.

VOCATIONAL TRAINING FOR CHILDREN WITH SPINA BIFIDA

To qualify for entitlement to a vocational training program an applicant must be a child:

- To whom VA has awarded a monthly allowance for spina bifida; and

- For whom VA has determined that achievement of a vocational goal is reasonably feasible.

A vocational training program may not begin before a child's 18th birthday, or the date of completion of secondary schooling, whichever comes first. Depending on the need, a child may be provided up to 24 months of full-time training.

VOCATIONAL TRAINING FOR CHILDREN OF FEMALE VIETNAM VETERANS BORN WITH CERTAIN BIRTH DEFECTS

Section 401 of P.L. 106-416, which became law on November 1, 2000 directed the Secretary of VA to identify birth defects of children of female Vietnam veterans that: (1) are associated with service during the Vietnam era; and (2) result in the permanent physical or mental disability of such children. The law excludes from such defects familial or birth-related defects or injuries. The law further directs the Secretary to provide to such children a monthly monetary allowance, as well as necessary health care to address the defect and any associated disability. It authorizes the Secretary to provide vocational training to such a child if the achievement of a vocational goal is reasonably feasible.

INDEPENDENT LIVING SERVICES

These services can help an individual with disabilities so severe that he or she cannot work. These services can lessen the individual's need to rely on others by giving him or her the skills needed to live as independently as possible at home and in the community.

Independent living services include:

- Extended evaluation of the individual's independent living needs;

- Training in activities of daily living;

- Case management;

- Personal adjustment counseling;

- Assistive technology;

- Training to improve the individual's chances of reaching a vocational goal.

APPLYING FOR BENEFITS

Interested veterans can apply by filling out VA Form 28-1900, Disabled Veterans Application for Vocational Rehabilitation, and mailing it to the VA regional office serving his or her area. (For a complete list of VA Regional Offices, refer to Chapter 36 of this book.)

CHAPTER 15

VET CENTERS

Vet Centers serve veterans and their families by providing a continuum of quality care that adds value for veterans, families, and communities. Care includes:

- Professional readjustment counseling;

- Professional counseling for posttraumatic stress disorder;

- Marital and family counseling;

- Substance abuse information and referral;

- Community education;

- Outreach to special populations, including disenfranchised and unserved veterans;

- The brokering of services with community agencies;

- Provides a key access link between the veteran and other services in the U.S. Department of Veterans Affairs;

- Promotion of wellness activities with veterans to help them reach quality health and life goals, and diminish the need for more intensive healthcare.

ELIGIBILITY

Legislation passed by Congress and signed into law by the President changed eligibility for Vet Center services, and extended the definition of the Vietnam era for war zone veterans (P.L. 104-262 and P.L. 104-275.)

Vet Centers serve the following veterans:

War Zone Veterans- all eras, including:

- **Vietnam War** – February 28, 1961 to May 7, 1975

- **Vietnam Era Veterans Not In The War Zone** – August 5, 1964 to May 7, 1975 (Veterans must request services at a Vet Center prior to January 1, 2004, to guarantee eligibility.)

- **Korean War** – June 27, 1950 to July 27, 1954 (eligible for the Korean Service Medal)

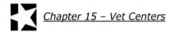

- **World War II** – There are 3 eligible categories:

  1. European-African-Middle Eastern Campaign Medal –
     December 7, 1941 to November 8, 1945

  2. Asiatic-Pacific Campaign Medal –
     December 7, 1941 to March 2, 1946

  3. American Campaign Medal –
     December 7, 1941 to March 2, 1946

- **Lebanon** – August 25, 1982 to February 26, 1984

- **Grenada** – October 23, 1983 to November 21, 1983

- **Panama** – December 20, 1989 to January 31, 1990

- **Persian Gulf** – August 2, 1990 to a date to be set by law or Presidential Proclamation

- **Somalia** – September 17, 1992 to a date to be set by law or Presidential Proclamation

- **Operation Joint Endeavor, Operation Joint Guard, & Operation Joint Forge** - Vet Center eligibility has been extended to veterans who participated in one or more of the three successive operations in the former Yugoslavia (Bosnia-Herzegovina and Croatia, aboard U.S. Naval vessels operating in the Adriatic Sea, or air spaces above those areas).

- **Global War on Terrorism** – Veterans who serve or have served in military expeditions to combat terrorism on or after September 11, 2001 and before a terminal date yet to be established.

Sexual Trauma And Harassment Counseling

Veterans of both sexes, all eras. Vet Center services include individual readjustment counseling, referral for benefits assistance, group readjustment counseling, liaison with community agencies, marital and family counseling, substance abuse information and referral, job counseling and placement, sexual trauma counseling, and community education.

Bereavement Counseling

The Department of Veteran Affairs (VA) offers bereavement counseling to parents, spouses and children of Armed Forces personnel who died in the service of their country. Also eligible are family members of reservists and National Guardsmen who die while on duty.

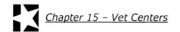

VET CENTER LOCATIONS

Alabama
Birmingham Vet Center
1500 5th Avenue South
Birmingham, AL 35205
(205) 731-0550

Mobile Vet Center
2577 Government Boulevard
Mobile, AL 36606
(251) 478-5906

Montgomery Vet Center Outstation
Colonial Park, Bldg. 600, #603
Montgomery, AL 35233
(334) 396-1986

Alaska
Anchorage Vet Center
4201 Tudor Centre Dr, Suite 115
Anchorage, AK 99508
(907) 563-6966

Fairbanks Vet Center
542 4th Avenue
Suite 100
Fairbanks, AK 99701
(907) 456-4238

Kenai Vet Center
Building F, Suite 4
Red Diamond Center
43335 K-Beach Road
Kenai, AK 99669
(907) 260-7640

Wasilla Vet Center
851 East Westpoint Ave, Suite 109
Wasilla, AK 99654
(907) 376-4318

Arizona
Chinle Vet Center Outstation
P.O. Box 1934
Chinle, AZ 86503
(928)-674-3682

Hopi Vet Center Outstation 2
P.O. Box 267
Keams Canyon, AZ 86034
(928)-738-5166

Phoenix East Valley Vet Center
1303 South Longmore, Suite 5
Mesa, AZ 85202
(480) 610-6727

Phoenix Vet Center
77 East Weldon Avenue, Suite 100
Phoenix, AZ 85012-2075
(602) 640-2981

Prescott Vet Center
161 South Granite Street
Prescott, AZ 86303
(928) 778-3469

Tucson Vet Center
3055 North 1st Avenue
Tucson, AZ 85719
(520) 882-0333

Arkansas
North Little Rock Vet Center
201 West Broadway
Suite A
Little Rock, AR 72114
(501) 324-6395

California
4B Pacific Western Regional Office
420 Executive Court North, Suite G
Fairfield, CA 94534
(707) 646-2988

Chico Vet Center
280 Cohasset Road
Chico, CA 95926
(530) 899-8549

Concord Vet Center
1899 Clayton Rd, Suite 140
Concord, CA 94520
(925) 680-4526

Corona Vet Center
800 Magnolia Avenue, Suite 110
Corona, CA 92879-8202
(909)-734-0525

East Los Angeles Vet Center
5400 E Olympic Blvd, #140
East Los Angeles, CA 90022
(323) 728-9966

Eureka Vet Center
2830 G Street, Suite A
Eureka, CA 95501
(707) 444-8271

Fresno Vet Center
3636 North 1st St, Suite 112
Fresno, CA 93726
(559) 487-5660

Los Angeles Vet Center
1045 W. Redondo Beach Blvd.,
Suite 150
Gardena, CA 90247
(310)-767-1221

Modesto Vet Center
1219 N. Carpenter Rd., Suite 12
Modesto, CA 95351
(209) 569-0713

Oakland Vet Center
1504 Franklin St, Suite 200
Oakland, CA 94612
(510) 763-3904

Redwood City Vet Center
2946 Broadway Street
Redwood City, CA 94062
(650) 299-0672

Rohnert Park Vet Center
6225 State Farm Drive
Suite 101
Rohnert Park, CA 94928
(707) 586-3295

Sacramento Vet Center
1111 Howe Avenue
Suite 390
Sacramento, CA 95825
(916) 566-7430

San Bernardino Vet Center
155 West Hospitality Lane
Suite #140
San Bernardino, CA 92408
(909) 890-0797

San Diego Vet Center
2900 6th Avenue
San Diego, CA 92103
(619) 294-2040

San Francisco Vet Center
505 Polk Street
San Francisco, CA 94102
(415) 441-5051

San Jose Vet Center
278 North 2nd Street
San Jose, CA 95112
(408) 993-0729

San Marcos Vet Center
One Civic Center Dr., Suite 140
San Marcos, CA 92069
(760) 744-6914

Santa Cruz County Vet Center
1350 41st Ave, Suite 102
Capitola, CA 95010
(831)-464-4575

Sepulveda Vet Center
9737 Hascle Street
Sepulveda, CA 91343
(818) 892-9227

Ventura Vet Center
790 E. Santa Clara St., Suite 100
Ventura, CA 93001
(805)-585-1860

West Los Angeles Vet Center
5730 Uplander Way, Suite 100
Culver City, CA 90230
(310) 641-0326

Colorado
Boulder Vet Center
2336 Canyon Blvd, Suite 130
Boulder, CO 80302
(303) 440-7306

Colorado Springs Vet Center
416 East Colorado Avenue
Colorado Springs, CO 80903
(719) 471-9992

4A Western Mountain
Regional Office
789 Sherman Street, Suite 570
Denver, CO 80203
(303) 393-2897

Denver Vet Center
7465 E Academy Boulevard
Denver, CO 80220
(303) 326-0645

Ft. Collins Vet Center Outstation
1100 Poudre River Dr. (Lower)
Ft. Collins, CO 80524
(970)-221-5176

Grand Junction Vet Center
2472 F. Road Unit 16
Grand Junction, CO 81505
(970) 245-4156

Pueblo Vet Center Outstation
509 E. 13th St.
Pueblo, CO 81001
(719) 546-6666

Connecticut
New Haven Vet Center
141 Captain Thomas Boulevard
New Haven, CT 06516
(203) 932-9899

Norwich Vet Center
5 Cliff Street
Norwich, CT 06360
(860) 887-1755

Wethersfield Vet Center
30 Jordan Lane
Wethersfield, CT 06109
(860) 563-2320

Delaware
Wilmington Vet Center
1601 Kirkwood Highway
Wilmington, DE 19805
(302) 994-1660

District of Columbia
Washington, D.C. Vet Center
1250 Taylor Street, NW
Washington, DC 20011
(202) 726-5212

Florida
Bay Pines Vet Center
789 Sherman Street, Suite 570
Denver, CO 80203
(303) 393-2897

Fort Lauderdale Vet Center
713 NE 3rd Avenue
Fort Lauderdale, FL 33304
(954) 356-7926

Ft. Myers Outstation Vet Center
3691 Evans
Ft. Myers, FL 33901
(239)-938-1100

Gainesville Vet Center
105 NW 75th Street, Suite #2
Gainesville, FL 32607
(352) 331-1408

Jacksonville Vet Center
300 East State Street
Jacksonville, FL 32202
(904) 232-3621

Key Largo Vet Center Outstation
105662 Overseas Hwy.
Key Largo, FL 33037
(305)-451-0164

Melbourne Vet Center
2098 Sarno Road
Melbourne, FL 32935
(321) 254-3410

Miami Vet Center
2700 SW 3rd Avenue
Suite 1A
Miami, FL 33129
(305) 859-8387

Orlando Vet Center
5575 S Semoran Blvd
Suite 36
Orlando, FL 32822
(407) 857-2800

Palm Beach Vet Center
2311 10th Avenue, North #13
Palm Beach, FL 33461
(561) 585-0441

Pensacola Vet Center
4501 Twin Oaks Drive
Pensacola, FL 32506
(850) 456-5886

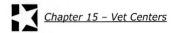

Sarasota Vet Center
4801 Swift Road
Sarasota, FL 34231
(941) 927-8285

St. Petersburg Vet Center
2880 1st Avenue, N.
St. Petersburg, FL 33713
(727) 893-3791

Tallahassee Vet Center
548 Bradford Road
Tallahassee, FL 32303
(850) 942-8810

Tampa Vet Center
8900N Armenia Ave, #312
Tampa, FL 33604
(813) 228-2621

Georgia
Atlanta Vet Center
1440 Dutch Valley Place
Suite G, Box 29
Atlanta, GA 30324
(404) 347-7264

Macon Vet Center
750 Riverside Drive
Macon, GA 31201
(478) 477-3813

North Atlanta Vet Center
930 River Centre Plaza
Lawrenceville, GA 30043
(770) 963-1809

Savannah Vet Center
8110A White Bluff Road
Savannah, GA 31406
(912) 652-4097

Guam
Agana Vet Center
222 Chalan Santo Papa Street
Reflection Center, Suite 102
Agana, Guam 96910
(671) 472-7160

Guam Vet Center
222 Chalan Santo Papa Reflection
Ctr. Ste 201
Hagatna, GU 96910
(671)-472-7160

Hawaii
Hilo Vet Center
120 Keawe Street
Suite 201
Hilo, HI 96720
(808) 969-3833

Honolulu Vet Center
1680 Kapiolani Boulevard
Suite F3
Honolulu, HI 96814
(808) 973-8387

Kailua-Kona Vet Center
Pottery Terrace, Fern Building
75-5995 Kuakini Highway, #415
Kailua-Kona, HI 96470
(808) 329-0574

Lihue Vet Center
3-3367 Kuhlo Highway
Suite 101
Lihue, HI 96766
(808) 246-1163

Wailuku Vet Center
35 Lunalilo
Suite 101
Wailuku, HI 96793
(808) 242-8557

Idaho
Boise Vet Center
5440 Franklin Road, Suite 100
Boise, ID 83705
(208) 342-3612

Pocatello Vet Center
1800 Garrett Way
Pocatello, ID 83201
(208) 232-0316

Illinois
Chicago Vet Center
2038 West 95th Street
Suite 200
Chicago, IL 60643
(773) 881-9900

Chicago Heights Vet Center
1600 Halsted Street
Chicago Heights, IL 60411
(708) 754-0340

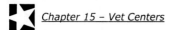

East St. Louis Vet Center
1265 North 89th Street, Suite 5
East St. Louis, IL 62203
(618) 397-6602

Evanston Vet Center
565 Howard Street
Evanston, IL 60202
(847) 332-1019

Moline Vet Center
1529 46th Avenue, #6
Moline, IL 61265
(309) 762-6954

Oak Park Vet Center
155 S Oak Park Blvd
Oak Park, IL 60302
(708) 383-3225

Peoria Vet Center
3310 North Prospect Street
Peoria, IL 61603
(309) 688-2170

Rockford Vet Center Outstation
4960 E. State St. #3
Rockford, IL 61108
(815)-395-1276

Springfield Vet Center
624 South 4th Street
Springfield, IL 62703
(217) 492-4955

Indiana
Evansville Vet Center
311 North Weinbach Avenue
Evansville, IN 47711
(812) 473-5993

Fort Wayne Vet Center
528 West Berry Street
Fort Wayne, IN 46802
(260) 460-1456

Gary Vet Center
6505 Broadway Ave.
Merrillville, IN 46410
219-736-5633

Indianapolis Vet Center
3833 Meridian, Suite 120
Indianapolis, IN 46208
(317) 927-6440

Iowa
Cedar Rapids Vet Center
1642 42nd Street, N.E.
Cedar Rapids, IA 52402
(319) 378-0016

Des Moines Vet Center
2600 Martin Luther King Jr.
Parkway
Des Moines, IA 50310
(515) 284-4929

Sioux City Vet Center
1551 Indian Hills Drive
Sioux City, IA 51104
(712) 255-3808

Kansas
Manhattan Vet Center
205 South 4th Street, Suite B
Manhattan, KS 66502
Phone: 785-587-8257

Wichita Vet Center
413 South Pattie
Wichita, KS 67211
(316) 265-3260

Kentucky
Lexington Vet Center
301 East Vine Street, Suite C
Lexington, KY 40507
(859) 253-0717

Louisville Vet Center
1347 South 3rd Street
Louisville, KY 40208
(502) 634-1916

Louisiana
Baton Rouge Vet Center
5207 Essen Lane, Suite 2
Baton Rouge, LA 70809
(225) 757-0042

New Orleans Vet Center
2200 Veterans Blvd, Suite 114
Kenner, LA 70062
(504) 464-4743

Shreveport Vet Center
2800 Youree Drive
Building 1, Suite 105
Shreveport, LA 71104
(318) 861-1776

Maine
Bangor Vet Center
352 Harlow Street
Bangor, ME 04401
(207) 947-3391

Caribou Vet Center
York Street Complex
Caribou, ME 04736
(207) 496-3900

Lewiston Vet Center
Parkway Complex
29 Westminster Street
Lewiston, ME 04240
(207) 783-0068

Portland Vet Center
475 Stevens Avenue
Portland, ME 04103
(207) 780-3584

Sanford Vet Center
628 Main Street
Springvale, ME 04083
(207) 490-1513

Maryland
Baltimore Vet Center
1777 Reisterstown Road
Suite 199
Baltimore, MD 21208
(410) 764-9400

Cambridge Vet Center
5510 West Shore Drive
Cambridge, MD 21613
(410) 228-6305

Elkton Vet Center
103 Chesapeake Blvd, Suite A
Elkton, MD 21921
(410) 394-4485

Harford County Vet Center
Outstation
223 W. Bel Air Avenue
Aberdeen, MD 21001
(410)-272-6771

Silver Spring Vet Center
1015 Spring St, Suite 101
Silver Spring, MD 20910
(301) 589-1073

Towson Vet Center
305 W. Chesapeake Ave
Suite 300
Towson, MD 21204
(410) 828-6619

Massachusetts
Boston Vet Center
665 Beacon Street
Boston, MA 02215
(617) 424-0665

Brockton Vet Center
1041-L Pearl Street
Brockton, MA 02401
(508) 580-2730

Hyannis Vet Center
474 West Main Street
Hyannis, MA 02601
(508) 778-0124

Lowell Vet Center
73 East Merrimack Street
Lowell, MA 01852
(978) 453-1151

New Bedford Vet Center
468 North Street
New Bedford, MA 02740
(508) 999-6920

Springfield Vet Center
1985 Main Street
Northgate Plaza
Springfield, MA 01103
(413) 737-5167

Worcester Vet Center
597 Lincoln Street
Worcester, MA 01605
(508) 856-7428

Michigan

Dearborn Vet Center
2881 Monroe Street
Suite 100
Deerborn, MI 48124
(313) 277-1428

Detroit Vet Center
4161 Cass Avenue
Detroit, MI 48201
(313) 831-6509

Escanaba Vet Center
3500 Ludington Street
Suite # 110
Escanaba , MI 49829
(906)-233-0244

Grand Rapids Vet Center
1940 Eastern SE
Grand Rapids, MI 48507
(616) 243-0385

Michigan Upper Peninsula Vet
Center
2600 College Ave.
Escanaba, MI 49829
(906)-789-9732

Minnesota

Duluth Vet Center
405 East Superior Street
Duluth, MN 55802
(218) 722-8654

St. Paul Vet Center
2480 University Avenue
St. Paul, MN 55114
(651) 644-4022

Mississippi

Biloxi Vet Center
288 Veterans Avenue
Biloxi, MS 39531
(228) 388-9938

Jackson Vet Center
4436 North State Street
Suite A3
Jackson, MS 39206
(601) 965-5727

Missouri

Kansas City Vet Center
3931 Main Street
Kansas City, MO 64111
(816) 753-1866

St. Louis Vet Center
2345 Pine Street
St. Louis, MO 63103
(314) 231-1260

Montana

Billings Vet Center
1234 Avenue C
Billings, MT 59102
(406) 657-6071

Missoula Vet Center
500 North Higgins Avenue
Missoula, MT 59802
(406) 721-4918

Nebraska

Lincoln Vet Center
920 L Street
Lincoln, NE 68508
(402) 476-9736

Omaha Vet Center
2428 Cuming Street
Omaha, NE 68131
(402) 346-6735

Nevada

Las Vegas Vet Center
1040 East Sahara Avenue
Suite 102
Las Vegas, NV 89104
(702) 388-6368

Reno Vet Center
1155 West 4th Street
Suite 101
Reno, NV 89503
(775) 323-1294

New Hampshire

Berlin Vet Center
515 Main Street
Gorham, NH 03581
(603) 752-2571

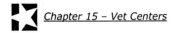

Manchester Vet Center
103 Liberty Street
Manchester, NH 03104
(603) 668-7060

New Jersey
Jersey City Vet Center
115 Christopher Columbus Drive
Room 200
Jersey City, NJ 07302
(201) 748-4467

Newark Vet Center
45 Academy Street
Suite 303
Newark, NJ 07102
(973) 645-5954

Trenton Vet Center
171 Jersey St., Building 36
Trenton, NJ 08611
(609) 989-2260

Ventnor Vet Center
6601 Ventnor Avenue, Suite 105
Ventnor, NJ 08406
(609) 487-8387

New Mexico
Albuquerque Vet Center
1600 Mountain Road, NW
Albuquerque, NM 87104
(505) 346-6562

Farmington Vet Center
4251 East Main, Suite B
Farmington, NM 87402
(505) 327-9684

Las Cruces Vet Center
230 S. Water Street
Las Cruces, NM 88001
(575) 523-9826

Santa Fe Vet Center
2209 Brothers Road, Suite 110
Santa Fe, NM 87505
(505) 988-6562

New York
Albany Vet Center
875 Central Avenue
Albany, NY 12206
(518) 438-2505

Babylon Vet Center
116 West Main Street
Babylon, NY 11702
(631) 661-3930

Binghamton Vet Center
53 Chenango Street
Binghamtom, NY 13901
(866) 716-8213

Bronx Vet Center
226 East Fordham Road
Room 220
Bronx, NY 10458
(718) 367-3500

Brooklyn Vet Center
25 Chapel Street, Suite 604
Brooklyn, NY 11201
(718) 330-2825

Buffalo Vet Center
564 Franklin Street
Buffalo, NY 14202
(716) 882-0505

Harlem Vet Center
55 West 125th Street
New York, NY 10027
(212) 426-2200

Manhattan Vet Center
32 Broadway, 2nd Floor
Suite 200
New York, NY 10004
(212) 742-9591

Middletown Vet Center
726 East Main Street, Suite 203
Middletown, NY 10940
(845) 342-9917

Rochester Vet Center
1867 Mount Hope Avenue
Rochester, NY 14620
(585) 232-5040

Staten Island Vet Center
150 Richmond Terrace
Staten Island, NY 10301
(718) 816-4499

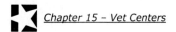

Syracuse Vet Center
716 East Washington Street
Syracuse, NY 13210
(315) 478-7127

Watertown Vet Center
210 Court Street
Watertown, NY 13601
(866) 610-0358

White Plains Vet Center
300 Hamilton Avenue
White Plains, NY 10601
(914) 682-6250

Woodhaven Vet Center
75-10B 91st Avenue
Woodhaven, NY 11421
(718) 296-2871

North Carolina
Charlotte Vet Center
223 South Brevard Street
Suite 103
Charlotte, NC 28202
(704) 333-6107

Fayetteville Vet Center
4140 Ramsey St., Suite 110
Fayetteville, NC 28311
(910) 488-6252

Greensboro Vet Center
2009 South Elm-Eugene Street
Greensboro, NC 27406
(336) 333-5366

Greenville Vet Center
150 Arlington Blvd., Suite B
Greenville, NC 27858
(252) 355-7920

Raleigh Vet Center
1649 Old Louisburg Road
Raleigh, NC 27604
(919) 856-4616

North Dakota
Bismarck Vet Center
1684 Capital Way
Bismarck, ND 58501
(701) 244-9751

Fargo Vet Center
3310 Fiechtner Drive, Suite 100
Fargo. MD 58103
(701) 237-0942

Minot Vet Center
2041 3rd Street, N.W.
Minot, ND 58701
(701) 852-0177

Ohio
Cincinnati Vet Center
801-B West 8th Street
Cincinnati, OH 45203
(513) 763-3500

Cleveland Heights Center
2022 Lee Road
Cleveland Heights, OH 44118
(216) 932-8471

Columbus Vet Center
30 Spruce Street
Columbus, OH 43215
(614) 257-5550

Dayton Vet Center
6th Floor, East Medical Plaza
627 Edwin
Dayton, OH 45408
(937) 461-9150

McCafferty Outstation Vet Center
4242 Lorain Avenue, Suite 201
Cleveland, OH 44113
(216)-939-0784

Parma Vet Center
5700 Pearl Rd., Suite 102
Parma, OH 44129
(440) 845-5023

Toledo Vet Center
1565 S. Byrne Road, Suite 104
Toledo, OH 43614
(419) 213-7533

Oklahoma
Oklahoma City Vet Center
3033 North Walnut, Suite 101W
Oklahoma City, OK 73105
(405) 270-5184

Tulsa Vet Center
1408 South Harvard
Tulsa, OK 74112
(918) 748-5105

Oregon
Eugene Vet Center
1255 Pearl Street
Eugene, OR 97403
(541) 465-6918

Grants Pass Vet Center
211 S.E. 10th Street
Grants Pass, OR 97526
(541) 479-6912

Portland Vet Center
8383 N.E. Sandy Blvd, Suite 110
Portland, OR 97220
(503) 273-5370

Salem Vet Center
617 Chemeketa St., N.E.
Salem, OR 97301
(503) 362-9911

Pennsylvania
DuBois Vet Center
100 Meadow Lane
Suite 8
DuBois, PA 15801
(814) 372-2095

Erie Vet Center
1001 State Street
Suites 1 & 2
Erie, PA 16501
(814) 453-7955

Harrisburg Vet Center
1500 N 2nd Street, Suite 2
Harrisburg, PA 17102
(717) 782-3954

McKeesport Vet Center
2001 Lincoln Way
McKeesport, PA 15131
(412) 678-7704

Philadelphia Vet Center
801 Arch Street, Suite 102
Philadelphia, PA 19107
(215) 627-0238

Philadelphia Vet Center
101 East Olney Avenue
Philadelphia, PA 19120
(215) 924-4670

Pittsburgh Vet Center
2500 Baldwick Road
Pittsburgh, PA 15205
(412) 920-1765

Scranton Vet Center
1002 Pittston Avenue
Scranton, PA 18505
(570) 344-2676

Williamsport Vet Center
805 Penn Street
Williamsport, PA 17701
(570) 327-5281

Puerto Rico
Arecibo Vet Center
52 Gonzalo Marin Street
Arecibo, Puerto Rico 00612-4702
(787) 879-4510

Ponce Vet Center
35 Mayor Street
Ponce, Puerto Rico 00730
(787) 841-3260

San Juan Vet Center
Condominio Medical Center Plaza
Suite LC8A and LC9
Rio Piedras, Puerto Rico 00921
(787) 749-4409

Rhode Island
Warwick Vet Center
2038 Warwick Avenue
Warwick, RI 02889
(401) 739-0167

South Carolina
Columbia Vet Center
1513 Pickens Street
Columbia, SC 29201
(803) 765-9944

Greenville Vet Center
14 Lavinia Avenue
Greenville, SC 29601
(864) 271-2711

North Charleston Vet Center
5603A Rivers Avenue
North Charleston, SC 29406
(843) 747-8387

South Dakota
Pine Ridge Vet Center Outstation
P.O. Box 910, 105 E. Hwy 18
Martin, SD 57747
(605) 685-1300

Rapid City Vet Center
621 Sixth Street, Suite 101
Rapid City, SD 57701
(605) 348-0077

Sioux Falls Vet Center
601 S. Cliff Ave., Suite C
Sioux Falls, SD 57104
(605) 330-4552

Tennessee
Chattanooga Vet Center
951 Eastgate Loop Road
Building 5700, Suite 300
Chattanooga, TN 37411
(423) 855-6570

Johnson City Vet Center
1615A West Market Street
Johnson City, TN 37604
(423) 928-8387

Knoxville Vet Center
2817 East Magnolia Avenue
Knoxville, TN 37914
(865) 545-4680

Memphis Vet Center
1835 Union, Suite 100
Memphis, TN 38104
(901) 544-0173

Nashville Vet Center
1420 Donelson Pike Suite A-5
Nashville, TN 37217
(615) 366-1220

Texas
Amarillo Vet Center
3414 Olsen Blvd., Suite E
Amarillo, TX 79109
(806) 354-9779

Austin Vet Center
1110 W William Cannon Dr
Suite 301
Austin, TX 78745
(512) 416-1314

Corpus Christi Vet Center
4646 Corona, Suite 250
Corpus Christi, TX 78411
(361) 854-9961

Dallas Vet Center
5232 Forest Lane, Suite 111
Dallas, TX 75244
(214) 361-5896

El Paso Vet Center
1155 Westmoreland
Suite 121
El Paso, TX 79925
(915) 772-0013

Fort Worth Vet Center
1305 West Magnolia, Suite B
Forth Worth, TX 76104
(817) 921-9095

Houston Vet Center
503 Westheimer
Houston, TX 77006
(713) 523-0884

Houston Vet Center
701 N. Post Oak Rd., Suite 102
Houston, TX 77024
(713) 682-2288

Killeen Heights Vet Center
302 Millers Crossing, Suite #4
Harker Heights, TX 76548
(254) 953-7100

Laredo Vet Center
6020 McPherson Road, #1A
Laredo, TX 78041
(956) 723-4680

Lubbock Vet Center
3208 34th Street
Lubbock, TX 79410
(806) 792-9782

McAllen Vet Center
801 Nolana Loop, Suite 115
McAllen, TX 78504
(956) 631-2147

Midland Vet Center
3404 W. Illinois, Suite 1
Midland, TX 79703
(432) 697-8222

San Antonio Vet Center
231 West Cypress Street
San Antonio, TX 78212
(210) 472-4025

Utah
Provo Vet Center
750 North 200 West
Suite 105
Provo, UT 84601
(801) 377-1117

Salt Lake City Vet Center
1354 East 3300 South
Salt Lake City, UT 84106
(801) 584-1294

Vermont
South Burlington Vet Center
359 Dorset Street
South Burlington, VT 05403
(802) 862-1806

White River Junction Vet Center
222 Holiday Drive
Gilman Office Center Building #2
White River Junction, VT 05001
(802) 295-2908

Virginia
Alexandria Vet Center
8796 Sacramento Drive
Suites D & E
Alexandria, VA 22309
(703) 360-8633

Norfolk Vet Center
2200 Colonial Avenue, Suite 3
Norfolk, VA 23517
(757) 623-7584

Richmond Vet Center
4202 Fitzhugh Avenue
Richmond, VA 23230
(804) 353-8958

Roanoke Vet Center
350 Albemarle Avenue, S.W.
Roanoke, VA 24016
(540) 342-9726

Virgin Islands
St. Croix Vet Center
The Village Mall
Rural Route 2
Box 10553, Kingshill
St. Croix, Virgin Islands 00850
(340) 778-5553

St. Thomas Vet Center
9800 Buccaneer Mall, Suite 8
St. Thomas, Virgin Islands 00802
(340) 774-6674

Washington
Bellingham Vet Center
3800 Byron Avenue, Suite 124
Bellingham, WA 98229
(360) 733-9226

Everett Vet Center
3311 Wetmore Avenue
Everett, WA 98201
(425)252-9701

Seattle Vet Center
2030 9th Avenue, Suite 210
Seattle, WA 98121
(206) 553-2706

Spokane Vet Center
100 North Mullan Road, Suite 102
Spokane, WA 99206
(509) 444-8387

Tacoma Vet Center
4916 Center Street, Suite E
Tacoma, WA 98409
(253) 565-7038

Yakima Valley Vet Center
1111 North 1st Street
Suite 1
Yakima, WA 98901
(509) 457-2736

West Virginia
Beckley Vet Center
101 Ellison Avenue
Beckley, WV 25801
(304) 252-8220

Charleston Vet Center
521 Central Avenue
Charleston, WV 25302
(304) 343-3825

Huntington Vet Center
3135 16th Street Road
Suite 11
Huntington, WV 25701
(304) 523-8387

Logan Vet Center Outstation
21 Main Street West
Henlawson, WV 25624
(304)-752-4453

Martinsburg Vet Center
900 Winchester Avenue
Martinsburg, WV 25401
(304) 263-6776

Morgantown Vet Center
1083 Greenbag Road
Morgantown, WV 26508
(304) 291-4303

Parkersburg Vet Center Outstation
2311 Ohio Avenue, Suite D
Pakersburg, WV 26101
(304) 485-1599

Princeton Vet Center
905 Mercer Street
Princeton, WV 24740
(304) 425-5653

Wheeling Vet Center
1206 Chapline Street
Wheeling, WV 26003
(304) 232-0587

Wisconsin
Madison Vet Center
147 South Butler Street
Madison, WI 53703
(608) 264-5342

Milwaukee Vet Center
5401 North 76th Street
Milwaukee, WI 53218
(414) 536-1301

Wyoming
Casper Vet Center
111 South Jefferson
Casper, WY 82601
(307) 261-5355

Cheyenne Vet Center
2424 Pioneer Avenue, Suite 103
Cheyenne, WY 82001
(307) 778-7370

CHAPTER 16

EDUCATION BENEFITS

The Veterans' Administration administers ten educational assistance programs, each with different eligibility criteria. Typically, a veteran's eligibility is based on his or her dates of active duty. Generally, only the VA can determine an applicant's eligibility. Specific information regarding educational benefits can be obtained from the Education Service of the VA (1-888-GI-BILL-1) or any VA regional office.

The basic categories of VA educational assistance programs are:

- Montgomery G.I. Bill - Active Duty (MGIB - Chapter 30)

- Montgomery G.I. Bill - Selected Reserve (Chapter 1606)

- Post-9/11 G.I. Bill – (GI Bill for the 21st Century, Chapter 33)

- Reserve Educational Assistance Program (REAP – Chapter 1607)

- Veterans' Educational Assistance Program (VEAP - Chapter 32)

- Educational Assistance Test Program (Section 901)

- Educational Assistance Pilot Program (Section 903)

- Survivors' and Dependents' Educational Assistance Program (Chapter 35)

- Restored Entitlement Program for Survivors (REPS)

- Vocational Rehabilitation (Chapter 31) (This topic is discussed in detail in Chapter 14 of this book.)

- Omnibus Diplomatic Security and Antiterrorism Act

MGIB, REAP, & MGIB-SR are discussed in the following three chapters. This chapter discusses the remaining seven educational assistance programs.

An individual can be eligible for more than one of the above education benefits. If so, he or she must elect which benefit to receive. Payments for more than one benefit at a time may not be made. *The VA strongly encourages individuals who qualify for more than one type of education benefit to discuss their education plans with a Veterans Benefits Counselor so that all options can be explored, and maximum benefits can be paid.*

VETERANS EDUCATIONAL ASSISTANCE PROGRAM (VEAP) – CHAPTER 32

> *Veterans who first entered active duty between January 1, 1977 and June 30, 1985 were able to voluntarily contribute to an education account to establish eligibility for this program.*

The Post-Vietnam Veterans' Educational Assistance Program is also known as VEAP or Chapter 32.

Veterans who first entered active duty between January 1, 1977 and June 30, 1985 were able to voluntarily contribute to an education account to establish eligibility for this program.

VEAP provides education and training opportunities to eligible persons who contributed to the program while on active duty. If an individual did not contribute, or received a refund of contributions, he or she is not eligible for VEAP benefits. The initial contribution must have been made by March 31, 1987. The maximum contribution by any individual participant is $2,700. A participating member's contributions are matched on a $2 for $1 basis by the Government.

VEAP Eligibility

To qualify for VEAP benefits, individuals must have:

- Entered active duty for the first time between January 1, 1977 and June 30, 1985; and

> *Benefits are generally payable for 10 years following a veteran's release from active duty.*

- Enrolled in and contributed to VEAP before April 1, 1987; and

- Served for a continuous period of 181 days or more (Individuals may be eligible if discharged from a shorter period of active duty for a service-connected disability.); and

- Been discharged or released from service under conditions other than dishonorable; and

- Completed 24 continuous months of active duty if enlisted for the first time after September 7, 1980, or entered active duty as an officer or enlistee after October 16, 1981. (Individuals meet this requirement if they completed a shorter period of active duty to which the service department called or ordered the individual.)

Individuals may be eligible for VEAP benefits if they did not complete 24 continuous months of active duty if they:

- Received VA disability compensation or military disability retirement; or

- Served a period of at least 24 continuous months of active duty before October 17, 1981; or

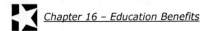

- Were discharged or released for early out, hardship, or service-connected disability.

Individuals may be eligible for VEAP benefits while still on active duty if they:

- Entered active duty for the first time after December 31, 1976, and before July 1, 1985; and

- Enrolled in and contributed to VEAP before April 1, 1987, and have at least three months of contributions available (For an elementary or high school program, at least one month of contributions must be available.); and

- Served for a continuous period of 181 days or more; and

- Completed their first active duty commitment.

The following types of active duty do not establish eligibility:

- Time assigned by the military to a civilian institution for the same course provided to civilians;

- Time served as a cadet or midshipman at a service academy;

- Time spent on active duty for training in the National Guard or Reserve.

NOTE: Individuals are not eligible for VEAP if they are eligible for the Montgomery GI Bill-Active Duty based on prior eligibility for Vietnam Ear Veterans' Educational Assistance.

Approved Courses

VEAP benefits may be received for a wide variety of training, including:

- Training for a high school diploma or the equivalent

- Undergraduate or graduate degrees from a college or university

- Cooperative training programs

- Accredited independent study programs leading to standard college degrees

- Courses leading to certificates or diplomas from business, technical or vocational schools

- Vocational flight training (Individuals must have a private pilot's license and meet the medical requirements for a desired license before beginning training, and throughout the flight training program)

- Apprenticeship or job training programs offered by a company or union

- Correspondence courses

- VA may approve programs offered by institutions outside of the United States, when they are pursued at educational institutions of higher learning, and lead to a college degree. Individuals must receive VA approval prior to attending or enrolling in any foreign programs.

- **Effective March 1, 2001**, benefits may be payable for licensing or certification tests. The tests are those needed to enter, maintain, or advance into employment in a civilian vocation or profession. The eligible veteran or family member may receive payment of the fee charged for the test or $2,000, whichever is less. *The tests must be approved for VA benefits.*

If an individual is seeking a college degree, the school must admit him or her to a degree program by the start of the third term.

Restrictions on Training

- Bartending and personality development courses

- Non-accredited independent study courses

- Any course given by radio

- Self-improvement courses such as reading, speaking, woodworking, basic seamanship, and English as a second language

- Any course which is avocational or recreational in character

- Farm cooperative courses

- Audited courses

- Courses not leading to an educational, professional, or vocational objective

- Courses an individual has previously taken and successfully completed

- Courses taken by a Federal government employee under the Government Employees' Training Act

- Courses paid for in whole or in part by the Armed Forces while on active duty

- Courses taken while in receipt of benefits for the same program from the Office of Workers' Compensation Programs

The VA must reduce benefits for individuals in Federal, State or local prisons after being convicted of a felony.

An individual may not receive benefits for a program at a proprietary school if he or she is an owner or official of the school.

Part-Time Training

Individuals unable to attend school full-time should consider going part-time. Benefit rates and entitlement charges are less than the full-time rates. For example, if a student receives full-time benefits for 12 months, the entitlement charge is 12 months. However, if the student receives ½ time benefits for 12 months, the charge is 6 months. VA will pay for less than ½ time training if the student is not receiving Tuition Assistance for those courses.

Remedial, Deficiency And Refresher Training

Remedial and deficiency courses are intended to assist a student in overcoming a deficiency in a particular area of study. In order for such courses to be approved, the courses must be deemed necessary for pursuit of a program of education.

Refresher training is for technological advances that occurred in a field of employment. The advance must have occurred while the student was on active duty, or after release.

There is an entitlement charge for these courses.

Tutorial Assistance

Students may receive a special allowance for individual tutoring if they entered school at one-half time or more. To qualify, the student must have a deficiency in a subject. The school must certify the tutor's qualifications, and the hours of tutoring. Eligible students may receive a maximum monthly payment of $100.00. The maximum total benefit payable is $1,200.00.

There is no entitlement charge for the first $600.00 of tutorial assistance.

To apply for tutorial assistance, students must submit VA Form 22-1990t, Application and Enrollment Certification for Individualized Tutorial Assistance. The form should be given to the certifying official in the office handling VA paperwork at the school for completion.

Months of Benefits / Entitlement Charged

> *Individuals are charged one full day of entitlement for each day of full-time benefits paid.*

Eligible members may be entitled to receive up to 36 months of VEAP benefits. Usually, the number of monthly payments for full-time training is the same as the number of months an individual contributed to VEAP.

Benefits are generally payable for 10 years following a veteran's release from active duty.

Individuals qualifying for more than one VA education program may receive a maximum of 48 months of benefits. For example, if a student used 30 months of Dependents' Educational Assistance, and is eligible for chapter 1606 benefits, he or she could have a maximum of 18 months of entitlement remaining.

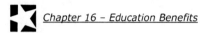

Individuals are charged one full day of entitlement for each day of full-time benefits paid.

For correspondence and flight training, one month of entitlement is charged each time VA pays one month of benefits. For cooperative programs, one month of entitlement is used for each month of benefits paid.

For apprenticeship and job training programs, the entitlement charge changes every 6 months. During the first 6 months, the charge is 75% of full time. For the second 6 months, the charge is 55% of full time. For the remainder of the program, the charge is 35% of full time.

Rates of Educational Assistance Pay

The total dollar amount of VEAP benefits is:

- An individual's total contributions, plus

- Matching funds equal to 2 times the individual's contributions, plus

- Any additional contributions or kickers made by the Department of Defense

The amount of money an individual receives each month depends on the type of training and the training time.

Institutional Training:

The monthly benefit payment will vary depending on the amount and number of contributions. Divide the total contributions by the number of months contributed, and this equals the full-time institutional rate.

> Example:
>
> **Step 1:**
> $1,800   individual contributions
> +3,600   matching funds (2 times individual contribution)
> + -0- kicker
> _____
> $5,400   TOTAL ENTITLEMENT
>
> **Step 2:**
> $5,400 divided by 36 months of contributions = $150 monthly full-time institutional rate
>
> (No amount in excess of an individual's total entitlement can be paid.)

Correspondence Training

An individual can be reimbursed for the entire established charges paid for a correspondence course. However, no amount in excess of an individual's total entitlement can be paid.

Flight Training

Individuals taking flight training will receive 60% of the approved charges for the course, including solo hours. (VA does not pay for solo hours before October 1, 1992.) No amount in excess of an individual's total entitlement can be paid.

Apprenticeship or Job Training

The monthly benefit amount is:

- 75% of the full-time rate for the first 6 months of training;
- 55% of the full-time rate for the second 6 months of training;
- 35% of the full-time rate for the rest of the training.

Monthly payments are reduced if an individual works less than 120 hours a month.

Cooperative Training

Individuals may receive payment at 80% of the rate to which he or she is entitled for institutional training.

Eligibility Periods

Benefits end 10 years from the date of the individual's last discharge or release from active duty.

VA can extend the 10-year period by the amount of time a service member was prevented from training during the period due to a disability or being held by a foreign government or power.

VA may extend the 10-year period if the individual reenters active duty for 90 days or more after becoming eligible. The extension ends 10 years from the date of discharge or release from the later period. Periods of active duty of less than 90 days can qualify for extensions only if discharge or release was due to:

> *Benefits end 10 years from the date of the individual's last discharge or release from active duty.*

- A service-connected disability; or
- A medical condition existing before active duty; or
- Hardship; or
- A reduction in force.

If a discharge is upgraded by the military, the 10-year period begins on the date of the upgrade.

Miscellaneous Information

- Any change in educational, professional or vocational objectives is considered a *"change of program."* The law permits one change of program without prior VA approval, provided an individual's attendance, conduct and progress in the last program were satisfactory. Additional *"changes of program"* require prior VA approval. VA will not charge a *change of program* if the individual enrolls in a new program after successful completion of the immediately preceding program.

- Once an individual starts receiving benefits, he must maintain satisfactory attendance, conduct and progress. The VA may stop benefits if an individual does not meet the standards set by the school. VA may later resume benefits if the individual reenters the same program at the same school, and the school approves the reentry, and certifies it to VA.

- If the individual does not reenter the same program at the same school, VA may resume benefits if the cause of unsatisfactory attendance, conduct or progress has been removed; and the program that the student intends to pursue is suitable to his or her abilities, aptitudes and interests.

- **Effective November 1, 2000,** VA education benefits can be paid (with some exceptions) for school breaks, if the breaks do not exceed 8 weeks; and the terms before and after the breaks are not shorter than the break. Prior to November 1 2000, VA education benefits could be paid only if the breaks did not exceed a calendar month.

Application For Benefits

When the individual finds a school, program, company, apprenticeship or job-training program, there are two important steps that must be followed:

1. Make sure the program is approved for VA training. Contact the local VA regional office if there are any questions.
2. Compete VA Form 22-1990, Application for Education Benefits. The completed form should be sent to the VA regional office with jurisdiction over the State where training will occur. (See the following section for Areas of VA jurisdiction.) Individuals not on active duty should send copy 4 of Form DD-214 along with the completed VA Form 22-1990.

Following receipt of an application, VA will review it and advise if anything else is needed.

If an individual has started training, the application and Notice of Basic Eligibility should be taken to the school, employer or union. The certifying official should complete VA Form 22-1999, Enrollment Certification, and send all the forms to VA.

Areas Of VA Jurisdiction

Eastern VA
Regional Office
PO Box 4616
Buffalo, NY
14240-4616

Connecticut
Delaware
District of Columbia
Maine
Maryland
Massachusetts
New Hampshire
New Jersey
New York
Ohio
Pennsylvania
Rhode Island
Vermont
Virginia
West Virginia
Foreign Schools

California
Hawaii
Idaho
Louisiana
New Mexico
Nevada
Oklahoma
Oregon
Philippines
Texas
Utah
Washington
American Samoa
Guam
Midway
Wake Island
Any of the islands in
the Federated
States of the
Marshall Islands,
the Republic of
Micronesia, or the
Republic of Palau

Southern VA
Regional Office
PO Box 100022
Decatur, GA 30031-7022

Alabama
Florida
Georgia
Mississippi
North Carolina
Puerto Rico
South Carolina
U.S. Virgin Islands

Western VA
Regional Office
PO Box 8888
Muskogee, OK
74402-8888

Alaska
Arizona
Arkansas

Central VA
Regional Office
PO Box 66830
St. Louis, MO
63166-6830

Colorado
Illinois
Indiana
Iowa
Kansas
Kentucky
Michigan
Minnesota
Missouri
Montana
Nebraska
North Dakota
South Dakota
Tennessee
Wisconsin
Wyoming

Procedures For Receipt of Monthly Payments

After selecting a school and submitting an application to VA, the school official must complete an enrollment certification, and submit it to the appropriate VA regional office. If a student meets the basic eligibility requirements for benefits, and the program or course is approved, VA will process the enrollment based on certified training time.

If a student is enrolled in a degree program at a college or university, he or she will receive payment after the first of each month for the training during the preceding month. If a student is enrolled in a certificate or diploma program at a business, technical, or vocational school, he or she will not receive payment until they have verified their attendance. Students will receive a *Student Verification of Enrollment Form 22-8979* each month, and must complete and return it to the appropriate VA regional office. After processing, VA will release a check.

If an individual is in an apprenticeship or job-training program, he or she will receive a form to report the hours worked each month. The form must be signed and given to the certifying official for the company or union. The certifying official must complete the form and send it to the appropriate VA regional office. After processing, VA will release a check.

If an individual is taking a correspondence course, he or she will receive a form each quarter, on which the student must show the number of lessons completed that quarter. The completed form should be sent to the school for certification of the number of lessons serviced during the quarter. The school will send the form to the appropriate VA regional office. After processing, VA will release a check. Payments are based on the number of lessons serviced by the school.

VA will send flight schools a supply of blank monthly certification of flight training forms. The school must complete the form by entering the number of hours, the hourly rate, and the total charges for flight training received during the month. The student should review and sign the completed form, and send it to the appropriate VA regional office. After processing, VA will release a check.

NOTE: It is against the law for schools to cash VA checks under a Power of Attorney Agreement.

Timely Receipt of Verification Forms And Checks

Once a completed verification form has been submitted, the student should receive a check within 2 weeks. If a check is not received by then, the VA should immediately be contacted so that appropriate action can be taken.

> *Once a completed verification form has been submitted, the student should receive a check within 2 weeks. If a check is not received by then, the VA should immediately be contacted so that appropriate action can be taken.*

Students taking courses leading to a degree at a college or university should receive their checks for each month by the fifth of the next month. If it is not received by then, the VA should be immediately contacted so that appropriate action can be taken.

Students taking courses leading to a certificate or diploma from a business, technical, or vocational school should receive their verification forms for each month by the fifth of the following month. If it is not received by then, the VA should be immediately contacted so that another form can be issued.

Advance Payments

An advance payment for the initial month, or partial month and the following month may be made, if:

- The school agrees to handle advance payments; and
- Training is one-half time or more; and
- A request is made by the individual in writing; and
- The VA receives the enrollment certification at least 30 days prior to the start of classes.

Advance payments are made out to the individual, and sent to the applicable school for delivery to the individual registration. VA cannot issue a check more than 30 days before classes start. Before requesting an advance payment, students should verify with the school certifying official that the school has agreed to process advance payments.

Requests for advance payments must be on VA Form 22-1999, Enrollment Certification, or a sheet of paper attached to the enrollment certification.

Once a student receives an advance payment at registration, the school must certify to VA that the student received the check. If a student reduces enrollment, or withdraws from all courses during the period covered by an advance payment, he or she must repay the overpayment to VA.

If an individual believes that the amount of a VA check is incorrect, the VA should be contacted before the check is cashed.

Direct Deposit

Payments can be sent directly to a student's savings or checking account through Direct Deposit (Electronic Funds Transfer). To sign up for direct deposit by phone, students must call 1-877-838-2778.

Student Responsibilities

To ensure timely receipt of correct payments, students should be sure to promptly notify the VA of:

- Any change in enrollment
- Any change in address

In addition, students should use reasonable judgment when accepting and cashing a check. All letters from VA about monthly rates and effective dates should be read carefully. If a student thinks the amount of a VA check is wrong, VA should be contacted *before* cashing the check. Any incorrect checks should be returned to VA.

If a student cashes a check for the wrong amount, he or she will be liable for repayment of any resulting overpayment.

Recovery of Overpayments

VA must take prompt and aggressive action to recover overpayments. Students have the right to request a waiver of the overpayment, or verification that the amount is correct. If an overpayment is not repaid or waived, VA may add interest and collection fees to the debt. VA may also take one or more of the following actions to collect the debt:

- Withhold future benefits to apply to the debt;
- Refer the debt to a private collection agency;
- Recover the debt from any Federal income tax refund;
- Recover the debt from the salary (if student is a Federal employee);
- File a lawsuit in Federal court to collect the debt;
- Withhold approval of a VA home loan guarantee.

An individual's reserve component will act to collect penalties caused by unsatisfactory participation in the reserve.

Changes in Enrollment

If a student withdraws from one or more courses after the end of the school's drop period, VA will reduce or stop benefits on the date of reduction or withdrawal. Unless the student can show that the change was due to *mitigating circumstances*, the student may have to repay **all** benefits for the course.

VA defines *mitigating circumstances* as "unavoidable and unexpected events that directly interfere with the pursuit of a course, and which are beyond the student's control.

Examples of reasons VA may accept include:

- Extended illness;
- Severe illness or death in immediate family;
- Unscheduled changes in employment; and
- Lack of child care.

Examples of reasons VA may not accept include:

- Withdrawal to avoid a failing grade;
- Dislike of the instructor; and
- Too many courses attempted.

(VA may ask the student to furnish evidence to support the reason for change, such as physician or employer written statements.)

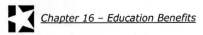

The first time a student withdraws from up to 6 credit hours, VA will "excuse" the withdrawal, and pay benefits for the period attended.

If a student receives a grade that does not count toward graduation, all benefits for the course may have to be repaid.

If a student receives a non-punitive grade, the school will notify VA, and VA may reduce or stop benefits. The student may not have to repay the benefits if he or she can show that the grades were due to mitigating circumstances.

Work-Study Programs

Students may be eligible for an additional allowance under a work-study program that allows students to perform work for VA in return for an hourly wage. Students may perform outreach services under VA supervision, prepare and process VA paperwork, work at a VA medical facility or National Cemetery, or perform other approved activities.

Students must attend school at the three-quarter of full-time rate.

VA will select students for the work-study program based on different factors. Such factors include:

- Disability of the student;
- Ability of the student to complete the work-study contract before the end of his or her eligibility for education benefits;
- Job availability within normal commuting distance to the student.

VA will give the highest priority to a veteran who has a service-connected disability or disabilities rated by VA at 30% or more

The number of applicants selected will depend on the availability of VA-related work at the school or at VA facilities in the area.

Students may work during or between periods of enrollment, and can arrange with VA to work any number of hours during his or her enrollment. However, the maximum number of hours a student may work is 25 times the number of weeks in the enrollment period.

Students will earn an hourly wage equal to the Federal or State minimum wage, whichever is greater. If a student works at a college or university, the school *may* pay the difference between the amount VA pays and the amount the school normally pays other work-study students doing the same job.

Students interested in taking part in a work-study program must complete VA Form 22,8691, Application for Work-Study Allowance. Completed forms should be sent to the nearest VA regional office.

Educational Counseling

VA can provide services to help eligible individuals understand their educational and vocational strengths and weaknesses and to plan:

- An educational or training goal, and the means by which the goal can be reached; or

- An employment goal for which an individual qualifies on the basis of present training or experience.

VA can also help plan an effective job search.

Counseling is available for:

- Service members eligible for VA educational assistance; or

- Service members on active duty and within 180 days of discharge; or

- Veterans with discharges that are not dishonorable, who are within one year from date of discharge.

Vocational Rehabilitation

Vocational rehabilitation helps disabled veterans become independent in daily living. Veterans may also receive assistance in selecting, preparing for, and securing employment that is compatible with their interests, talents, skills, physical capabilities, and goals.

Veterans may qualify for Training and Rehabilitation under Chapter 31 of Title 38, United States Code, if:

> *Vocational rehabilitation helps disabled veterans become independent in daily living. Veterans may also receive assistance in selecting, preparing for, and securing employment that is compatible with their interests, talents, skills, physical capabilities, and goals.*

- The veteran has a service-connected disability or disabilities rated by VA at 20% or more; and

- The veteran received a discharge from active duty that was not dishonorable; and

- The veteran has an employment handicap.

Veterans may also qualify with a service-connected disability or disabilities rated by VA at 10%, and:

- The veteran has a serious employment handicap; or

- The veteran first applied for vocational rehabilitation benefits before November 1, 1990, reapplied after that date, and has an employment handicap.

To apply for vocational rehabilitation, VA for 28-1900, Disabled Veterans Application for Vocational Rehabilitation, must be completed and sent to the nearest VA regional office.

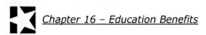

For detailed information on vocational rehabilitation, refer to Chapter 14 of this book.

Refund of VEAP Benefits

If a service member does not wish to use his or her VEAP benefits, he or she must apply to the nearest VA regional office for a refund of his or her contributions.

Appeal of VA Decision

VA decisions on education benefits may be appealed within one year of the date an individual receives notice of a VA decision.

For detailed information on filing an appeal, please refer to Chapter 35 of this book.

EDUCATIONAL AND ASSISTANCE TEST PROGRAM (SECTION 901)

This program was included as part of the "Department of Defense Authorization Act of 1981". The test program is funded by the Department of Defense, and administered by the VA. "Section 901" has been used to identify the program since its inception. However, the title "chapter 107" may also be used.

Section 901 is a noncontributory program in which an eligible participant, or in some cases his or her dependent(s), may receive an educational assistance and subsistence allowance while training at an accredited institution.

Basic eligibility to section 901 benefits was limited to a small group of servicepersons who enlisted between September 30, 1980 and October 1, 1981, met strict guidelines and were selected by the Department of Defense. The Waco Regional Office processes all section 901 payments.

EDUCATIONAL ASSISTANCE PILOT PROGRAM (SECTION 903)

Section 903 is a modified Chapter 32 (VEAP) program, in which the Service Department makes the individual's monthly contributions. Eligibility was limited to a small group of participants, selected by the service department, who enlisted between November 30, 1980 and October 1, 1981. Individuals must have been selected for the pilot program.

SURVIVORS' AND DEPENDENTS EDUCATIONAL ASSISTANCE PROGRAM (DEA) – CHAPTER 35

The Survivors' and Dependents Educational Assistance Program (DEA) was enacted by Congress to provide education and training opportunities to eligible dependents of certain veterans. The program offers up to 45 months of education benefits.

ELIGIBILITY REQUIREMENTS

To qualify, one must be the son, daughter or spouse of:

- A veteran who died, or is permanently and totally disabled as the result of a service-connected disability, which arose out of active service in the Armed Forces.

- A veteran who died from any cause while such service-connected disability was in existence.

- A service member who is missing in action or captured in the line of duty by a hostile force.

- A service member who is being forcibly detained or interned in the line of duty by a foreign power.

- A service member who is hospitalized or receiving outpatient treatment for a service connected permanent and total disability and is likely to be discharged for that disability. This change is effective December 23, 2006.

Important update for service members who are hospitalized or receiving outpatient medical care <u>before their discharge for a total and permanent service-connected disability.</u>

Section 301 of Public Law 109-461 adds a new category to the definition of "eligible person" for DEA benefits . The new category includes the spouse or child of a person who:

- VA determines has a service-connected permanent and total disability; and

- at the time of VA's determination is a member of the Armed Forces who is hospitalized or receiving outpatient medical care, services, or treatment; and

- is likely to be discharged or released from service for this service-connected disability.

Persons eligible under this new provision may be eligible for DEA benefits effective December 23, 2006, the effective date of the law.

ELIGIBILITY PERIOD: SON OR DAUGHTER

As a son or daughter (including stepchild or adopted child), as long as the individual has entitlement left, he or she may generally receive benefits under this program from age 18 to 26 (8 years).

However, in certain instances, benefits may begin before age 18 and continue after age 26. In some instances, the individual may choose among possible beginning dates.

Effect of Active Duty on Eligibility

Following are the effects of active duty on an individual's period of eligibility. (See also **Effect of Active Duty on Entitlement.**)

- Individuals may not receive DEA benefits while on active duty in the Armed Forces.

- To receive DEA benefits after military service, discharge must not be under dishonorable conditions.

- The eligibility period can generally extend for eight years from the date of the individual's first unconditional release from active duty, if his or her service was between ages 18 and 26. But this extension can't go beyond the individual's 31st birthday.

- If, on or after September 11, 2001, an individual is called to active duty under title 10, or if he or she was involuntarily ordered to full-time National Guard duty under section 502 (f) of title 32 (State authority), in most cases VA can extend the eligibility period for DEA by the number of months and days spent on active duty plus four months. This extension may go beyond the 31st birthday, depending on the facts in the claim.

Other Extensions of The Eligibility Period

Circumstances Beyond An Individual's Control

If evidence is provided that training had to stop because of conditions beyond an individual's control, in some cases VA can extend eligibility for the period he or she had to stop training.

Circumstances that may be considered beyond control (if verified by evidence) include:

- Service in an official missionary capacity;

- Immediate family or financial obligations that require the individual to stop training, for example, to take employment;

- Unavoidable conditions of employment that require the individual to stop training;

- The individual's illness or death; or illness in his or her immediate family.

In Training When Eligibility Ends

If an individual is enrolled in training when eligibility ends, in most cases VA can extend his or her eligibility to the end of the semester or quarter, or to the end of twelve weeks if the course isn't operated on a semester or quarter basis.

Marriage

As a son or daughter, marriage doesn't affect the period of eligibility.

ELIGIBILITY PERIOD: SPOUSE

If a spouse is eligible because the veteran has a permanent and total service-connected disability, benefits generally end 10 years from one of the following dates:

- Effective date of the veteran's permanent and total disability evaluation;
- Date VA notifies the veteran of the permanent and total disability evaluation;
- Beginning date chosen by the spouse, between the date the spouse become eligible and the date VA notifies the veteran of the permanent and total disability evaluation.

2008 UPDATE:

If the VA rated the veteran permanently and totally disabled with an effective date of 3 years from discharge a spouse will remain eligible for 20 years from the effective date of the rating. This change is effective October 10, 2008 and no benefits may be paid for any training taken prior to that date.

Service member held captive or missing

If a spouse is eligible because the veteran or service member is being held or is missing, as:

- A prisoner of war;
- Missing in action; or
- Forcibly held by a foreign government or power;

His or her 10-year period of eligibility begins on the 91st day after the date the service member was listed as a captive or missing.

If the veteran or service member is released from captivity, or is determined to be alive and no longer missing, the spouse's period of eligibility ends on that date. If the spouse is enrolled in training on that date, his or her eligibility may be extended to the end of the term or course.

Veteran Died on Active Duty

If a spouse is eligible because the veteran died on active duty, his or her eligibility period is 20 years from the date of death.

Effect of Active Duty on Eligibility

Following are the effects of active duty on the eligibility period:

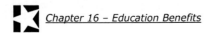

- Individuals may not receive DEA benefits while on active duty in the Armed Forces.
- To receive DEA benefits after military service, his or her discharge must not be under dishonorable conditions.
- If, on or after September 11, 2001, the individual was called to active duty under title 10, or involuntarily ordered to full-time National Guard duty under section 502 (f) of title 32 (State authority), in most cases VA can extend the eligibility period for DEA by the number of months and days spent on active duty plus four months.

Effect of Divorce on Eligibility

If marriage to the veteran ends in divorce, the spouse's eligibility for DEA benefits ends on that date. But if he or she is in training, and the divorce occurs through no fault of him or her, VA can extend the eligibility as explained in the next section under ***While in Training.***

Extensions of Eligibility Period

Disability

VA may be able to extend the 10-year eligibility period by the amount of time the spouse was prevented from training during that period because of a disability he or she incurred.

While in Training

If the spouse is enrolled in training when his or her eligibility ends, in most cases VA can extend eligibility to the end of the semester or quarter, or to the end of twelve weeks if the course isn't operated on a semester or quarter basis.

Effect of Remarriage

<u>**Before age 57:**</u>

- If a surviving spouse remarries before age 57, his or her eligibility ends on the date of remarriage.
- If an individual remarried after November 30, 1999, and the remarriage ends, VA may reinstate eligibility to DEA. The remarriage must be ended by death, divorce, or because the individual stopped living with his or her spouse and stopped holding him or herself out to the public as the person's spouse.
- If a surviving spouse remarried after October 31, 1990, but before November 30, 1999, VA can't reinstate eligibility, even if remarriage ends.

<u>**After age 57:**</u>

- If a surviving spouse remarries on or after January 1, 2004, and is 57 or older, he or she can still be eligible for DEA benefits.

- (If the surviving spouse remarried after age 57 and before December 16, 2003, **he or she must have applied in writing before December 16, 2004,** for eligibility to be reinstated.)

Note: Remarrying after age 57 doesn't extend the 10-year period of eligibility that was established before remarriage.

Example: A surviving spouse established eligibility for a 10-year period ending on November 15, 2005, which is 10 years from the date of the veteran's death. She remarried in April 2004 at age 58. She will keep her eligibility for DEA through November 15, 2005.

MONTHS OF BENEFITS PAYABLE

The following applies to sons and daughters (including stepchildren and adopted children), spouses and surviving spouses.

Individuals may be entitled to receive up to 45 months of DEA benefits. They may receive a maximum of 48 months of benefits combined if they are eligible under more than one VA education program.

Individuals are charged one full day for each day of full-time benefits paid. Entitlement is charged in months and days. Each month is counted as 30 days. If he or she trains part-time, VA adjusts the entitlement charge according to the training time

Effect of Active Duty on Available Months of Benefits

- If an individual is called up to active duty under title 10 (federal authority) while he or she is receiving benefits, and has to drop out of school without receiving credit, VA will restore (give back) the months of benefits used for that period of training.

- If called up under title 32 (State authority), VA can't restore the months of benefits used.

Pension, Compensation, and DIC Programs

A son or daughter who is eligible for Chapter 35 benefits, as well as pension, compensation, or Dependency & Indemnity Compensation (DIC) based on school attendance, must elect which benefit to receive. An election of Chapter 35 benefits is a bar to further payment of pension, compensation, or DIC after the age of 18.

NOTE: If a program will last longer than 45 months, the son or daughter may find it to his or her advantage to defer Chapter 35 benefits. He or she could continue to receive pension, compensation, or DIC benefits which are payable as a result of school attendance. *The VA strongly encourages individuals who qualify for more than one type of education benefit to discuss their education plans with a Veterans Benefits Counselor so that all options can be explored, and maximum benefits can be paid.*

Approved Courses

A State agency or VA must approve each program offered by a school or company.

Individuals may receive benefits for a wide variety of training, including:

- Undergraduate degrees from a college or university

- Graduate degrees from a college or university

- Cooperative training programs

- Accredited independent study programs leading to a college degree

- Courses leading to a certificate or diploma from business, technical, or vocational schools

- Apprenticeship or job training program offered by a company or union

- Correspondence courses (spouses only)

- Farm cooperative courses

- Secondary school programs for individuals who are not high school graduates

- Secondary school deficiency or remedial courses to qualify for admission to an educational institution

- Effective November 1, 2000, persons eligible for DEA can receive benefits for VA-approved preparation courses for college and graduate school entrance exams. (The law also allows children to pursue these courses before age 18.)

- Effective March 1, 2001, benefits may be payable for licensing or certification tests. The tests are those needed to enter, maintain, or advance into employment in a civilian vocation or profession. The eligible veteran or family member may receive payment of the fee charged for the test or $2,000, whichever is less. *The tests must be approved for VA benefits.* Contact the VA for a complete list of approved certification tests.

VA may approve programs offered by institutions outside of the United States, when they are pursued at educational institutions of higher learning, and lead to a college degree. Individuals must receive VA approval prior to attending or enrolling in any foreign programs.

An eligible son or daughter who is handicapped by a physical or mental disability that prevents pursuit of an educational program may receive Special Restorative Training. This may involve speech and voice correction, language retraining, lip reading, auditory training, Braille reading and writing, etc.

An eligible spouse or son or daughter over age 14 who is handicapped by a physical or mental disability that prevents pursuit of an educational program may receive Specialized Vocational Training. This includes specialized courses, alone or in combination with other courses, leading to a vocational objective that is suitable for the person and required by reason of physical or mental handicap.

> *A State agency or VA must approve each program offered by a school or company.*

If an individual is seeking a college degree, the school must admit the individual to a degree program by the start of the individual's third term.

Restrictions on Training

Benefits are not payable for the following courses:

- Non-accredited independent study courses
- Bartending and personality development courses
- Correspondence courses (if you are a dependent or surviving child)
- Any course given by radio
- Vocational flight training
- Self-improvement courses such as reading, speaking, woodworking, basic seamanship, and English as a 2nd language
- Any course which is avocational or recreational in character
- Audited courses
- Courses not leading to an educational, professional, or vocational objective
- Courses previously taken and successfully completed
- Courses taken by a Federal government employee under the Government Employee's Training Act
- Courses taken while in receipt of benefits for the same program from the Office of Workers' Compensation Programs

VA must reduce benefits for individuals in Federal, State, or local prisons after being convicted of a felony.

An individual may not receive benefits for a program at a proprietary school if her or she is an owner or official of the school.

An individual may not receive benefits under this program while serving on active duty in the Armed Forces.

Part-Time Training

Individuals unable to attend school full-time should consider going part-time. Benefit rates and entitlement charges are less than the full-time rates. For example, if a student receives full-time benefits for 12 months, the entitlement charge is 12 months. However, if the student receives ½ time benefits for 12 months, the charge is 6 months. VA will pay for less than ½ time training if the student is not receiving Tuition Assistance for those courses.

Remedial, Deficiency and Refresher Training

Remedial and deficiency courses are intended to assist a student in overcoming a deficiency in a particular area of study.

Refresher training is available only at the elementary or secondary level. It is for reviewing or updating material previously covered in a course satisfactorily completed.

There is no entitlement charge for these courses for the first 5 months of training.

Tutorial Assistance

Students may receive a special allowance for individual tutoring performed after September 30, 1992, if they entered school at one-half time or more. To qualify, the student must have a deficiency in a subject. The school must certify the tutor's qualifications, and the hours of tutoring. Eligible students may receive a maximum monthly payment of $100.00. The maximum total benefit payable is $1,200.00.

There is no entitlement charge for the first $600.00 of tutorial assistance.

To apply for tutorial assistance, students must submit VA Form 22-1990t, Application and Enrollment Certification for Individualized Tutorial Assistance. The form should be given to the certifying official in the office handling VA paperwork at the school for completion.

Rates of Educational Assistance

The following basic monthly rates are effective October 1, 2010:

Basic Monthly Rates Survivors' And Dependents Educational Assistance Program (DEA)

Type of Training	Full-Time	Three-Quarter Time	One-Half Time	Less than ½ Time, But More Than ¼ Time	One-Quarter Time
Institutional	$936.00	$702.00	$466.00	Tuition & Fees, not to exceed $466.00	Tuition & Fees, not to exceed $234.00
Farm Cooperative Training	$753.00	$565.00	$466.00		
Correspondence Training	Entitlement charged at the rate of one month for each $936.00 paid.				
Apprenticeship On-The-Job Training -	First six months: $682.00 Second six months: $511.00 Third six months: $337.00 Remainder of program: $170.00				
Special Restorative Training:	$936.00				
Accelerated Charges: Cost of Tuition & Fees in Excess of:	$290.00				
Entitlement Reduced 1 Day For Each	$31.20 (1/30th of Full-Time Rate)				

Change of Program

Any change in educational, professional or vocational objectives is considered a *"change of program."* VA will not charge a change of program when a student enrolls in a new program, provided he or she successfully completed the immediately preceding program.

Spouse, Widow or Widower of Veteran

A spouse, widow, or widower of a veteran may make one change of program without prior VA approval if attendance, conduct, and progress in the last program were satisfactory. VA may approve additional changes if the proposed programs are suitable to the student's abilities, aptitudes, and interests.

Child of Veteran

VA may approve a change of program for sons or daughters if it finds that the new program is suitable to the student's abilities, aptitudes, and interests.

Attendance, Conduct and Progress

Once an individual starts receiving benefits, he must maintain satisfactory attendance, conduct and progress. The VA may stop benefits if an individual does not meet the standards set by the school. VA may later resume benefits if the individual reenters the same program at the same school, and the school approves the reentry, and certifies it to VA.

If the individual does not reenter the same program at the same school, VA may resume benefits if the cause of unsatisfactory attendance, conduct or progress has been removed; and the program that the student intends to pursue is suitable to his or her abilities, aptitudes and interests.

Application For Benefits

When the individual finds a school, company or apprenticeship, there are two important steps that must be followed:

1. Make sure the program is approved for VA training. Contact the local VA regional office if there are any questions.

2. Compete VA Form 22-5490, Application for Survivors' and Dependents' Educational Assistance. The completed form should be sent to the VA regional office with jurisdiction over the State where training will occur. Sons or daughters under legal age must have the application signed by a parent or guardian. Sons or daughters of age can apply alone.

Following receipt of an application, VA will review it and advise if anything else is needed.

If an individual has started training, the application and Notice of Basic Eligibility should be taken to the school, employer or union. The certifying official should complete VA Form 22-1999, Enrollment Certification, and send all the forms to VA.

Procedures For Receipt of Monthly Payments

After selecting a school and submitting an application to VA, the school official must complete an enrollment certification, and submit it to the appropriate VA regional office. If a student meets the basic eligibility requirements for benefits, and the program or course is approved, VA will process the enrollment based on certified training time.

If a student is enrolled in a degree program at a college or university, he or she will receive payment after the first of each month for the training during the preceding month. If a student is enrolled in a certificate or diploma program at a business, technical, or vocational school, he or she will not receive payment until they have verified their attendance. Students will receive a *Student Verification of Enrollment Form 22-8979* each month, and must complete and return it to the appropriate VA regional office. After processing, VA will release a check.

If an individual is in an apprenticeship or job-training program, he or she will receive a form to report the hours worked each month. The form must be signed and given to the certifying official for the company or union. The certifying official must complete the form and send it to the appropriate VA regional office. After processing, VA will release a check.

If an individual is taking a correspondence course, he or she will receive a form each quarter, on which the student must show the number of lessons completed that quarter. The completed form should be sent to the school for certification of the number of lessons serviced during the quarter. The school will send the form to the appropriate VA regional office. After processing, VA will release a check. Payments are based on the number of lessons serviced by the school.

NOTE: It is against the law for schools to cash VA checks under a Power of Attorney Agreement.

Effective November 1, 2000, VA education benefits can be paid (with some exceptions) for school breaks, if the breaks do not exceed 8 weeks; and the terms before and after the breaks are not shorter than the break. Prior to November 1 2000, VA education benefits could be paid only if the breaks did not exceed a calendar month.

Timely Receipt of Verification Forms And Checks

Students taking courses leading to a degree at a college or university should receive their checks for each month by the fifth of the next month. If it is not received by then, the VA should be immediately contacted so that appropriate action can be taken.

Students taking courses leading to a certificate or diploma from a business, technical, or vocational school should receive their verification forms for each month by the fifth of the following month. If it is not received by then, the VA should be immediately contacted so that another form can be issued.

One a completed verification form has been submitted, the student should receive a check within 2 weeks. If a check is not received by then, the VA should immediately be contacted so that appropriate action can be taken.

Advance Payments

An advance payment for the initial month, or partial month and the following month may be made, if:

- The school agrees to handle advance payments; and
- Training is one-half time or more; and
- A request is made by the individual in writing; and
- The VA receives the enrollment certification at least 30 days prior to the start of classes.

Requests for advance payments must be on VA Form 22-1999, Enrollment Certification, or a sheet of paper attached to the enrollment certification.

Advance payments are made out to the individual, and sent to the applicable school for delivery to the individual registration. VA cannot issue a check more than 30 days before classes start.

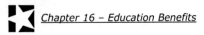

Before requesting an advance payment, students should verify with the school certifying official that the school has agreed to process advance payments.

Requests for advance payments must be on VA Form 22-1999, Enrollment Certification, or a sheet of paper attached to the enrollment certification.

Once a student receives an advance payment at registration, the school must certify to VA that the student received the check. If a student reduces enrollment, or withdraws from all courses during the period covered by an advance payment, he or she must repay the overpayment to VA.

If an individual believes that the amount of a VA check is incorrect, the VA should be contacted before the check is cashed.

Direct Deposit

Payments can be sent directly to a student's savings or checking account through Direct Deposit (Electronic Funds Transfer). To sign up for direct deposit by phone, students must call 1-877-838-2778.

Student Responsibilities

To ensure timely receipt of correct payments, students should be sure to promptly notify the VA of:

- Any change in enrollment;

- Any change in address;

- Any change in marital status (separation from the veteran, divorce from the veteran, or remarriage following the death of the veteran).

In addition, students should use reasonable judgment when accepting and cashing a check. All letters from VA about monthly rates and effective dates should be read carefully. If a student thinks the amount of a VA check is wrong,

VA should be contacted **before** cashing the check. Any incorrect checks should be returned to VA.

If a student cashes a check for the wrong amount, he or she will be liable for repayment of any resulting overpayment.

Recovery of Overpayments

VA must take prompt and aggressive action to recover overpayments. Students have the right to request a waiver of the overpayment, or verification that the amount is correct. If an overpayment is not repaid or waived, VA may add interest and collection fees to the debt. VA may also take one or more of the following actions to collect the debt:

- Withhold future benefits to apply to the debt;

- Refer the debt to a private collection agency;

- Recover the debt from any Federal income tax refund;

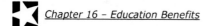

- Recover the debt from the salary (if student is a Federal employee);
- File a lawsuit in Federal court to collect the debt;
- Withhold approval of a VA home loan guarantee.

Changes in Enrollment

If a student withdraws from one or more courses after the end of the school's drop period, VA will reduce or stop benefits on the date of reduction or withdrawal. Unless the student can show that the change was due to *mitigating circumstances*, the student may have to repay **all** benefits for the course.

VA defines *mitigating circumstances* as "unavoidable and unexpected events that directly interfere with the pursuit of a course, and which are beyond the student's control.

Examples of reasons VA may accept include:

- Extended illness;
- Severe illness or death in immediate family;
- Unscheduled changes in employment; and
- Lack of child care.

Examples of reasons VA may not accept include:

- Withdrawal to avoid a failing grade;
- Dislike of the instructor; and
- Too many courses attempted.

(VA may ask the student to furnish evidence to support the reason for change, such as physician or employer written statements.)

The first time a student withdraws from up to 6 credit hours, VA will "excuse" the withdrawal, and pay benefits for the period attended.

If a student receives a grade that does not count toward graduation, all benefits for the course may have to be repaid.

If a student receives a non-punitive grade, the school will notify VA, and VA may reduce or stop benefits. The student may not have to repay the benefits if he or she can show that the grades were due to mitigating circumstances.

Work-Study Programs

Students may be eligible for an additional allowance under a work-study program that allows students to perform work for VA in return for an hourly wage. Students may perform outreach services under VA supervision, prepare and process VA paperwork, work at a VA medical facility or National Cemetery, or perform other approved activities.

Students must attend school at the three-quarter of full-time rate.

VA will select students for the work-study program based on different factors. Such factors include:

- Disability of the student;
- Ability of the student to complete the work-study contract before the end of his or her eligibility for education benefits;
- Job availability within normal commuting distance to the student;
- VA will give the highest priority to a veteran who has a service-connected disability or disabilities rated by VA at 30% or more.

The number of applicants selected will depend on the availability of VA-related work at the school or at VA facilities in the area.

Students may work during or between periods of enrollment, and can arrange with VA to work any number of hours during his or her enrollment. However, the maximum number of hours a student may work is 25 times the number of weeks in the enrollment period.

Students will earn an hourly wage equal to the Federal or State minimum wage, whichever is greater. If a student works at a college or university, the school **may** pay the difference between the amount VA pays and the amount the school normally pays other work-study students doing the same job.

Students interested in taking part in a work-study program must complete VA Form 22,8691, Application for Work-Study Allowance. Completed forms should be sent to the nearest VA regional office.

Educational Counseling

Upon request, VA will provide counseling services, including testing, to help qualified individuals:

- Select an educational, vocational, or professional objective;
- Develop a plan to achieve the above objective;
- Overcome any personal or academic problems that may interfere with the successful achievement of the stated objective.

Qualified VA personnel are available to provide counseling services free of charge to qualified individuals. Individuals must pay the cost of any travel to and from the place at which VA provides counseling.

VA requires and provides counseling for each disabled child who needs special services to pursue a program of education and for certain other eligible children.

VA requires and provides counseling for disabled spouses and those who need specialized programs of vocational training as a result of the handicapping effects of their disabilities.

Individuals should contact the nearest VA regional office to make counseling appointments.

Appeal of VA Decision

VA decisions on education benefits may be appealed within one year of the date an individual receives notice of a VA decision.

For detailed information on filing an appeal, please refer to Chapter 35 of this book.

RESTORED ENTITLEMENT PROGRAM FOR SURVIVORS (REPS)

The Restored Entitlement Program for Survivors (REPS) is authorized by Section 156 of Public Law 97-377. This program restores social security benefits that were reduced or terminated by Public Law 97-35, the Omnibus Budget Reconciliation Act of 1981. This act eliminated the "parent with child in care" benefit when a surviving spouse's last child in care attained age 16. REPS restores the benefit until the youngest child in care attains 18, unless entitled to another Social Security benefit of equal or greater value.

The REPS program is funded by the Department of Defense, based on Social Security rules, and administered by the VA.

REPS benefits are payable to certain spouses and children of veterans who died while on active duty before August 13, 1981, or died from disabilities incurred in active duty before August 13, 1981. If a surviving spouse remarries, his or her benefits are terminated. If the child in care leaves the parent's custody, marries or dies, REPS entitlement ends. REPS benefits are reduced by $1 for each $2 of earned income over the exempt amount for Social Security (announced by Social Security Administration at the beginning of each calendar year).

REPS benefits are payable to unmarried children between the ages of 18 and 22 who are full-time students at approved schools beyond the high school level. Benefits are awarded on a school year basis. Each year verification must be received before any additional benefits can be awarded. If the child marries or reduces to less than full-time attendance, benefits will be discontinued. If the child has earned income or wages, REPS benefits are reduced.
REPS benefits are not payable based on service in the commissioned corps of the National Oceanic and Atmospheric Administration, or the Public Health Service.

To apply for REPS benefits, VA Form 21-8924, Application of Surviving Spouse or Child for REPS Benefits must be completed and sent to the local VA regional VA office for basic eligibility determination.

Once completed, the application will be forwarded to the St. Louis office for processing. A *Student Beneficiary Report* is mailed to each student receiving

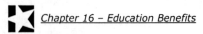

REPS benefits each March. The report confirms enrollment, and allows students to report any earnings.

For specific information, contact the nearest regional VA office.

VOCATIONAL REHABILITATION (CHAPTER 31)

This topic is discussed in detail in Chapter 14 of this book.

OMNIBUS DIPLOMATIC SECURITY AND ANTITERRORISM ACT

Public Law 99-399, The Omnibus Diplomatic Security and Antiterrorism Act of 91986 (the Antiterrorism Act) became effective January 21, 1981. This program is designed to provide educational assistance for persons held as captives, and their dependents.

Under this Act, VA may provide education benefits to:

- Former captives who were employees of the United States Government. Individuals providing personal services to the United States similar to that provided by civil service employees may also be eligible. This includes foreign nationals and resident aliens of the United States.

- Former captives taken during hostile action resulting from their relationship with the United States.

- Family members of individuals in captivity or individuals who die while in captivity.

VA will provide educational benefits to persons eligible under the Antiterrorism Act that are identical to those provided to eligible persons under Chapter 35 of title 38, U.S. Code (Survivors' and Dependents' Educational Assistance Program).

All inquiries regarding this Act should be directed to the nearest VA regional office.

CHAPTER 17

EDUCATION BENEFITS - MONTGOMERY G.I. BILL (MGIB), CHAPTER 30

ELIGIBILITY REQUIREMENTS

The Montgomery G.I. Bill (MGIB) establishes education benefits for four categories of individuals, based on active duty service. The benefits available under each category may vary depending on individual situations and lengths of active duty service. The eligibility requirements for each category are described below. However, the following two requirements must be met by all individuals, no matter which category his or her eligibility falls under:

1. **Character Of Discharge:**

    To use MGIB after an individual is separated from active duty, an individual's discharge must be fully honorable. Discharges "under honorable conditions" and "general" discharges don't establish eligibility for MGIB.

2. **Completed High School:**

    To use MGIB as an active duty member, or after separation from active duty, an individual must obtain a high school diploma or equivalency certificate before applying for benefits.

    Completing 12 hours toward a college degree before applying for benefits also meets this requirement. This is a change in eligibility rules that became effective November 1, 2000. If an individual wasn't previously eligible because he or she did not meet the high school requirement, the change provides a second chance.

In addition to the above requirements, individuals must meet requirements from one of the four following categories. (Individuals who entered active duty before July 1, 1985 may only qualify under Categories 2, 3, or 4.)

Category I

- The veteran must have entered active duty for the first time on or after July 1, 1985.

- The veteran must have enrolled in MGIB (didn't decline MGIB in writing upon entry into active duty).

Exception: If an individual declined MGIB in writing, he or she may not change this decision at a later date unless:

- The individual qualifies under Category 3; or

- The individual withdrew his or her election not to participate during the "open period" for withdrawal (December 1, 1988 through June 30, 1989).

- Individuals who graduated from a service academy and received a commission are not eligible.

- Individuals who became commissioned upon completing an ROTC scholarship program are not eligible, unless one of the following exceptions applies:

- The individual received a commission after becoming eligible for MGIB.

- The individual received a commission after September 30, 1996, and received less than $3,400 during any one year of his or her ROTC program.

- Individuals who received loan repayment from the military for their education are not eligible. (Note: Individuals who received loan repayment for one period of active duty, may still be eligible based on another period of active duty, as long as they did not decline MGIB when they first entered active duty.

- To use MGIB while on active duty, an individual must serve two continuous years of active duty.

- To use MGIB after separation from active duty, the individual must have served 3 continuous years of active duty, unless discharged early for one of the following reasons:

- Convenience of the government (veteran must have served 30 months if he had a 3-year obligation)

- Service-connected disability

- Hardship

- A medical condition the individual had before service

- A condition that interfered with performance of duty

- Certain reductions in force (RIF)

Exception: To use MGIB after separation from active duty, the individual may only need 2 years of active duty if:

- He or she first enlisted for 2 years of active duty; or

- The individual has an obligation to serve 4 years in the Selected Reserve (the 2 X 4 program). The individual must enter the Selected Reserve within one year of release from active duty; or

- The individual was separated early for one of the following reasons:

- Convenience of the government (veteran must have served 20 months if he had a 2-year obligation)

- Service-connected disability

- Hardship

- A medical condition the individual had before service

- A condition that interfered with performance of duty

- Certain reductions in force (RIF)

Note: Until November 1, 2000, the above "length of service" requirements had to be met during an individual's *initial* period of active duty.

Effective November 1, 2000, the above "length of service" requirements are no longer based on the *initial* period of active duty - any period of active duty may establish eligibility. Veterans still have to serve their obligated period of service, but that time does not have to be only from their first period of service. They can now serve the required number of years in a later period of service.

Likewise, veterans who were discharged for convenience of the government still have to serve 20 months, if they had a 2-year obligation, or 30 months, if they had an obligation of 3 years or more. However, effective November 1, 2000, that time can now be from a later period of service.

Service In The National Guard Or Reserve

Service in the National Guard or reserve is qualifying as active duty for MGIB benefits only under the following conditions:

1. Full-time National Guard or Reserve service authorized under title 10, U.S. Code (Active Guard/Reserve, or AGR) is considered active duty for purposes of qualifying for VA education benefits, unless the service is active duty for training.
2. Full-time National Guard service under title 32, U.S. Code (State authority) is considered active duty for purposes of qualifying for VA education benefits, provided the service was first performed after November 29, 1989 (with no previous active duty); and is for the purpose of organizing, administering, recruiting, instructing, or training the National Guard. Duty for the purpose of performing operations (such as drug interdiction, for example) is not considered active duty for MGIB benefits.

Category II

- The veteran had remaining entitlement under the Vietnam Era Veterans' Educational Assistance Program (chapter 34 of Title 38, U.S. Code) on December 31, 1989; and

- The veteran served on active duty for any number of days during the period October 19, 1984 to June 30, 1985, and then continued on active duty without a break from July 1, 1985 through:

- June 30, 1988, or

- June 30, 1987, and then served four years in the Selected Reserve after release from active duty. The individual must have entered the Selected Reserve within one year of his or her release from active duty.

  (This option became effective December 27, 2001.)

- The individual wasn't on active duty on October 19, 1984, but reentered active duty after that date, and served three continuous years on active duty on or after July 1, 1985, or two years on active duty followed by four years in the Selected Reserve on or after July 1, 1985. *(This option became effective December 27, 2001.)*

- Individuals who graduated from a service academy and received a commission after December 31, 1976 are not eligible.

- Individuals who received a commission after September 30, 1996 upon completing an ROTC scholarship program are not eligible, unless one of the following exceptions applies:

- The individual received a commission after becoming eligible for MGIB.

- The individual completed ROTC without a full scholarship.

- The individual received a commission after September 30, 1996, and received less than $3,400 during any one year of his or her ROTC program.

Category III

Effective February 3, 1991, the law was amended to allow certain individuals who were involuntarily separated from service as a result of reduction in personnel, who would not otherwise be eligible, to have the opportunity to elect MGIB benefits before separation. A veteran may qualify if:

- The veteran was on active duty on September 30, 1990, and was involuntarily separated after February 2, 1991; or

- The veteran was involuntarily separated on or after November 30, 1993.

- Effective October 23, 1992, the law was expanded to allow the same opportunity to elect MGIB benefits before separation to members voluntarily separated under either the Voluntary Separation Incentive (VSI) or Special Separation Benefit (SSB) program.

- If the member was eligible for the Post Vietnam Era Veterans' Educational Assistance Program (VEAP), he must elect to receive MGIB benefits, and apply for a refund of contributions to Chapter 32.

- The member must have had his military pay reduced by $1,200 before discharge.

Members qualifying under Category III based on a voluntary or involuntary separation are not eligible for MGIB benefits until the day following discharge.

(If a veteran eligible under Category 3 had a chapter 32 _kicker,_ VA will pay the basic chapter 30 rate and an additional amount based upon the amount of the remaining kicker.)

Category IV

Individuals may qualify under Category IV if they were on active duty on October 9, 1996, and were VEAP participants with money in the VEAP fund. These individuals must have elected MGIB, and paid $1,200 by October 9, 1997.

Individuals may also be eligible if they served on full time active duty in the National Guard between June 10, 1985 and November 29, 1989, and elected to have their National Guard service count toward establishing eligibility for MGIB benefits by July 9, 1997.

Effective November 1, 2000, VEAP participants, whether they had contributions in their accounts or not, could become eligible for MGIB if they:

- Made an irrevocable election to receive MGIB; and

- Were VEAP participants on or before October 9, 1996; and

- Continuously served on active duty from October 9, 1996 through April 1, 2000; and

- Made a payment of $2,700. The payment will be made by reducing their basic pay before their discharge from service. If $2,700 is not collected before discharge from pay reductions, veterans must make payments to the military service in the amount needed to bring the total to $2,700. DoD can also collect the additional amount by reducing retired or retainer pay.

  (NOTE: This payment, unlike earlier contributions to VEAP is _not refundable._ The payment does not go into the VEAP account, it is deposited into the Treasury of the United States as miscellaneous receipts; and

- Met other VEAP eligibility requirements.

- VEAP participants must have made this election on or before October 31, 2001.

Important Information Regarding Eligibility For Increased Payments:

The Floyd D. Spence National Defense Authorization Act for Fiscal Year 2001 (Public Law 106-398), which was signed into law on October 30, 2000, gives many members of the Armed Forces a chance to receive increased payment for off-duty training and education.

- **Before this law—**the military services in most cases could pay up to 75% of the tuition or expenses charged by the school. This program is known as Tuition Assistance. Eligible service members had to find additional financing, or pay the remaining expenses, from their own pockets. A service member eligible for the Montgomery GI Bill (MGIB), a VA education benefit, wasn't allowed to receive both Tuition Assistance and the MGIB for the same course.

- **Now, with this law—**the military services can pay up to 100% of the tuition and expenses charged by the school, up to limits determined by the Department of Defense. If the tuition and expenses are more than the amount a service department will pay, a service member eligible for MGIB can elect to receive MGIB benefits for all or a part of the remaining expenses. This add-on payment is referred to as a "Top-up" benefit by VA. Top-up benefits are limited to 36 months.

A service member who receives MGIB benefits as a result of the provision will receive a lower rate once he or she is discharged. The full-time monthly rate will be the rate that would have been payable to him or her had he or she not used the MGIB in service for tuition assistance, reduced by the amount of payments received in service, divided by 36.

IMPORTANT UPDATE EFFECTIVE NOVEMBER 1, 2007 -

Army Makes Changes to its Program offering Transferability of GI Bill to Dependents

Effective November 1, 2007 the **Army** has made changes to its GI Bill transferability program. Eligible soldiers may now transfer up to 18 months of their GI Bill to spouses or children.

This pilot program is authorized under Title 38, U.S. Code, Chapter 30 (amended by PL 107-107), the Montgomery GI Bill (MGIB).

ELIGIBILITY REQUIREMENTS

Participants must ensure they meet the following eligibility requirements and take the following actions to participate in the program:

- MGIB-era Soldiers who are eligible for MGIB must have enrolled in the MGIB upon initial entry to active duty and paid the $1,200 for MGIB enrollment. (Not eligible are Vietnam Ear-Rollover, VEAP conversion, and Involuntary Separation.)

- Completed at least 6 years of service in the Armed Forces at the time of reenlistment.

- Reenlist for a period of at least 4 years and complete DD Form 2366-2 with their servicing Army Retention Career Counselor.

- Qualify for a MOS Specific Selective Reenlistment Bonus (SRB) and entitled to a Zone B or Zone C bonus at the time of reenlistment.

The following individuals may receive transfer of entitlement:

- The spouse of the individual making the transfer;

- One or more of the children of the individual making the transfer; or

- A combination of the individuals referred above.

A dependent to whom the entitlement is transferred may not begin using the entitlement until:

Spouse:
The Soldier has completed at least six years of service in the Armed Forces.

Child:
The Soldier has completed at least 10 years of service in the Armed Forces, and either:

- The completion by the child of the requirement of a secondary school diploma (or equivalency certificate); or

- The attainment by the child of 18 years of age.

DISCHARGES AND SEPARATIONS

As previously mentioned, if the veteran is separated from active duty, the character of discharge must specifically be listed as "Honorable." "Under Honorable Conditions," or a "General" discharge do not establish eligibility. A discharge for one of the following reasons may result in a reduction of the required length of active duty to qualify for benefits under the MGIB:

- Convenience of the Government; or

- Disability; or

- Hardship; or

- Medical conditions existing before entry into Service; or

- Force reductions; or

- Medical condition which is not a disability due to misconduct, but which prevents satisfactory performance of duty.

CERTAIN TYPES OF ACTIVE DUTY WHICH DO NOT ESTABLISH ELIGIBILITY

The following types of active duty do not establish eligibility for MGIB benefits:

- Time assigned by the military to a civilian institution to take the same course provided to civilians.

- Time served as a cadet or a midshipman at a service academy.

- Time spent on active duty for training in the National Guard or Reserve.

(Please note: Time assigned by the military to a civilian institution, and time served at a service academy does not break the continuity of active duty required to establish eligibility for MGIB benefits. Active duty for training does count toward the four years in the Selected Reserve under the 2 by 4 program.)

APPROVED COURSES

This program provides veterans up to 36 months of education benefits. The benefits may be used for:

- Undergraduate or graduate degrees from a college or university;

- Cooperative training programs;

- Accredited independent study programs leading to standard college degrees;

- Courses leading to certificates or diplomas from business, technical or vocational schools;

- Vocational flight training (from September 30, 1990 only – Individuals must have a private pilot's license and meet the medical requirements for a desired license before beginning training, and throughout the flight training program);

- Apprenticeship / job training programs offered by a company or union;

- Correspondence courses;

- VA may approve programs offered by institutions outside of the United States, when they are pursued at educational institutions of higher learning, and lead to an associate or higher degree, or the equivalent. Individuals must receive VA approval prior to attending or enrolling in any foreign programs;

- Effective March 1, 2001, benefits can be payable for licensing or certification tests. The tests are those needed to enter, maintain, or advance into employment in a civilian vocation or profession. The eligible veteran or family member may receive payment of the fee charged for the test or $2,000, whichever is less. Individuals may take as many tests as needed. They do not have to pass the test to receive benefits. Individuals can receive benefits to retake a failed test, and to renew or update a license or certificate. *The tests must be approved for VA benefits.* Contact the VA for a complete list of approved certification tests.

UPDATE – Public Law 108-183, The Veterans Benefits Act of 2003, expands, effective June 16, 2004, the MGIB program to cover self-employment training programs of less than six months, and entrepreneurship courses at approved institutions.

If an individual is seeking a college degree, the school must admit the individual to a degree program by the start of the individual's third term.

Under certain circumstances, remedial, deficiency and refresher courses may be approved. A special allowance for tutorial assistance, vocational counseling, and work-study programs may also be payable to individuals.

RESTRICTIONS ON TRAINING

- Bartending and personality development courses;
- Non-accredited independent study courses;
- Any course given by radio;
- Self-improvement courses such as reading, speaking, woodworking, basic seamanship, and English as a second language;
- Any course which is avocational or recreational in character;
- Farm cooperative courses;
- Audited courses;
- Courses not leading to an educational, professional, or vocational objective;
- Courses an individual has previously completed;
- Courses taken by a Federal government employee under the Government Employees' Training Act;
- Courses paid for in whole or in part by the Armed Forces while on active duty;
- Courses taken while in receipt of benefits for the same program from the Office of Workers' Compensation Programs.

The VA must reduce benefits for individuals in Federal, State or local prisons after being convicted of a felony.

An individual may not receive benefits for a program at a proprietary school if he or she is an owner or official of the school.

Benefits are generally payable for 10 years following a veteran's release from active duty.

PART-TIME TRAINING

Individuals unable to attend school full-time should consider going part-time. Benefit rates and entitlement charges are pro-rated as follows:

- Individuals who are on active duty or training at less than one-half time, will receive the lesser of:
  - The monthly rate based on tuition and fees for the course(s); or

  - The maximum monthly rate based on training time.

- Individuals training at less than one-half time will receive payment in one sum for the whole enrollment period.

REMEDIAL, DEFICIENCY AND REFRESHER TRAINING

Remedial and deficiency courses are intended to assist a student in overcoming a deficiency in a particular area of study. In order for such courses to be approved, the courses must be deemed necessary for pursuit of a program of education.

Refresher training is for technological advances that occurred in a field of employment. The advance must have occurred while the student was on active duty, or after release.

There is an entitlement charge for these courses.

TUTORIAL ASSISTANCE

Students may receive a special allowance for individual tutoring, if attending school at one-half time or more. To qualify, the student must have a deficiency in a subject. The school must certify the tutor's qualifications, and the hours of tutoring. Eligible students may receive a maximum monthly payment of $100.00. The maximum total benefit payable is $1,200.00.

There is no entitlement charge for the first $600.00 of tutorial assistance.

To apply for tutorial assistance, students must submit VA Form 22-1990t, Application and Enrollment Certification for Individualized Tutorial Assistance. The form should be given to the certifying official in the office handling VA paperwork at the school for completion.

MONTHS OF BENEFITS / ENTITLEMENT CHARGED

Individuals who complete their full period of enlistment may receive up to 36 months of MGIB benefits.

Individuals are considered to have completed their full enlistment period if they are discharged for the convenience of the government after completing 20 months of an enlistment of less than three years; or 30 months of an enlistment of three years or more.

Individuals will earn only one month of entitlement for each month of active duty after June 39, 1985, if they are discharged for other specific reasons (i.e. service-connected disability, reduction in force, hardship, etc.) before completing the enlistment period.

Individuals will earn one month of entitlement for each four months in the Selected Reserve after June 30, 1985.

Individuals qualifying for more than one VA education program may receive a maximum of 48 months of benefits. For example, if a student used 30 months of Dependents' Educational Assistance, and is eligible for chapter 1606 benefits, he or she could have a maximum of 18 months of entitlement remaining.

Individuals are charged one full day of entitlement for each day of full-time benefits paid. For correspondence and flight training, individuals use one month of entitlement each time the VA pays the equivalent of one month of full-time benefits. Individuals pursuing a cooperative program use one month for each month of benefits paid.

For apprenticeship and job-training programs, the entitlement charge during the first 6 months is 75% of full-time. For the second six months, the charge is 55% of full-time. For the rest of the program, the charge is 35% of full-time.

VA can extend entitlement to the end of a term, quarter, or semester if the ending date of an individual's entitlement falls within such period. If a school does not operate on a term basis, entitlement can be extended for 12 weeks.

RATES OF EDUCATIONAL ASSISTANCE AFTER SEPARATION FROM ACTIVE DUTY

The basic monthly rates increase October 1 every year with the Consumer Price Index (CPI) increase. While in training, students receive a letter with the current rates when the increase goes into effect each year. The rates may increase at other times by an act of Congress.

Basic Monthly Rates for College and Vocational School

For approved programs in college and vocational or technical schools, basic payments are monthly and the rates are based on training time. When students train at less than half time, they will be paid tuition and fees. But if tuition and fees amount to more than would be paid at the half-time rate (or the quarter-time rate if training at quarter-time or less), payments will be limited to the half time (or the quarter-time rate).

For on-the-job training (OJT) and apprenticeship programs, rates are monthly and based on the length of time in the program. MGIB rates decrease as the student's wages increase according to an approved wage schedule.

Rates For Other Types of Training

For correspondence courses, students receive 55% of the approved charges for the course.

For flight training, students receive 60% of the approved charges for the course. For reimbursement of tests for licenses or certifications, students receive 100% of the charges up to a maximum of $2,000 per test.

RATES OF EDUCATIONAL ASSISTANCE *WHILE ON ACTIVE DUTY*

If a service member goes to school while on active duty, he or she may have two options for using MGIB benefits. The may be eligible to receive:
- "Regular" MGIB; or
- Tuition Assistance plus MGIB, or Tuition Assistance "Top-Up"

Using "Regular" MGIB on Active Duty

If a service member uses "regular" MGIB while on active duty, VA can pay whichever is less:
- The monthly rate based on tuition and fees for your course(s); or
- The maximum monthly MGIB rate (basic rate plus any increases he or she may qualify for).

The basic monthly rates increase October 1 every year with the Consumer Price Index (CPI) increase. While in training, students receive a letter with the current rates when the increase goes into effect each year. The rates may increase at other times by an act of Congress.

Using Tuition Assistance "Top-Up"

If a student is on active duty, he or she may be eligible to receive Tuition Assistance (TA) from his or her branch of service. If the student has been on active duty for two years, he or she may also be eligible to use MGIB to supplement, or "top up," the TA. Top-up covers the remaining percentage of costs approved for TA that TA alone doesn't' cover—**up to specified limits**. For example, if a student's service authorizes 75% of costs, top-up can pay the remaining 25% of costs approved for TA.

Following are some questions and answers provided by VA regarding the "Top-Up" program.

(From the Floyd D. Spence National Defense Authorization Act for Fiscal Year 2001 - Public Law 106-398)

Question: What does this provision change?
Answer: Before this law, the military services, through their Tuition Assistance program, generally could pay up to 75% of the tuition or expenses charged by

the school. Eligible service members had to find additional financing, or pay the remaining expenses from their own pockets. A service member eligible for the Montgomery GI Bill (MGIB), a VA education benefit, wasn't allowed to receive both Tuition Assistance and the MGIB for the same course.

Because of the new law, the military services can now pay up to 100% of the tuition and expenses charged by the school up to limits established by DOD. If the tuition and expenses are more than the amount a service department will pay, a service member eligible for MGIB can elect to receive MGIB benefits for all or a part of the remaining expenses. VA is calling this add-on payment "Top-up."

Question: What does this provision mean to me?
Answer: If you're eligible for MGIB, and plan to use Tuition Assistance (TA), and your service will not pay 100% of tuition and fees, you can use MGIB Top-up to pay the balance.

Question: Can VEAP converters and service members eligible for MGIB based on Vietnam Era service receive the Top-up?
Answer: Yes, anyone who is eligible for MGIB – Active Duty (not MGIB – Selected Reserves) can receive the Top-up benefits.

Question: Is this a good deal for me?
Answer: Using Top-up is a good deal if you plan to use TA to complete a degree program while on active duty, and don't plan to continue your education after service. Top-up can also be helpful for just taking a few courses with TA while on active duty. Then you can save most of your MGIB to use after service to complete your education program.

You need to consider carefully your own situations, and check with your education officer or counselor, before applying for Top-up. For example, if you plan to take expensive courses using Top-up, you need to consider whether you'll take additional training after you're discharged from active duty. If so, you need to understand the effect of using the Top-up. You can then calculate whether your remaining benefits will cover the additional training you might need.

Question: Is there a limit to the amount of Top-up I can use?
Answer: Yes, Top-up is limited to 36 months of payments. For example, if you are paid Top-up for a 3-month course, you use 3 of the 36 months.

Question: Does this mean if I use 36 months of Top-up, I've used up all my MGIB benefits?
Answer: Probably not. The 36-month limit for Top-up is based on 1 month used for each month of Top-up paid no matter how much is paid. Your regular MGIB entitlement is based on your full-time monthly rate. For example, if your full-time rate is $600 and you are paid $300 Top-up, you only use 1/2 month of your MGIB ($300 is 1/2 of $600).

Question: Can the Top-up apply retroactively, to training already received?
Answer: Yes, the Top-up can apply retroactively, **but** you must be eligible for the Montgomery GI Bill, **and** we can only go back one year from the date your claim was/is received in VA **and** only for training in terms that began on or after October 30, 2000, which is the effective date of the law.

Question: Will DoD pay 100% tuition assistance?
Answer: DoD will encourage services to pay 100% TA if their budgets permit, but this could vary from service to service. Of course, if DoD does pay 100%, you won't need to use MGIB Top-up.

Question: What should I do to apply for Top-up?
Answer: If you want to use Top-up for winter term 2001 or later, go ahead and file the claim following the instructions below.

If you haven't previously filed a claim for MGIB, you should do the following:

Request TA from your branch of service. See your education services officer or education counselor.

Complete an application for VA education benefits, VA Form 22-1990. Indicate "Top-up" on the VA application in item 1A under the MGIB–Active Duty block.
Send your TA approval form, along with the application for VA education benefits, to the VA Regional Processing Office that handles your claim. The address is on the form.

If you've previously filed a claim for MGIB and weren't denied benefits, simply submit your signed TA approval form to the VA Regional Processing Office that handles your claim.

Important: These claims are handled differently from claims for MGIB without TA. For Top-up claims, you **won't** need to check in with the school official who certifies VA benefits. VA won't need an enrollment certification on VA Form 22-1999. You won't need to check for approval of the program for VA benefits; approval isn't an issue. That's because Top-up is payable for any course for which TA is payable under DOD criteria.

VA determines your eligibility for MGIB. If you're eligible for MGIB, the TA approval form establishes your eligibility for Top-up. No certifications from the school are needed.

What about the signatures on the TA approval form? The TA approval form must be signed by the approving DoD officials. Some branches of service require the commanding officer's signature; some require the education service officer's signature.

DETAILED RATES OF EDUCATIONAL ASSISTANCE

The rates, effective October 1, 2010, are detailed in the following charts.

BASIC MONTHLY RATES EFFECTIVE OCTOBER 1, 2010 Montgomery G.I. Bill - Active Duty (MGIB), Chapter 30					
Type of Training	**Full- Time**	**Three- Quarter Time**	**One-Half Time**	**Less than ½ Time, but More Than ¼ Time**	**One- Quarter Time**
Institutional	$1426.00	$1069.50	$713.00	Tuition & Fees, not to exceed $713.00	$356.50
Cooperative Training	$1426.00 (Full-Time Only)				
Correspondence Training	Entitlement charged at the rate of one month for each $1426.00 paid				
Apprenticeship On-The-Job Training -	First six months: $1069.50 Second six months: $784.30 Remainder of program: $499.10				
Flight Training	Entitlement charged at the rate of one month for each $1426.00 paid				

**BASIC MONTHLY RATES EFFECTIVE OCTOBER 1, 2010
FOR PERSONS WHOSE INITIAL ACTIVE DUTY OBLIGATION WAS LESS
THAN THREE YEARS, AND WHO SERVED LESS THAN THREE YEARS
(EXCLUDING 2 X 4 PARTICIPANTS)**

Type of Training	Full-Time	Three-Quarter Time	One-Half Time	LESS THAN ½ TIME, BUT MORE THAN ¼ TIME	One-Quarter Time
Institutional	$1158.00	$868.50	$579.00	Tuition & Fees, not to exceed $579.00	$289.50
Cooperative Training	$1158.00 (Full-Time Only)				
Correspondence Training	Entitlement charged at the rate of one month for each $1158.00 paid				
Apprenticeship On-The-Job Training -	First six months: $868.50 Second six months: $636.90 Remainder of program: $405.30				
Flight Training	Entitlement charged at the rate of one month for each $1158.00 paid				

**BASIC INSTITUTIONAL RATES EFFECTIVE OCTOBER 1, 2010
FOR PERSONS WITH REMAINING ENTITLEMENT
UNDER CHAPTER 34 OF TITLE 38, U.S.C.**

Time	No Dependents	One Dependent	Two Dependents	EACH ADD'L DEPENDENT
Full	$1614.00	$1650.00	$1681.00	$16.00
Three-Quarter	$1211.00	$1237.50	$1261.00	$12.00
One-Half	$807.00	$825.00	$840.00	$8.50
Less Than 1/2, But More Than 1/4	Tuition and fees, not to exceed the rate of $807.00			
One-Quarter	Tuition and fees, not to exceed the rate of $403.50			
Cooperative	$1614.00	$1650.00	$1681.00	$16.00

BASIC JOB TRAINING RATES
EFFECTIVE OCTOBER 1, 2010
FOR PERSONS WITH REMAINING ENTITLEMENT
UNDER CHAPTER 34 OF TITLE 38, U.S.C.

Apprenticeship and On-The-Job Training

Time	No Dependents	One Dependent	Two Dependents	EACH ADD'L DEPENDENT
First six months	$1172.25	$1184.63	$1195.50	$5.25
Second six months	$840.68	$850.03	$857.73	$3.85
Third six months	$522.90	$529.03	$533.75	$2.45
Remainder	$511.00	$516.78	$522.03	$2.45

SPECIAL NOTES:
- Cooperative Training is full time only.

- Individuals taking correspondence courses will receive 55% of the approved charges for the course.

- Individuals taking flight training will receive 60% of the approved charges for the course, including solo hours.

Increases Above Basic Rates

Individuals may qualify for the following increases above their basic monthly rates. These increases don't apply to correspondence courses, the test for a license or certification, or flight training.

College Fund

Certain branches of service may offer the College Fund. The College Fund money, or "kicker," is an additional amount of money that increases the basic MGIB monthly benefit and is included in the VA payment.

Important: Students can't receive College Fund money without receiving MGIB. A common misunderstanding is that the College Fund is a separate benefit from MGIB. The College Fund is an add-on to the MGIB benefit.

VEAP "KICKER."

VA pays an additional amount, commonly known as a "kicker," if directed by the Department of Defense (DoD). If an individual is eligible under Category 3 or Category 4 and has a VEAP kicker, he or she can receive the amount of the VEAP kicker contributed by the service department divided by the total months of MGIB eligibility.

Increase based on contributions made up to $600.
Individuals may be eligible to make these contributions if they are eligible for MGIB under Category 1, and on active duty, or were separated from active duty during the period November 1, 2000, to May 1, 2001.

This "Buy-Up" feature can allow active duty servicemembers to **Get up to an extra $150 per month** increase above the standard MGIB "pay rate." (Note: The Air Force calls this program a GI Bill kicker.)

Important: If an individual was separated during this period, **he or she must have made these contributions by July 31. 2001.**

Unfortunately, the law doesn't allow these contributions from individuals who are eligible for MGIB under Categories 2, 3, or 4.

If a service member was originally eligible under Category 1 and made contributions, but later becomes eligible under Category 3 because of the type of separation, he or she can still use the contributions to increase the MGIB rate.

Caution: Unless a student takes expensive courses, he or she won't receive the increases while training on active duty (or while training at less than half time after discharged) because VA can't pay more than the tuition and fees charged for the course.

ACCELERATED PAYMENTS FOR EDUCATION LEADING TO EMPLOYMENT IN HIGH TECHNOLOGY

One of the provisions contained in the Veterans Education and Benefits Expansion Act of 2001 (Public Law 107-103) called for accelerated payments for education leading to employment in high technology, effective October 1, 2002. Following are questions and answers provided by the VA regarding this provision.

What is an Accelerated Payment?

An accelerated payment is a lump sum payment of 60% of tuition and fees for certain high cost, high tech programs. If a participant does not have sufficient entitlement to cover 60% of tuition and fees, he or she will receive pay based on the actual remaining entitlement.

VA will make accelerated payments for one term, quarter, or semester at a time. However, if the program is not offered on a term, quarter or semester basis, the accelerated payment is paid for the entire program. To qualify, a participant must be enrolled in a high tech program and must certify that he or she intends to seek employment in a high tech industry as defined by VA. Accelerated payment is paid instead of Montgomery GI Bill benefits that would otherwise have been received.

Who qualifies for accelerated payments?

Only individuals eligible for the Montgomery GI Bill - Active Duty (Chapter 30) qualify for accelerated payments.

How high do the tuition and fees have to be?

To receive accelerated payment, the tuition and fees must be more than double the Montgomery GI Bill benefits that a participant would otherwise receive for that term. For example, if the full-time rate is $732 and a participant is enrolled in a 4-month semester, the tuition and fees must be over $5,856 (4 months x $732=$2,928; $5,856=2 x $2,928) before he or she could receive an accelerated payment.

If a participant receives $900 in monthly benefits, the tuition and fees must be over $7,200 (4 months x $900=$3,600; $7,200= 2 x $3,600).

If a participant receives $1,050 in monthly benefits, the tuition and fees must be over $8,400 (4 months x $1,050 = $4,200; 2 x $4,200 = $8,400).

What programs qualify for accelerated payment?

Both degree and non-degree programs qualify. A participant must be enrolled in a program in one of the following categories:

- Life science or physical science (but not social science);
- Engineering (all fields);
- Mathematics;
- Engineering and science technology;
- Computer specialties; and·
- Engineering, science, and computer management

What industries qualify for accelerated payments?

A participant must intend to seek employment in one of the following industries:

- Biotechnology;
- Life Science Technologies;
- Opto-electronics;
- Computers and telecommunications;
- Electronics;
- Computer-integrated manufacturing;
- Material Design;
- Aerospace;
- Weapons;

- Nuclear technology

How does a participant apply for accelerated payments?

The individual must ask the school to include his or her request for accelerated payment to VA when it sends the enrollment information to VA for processing. The individual's request must include his or her certification of intent to seek employment in a high technology industry.

How is the education entitlement charged?

VA will divide the accelerated payment by the amount of the individual's full-time monthly rate (including kickers and additional contributions) and will reduce the entitlement by the resulting number of months and days.

Example: Jill received an accelerated payment of $3,600. Her full-time rate is $900. VA will charge her entitlement as follows: $3,600/$900 = 4 months.

When can accelerated payments be made?

Accelerated payments may only be made for terms or other enrollment periods that begin on or after October 1, 2002.

Can school related expenses (such as books, supplies, and living expenses) be counted as tuition and fees for accelerated payments?

No. Only the school's tuition and fees can be considered for accelerated payment.

Can an individual receive accelerated payments for short, non-degree course?

Yes, as long as they are approved for VA benefits. Short, expensive, IT courses offered by businesses typically are not approved for VA benefits.

Can an individual receive accelerated payments for non-technical courses (such as English, history, etc.) when taking those courses as part of a high technology program?

Yes. However, the degree or certificate must require the completion of these other non-technical courses.

Is it possible to receive an accelerated payment check before a school term begins?

No. VA needs to verify that the individual has enrolled before sending out the large payment. VA will pay the student as soon after the start of the term as possible. Individuals will receive payment faster if they receive direct deposit.

Does a student have to verify enrollment each month if he or she receives an accelerated payment?

No. After the individual completes his or her enrollment, VA will ask the student to verify that he or she have received the accelerated payment. VA will also ask the individual to indicate how he or she used the accelerated payment (such as toward tuition, fees and books and supplies). VA is asking the latter question for statistical purposes only because the law requires them to collect this information. A student's answer will have no bearing on his or her entitlement to the accelerated payment. The student must respond to these questions within 60 days from the end of the enrollment period or VA will create an overpayment equal to the accelerated payment. As with any course, the student must notify VA of any change in his or her enrollment. The student's school must report any changes as well.

Is there any financial risk with accelerated payment?

Yes. If a student receives a grade, which does not count toward graduation requirements, he or she may have to repay all or part of the accelerated payment, depending on the circumstances. This could be a large amount of money.

Do the accelerated payments have to be paid back if the individual fails to find employment in a high technology industry?

No. The fact that he or she intended to find employment in a high technology industry is sufficient.

List Of Approved High Technology Programs

1.09 Animal Sciences
01.0901 Animal Sciences, General
01.0902 Agricultural Animal Breeding
01.0903 Animal Health
01.0904 Animal Nutrition
01.0905 Dairy Science
01.0906 Livestock Management
01.0907 Poultry Science

01.10 Food Science and Technology
01.1001 Food Science
01.1002 Food Technology and Processing
01.1099 Food Science and Technology
01.1101 Plant Sciences General
01.1102 Agronomy and Crop Science
01.1103 Horticultural Science
01.1104 Agricultural and Horticultural Plant Breeding
01.1105 Plant Protection and Integrated Pest Management
01.1106 Range Science Management

01.12 Soil Sciences
01.1201 Soil Science and Agronomy General
01.1202 Soil Chemistry and Physics
01.1203 Soil Microbiology
01.1299 Soil Sciences

03.01 Natural Resources Conservation and Research
03.0104 Environmental Science

03.03 Fishing and Fisheries Sciences and Management

03.05 Forestry
03.0501 Forestry, General
03.0502 Forest Sciences and Biology
03.0506 Forest Management/Forest Resources Management
03.0508 Urban Forestry
03.0509 Wood Science and Wood Products/Pulp and Paper Technology
03.0510 Forest Resources Production and Management
03.0511 Forest Technology/Technician

03.06 Wildlife and Wildlands Science and Management

09.07 Radio, Television, and Digital Communication
09.0702 Digital Communication and Media/Multimedia

11.0101 Computer and Information Sciences, General
11.0102 Artificial Intelligence and Robotics
11.0103 Information Technology
11.0199 Computer and Information Sciences

11.02 Computer Programming
11.0201 Computer Programming/Programmer General
11.0202 Computer Programming Specific Applications

11.03 Data Processing
11.0301 Data Process and Data Processing Technology/Technician

11.04 Information Science/Studies

11.05 Computer Systems Analysis

11.07 Computer Science

11.08 Computer Software and Media Application
11.0801 Web Page, Digital/Multimedia and Information Resources Design
11.0802 Data Modeling/Warehousing and Database Administration
11.0803 Computer Graphics
11.0899 Computer Software and Media Applications, Other.

11.09 Computer System Networking and Telecommunications

11.10 Computer/Information Technology Administration and Management
11.1001 System Administration/Administrator
11.1002 System, Networking and LAN/WAN Management/Manager
11.1003 Computer and Information Systems Security
11.1004 Web/Multimedia Management and Webmaster

*14. Engineering.
Instructional program that prepare individuals to apply mathematical and scientific principles to the solution of practical problems.

*15. Engineering Technologies/Technicians.

Instructional programs that prepare individuals to apply basic engineering principles and technical skills in support of engineering and related projects.

*26. Biological and Biomedical Sciences.
Instructional programs that focus on the biological sciences and the non-clinical biomedical sciences, and that prepare individuals for research and professional careers as biologist and biomedical scientist.

*27. Mathematics and Statistics.
Instructional programs that focus on the systematic study of logical symbolic language and its applications.

*29. Military Technologies.
A program that prepares individuals to undertake advanced and specialized leadership and technical responsibilities for the armed services and related national security organizations. Includes instruction in such areas as weapons systems and technology, communications, intelligence, management, logistics and strategy.

30.01 Biological and Physical Sciences

30.06 System Science and Theory

30.08 Mathematics and Computer Science

30.10 Biopsychology

30.11 Gerontology

30.16 Accounting and Computer Science

30.17 Behavioral Sciences

30.18 Natural Sciences

30.19 Nutrition Sciences

30.24 Neuroscience

30.25 Cognitive Science

*40. Physical Sciences.
Instructional programs that focus on the scientific study of inanimate objects, processes of matter and energy, and associated phenomena.

*41. Science Technologies/Technicians.
Instructional programs that prepare individuals to apply scientific principles and technical skills in support of scientific research and development.

42.11 Physiological Psychology/Psychobiology

42.19 Psychometrics and Quantitative Psychology

42. 24 Psychopharmacology

42.26 Forensic Psychology

*51.14 Medical Clinical Sciences/Graduate Medical Studies
51.1401 Medical Scientist (MS, PhD)

NOTE: "*" means all programs are considered high technology programs within that discipline.

ELIGIBILITY PERIODS

Benefits generally end 10 years from the date of an individual's last discharge or release from active duty. The VA may extend the 10-year period by the amount of time an individual is prevented from training due to a disability, or the individual is being held by a foreign government or power.

The VA may extend the 10-year period if an individual reenters active duty for 90 days or more after becoming eligible. The extension ends 10 years from the date of discharge or release from the later period. Periods of active duty of less than 90 days may qualify for extensions, only if the discharge or release was for:

- A service-connected disability; or

- A medical condition existing before active duty; or

- Hardship; or

- A reduction in force.

If an individual's discharge is upgraded by the military, the 10-year period begins on the date of the upgrade.

Special Note For Individuals Eligible Under Category II:

If an individual is eligible under Category II, and discharge was before December 31, 1989,he had until January 1, 2000 to use his entitlement. In most cases, the VA will subtract periods an individual was not on active duty between January 1, 1977 and June 30, 1985, from the individual's 10-year period.

Special Note For Individuals Eligible Under The 2 By 4 Program

If an individual is eligible based upon two years of active duty followed by four years in the Selected Reserve, the individual may have 10 years from release from active duty, or 10 years from the completion of the four-year Selected Reserve obligation to use benefits, whichever is later.

Miscellaneous Information

- Any change in educational, professional or vocational objectives is considered a *"change of program."* The law permits one change of program without prior VA approval, provided an individual's attendance, conduct and progress in the last program were satisfactory. Additional *"changes of program"* require prior VA approval. VA will not charge a *change of program* if the individual enrolls in a new program after successful completion of the immediately preceding program.

- Once an individual starts receiving benefits, he must maintain satisfactory attendance, conduct and progress. The VA may stop benefits if an individual does not meet the standards set by the school. VA may later resume benefits if the individual reenters the same program at the same school, and the school approves the reentry, and certifies it to VA.

- If the individual does not reenter the same program at the same school, VA may resume benefits if the cause of unsatisfactory attendance, conduct or progress has been removed; and the program that the student intends to pursue is suitable to his or her abilities, aptitudes and interests.

- **Update: Effective November 1, 2000,** VA education benefits can be paid (with some exceptions) for school breaks, if the breaks do not exceed 8 weeks; and the terms before and after the breaks are not shorter than the break. Prior to November 1 2000, VA education benefits could be paid only if the breaks did not exceed a calendar month.

APPLICATION FOR BENEFITS

VA Form 22-1990, "Application for Education Benefits" must be completed. The form may be obtained from individual schools, from any VA regional office, or by calling 1-888-GIBILL-1.

The completed form should be sent to the VA regional office with jurisdiction over the state in which the individual will train.

If an individual is not on active duty, copy 4 of DD Form 214 (Certificate of Release or Discharge from Active Duty), must also be sent to the VA. If an individual is on active duty, enrollment must be approved by the Base Education Services Officer, and service must be verified by the Commanding Officer.

If training has already started, the school, employer, or union should complete VA Form 22-1999 (Enrollment Certification) and submit it along with the application.

PROCEDURES FOR RECEIPT OF MONTHLY PAYMENTS

> *Students will receive a Student Verification of Enrollment Form 22-8979 each month, and must complete and return it to the appropriate VA regional office. After processing, VA will release a check.*

After selecting a school and submitting an application to VA, the school official must complete an enrollment certification, and submit it to the appropriate VA regional office. If a student meets the basic eligibility requirements for benefits, and the program or course is approved, VA will process the enrollment based on certified training time.

If a student is enrolled in a degree program at a college or university, or a certificate or diploma program at a business, technical, or vocational school, they will not receive payment until they have verified their attendance. Students will receive a *Student Verification of Enrollment Form 22-8979* each month, and must complete and return it to the appropriate VA regional office. After processing, VA will release a check.

Beginning in the Fall of 2000, VA announced a new way to verify enrollment. **All students who are receiving MGIB Active Duty (chapter 30) education benefits are now able to certify their monthly Verification of Enrollment (VAF 22-8979) over the by using a toll free phone system (Interactive Voice Response - IVR) or the internet (Web Automated Verification of Enrollment (WAVE).** Use of these systems eliminates the need for the student to sign and return the VA Form 22-8979 every month.

Once the IVR or WAVE system tells the student that he or she is certified, it is not necessary to return the Verification of Enrollment form.

If an individual is in an apprenticeship or job-training program, he or she will receive a form to report the hours worked each month. The form must be signed and given to the certifying official for the company or union. The certifying official must complete the form and send it to the appropriate VA regional office. After processing, VA will release a check.

If an individual is taking a correspondence course, he or she will receive a form each quarter, on which the student must show the number of lessons completed that quarter. The completed form should be sent to the school for certification of the number of lessons serviced during the quarter. The school will send the form to the appropriate VA regional office. After processing, VA will release a check. Payments are based on the number of lessons serviced by the school.

VA will send flight schools a supply of blank monthly certification of flight training forms. The school must complete the form by entering the number of hours, the hourly rate, and the total charges for flight training received during the month. The student should review and sign the completed form, and send it to the appropriate VA regional office. After processing, VA will release a check.

NOTE: It is against the law for schools to cash VA checks under a Power of Attorney Agreement.

TIMELY RECEIPT OF VERIFICATION FORMS AND CHECKS

Students should receive their verification forms for each month by the fifth of the following month. If it is not received by then, the VA should be immediately contacted so that another form can be issued.

One a completed verification form has been submitted, the student should receive a check within 2 weeks. If a check is not received by then, the VA should immediately be contacted so that appropriate action can be taken.

ADVANCE PAYMENTS

An advance payment for the initial month, or partial month and the following month may be made, if:

1. The school agrees to handle advance payments; and
2. Training is one-half time or more; and
3. A request is made by the individual in writing; and
4. The VA receives the enrollment certification at least 30 days prior to the start of classes.

Advance payments are made out to the individual, and sent to the applicable school for delivery to the individual registration. VA cannot issue a check more than 30 days before classes start. Before requesting an advance payment, students should verify with the school certifying official that the school has agreed to process advance payments.

Requests for advance payments must be on VA Form 22-1999, Enrollment Certification, or a sheet of paper attached to the enrollment certification.

Once a student receives an advance payment at registration, the school must certify to VA that the student received the check. If a student reduces enrollment, or withdraws from all courses during the period covered by an advance payment, he or she must repay the overpayment to VA.

If an individual believes that the amount of a VA check is incorrect, the VA should be contacted before the check is cashed.

DIRECT DEPOSIT

Chapter 30 payments can be sent directly to a student's savings or checking account through Direct Deposit (Electronic Funds Transfer). To sign up for direct deposit by phone, students must call 1-877-838-2778.

STUDENT RESPONSIBILITIES

To ensure timely receipt of correct payments, students should be sure to promptly notify the VA of:

- Any change in enrollment;
- Any change in address;
- Any change in selected reserve status;
- Any changes affecting a student's dependents (if a student is receiving an allowance which includes an additional amount for dependents).

In addition, students should use reasonable judgment when accepting and cashing a check. All letters from VA about monthly rates and effective dates should be read carefully. If a student thinks the amount of a VA check is wrong, VA should be contacted **before** cashing the check. Any incorrect checks should be returned to VA.

If a student cashes a check for the wrong amount, he or she will be liable for repayment of any resulting overpayment.

RECOVERY OF OVERPAYMENTS

VA must take prompt and aggressive action to recover overpayments. Students have the right to request a waiver of the overpayment, or verification that the amount is correct. If an overpayment is not repaid or waived, VA may add interest and collection fees to the debt. VA may also take one or more of the following actions to collect the debt:

- Withhold future benefits to apply to the debt;
- Refer the debt to a private collection agency;
- Recover the debt from any Federal income tax refund;
- Recover the debt from the salary (if student is a Federal employee);
- File a lawsuit in Federal court to collect the debt;
- Withhold approval of a VA home loan guarantee.

CHANGES IN ENROLLMENT

If a student withdraws from one or more courses after the end of the school's drop period, VA will reduce or stop benefits on the date of reduction or withdrawal. Unless the student can show that the change was due to *mitigating circumstances*, the student may have to repay **all** benefits for the course.

VA defines *mitigating circumstances* as "unavoidable and unexpected events that directly interfere with the pursuit of a course, and which are beyond the student's control.

Examples of reasons VA may accept include:

- Extended illness;
- Severe illness or death in immediate family;
- Unscheduled changes in employment; and
- Lack of child care.

Examples of reasons VA may not accept include:

- Withdrawal to avoid a failing grade;
- Dislike of the instructor; and
- Too many courses attempted.

(VA may ask the student to furnish evidence to support the reason for change, such as physician or employer written statements.)

The first time a student withdraws from up to 6 credit hours, VA will "excuse" the withdrawal, and pay benefits for the period attended.

If a student receives a grade that does not count toward graduation, all benefits for the course may have to be repaid. Affected students should check the school's grading policy with the office handling VA paperwork.

If a student receives a non-punitive grade, the school will notify VA, and VA may reduce or stop benefits. The student may not have to repay the benefits if he or she can show that the grades were due to mitigating circumstances.

WORK-STUDY PROGRAMS

Students may be eligible for an additional allowance under a work-study program that allows students to perform work for VA in return for an hourly wage. Students may perform outreach services under VA supervision, prepare and process VA paperwork, work at a VA medical facility or National Cemetery, or perform other approved activities.

Students must attend school at the three-quarter of full-time rate.

VA will select students for the work study program based on different factors. Such factors include:

- Disability of the student;
- Ability of the student to complete the work-study contract before the end of his or her eligibility for education benefits;
- Job availability within normal commuting distance to the student;
- VA will give the highest priority to a veteran who has a service-connected disability or disabilities rated by VA at 30% or more.

The number of applicants selected will depend on the availability of VA-related work at the school or at VA facilities in the area.

Students may work during or between periods of enrollment, and can arrange with VA to work any number of hours during his or her enrollment. However, the maximum number of hours a student may work is 25 times the number of weeks in the enrollment period.

Students will earn an hourly wage equal to the Federal or State minimum wage, whichever is greater. If a student works at a college or university, the school **may** pay the difference between the amount VA pays and the amount the school normally pays other work-study students doing the same job.

Students may elect to be paid in advance for 40% of the number of hours in the work-study agreement, or for 50 hours, whichever is less. After completion of the hours covered by the first payment, VA will pay the student after completion of each 50 hours of service.

Students interested in taking part in a work-study program must complete VA Form 22,8691, Application for Work-Study Allowance. Completed forms should be sent to the nearest VA regional office.

EDUCATIONAL COUNSELING

VA can provide services to help eligible individuals understand their educational and vocational strengths and weaknesses and to plan:

- An educational or training goal, and the means by which the goal can be reached; or
- An employment goal for which an individual qualifies on the basis of present training or experience.

VA can also help plan an effective job search.

Counseling is available for:

- Service members who are on active duty, and are within 180 days of discharge, and are stationed in the United States; or
- Veterans with discharges that are not dishonorable, who are within one year from date of discharge.

VOCATIONAL REHABILITATION

Veterans may qualify for Training and Rehabilitation under Chapter 31 of Title 38, United States Code, if:

- The veteran has a service-connected disability or disabilities rated by VA at 20% or more; and

- The veteran received a discharge from active duty that was not dishonorable; and

- The veteran has an employment handicap.

Veterans may also qualify with a service-connected disability or disabilities rated by VA at 10%, and:

- The veteran has a serious employment handicap; or

- The veteran first applied for vocational rehabilitation benefits before November 1, 1990, reapplied after that date, and has an employment handicap.

Vocational rehabilitation helps disabled veterans become independent in daily living. Veterans may also receive assistance in selecting, preparing for, and securing employment that is compatible with their interests, talents, skills, physical capabilities, and goals.

To apply for vocational rehabilitation, VA for 28-1900, Disabled Veterans Application for Vocational Rehabilitation, must be completed and sent to the nearest VA regional office.

For detailed information on vocational rehabilitation refer to Chapter 14 of this book.

APPEAL OF VA DECISION

VA decisions on education benefits may be appealed within one year of the date an individual receives notice of a VA decision.

For detailed information on filing an appeal, please refer to Chapter 35 of this book.

CHAPTER 18

EDUCATION BENEFITS –
POST-9/11 G.I. BILL, CHAPTER 33

The Post-9/11 GI Bill (or so-called *GI Bill for the 21st century*) is a new education benefit program for individuals who served on active duty on or after September 11, 2001. It boasts the most comprehensive education benefits package since the original GI Bill was signed into law in 1944.

The new bill goes well beyond helping to pay for tuition; many veterans who served after September 11, 2001, will get full tuition and fees, a new monthly housing stipend, and a $1,000 a year stipend for books and supplies. **The new bill also gives Reserve and Guard members who have been activated for more than 90 days since 9/11 access to the same GI Bill benefits.**

Post-9/11 GI Bill benefits are payable for training pursued on or after August 1, 2009. No payments can be made under this program for training pursued before this date.

IMPORTANT UPDATE

The Veterans Educational Assistance Improvements Act of 2010 was signed into law on January 4, 2011. At the time of this publication, the following information was available regarding this legislation:

Effective August 1, 2009, but not payable until October 1, 2011:

▪   Certain National Guard members mobilized on Title 32 orders on-or-after September 11, 2001 are now eligible for the Post-9/11 GI Bill and any qualifying Title 32 mobilization may be used to increase his or her percentage of eligibility.

Effective March 5, 2011:

▪   Limits active duty members to the net cost for tuition and fees prorated based on the eligibility tiers (40%-100%) previously established for Veterans. (Same limitations apply to transferee spouses of active duty servicemembers.)

Effective August 1, 2011:

- The Post-9/11 GI Bill will now pay all public school in-state tuition and fees; this includes graduate training, etc.

- For students attending private institutions of higher learning or foreign schools, the tuition and fee reimbursement is capped at the lesser of net out-of-pocket cost or $17,500 annually - however the Yellow Ribbon Program still exists.

- MGIB-AD & MGIB-SR College fund payments will now be paid on a monthly basis instead of a lump-sum at the beginning of the term.

- Reimbursement is now available for multiple Licensing and Certification Tests.

- Reimbursement is now available for fees paid to take national examinations used for admission to an institution of higher learning (e.g. SAT, LSAT, ACT, GMAT, etc).

- Vocational Rehabilitation participants may now elect the higher housing allowance offered by the Post-9/11 GI Bill if otherwise eligible for the Post-9/11 GI Bill.

- If training at greater than ½ time the housing allowance is now prorated according to the training time the individual is enrolled (rounded to the nearest tenth). So, if a student's full housing allowance is $1000, and he or she is attending ¾ time - the housing allowance would be $800 (80% of $1000).

- Break or interval pay is no longer payable under any VA education benefit program unless under an Executive Order of the President or due to an emergency situation such as a natural disaster or strike. Entitlement which previously would have been used for break pay will be available for use during a future enrollment.

  This means that if the semester ends December 15, the housing allowance is paid for the first 15 days of December only. Benefits will begin again when the new semester begins (e.g. January 15), and the student will be paid for the remaining days of that month and term.

  Students using other VA education programs are included in this change. Monthly benefits will be prorated in the same manner.

- NOAA and PHS personnel are now eligible to transfer their entitlement to eligible dependents

Effective October 1, 2011:

- If a student is training at greater than ½ time, his or her housing allowance is now prorated according to the training time he or she is enrolled. For example, if full housing allowance for is $1000, and the student is attending ¾ time - the housing allowance would be $750 (¾ of $1000)

- Housing allowance is now payable to students enrolled solely in distance learning. The housing allowance is ½ the national average BAH for an E-5 with dependents (the rate would be $673.50 for 2011).

- Non-college degree programs, on-the-job training, and flight training programs are now covered under the Post-9/11 GI Bill.

- The book stipend is now payable to active duty members.

ELIGIBILITY

If an individual has served a total of at least 90 consecutive days on active duty in the Armed Forces since September 11, 2001, he or she is eligible. However, the amount of benefits received under this program is determined by the actual amount of accumulated post 9/11 service the individual has.

An individual may be eligible if he or she has served at least 90 aggregate days on active duty after September 10, 2001, and is still on active duty, or was honorably:

- Discharged from the active duty; or

- Released from active duty and placed on the retired list or temporary disability retired list; or

- Released from active duty and transferred to the Fleet Reserve or Fleet Marine Corps Reserve; or

- Released from the active duty for further service in a reserve component of the Armed Forces.

Individuals may also be eligible if they were honorably discharged from active duty for a service-connected disability, and served 30 continuous days after September 10, 2001.

Some periods of active duty service are excluded. Periods of service under the following do not count toward qualification for the Post 9/11 GI Bill:

- NOAA, PHS, or Active Guard Reserve;

- ROTC under 10 U.S.C. 2107(b);

- Service academy contract period;

- Service terminated due to defective enlistment agreement;

- Service used for loan repayment; *and*

- Selected reserve service used to establish eligibility under the Montgomery GI Bill (MGIB chapter 30), MGIB for Selected Reserve (MGIB-SR Chapter 1606), or the Reserve Education Assistance Program (REAP chapter 1607).

Under the MGIB, officers who received their commission through a service academy, or an ROTC scholarship were ineligible. There are no such restrictions under the new program. Any officer, who was previously ineligible, will be eligible for the new program, assuming they have at least 90 days of post 9/11 active duty service.

Similarly, military members who previously declined the MGIB are eligible for the new program.

If, on August 1, 2009, a servicemember was eligible for MGIB-SR or REAP, and he or she qualifies for the Post-9/11 GI Bill, he or she must make an irrevocable election to receive benefits under the Post-9/11 GI Bill. The individual then loses any right to future MGIB-SR or REAP benefits.

BENEFIT AMOUNT PAYABLE

The new rates depend on the length of post 9/11 active duty service, the state of residence, and the number of courses taken. Like the MGIB, the Post-9/11 GI Bill pays 36 months of full time education benefits. So, if an individual goes to school full-time, he or she will receive the full benefit rates for 36 months. If he or she goes to school 1/2 time, he or she will receive half of the monthly entitlement for 72 months, etc.

Based on the length of active duty service, eligible participants are entitled to receive a percentage of the following:

- Cost of tuition and fees, not to exceed the most expensive in-state undergraduate tuition at a public institution of higher education (paid directly to the school);

- Monthly housing allowance equal to the basic allowance for housing payable to a military E-5 with dependents, in the same zip code as the primary school (paid directly to the servicemember or veteran);

- Yearly books and supplies stipend of up to $1,000 per year (paid directly to the servicemember or veteran); and

- A one-time payment of $500 paid to certain individuals relocating from highly rural areas.

(The housing allowance and books and supplies stipend are not payable to individuals on active duty. The housing allowance is not payable to those pursuing training at half time or less or to individuals enrolled solely in distance learning programs.)

The following chart outlines the breakdown of benefits based on amount of service:

Member Serves	Percentage of Maximum Benefit Payable
At least 36 months	100%
At least 30 continuous days on active duty and must be discharged due to service-connected disability	100%
At least 30 months, but less than 36 months	90%
At least 24 months, but less than 30 months	80%
At least 18 months, but less than 24 months	70%
At least 12 months, but less than 18 months	60%
At least 06 months, but less than 12 months	50%
At least 90 days, but less than 06 months	40%

2010-2011 MAXIMUM IN-STATE TUITION & FEES

We are providing the final figures that have been confirmed by State Approving Agencies in accordance with VA's statutory requirement to determine the **highest** in-state, undergraduate, public tuition as specified in 38 USC 3313(c)(1)(A). This information has no relationship to, and should not be compared with, average costs of tuition and fees of public institutions within any state commonly referred to when considering educational options.

Table last updated August 31, 2010

State	Maximum Charge per Credit Hour	Maximum Total Fees per Term
Alabama	$329.17	$20,787.00
Alaska	$170.00	$19,455.00
Arizona	$725.00	$15,000.00
Arkansas	$210.15	$1,774.78
California	$391.75	$2,264.75
Colorado	$529.50	$45,774.25
Connecticut	$543.00	$2,660.50
Delaware	$425.33	$584.00
District of Columbia	$265.83	$310.00
Florida	$295.00	$43,660.00
Guam	$190.00	$249.00
Georgia	$505.00	$15,440.00
Hawaii	$316.00	$1,325.70
Idaho	$273.00	$2,428.24
Illinois	$629.75	$16,367.00
Indiana	$338.50	$13,063.00
Iowa	$343.66	$17,222.00
Kansas	$420.05	$50,752.96
Kentucky	$456.30	$11,235.00
Louisiana	$473.00	$2,884.70
Maine	$345.00	$5,500.00
Maryland	$471.86	$16,308.00
Massachusetts	$340.00	$20,793.50
Michigan	$1,001.00	$19,374.50
Minnesota	$450.00	$37,808.00
Mississippi	$584.75	$805.00
Missouri	$373.00	$11,898.00
Montana	$205.40	$13,646.00
Nebraska	$251.00	$1,589.55
Nevada	$156.75	$4,072.46
New Hampshire	$1,003.75	$5,197.00
New Jersey	$468.66	$7,962.00
New Mexico	$229.40	$6,104.00
New York	$1,010.00	$12,293.00

State	Maximum Charge per Credit Hour	Maximum Total Fees per Term
North Carolina	$606.63	$2,293.40
North Dakota	$464.46	$25,686.00
Ohio	$508.25	$15,134.00
Oklahoma	$188.60	$15,058.05
Oregon	$407.00	$25,669.00
Pennsylvania	$934.00	$6,110.00
Puerto Rico	$90.00	$25.00
Rhode Island	$376.00	$5,187.00
South Carolina	$829.00	$2,798.00
South Dakota	$99.80	$25,685.00
Tennessee	$270.00	$13,426.00
Texas	$1,549.00	$12,130.00
Utah	$238.70	$85,255.00
Vermont	$512.00	$5,106.00
Virgin Islands	$125.00	$706.00
Virginia	$353.50	$3,969.50
Washington	$430.00	$9,648.00
West Virginia	$268.67	$4,276.67
Wisconsin	$673.00	$30,963.00
Wyoming	$99.00	$4,335.00
Overseas	$439.69	$13,713.88

CONTRIBUTIONS

Unlike the MGIB and VEAP, the new MGIB does not require the servicemember to elect or decline, nor make monthly contributions. Unfortunately, if someone has already contributed to the GI Bill, he or she won't get their money back, unless they use all of their new GI Bill entitlements. If they do, the $1,200 contribution to the MGIB (or a proportional amount, if they used any of their MGIB entitlement) will be added to his or her final new GI Bill education payment. If an individual is currently paying into the MGIB, he or she can stop now, and still be eligible for the new program, beginning in August 2009.

IRREVOCABLE ELECTION

If, on August 1, 2009, the servicemember or veteran is eligible for the Montgomery GI Bill; the Montgomery GI Bill-Selected Reserve; or the Reserve Educational Assistance Program, and qualifies for the Post-9/11 GI Bill, an irrevocable election must be made to receive benefits under the Post-9/11 GI Bill. In most instances, once the election to receive benefits under the Post-9/11 GI Bill is made, the individual will no longer be eligible to receive benefits under the relinquished program.

COVERED EXPENSES

The plan covers any approved programs offered by a school in the United States that is authorized to grant an associate (or higher) degree.

The plan may also pay for tutorial assistance, or up to $2,000 for the reimbursement of one licensing or certification test.

If a servicemember transferred to the Post-9/11 GI Bill from MGIB-Active Duty, MGIB-SR, or REAP, he or she may also receive Post-9/11 benefits for flight training, apprenticeship, or on-the-job training programs, and correspondence courses.

COLLEGE FUNDS

If the member is eligible for a "kicker," such as the Army or Navy College Fund, or a Reserve "Kicker," he or she will still receive the extra monthly benefit under the new GI bill. This monthly amount will be paid to the member, not to the university.

COLLEGE LOAN REPAYMENT

Individuals, who were previously ineligible for the MGIB because they elected the College Loan Repayment Program (CLRP), are eligible for the new GI Bill, but only active duty service performed after their initial active duty service obligation counts toward the new benefits. In other words, if they were initially enlisted for five years and received the CLRP, they would have to reenlist or extend their enlistment in order to take advantage of the new GI Bill.

TRANSFERRING BENEFITS TO DEPENDENTS

While the Post-9/11 GI Bill offers a very generous post-service education benefit, a special provision of the program allows career service members the opportunity to share their education benefits with immediate family members.

Allowing career service members to transfer their GI Bill benefits to family members has long been one of the most requested items among military family readiness and advocacy groups.

Eligible Individuals

Any member of the Armed Forces (active duty or Selected Reserve, officer or enlisted) on or after August 1, 2009, who is eligible for the Post-9/11 GI Bill, and:

- Has at least 6 years of service in the Armed Forces on the date of election and agrees to serve 4 additional years in the Armed Forces from the date of election.

- Has at least 10 years of service in the Armed Forces (active duty and/or selected reserve) on the date of election, is precluded by either standard policy (service or DoD) or statute from committing to 4 additional years, and agrees to serve for the maximum amount of time allowed by such policy or statute, or

  o Is (or becomes) retirement eligible during the period from August 1, 2009, through August 1, 2013. A service member is considered to be retirement eligible if he or she has completed 20 years of active duty or 20 qualifying years of reserve service.

    o For those individuals eligible for retirement on August 1, 2009, no additional service is required.

    o For those individuals who have an approved retirement date after August 1, 2009, and before July 1, 2010, no additional service is required.

    o For those individuals eligible for retirement after August 1, 2009, and before August 1, 2010, 1 year of additional service after approval of transfer is required.

    o For those individuals eligible for retirement on or after August 1, 2010, and before August 1, 2011, 2 years of additional service after approval of transfer are required.

    o For those individuals eligible for retirement on or after August 1, 2011, and before August 1, 2012, 3 years of additional service after approval of transfer required.

Eligible Family Members

An individual approved to transfer an entitlement to educational assistance under this section may transfer the individual's entitlement to:

- The individual's spouse.

- One or more of the individual's children.

- Any combination of spouse and child.

A family member must be enrolled in the Defense Eligibility Enrollment Reporting System (DEERS) and be eligible for benefits, at the time of transfer to receive transferred educational benefits.

A child's subsequent marriage will not affect his or her eligibility to receive the educational benefit; however, after an individual has designated a child as a transferee under this section, the individual retains the right to revoke or modify the transfer at any time.

A subsequent divorce will not affect the transferee's eligibility to receive educational benefits; however, after an individual has designated a spouse as a transferee under this section, the eligible individual retains the right to revoke or modify the transfer at any time.

Nature of Transfer

An eligible Service member may transfer up to the total months of unused Post-9/11 GI Bill benefits, or the entire 36 months if the member has used none.

Family member use of transferred educational benefits is subject to the following:

Spouse:

*   May start to use the benefit immediately.

*   May use the benefit while the member remains in the Armed Forces or after separation from active duty.

*   Is not eligible for the monthly stipend or books and supplies stipend while the member is serving on active duty.

*   Can use the benefit for up to 15 years after the service member's last separation from active duty.

Child:

*   May start to use the benefit only after the individual making the transfer has completed at least 10 years of service in the Armed Forces.

*   May use the benefit while the eligible individual remains in the Armed Forces or after separation from active duty.

*   May not use the benefit until he/she has attained a secondary school diploma (or equivalency certificate), or reached 18 years of age.

*   Is entitled to the monthly stipend and books and supplies stipend even though the eligible individual is on active duty.

*   Is not subject to the 15-year delimiting date, but may not use the benefit after reaching 26 years of age.

VEAP & THE POST 9/11 BENEFIT

If someone is eligible for both VEAP and the Post-9/11 GI Bill he or she may disenroll from VEAP and receive a refund of contributions, or leave the remaining contributions in the VEAP account and remain eligible for both benefit programs.

NOTE: Students may not receive benefits under more than one program at the same time.

EXPIRATION DATE

Eligibility for the new GI Bill expires 15 years from the last period of active duty of at least 90 consecutive days. If released for a service-connected disability after at least 30 days of continuous service, eligibility ends 15 years from when the member is released for the service-connected disability.

YELLOW RIBBON PROGRAM

The Post-9/11 GI Bill pays up to the highest public in-state undergraduate tuition. Tuition and fees may exceed that amount for individuals attending a private institution, graduate school or attending in a non-resident status.

The Yellow Ribbon Program is a provision of the Post-9/11 Veterans Education Assistance Act of 2008. Its purpose is to address enrollment at institutions that cost more than the Post-9/11 GI Bill's tuition benefit cap.

This program allows institutions of higher learning (degree granting institutions) in the United States to voluntarily enter into an agreement with VA to fund tuition expenses that exceed the highest public in-state undergraduate tuition rate. The institution can waive up to 50% of those expenses and VA will match the same amount as the institution.

To be eligible, the student must be:

- A veteran receiving benefits at the 100% benefit rate payable;

- A transfer-of-entitlement eligible dependent child; or

- A transfer-of-entitlement eligible spouse of a veteran.

The Institution of Higher Learning (IHL) must agree to:

- Provide contributions to eligible individuals who apply for the Yellow Ribbon Program on a first-come first-served basis, regardless of the rate at which the individual is pursuing training in any given academic year;

- Provide contributions during the current academic year and all subsequent academic years in which the student maintains satisfactory progress, conduct, and attendance;

- Make contributions toward the program on behalf of the individual in the form of a waiver;

- Choose the percentage that will be waived and waive the same percentage (up to 50%) of established charges that exceed the in-State maximum for each student eligible;

- State the maximum number of individuals for whom contributions will be made in any given academic year.

WORK-STUDY PROGRAM

Veterans and eligible transfer-of-entitlement recipients who train at the three-quarter rate of pursuit or higher may be eligible for a work study program in which they work for VA and receive hourly wages. Students under the work-study program must be supervised by a VA employee and all duties performed must relate to VA. The types of work allowable include:

- VA paperwork processing at schools or other training facilities.

- Assistance with patient care at VA hospitals or domiciliary care facilities.

- Work at national or state veterans' cemeteries.

- Other VA-approved activities.

CHAPTER 19

EDUCATION BENEFITS – RESERVE EDUCATIONAL ASSISTANCE PROGRAM (REAP) CHAPTER 1607

H.R. 4200 created a new education benefit called the **"Reserve Educational Assistance Program" (REAP)** or Chapter 1607. This new program makes certain individuals who were activated after September 11, 2001 either eligible for education benefits or eligible for increased benefits.

Purpose

Chapter 1607 was established as a part of the Ronald W. Reagan National Defense Authorization Act for Fiscal Year 2005. It is a new Department of Defense education benefit program designed to provide educational assistance to members of the Reserve components called or ordered to active duty in response to a war or national emergency (contingency operation) as declared by the President or Congress. The Department of Defense and the Department of Homeland Security will determine who is eligible for this program. The Department of Veterans Affairs will administer the program and pay benefits from funds contributed by DOD.

Chapter 1607 provides educational assistance to members of the reserve components called or ordered to active duty in response to a war or national emergency (contingency operations) as declared by the President or Congress.

Note: "Contingency operations" as defined in title 10 U.S. Code means "military operations that are designated by the Secretary of Defense as an operation in which members of the armed forces are or may become involved in military actions, operations or hostilities against an enemy of the United States or against opposing military force; or results in the call or order to, or retention on active duty of members of the uniformed services...."

Eligibility

The Secretaries of each military service, Department of Defense, and Department of Homeland Security (Coast Guard) will determine eligibility.

The law requires DoD to give individuals written notification of eligibility for REAP.

- Unlike the MGIB-Active Duty, service members do not have to pay anything to participate in Chapter 1607.

- A member of a reserve component who serves on active duty on or after September 11, 2001 under title 10 U.S. Code for a contingency operation and who serves at least 90 consecutive days or more is eligible for chapter 1607.

- National Guard members also are eligible if their active duty is under section 502(f), title 32 U.S.C. and they serve for 90 consecutive days when authorized by the President or Secretary of Defense for a national emergency and is supported by federal funds. Individuals are eligible as soon as they reach the 90-day point whether or not they are currently on active duty. DoD will fully identify contingency operations that qualify for benefits under chapter 1607.

- Disabled members who are injured or have an illness or disease incurred or aggravated in the line of duty and are released from active duty before completing 90 consecutive days are also eligible.

  (Members released early for disability incurred or aggravated in the line of duty may receive Chapter 1607 benefits at the 40% rate. The member is entitled to Chapter 1607 benefits for 10 years from the date of eligibility.)

Payment Rates

The benefit amount payable under Chapter 1607 is a percentage of the MGIB (Chapter 30) 3-year rate, based on the number of continuous days served on active duty.

Time Reserve Member Serves on Active Duty	Percentage of Ch 30 (3-Year Rate)
90 days but less than one year	40%
One year but less than two years	60%
Two years or more	80%

The following basic monthly rates are effective October 1, 2010:

INSTITUTIONAL TRAINING			
Training Time	Consecutive service of 90 days but less than one year	Consecutive service of 1 year or more	Consecutive service of 2 years or more
Full Time	$570.40	$855.60	$1140.80
¾ Time	427.80	641.70	855.60
½ Time	285.20	427.80	570.40
Less than ½ time, but more than ¼ time	285.20 (tuition & fees only)	427.80 (tuition & fees only)	570.40 (tuition & fees only)
¼ time or less	142.60 (tuition & fees only)	213.90 (tuition & fees only)	285.20 (tuition & fees only)

CORRESPONDENCE TRAINING	
40% Level	22% of the approved cost of course
60% Level	33% of the approved cost of course
80% Level	44% of the approved cost of course

FLIGHT TRAINING	
40% Level	24% of the approved cost of course
60% Level	36% of the approved cost of course
80% Level	48% of the approved cost of course

APPRENTICESHIP AND ON-THE-JOB TRAINING

Rates Effective October 1, 2010

Training Period	Consecutive service of 90 days, but less than one year	Consecutive service of 1 year or more	Consecutive service of 2 years or more
First six months of training	$427.80	$641.70	$855.60
Second six months of training	313.72	470.58	627.44
Remaining pursuit of training	199.64	299.46	399.28

COOPERATIVE TRAINING

Training Time	Service of 90 days, but less than one year	Service of 1 year or more	Service of 2 years or more
Monthly Rate	$570.40	$855.60	$1140.80

Note: Some reservists may contribute up to an additional $600 to the GI Bill to receive increased monthly benefits. For an additional $600 contribution, they may receive up to $5400 in additional GI Bill benefits

Applying For Benefits

VA Regional Processing Offices in Atlanta, St. Louis, Buffalo, and Muskogee will accept applications and supporting documents for Chapter 1607 claims. <u>VA will take action on your claim at this time.</u>

Individuals who have never submitted an Education Claim to VA:

Submit an **Application for VA Education Benefits (VA Form 22-1990)** and submit any available documents such as Discharge from Military Service (DD Form 214), copies of orders to active duty and anything else available as evidence of qualifying service.

Annotate "Chapter 1607" prominently on all correspondence and documents.

Individuals who have previously filed a claim for Education benefits:

A new application form is not required. However, individuals should submit any available documents such as Discharge from Military Service (DD Form

214), copies of orders to active duty and anything else available as evidence of qualifying service to help establish eligibility for this program. Individuals should also submit a **Request For Change of Program or Place of Training (VA form 22-1995)** which should be annotated "1607."

Annotate "Chapter 1607" prominently on all correspondence and documents.

Earliest Eligibility Date

Chapter 1607 benefits may be paid before the date of enactment the law, which was October 28, 2004. Chapter 1607 benefits are **potentially** payable from December 9, 2001 (90 days after September 11, 2001) for persons who were serving on a contingency operation on September 11, 2001 and who were in school on December 9, 2001.

Months of Benefits Payable

Individuals may receive 36 months of full time entitlement at his or her given rate. A Chapter 1607 participant may not use more than 48 months of entitlement under any combination of VA Educational programs. For example, if he or she has already used 20 months of Chapter 1606, he or she will only receive 28 months of Chapter 1607.

Benefit Ending Date

Individuals may use benefits under Chapter 1607 as long as they remain within their component. Benefits must be terminated if an individual leaves the Reserves or participates in a ROTC program under Title 10 Section 2107.

Note: There is no fixed delimiting period (ending date) for persons eligible under chapter 1607, as there is for all of the other VA education programs so long as an individual does not leave his or her Reserve component. There is one exception: If an individual is separated from the Ready Reserve for a disability which was not the result of his or her own willful misconduct, he or she is entitled to chapter 1607 benefits for 10-years after the date of entitlement.

2008 UPDATE:

As previously stated, under previous law, benefits ended upon separation from the Reserves. Section 530 of the National Defense Authorization Act of 2008 *increased the time period where a reservist may use SRMGIB benefits to ten years after separation from the Reserves*, as long as the member's discharge characterization is honorable. *This revision is backdated to October 28, 2004.*

Receipt of Other VA Education Benefits

Individuals must make an irrevocable election choosing which program they want their military service to count towards. Individuals also cannot receive assistance under more than one VA Education program at one time.

If an individual is eligible for a Chapter 1606 kicker, he or she can still be paid that kicker while receiving Chapter 1607.

Approved Courses

The following programs are available:

- College or University Degree Programs
- Vocational Programs
- Independent Study or Distance Learning Programs
- Correspondence Courses
- Flight Training
- On-the-Job Training and Apprenticeship Programs
- Tuition Assistance Top-Up Program
- Entrepreneurship Courses

(NOTE: VA does not approve schools or programs for benefits. Each individual state approves schools and courses. To find out if your school or program is approved for VA Educational Benefits under REAP, contact your school's VA Certifying Official, or call VA at 1-888-442-4551.)

CHAPTER 20

EDUCATION BENEFITS - MONTGOMERY G.I. BILL – SELECTED RESERVE (MGIB-SR), CHAPTER 1606

The Montgomery GI Bill-Selected Reserve Program is for members of the Selected Reserve, including the Army Reserve, Navy Reserve, Air Force Reserve, Marine Corps Reserve, Coast Guard Reserve, Army National Guard and Air National Guard. While the reserve components decide who is eligible for the program, VA makes the payments for the program. Chapter 1606 is the first educational program that does not require service in the *active* Armed Forces in order to qualify.

ELIGIBILITY REQUIREMENTS

- Member must have signed a 6-year obligation to serve in the Selected Reserve after June 30, 1985. (Officers must have agreed to serve 6 years in addition to his or her original obligation.) For some types of training, it is necessary to have a 6-year commitment that began after September 30, 1990. Call 1-888-GIBILL-1 for more information;

- Member must have completed his or her Initial Active Duty for Training (IADT);

- Member must maintain *Selected Reserve Status* - Serve in a drilling Selected Reserve unit and remain in good standing;

- Member must meet the requirement to receive a high school diploma or equivalency certificate before completing IADT. Member must remain in good standing while serving in an active Selected Reserve Unit;

- Effective November 1, 2000, veterans and reservists can apply for MGIB-SR benefits *any time* after receiving their high school diploma or equivalency certificate. It no longer has to be received prior to the end of the individual's first period of active duty.

Beginning on October 1, 1990, a member of the Selected Reserve with a bachelor's degree can become eligible by signing a new contract that will result in a 6 year reserve obligation. Beginning on November 30, 1993, a member of the Selected Reserve can become eligible for graduate degree training. A new 6 year contract is not required in order to pursue graduate training.

If an individual enters active duty in the Selected Reserve (AGR, TAR, FTS) after November 29, 1989, he or she must have been eligible *before* November 29, 1989 in order to remain eligible.

ELIGIBILITY RESTRICTIONS

MGIB – AD:
An individual can't be eligible for MGIB – SR if he or she elected to have his or her service in the Selected Reserve credited toward establishing eligibility under the Montgomery GI Bill – Active Duty

ROTC (Reserve Officers' Training Corps) scholarship under section 2107 of title 10, U.S. Code:
An individual can't be eligible for MGIB – SR if he or she is receiving financial assistance through the Senior ROTC program under this section of the law.

Note: However, an individual may still be eligible for MGIB – SR if he or she receives financial assistance under **Section 2107a** of title 10, U.S. Code. This financial assistance program is for specially selected members of the Army Reserve and National Guard only. Individuals should check with their ROTC advisor for more information.

Note: There's no restriction on service academy graduates receiving MGIB – SR. Service academy graduates who received a commission aren't eligible under MGIB – AD.

If an individual enters Active Guard and Reserve (AGR) status, his or her eligibility for MGIB – SR will be suspended. He or she may be eligible for MGIB – AD. The individual may resume MGIB – SR eligibility after AGR status ends.

APPROVED COURSES

Individuals may receive benefits for a wide variety of training, including:

- Undergraduate degrees from a college or university;

- Beginning November 30, 1993, graduate degrees from a college or university;

- Accredited independent study programs leading to standard college degrees;

- Technical courses for a certificate at a college or university.

Individuals with 6-year commitments beginning after September 30, 1990 may take the following types of training:

- Courses leading to a certificate or diploma from business, technical, or vocational schools;

- Cooperative training;

- Apprenticeship or job training programs offered by companies;

- Correspondence training;

- Independent study programs;

- Flight training (Individuals must have a private pilot's license, and must meet the medical requirements for the desired license program before beginning training, and throughout the flight training program.)

VA may approve programs offered by institutions outside of the United States, when they are pursued at educational institutions of higher learning, and lead to a college degree. Individuals must receive VA approval prior to attending or enrolling in any foreign programs.

Eligibility for this program is determined by the Selected Reserve components. Payments for the program are made by the VA.

A State agency or VA must approve each program offered by a school or company.

If an individual is seeking a college degree, the school must admit the individual to a degree program by the start of the individual's third term.

RESTRICTIONS ON TRAINING

Benefits are not payable for the following courses:

- Courses paid by the military Tuition Assistance program, if student is enrolled at less than ½ time;

- Courses taken while student is receiving a Reserve Officers' Training Corps scholarship;

- Non-accredited independent study courses;

- Bartending and personality development courses;

- Any course given by radio;

- Self-improvement courses such as reading, speaking, woodworking, basic seamanship, and English as a 2nd language;

- Any course which is avocational or recreational in character;

- Farm-cooperative courses;

- Audited courses;

- Courses not leading to an educational, professional, or vocational objective;

- Courses previously taken and successfully completed;

- Courses taken by a Federal government employee under the Government Employee's Training Act;

- Courses taken while in receipt of benefits for the same program from the Office of Workers' Compensation Programs.

VA must reduce benefits for individuals in Federal, State, or local prisons after being convicted of a felony.

An individual may not receive benefits for a program at a proprietary school if her or she is an owner or official of the school.

PART-TIME TRAINING

Individuals unable to attend school full-time should consider going part-time. Benefit rates and entitlement charges are less than the full-time rates. For example, if a student receives full-time benefits for 12 months, the entitlement charge is 12 months. However, if the student receives ½ time benefits for 12 months, the charge is 6 months. VA will pay for less than ½ time training if the student is not receiving Tuition Assistance for those courses.

REMEDIAL, DEFICIENCY AND REFRESHER TRAINING

Remedial and deficiency courses are intended to assist a student in overcoming a deficiency in a particular area of study. Individuals may qualify for benefits for remedial, deficiency, and refresher courses if they have a 6-year commitment that began after September 30, 1990. In order for such courses to be approved, the courses must be deemed necessary for pursuit of a program of education.

Refresher training is for technological advances that occurred in a field of employment. The advance must have occurred while the student was on active duty, or after release.

There is an entitlement charge for these courses.

TUTORIAL ASSISTANCE

Students may receive a special allowance for individual tutoring performed after September 30, 1992, if they entered school at one-half time or more. To qualify, the student must have a deficiency in a subject. The school must certify the tutor's qualifications, and the hours of tutoring. Eligible students may receive a maximum monthly payment of $100.00. The maximum total benefit payable is $1,200.00.

There is no entitlement charge for the first $600.00 of tutorial assistance.

To apply for tutorial assistance, students must submit VA Form 22-1990t, Application and Enrollment Certification for Individualized Tutorial Assistance. The form should be given to the certifying official in the office handling VA paperwork at the school for completion.

MONTHS OF BENEFITS / ENTITLEMENT CHARGED

Eligible members may be entitled to receive up to 36 months of education benefits. Benefit entitlement ends 10 years from the date the member becomes eligible for the program, or on the day the member leaves the Selected Reserve. (If a member's Reserve or National Guard unit was deactivated during the period October 1, 1991 through September 30, 1999, or if the member was involuntarily separated from service during this same period, eligibility for MGIB-SR benefits is retained for the full 10-year eligibility period. Eligibility for MGIB-SR benefits is also retained if a member is discharged due to a disability that was not caused by misconduct. Eligibility periods may be extended if a member is ordered to active duty.)

Individuals qualifying for more than one VA education program may receive a maximum of 48 months of benefits. For example, if a student used 30 months of Dependents' Educational Assistance, and is eligible for chapter 1606 benefits, he or she could have a maximum of 18 months of entitlement remaining.

Individuals are charged one full day of entitlement for each day of full-time benefits paid. For correspondence and flight training, one month of entitlement is charged each time VA pays one month of benefits. For cooperative programs, one month of entitlement is used for each month of benefits paid.

For apprenticeship and job training programs, the entitlement charge changes every 6 months. During the first 6 months, the charge is 75% of full time. For the second 6 months, the charge is 55% of full time. For the remainder of the program, the charge is 35% of full time.

RATES OF EDUCATIONAL ASSISTANCE PAY

The following basic monthly rates are effective October 1, 2010:

BASIC MONTHLY RATES MONTGOMERY G.I. BILL – SELECTED RESERVE (MGIB-SR), CHAPTER 1606				
Type of Training	**Full-Time**	**Three-Quarter Time**	**One-Half Time**	**Less than ½ Time**
Institutional	$337.00	$252.00	$167.00	$84.25
Cooperative Training	$337.00 (Full-Time Only)			
Correspondence Training	Entitlement charged at the rate of one month for each $337.00 paid *(Payment for correspondence courses is made at 55% of the approved charges for the course.)*			
Apprenticeship On-The-Job Training -	First six months: $252.75 Second six months: $185.35 Remainder of program: $117.95			
Flight Training	Entitlement charged at the rate of one month for each $337.00 paid *(Payment for flight training is made at 60% of the approved charges for the course, including solo hours.)*			

ELIGIBILITY PERIODS

2008 UPDATE:

Under previous law, benefits typically ended upon separation from the Reserves. Section 530 of the National Defense Authorization Act of 2008 ***increased the time period that a reservist may use SRMGIB benefits to ten years after separation from the Reserves***, as long as the member's discharge characterization is honorable. ***This revision is backdated to October 28, 2004.***

For individuals who separated from the Selected Reserve prior to 10/28/2004, generally benefits end the day of separation. For individuals who stayed in the Selected Reserve, generally benefits ended 14 years from the date the individual became eligible for the program.

Exceptions: *If an individual stayed in the Selected Reserve*, VA could generally extend the 14-year period if:

- The individual couldn't train due to a disability caused by Selected Reserve service; or

- The individual was activated for service in the Persian Gulf Era (which hasn't ended for purposes of VA education benefits); or

- The individual's eligibility expired during a period of his or her enrollment in training .

MISCELLANEOUS INFORMATION

- Any change in educational, professional or vocational objectives is considered a *"change of program."* The law permits one change of program without prior VA approval, provided an individual's attendance, conduct and progress in the last program were satisfactory. Additional *"changes of program"* require prior VA approval. VA will not charge a *change of program* if the individual enrolls in a new program after successful completion of the immediately preceding program.

- Once an individual starts receiving benefits, he must maintain satisfactory attendance, conduct and progress. The VA may stop benefits if an individual does not meet the standards set by the school. VA may later resume benefits if the individual reenters the same program at the same school, and the school approves the reentry, and certifies it to VA.

- If the individual does not reenter the same program at the same school, VA may resume benefits if the cause of unsatisfactory attendance, conduct or progress has been removed; and the program that the student intends to pursue is suitable to his or her abilities, aptitudes and interests.

- Effective November 1, 2000, VA education benefits can be paid (with some exceptions) for school breaks, if the breaks do not exceed 8 weeks; and the terms before and after the breaks are not shorter than the break. Prior to November 1 2000, VA education benefits could be paid only if the breaks did not exceed a calendar month.

APPLICATION FOR BENEFITS

When an individual becomes eligible for the program, his or her unit will provide the individual with a Notice of Basic Eligibility, DD Form 2384, or DD Form 2384-1 (for persons who establish eligibility on or after October 1, 1990). The unit will also code the eligibility into the Department of Defense personnel system.

When the individual finds a school, program, company, apprenticeship or job-training program, there are two important steps that must be followed:

- Make sure the program is approved for VA training. Contact the local VA regional office if there are any questions.
- Compete VA Form 22-1990, Application for Education Benefits. The completed form should be sent to the VA regional office with jurisdiction over the State where training will occur.

Following receipt of an application, VA will review it and advise if anything else is needed.

If an individual has started training, the application and Notice of Basic Eligibility should be taken to the school, employer or union. The certifying official should complete VA Form 22-1999, Enrollment Certification, and send all the forms to VA.

PROCEDURES FOR RECEIPT OF MONTHLY PAYMENTS

After selecting a school and submitting an application to VA, the school official must complete an enrollment certification, and submit it to the appropriate VA regional office. If a student meets the basic eligibility requirements for benefits, and the program or course is approved, VA will process the enrollment based on certified training time.

VA will accept the Notice of Basic Eligibility to pay benefits for 120 days after an individual's eligibility date. If the eligibility date is more than 120 days before the training program starts, VA will not approve the claim unless the Department of Defense personnel system shows that the individual is eligible. Only a student's reserve component can update the DoD personnel system. VA cannot change an individual's eligibility record.

When VA approves a claim, it will issue a letter with the details of the benefits payable. The first payment should be received within a few days of receipt of the letter.

If a student is enrolled in a degree program at a college or university, he or she will receive payment after the first of each month for the training during the preceding month. If a student is enrolled in a certificate or diploma program at a business, technical, or vocational school, he or she will not receive payment until they have verified their attendance. Students will receive a *Student Verification of Enrollment Form 22-8979* each month, and must complete and return it to the appropriate VA regional office. After processing, VA will release a check.

If an individual is in an apprenticeship or job-training program, he or she will receive a form to report the hours worked each month. The form must be signed and given to the certifying official for the company or union. The certifying official must complete the form and send it to the appropriate VA regional office. After processing, VA will release a check.

If an individual is taking a correspondence course, he or she will receive a form each quarter, on which the student must show the number of lessons completed that quarter. The completed form should be sent to the school for certification of the number of lessons serviced during the quarter. The school will send the form to the appropriate VA regional office. After processing, VA will release a check. Payments are based on the number of lessons serviced by the school.

VA will send flight schools a supply of blank monthly certification of flight training forms. The school must complete the form by entering the number of hours, the hourly rate, and the total charges for flight training received during the month. The student should review and sign the completed form, and send it to the appropriate VA regional office. After processing, VA will release a check.

NOTE: It is against the law for schools to cash VA checks under a Power of Attorney Agreement.

TIMELY RECEIPT OF VERIFICATION FORMS AND CHECKS

Students taking courses leading to a degree at a college or university should receive their checks for each month by the fifth of the next month. If it is not received by then, the VA should be immediately contacted so that appropriate action can be taken.

Students taking courses leading to a certificate or diploma from a business, technical, or vocational school should receive their verification forms for each month by the fifth of the following month. If it is not received by then, the VA should be immediately contacted so that another form can be issued.

One a completed verification form has been submitted, the student should receive a check within 2 weeks. If a check is not received by then, the VA should immediately be contacted so that appropriate action can be taken.

ADVANCE PAYMENTS

An advance payment for the initial month, or partial month and the following month may be made, if:

- The school agrees to handle advance payments; and

- Training is one-half time or more; and

- A request is made by the individual in writing; and

- The VA receives the enrollment certification at least 30 days prior to the start of classes.

Advance payments are made out to the individual, and sent to the applicable school for delivery to the individual registration. VA cannot issue a check more than 30 days before classes start. Before requesting an advance payment, students should verify with the school certifying official that the school has agreed to process advance payments.

Requests for advance payments must be on VA Form 22-1999, Enrollment Certification, or a sheet of paper attached to the enrollment certification.

Once a student receives an advance payment at registration, the school must certify to VA that the student received the check. If a student reduces enrollment, or withdraws from all courses during the period covered by an advance payment, he or she must repay the overpayment to VA.

If an individual believes that the amount of a VA check is incorrect, the VA should be contacted before the check is cashed.

DIRECT DEPOSIT

Payments can be sent directly to a student's savings or checking account through Direct Deposit (Electronic Funds Transfer). To sign up for direct deposit by phone, students must call (877) 838-2778.

STUDENT RESPONSIBILITIES

To ensure timely receipt of correct payments, students should be sure to promptly notify the VA of:

- Any change in enrollment;

- Any change in address;

- Any change in selected reserve status (If an individual changes units or components, both the old and new units must report the change to VA through the components' eligibility data systems.)

In addition, students should use reasonable judgment when accepting and cashing a check. All letters from VA about monthly rates and effective dates should be read carefully. If a student thinks the amount of a VA check is wrong,

VA should be contacted **before** cashing the check. Any incorrect checks should be returned to VA.

If a student cashes a check for the wrong amount, he or she will be liable for repayment of any resulting overpayment.

If an individual does not participate satisfactorily in the Selected Reserve, his or her eligibility ends. His or her component can require that a penalty be paid, based on a portion of payments received.

RECOVERY OF OVERPAYMENTS

VA must take prompt and aggressive action to recover overpayments. Students have the right to request a waiver of the overpayment, or verification that the amount is correct. If an overpayment is not repaid or waived, VA may add interest and collection fees to the debt. VA may also take one or more of the following actions to collect the debt:

- Withhold future benefits to apply to the debt;
- Refer the debt to a private collection agency;
- Recover the debt from any Federal income tax refund;
- Recover the debt from the salary (if student is a Federal employee);
- File a lawsuit in Federal court to collect the debt;
- Withhold approval of a VA home loan guarantee.

An individual's reserve component will act to collect penalties caused by unsatisfactory participation in the reserve.

CHANGES IN ENROLLMENT

If a student withdraws from one or more courses after the end of the school's drop period, VA will reduce or stop benefits on the date of reduction or withdrawal. Unless the student can show that the change was due to *mitigating circumstances*, the student may have to repay **all** benefits for the course.

VA defines *mitigating circumstances* as "unavoidable and unexpected events that directly interfere with the pursuit of a course, and which are beyond the student's control.

Examples of reasons VA may accept include:

- Extended illness;
- Severe illness or death in immediate family;
- Unscheduled changes in employment; and
- Lack of child care.

Examples of reasons VA may not accept include:

- Withdrawal to avoid a failing grade;
- Dislike of the instructor; and
- Too many courses attempted.

(VA may ask the student to furnish evidence to support the reason for change, such as physician or employer written statements.)

The first time a student withdraws from up to 6 credit hours, VA will "excuse" the withdrawal, and pay benefits for the period attended.

If a student receives a grade that does not count toward graduation, all benefits for the course may have to be repaid.

If a student receives a non-punitive grade, the school will notify VA, and VA may reduce or stop benefits. The student may not have to repay the benefits if he or she can show that the grades were due to mitigating circumstances.

WORK-STUDY PROGRAMS

Students may be eligible for an additional allowance under a work-study program that allows students to perform work for VA in return for an hourly wage. Students may perform outreach services under VA supervision, prepare and process VA paperwork, work at a VA medical facility or National Cemetery, or perform other approved activities.

Students must attend school at the three-quarter of full-time rate.

VA will select students for the work-study program based on different factors. Such factors include:

- Disability of the student;
- Ability of the student to complete the work-study contract before the end of his or her eligibility for education benefits;
- Job availability within normal commuting distance to the student;
- VA will give the highest priority to a veteran who has a service-connected disability or disabilities rated by VA at 30% or more.

The number of applicants selected will depend on the availability of VA-related work at the school or at VA facilities in the area.

Students may work during or between periods of enrollment, and can arrange with VA to work any number of hours during his or her enrollment. However, the maximum number of hours a student may work is 25 times the number of weeks in the enrollment period.

Students will earn an hourly wage equal to the Federal or State minimum wage, whichever is greater. If a student works at a college or university, the school **may** pay the difference between the amount VA pays and the amount the school normally pays other work-study students doing the same job.

Students interested in taking part in a work-study program must complete VA Form 22,8691, Application for Work-Study Allowance. Completed forms should be sent to the nearest VA regional office.

EDUCATIONAL COUNSELING

VA can provide services to help eligible individuals understand their educational and vocational strengths and weaknesses and to plan:

- An educational or training goal, and the means by which the goal can be reached; or

- An employment goal for which an individual qualifies on the basis of present training or experience.

VA can also help plan an effective job search.

Counseling is available for:

- Service members eligible for VA educational assistance; and

- Service members on active duty and within 180 days of discharge; or

- Veterans with discharges that are not dishonorable, who are within one year from date of discharge.

VOCATIONAL REHABILITATION

Veterans may qualify for Training and Rehabilitation under Chapter 31 of Title 38, United States Code, if:

- The veteran has a service-connected disability or disabilities rated by VA at 20% or more; and

- The veteran received a discharge from active duty that was not dishonorable; and

- The veteran has an employment handicap.

Veterans may also qualify with a service-connected disability or disabilities rated by VA at 10%, and:

- The veteran has a serious employment handicap; or
- The veteran first applied for vocational rehabilitation benefits before November 1, 1990, reapplied after that date, and has an employment handicap.

Vocational rehabilitation helps disabled veterans become independent in daily living. Veterans may also receive assistance in selecting, preparing for, and securing employment that is compatible with their interests, talents, skills, physical capabilities, and goals.

To apply for vocational rehabilitation, VA for 28-1900, Disabled Veterans Application for Vocational Rehabilitation, must be completed and sent to the nearest VA regional office.

For detailed information on vocational rehabilitation, refer to Chapter 14 of this book.

APPEAL OF VA DECISION

VA decisions on education benefits may be appealed within one year of the date an individual receives notice of a VA decision. Examples of *VA decisions* include:

- Training time,
- Change of program,
- School or course approval.

If a service member disagrees with a decision about his or her basic eligibility, he or she must contact the unit, National Guard Education Officer, or Army Reserve Education Services Officer. VA does not have authority under the law to reverse eligibility determinations. If the eligibility status is corrected, VA will pay benefits for periods during which the individual was eligible.

For detailed information on filing an appeal, please refer to Chapter 35 of this book.

CHAPTER 21

LIFE INSURANCE

VA insurance programs were developed to provide insurance benefits for veterans and servicemembers who may not be able to get insurance from private companies because of a service connected disability or because of the extra risks involved in military service.

VA has responsibility for veterans' and servicemembers' life insurance programs. Listed below are the eight life insurance programs managed by VA. The first four programs listed are closed to new issues. The last four are still issuing new policies.

WAR RISK INSURANCE ACT (1914)

The United States Government first became involved in the insurance business when war broke out in Europe in 1914. Although President Wilson declared America neutral, commercial merchant ships supplied war materials to the allies in the war against Germany. Owners of these merchant ships could not get marine insurance from commercial companies. Congress passed the War Risk Insurance Act on September 2, 1914, providing marine insurance protection for merchant ships supplying the allies.

America entered the war against Germany in April 1917. Life insurance issued by commercial life insurers either excluded protection against the extra hazards of war, or if such protection was included, the premium rates were much higher than the normal rate. The War Risk Insurance Act was amended on June 12, 1917, to cover merchant marine personnel. The act was again amended on October 6, 1917, authorizing, for the first time, issuance of government life insurance to members of the armed forces. Over 4 million policies were issued during World War I.

UNITED STATES GOVERNMENT LIFE INSURANCE – USGLI (1919-1940) POLICY PREFIX – K

The United States Government Life Insurance program (USGLI) was established in 1919 and replaced War Risk policies. Individuals could keep this coverage after separation from service.

The program was established to meet the needs of World War I veterans, but remained open to servicemembers and veterans with service before October 8, 1940. The government became a self-insurer, since private insurance companies were unwilling to assume the unpredictable risks associated with a war.

Premiums No Longer Paid

Because of the strong financial position of this program, all USGLI policies were declared paid-up as of January 1, 1983. *Premiums are no longer collected from policyholders in this program.*

Dividends Paid To USGLI Policyholders

Dividends are paid on all but a few USGLI policies.

Reserves set aside in the trust funds continue to earn interest each year in excess of what is needed to pay future claims allowing VA to pay dividends.

Disability Provisions

USGLI policies (except Special Endowment at Age 96) contain a provision that matures the policy upon the insured's total permanent disability. Under this provision:

- Proceeds are payable in installments of $5.75 monthly per $1,000 of insurance, as long as the insured remains totally and permanently disabled, with 240 payments guaranteed.

- If the insured dies before all guaranteed installments have been paid, the balance is payable to his or her named beneficiary.

- No additional premium is charged.

- There is no limit as to the age at which a disability may occur.

Filing a Death Claim

To file a death claim, the beneficiary should complete *VA Form 29-4125, Claim for One Sum Payment.* The completed form should be mailed or faxed, along with a death certificate to:

Department of Veterans Affairs
Regional Office and Insurance Center
PO Box 7208
Philadelphia, PA 19101
Fax: (215) 381-3561

If the beneficiary desires monthly payments instead of one lump sum, additional information is needed. The beneficiary should call the Insurance Center at (800) 669-8477 for instructions.

Customer Service

Any questions regarding USGLI should be directed to the VA Life Insurance Program at (800) 669-8477.

NATIONAL SERVICE LIFE INSURANCE (1940-1951)
POLICY PREFIX - V, H, N OR AN

The National Service Life Insurance program (NSLI) was established on October 8, 1940 to meet the insurance needs of World War II military personnel and veterans. Like USGLI coverage, insureds could keep their NSLI coverage after discharge from service.

> *Any questions regarding NSLI should be directed to the VA Life Insurance Program at (800) 669-8477.*

Over 22 million policies were issued under the NSLI program. The majority of policies VA administers directly are NSLI policies. This program remained open until April 25, 1951, when two new programs were established for Korean War servicemembers and veterans.

The NSLI program provides for:

- A maximum amount of $10,000 insurance coverage. (However, this limit does not include *paid-up additional insurance* which can be purchased with the annual dividends.);

- Individual policies issued to each policyholder;

- Certain contractual rights whereby a policyholder can bring a suit against VA in a US District Court. Administrative decisions of the Board of Veterans Appeals can be appealed to the Court of Veterans Appeals.

Premium Rates "Capped" For Term Policies

NSLI "V" term policies can be renewed indefinitely. At the older ages, premium rates increase significantly to cover the higher death rates at those ages.

In 1984, the VA "capped" premium rates at the age 70 rate. This means that a term policyholder's premium will never increase over the age 70 -premium rate.

Effective September 11, 2000, "capped" NSLI term policies receive a termination dividend if a policy lapses, or if the policyholder voluntarily cancels their policy. The termination dividend will be used to purchase paid-up additional whole life insurance.

Dividends Paid To NSLI Policyholders

After the reserve level requirements are determined by the Insurance Actuarial Staff, any surplus funds are returned to policyholders as a dividend.

Disability Provisions

All NSLI policies provide for
- A waiver of premiums at no extra cost if the insured becomes totally disabled for six months or longer prior to age 65.

- An optional "Total Disability Income Provision" covering disability before age 65, providing a monthly income of up to $100 per month, as long as total disability continues.

"H" Insurance

"H" policies were issued between August 1, 1946, and December 31, 1949, to veterans with service-incurred disabilities.

On November 11, 1998, the President signed into law the 'Veterans Programs Enhancement Act of 1998' (Public Law 105-368), which contained provisions affecting VA benefits. Included in the legislation was the merger of "H" policies into the regular NSLI "V" policies. Under the new law:
- All "H" policies were to be converted to "V" policies by January 1999.

- Converted policies now have the same premium rates and policy provisions as "V" policies.

- "H" policyholders now receive dividends.

Filing a Death Claim

To file a death claim, the beneficiary should complete *VA Form 29-4125, Claim for One Sum Payment*. The completed form should be mailed or faxed, along with a death certificate to:

Department of Veterans Affairs
Regional Office and Insurance Center
PO Box 7208
Philadelphia, PA 19101
Fax: (215) 381-3561

If the beneficiary desires monthly payments instead of one lump sum, additional information is needed. The beneficiary should call the Insurance Center at 1-800-669-8477 for instructions.

Customer Service

Any questions regarding NSLI should be directed to the VA Life Insurance Program at (800) 669-8477.

SERVICEMEN'S INDEMNITY INSURANCE (1951-1956)

In 1951, NSLI was replaced by Servicemen's Indemnity Insurance, which automatically covered active duty servicemembers for $10,000 at no cost to the individual. Servicemembers remained covered for 120 days after their discharge.

VETERANS' SPECIAL LIFE INSURANCE – VSLI (1951-1956)
POLICY PREFIX – RS OR W

Discharged servicemembers who had Servicemen's Indemnity Insurance could replace their coverage with Veterans' Special Life Insurance (VSLI). VSLI was established in 1951 to meet the insurance needs of veterans who served during

> *The Veterans' Special Life Insurance program was closed to new issues at the end of 1956.*

the Korean Conflict, and the post Korean period through January 1, 1957. The VSLI program allowed these newly discharged servicemembers to apply for $10,000 of contract term insurance. Application had to be made during the 120-day period during which they remained covered by Servicemen's Indemnity Insurance. (The $10,000 policy limit does not include *paid-up additional insurance*, which can be purchased with the annual dividends.)

In the early 1950's, commercial life insurance companies began to view the government's life insurance programs for veterans as competition for their business and began lobbying Congress to remove the government from the life insurance business. As a result, the Veterans' Special Life Insurance program was closed to new issues at the end of 1956.

Features Of "RS" And "W" Policies:

There are two types of VSLI policies:

"RS" - five-year level premium term policies:

- These were the original policies available in this program.

- "RS" policies could remain in force as 5 Year Level Premium Term beyond the age of 50.

- To provide financial relief from the high premium rates at advanced ages, "RS" term premiums were capped at the age 70-renewal rate effective May 1, 1989. This meant that the annual premium for these policies would not exceed $69.73 per $1,000 of coverage.

Effective September 11, 2000, "capped" VSLI term policies receive a termination dividend if a policy lapses, or if the policyholder voluntarily cancels their policy. The termination dividend will be used to purchase paid-up additional whole life insurance.

"W" - five-year level premium term policies:

- A 1959 legislative change permitted "RS" policyholders to convert to permanent plans or to exchange their policies for a special lower premium term policy. These newer policies are identified by the prefix "W."

- To avoid "W" term policyholders from keeping their policies into advanced ages (when premiums are very high), these policies had to be converted to permanent plans before age 50, or coverage ceased. There are no longer any "W" term policyholders eligible for this conversion.

Disability Provisions

All VSLI policies provide for:

- A waiver of premiums at no extra cost based on the insured's total disability lasting six months or longer and starting before age 65.

- An optional Total Disability Income Provision covering disability before age 65, providing a monthly income of $10 per $1,000 of insurance, is available at an extra cost.

Filing a Death Claim

To file a death claim, the beneficiary should complete *VA Form 29-4125, Claim for One Sum Payment*.

The completed form should be mailed or faxed, along with a death certificate to:

Department of Veterans Affairs
Regional Office and Insurance Center
PO Box 7208
Philadelphia, PA 19101
Fax: (215) 381-3561

If the beneficiary desires monthly payments instead of one lump sum, additional information is needed. The beneficiary should call the Insurance Center at (800) 669-8477 for instructions.

Customer Service

Any questions regarding VSLI should be directed to the VA Life Insurance Program at (800) 669-8477.

SERVICE-DISABLED VETERANS INSURANCE-
S-DVI
(1951-PRESENT)
(POLICY PREFIX - RH OR ARH)

The only new insurance issued between 1957 and 1965 to either servicemembers or veterans was Service-Disabled Veterans Insurance. This insurance was (and still is) available to veterans with a service-connected disability.

S-DVI, also called "RH Insurance" is available in a variety of permanent plans, as well as term insurance. Policies are issued for a maximum face amount of $10,000.

S-DVI is open to veterans separated from the service on or after April 25, 1951, who receive a service-connected disability rating of 0% or greater. New policies are still being issued under this program.

Eligibility For S-DVI Insurance ("RH")

Veterans are eligible to apply for S-DVI if:

- They have received a rating for a service-connected disability.

- They apply for the insurance within two years from the date service-connection is established. (Public Law 102-86 extended the initial one-year limit for service-connection grants made on or after September 1, 1991.)

Eligibility For Supplemental S-DVI ("Supplemental RH")

The Veterans' Benefits Act of 1992, provided for $20,000 of supplemental coverage to S-DVI policyholders. (Effective October 1, 2011 this amount will increase to $30,000.)

Premiums may not be waived on this supplemental coverage.

S-DVI policyholders are eligible for this supplemental coverage if:

- They are eligible for a waiver of premiums.

- They apply for the coverage within one year from notice of the grant of waiver.

Gratuitous S-DVI ("ARH")

Congress enacted legislation in 1959 to protect veterans who become incompetent from a service-connected disability while eligible to apply for S-DVI, but who die before an application is filed. "ARH" insurance is:

- Issued posthumously;
- Payable to a preferred class of the veteran's relatives;
- Payable in a lump sum only.

Premiums For S-DVI Insurance

The premiums charged for this coverage are:

- Based on the rates a healthy individual would have been charged when the program began in 1951.
- Insufficient to pay all of the claims because the program insures many veterans with severe disabilities.
- Waived for totally disabled veterans (27% of S-DVI policyholders).
- Supplemented on an annual basis by Congressional appropriations.

Effective November 1, 2000, the VA "capped" premium rates at the age 70 rate. This means that a term policyholder's premium will never increase over the age 70 -premium rate.

There are no reserves or surplus funds in this program. Therefore, dividends are *not* paid.

Disability Provisions

S-DVI policies (except supplemental coverage) provide for the following disability benefits:

- A waiver of premiums at no extra premium based on the insured's total disability lasting six months or longer and starting before age 65;
- A total disability premium waiver in cases where the disability commenced prior to the effective date of the policy, providing the disability is service-connected.

The optional Total Disability Income Provision is not available under this program.

Filing a Death Claim

To file a death claim, the beneficiary should complete _VA Form 29-4125, Claim for One Sum Payment_. The completed form should be mailed or faxed, along with a death certificate to:

Department of Veterans Affairs
Regional Office and Insurance Center
PO Box 7208
Philadelphia, PA 19101
Fax: (215) 381-3561

If the beneficiary desires monthly payments instead of one lump sum, additional information is needed. The beneficiary should call the Insurance Center at (800) 669-8477 for instructions.

Customer Service

Any questions regarding USGLI should be directed to the VA Life Insurance Program at (800) 669-8477.

VETERANS' REOPENED INSURANCE - VRI (1965-1966) POLICY PREFIX - J, JR, OR JS

In 1964, Congress enacted legislation providing for a limited reopening of NSLI and VSLI. Beginning May 1, 1965, veterans who had been eligible to obtain insurance between October 8, 1940 and January l, 1957, could once again apply for government life insurance. They had one year to apply for this "reopened" insurance, which was available _only_ to disabled veterans. Approximately 228,000 VRI policies were issued. No term insurance policies were issued in this program.

The maximum face amount of a policy is $10,000. However, this limit does not include _paid-up additional insurance_, which can be purchased with the dividends that are paid annually on these policies.

Premium Rates

Premium rates for this insurance depend on the nature and severity of the disability.

Disability Provisions

VRI policies provide for:

- A waiver of premium at no extra premium based on the insured's total disability lasting six months or longer, and starting prior to age 65.

- An optional total disability income benefit covering disability occurring before age 65 for "J" policyholders. (This is **not** available on policies prefixed by "JR" or "JS".) Payments are made at the rate of $10 monthly per $1,000 of coverage, as long as the insured remains totally disabled.

Dividends Paid To VRI Policyholders

The VRI program began paying dividends in 1980 in order to more equitably distribute the surplus earnings of the program.

Filing a Death Claim

To file a death claim, the beneficiary should complete *VA Form 29-4125, Claim for One Sum Payment*. The completed form should be mailed or faxed, along with a death certificate to:

Department of Veterans Affairs
Regional Office and Insurance Center
PO Box 7208
Philadelphia, PA 19101
Fax: (215) 381-3561

If the beneficiary desires monthly payments instead of one lump sum, additional information is needed. The beneficiary should call the Insurance Center at (800) 669-8477 for instructions.

Customer Service

Any questions regarding VRI should be directed to the VA Life Insurance Program at (800) 669-8477.

SERVICEMEMBERS' GROUP LIFE INSURANCE - SGLI
(1965-PRESENT)

To meet the insurance needs of Vietnam Era servicemembers, the government entered into a cooperative effort with the private insurance industry. In 1965, the Servicemembers' Group Life Insurance (SGLI) program was established. This program provides low-cost term insurance protection to servicemembers through a group policy issued by a commercial life insurance company. Under this policy, the government agrees to pay the claim costs resulting from of the extra hazards of service. All other costs of the program are covered by the premiums deducted from the service member's pay.

SGLI is supervised by the Department of Veterans Affairs and is administered by the Office of Servicemembers' Group Life Insurance (OSGLI) under terms of a group insurance contract.

Effective December 1, 2005, a new program of insurance was created under SGLI, called Traumatic Servicemembers' Group Life Insurance (TSGLI). This coverage provides servicemembers protection against loss due to traumatic injuries and is designed to provide financial assistance to members so their loved ones can be with them during their recovery from their injuries. The coverage ranges from $25,000 to $100,000 depending on the nature of the injury.

(See following section for further information regarding Traumatic Injury Coverage.)

Eligibility For SGLI

Full-time coverage is available for:

- Commissioned, warrant and enlisted members of the Army, Navy, Air Force, Marine Corps and Coast Guard;

- Commissioned members of the National Oceanic and Atmospheric Administration and the Public Health Service;

- Cadets or midshipmen of the four United States Service Academies;

- Ready Reservists scheduled to perform at least 12 periods of inactive training per year.

- Members of the Individual Ready Reserves who volunteer for assignment to a mobilization category.

- Part-time coverage is available for eligible members of the Reserves who do not qualify for full-time coverage.

Coverage Amounts

- Effective September 1, 2005 coverage in the SGLI Program increased from $250,000 to $400,000. As of September 1, 2005, coverage must be elected in $50,000 increments.   (Prior to September 1, 2005, coverage could be elected in $10,000 increments.)

- A special death gratuity of $150,000 was approved for survivors of servicemembers who:

- Died from October 7, 2001 to September 1, 2005, and

- Died while on active duty.

SGLI coverage is:

- Automatic at the time of entry into a period of active duty or reserve status.

- Available in $50,000 increments up to the maximum of $400,000 of insurance.

Members may decline coverage or may elect reduced coverage by contacting their personnel officer and completing Form 8286, SGLI Election and Certificate. If such a member later wishes to obtain or increase coverage, proof of good health will be required.

NOTE: *Reservists called to active duty, are* **automatically** *insured for $400,000 regardless of whether or not they had previously declined coverage, or elected a lesser amount of coverage while on reserve duty.*

Coverage Periods

Full-time SGLI coverage for members on active duty or active duty for training and members of the Ready Reserve will terminate:

1. The 120th day after separation or release from duty, or separation or release from assignment to a unit or position of the Ready Reserve;
2. For members who are totally disabled on the date of separation or release, at the end of the last day of one year following separation or release or at the end of the day on which the insured ceases to be totally disabled, whichever is earlier, but in no event earlier than 120 days following separation or release from such duty; **(NOTE: Refer to important updated information following #4, below.)**

3. At the end of the 31st day of a continuous period of:

    a. Absence without leave;
    b. Confinement by military authorities under a court-martial sentence involving total forfeiture of pay and allowances; or
    c. Confinement by civilian authorities under sentence adjudged by a civilian court. Note: Any insurance terminated as the result of the absence or confinement, together with any beneficiary designation in effect at the time the insurance was terminated, will be automatically restored as of the date the member returns to duty with pay.

4. The last day of the month in which the member files with the uniformed service, written notice of an election not to be insured.

UPDATE - SGLI Disability Extension Increased to Two Years

On June 15, 2006, the President signed P.L. 109- 233, the Veterans' Housing Opportunity & Benefits Improvement Act of 2006. The Law extends the period of Servicemembers' Group Life Insurance (SGLI) coverage for totally disabled veterans following separation from active duty or active duty for training to the earlier of:

- The date on which the insured ceases to be totally disabled; or

- The date that is two years after separation or release,

The Law makes identical changes with respect to certain reserve assignments in which the individual performs active duty or volunteers for assignment to a mobilization category.

The SGLI Disability Extension is available to you if you are totally disabled at time of discharge. To be considered totally disabled, you must have a disability that prevents you from being gainfully employed OR have one of the following conditions, regardless of your employment status:

- Permanent loss of use of both hands
- Permanent loss of use of both feet
- Permanent loss of use of both eyes
- Permanent loss of use of one hand and one foot
- Permanent loss of use of one foot and one eye
- Permanent loss of use of one hand and one eye
- Total loss of hearing in both ears
- Organic loss of speech (lost ability to express oneself, both by voice and whisper, through normal organs for speech - being able to speak with an artificial appliance is disregarded in determination of total disability)

Part-time coverage terminates as follows:

1. Part-time coverage is in effect only on the days of active duty or active duty for training, and the hours of inactive duty training, including period of travel to and from duty. A temporary termination of coverage occurs at the end of each such period of duty, including travel time, and coverage is resumed at the commencement of the next period of covered duty or travel.
2. When part-time coverage is extended for 120 days as the result of a disability, the extended coverage terminates at the end of the 120th day following the Reservist active or inactive period during which the disability was incurred or aggravated.
3. Unless extended for 120 days because of disability as referred to above, eligibility for part-time coverage terminates at the end of the last day of the member's obligation to perform such duty.
4. If a member files with the uniformed service a written notice of an election not to be insured, coverage terminates on the last day of the period of active duty or active duty for training, or at the end of the period of inactive duty training, including travel time while returning from such duty during which the election is filed. If the election is filed with a member's uniformed service other than during a period of active duty, active duty for training, or inactive duty the coverage is terminated immediately.

Beneficiary Selection

Any beneficiary can be named. If none is selected, the insurance is distributed, by law, in the following order:

- Spouse; or
- Children; or
- Parents; or
- Executor of estate; or
- Other next of kin.

An insured should designate a beneficiary by completing *Form SGVL 8286, Servicemembers' Group Life Insurance Election and Certificate.* The completed form should be submit to the individual's uniformed service.

Options For Payment Of Policy Proceeds

SGLI proceeds can be paid in a lump sum *or* over a 36-month period.

Alliance Account

If the proceeds are to be paid in a lump sum then beneficiaries of SGLI and VGLI will receive the payment of their insurance proceeds via an *"Alliance Account"*. Rather than the traditional single check for the full amount of insurance proceeds, the beneficiary receives a checkbook for an interest bearing account from which the beneficiary can write a check for any amount from $250 up to the full amount of the proceeds. The Alliance Account :

- Earns interest at a competitive rate;
- Is guaranteed by Prudential;
- Gives the beneficiary time to make important financial decisions while their funds are secure and earning interest ;
- Gives them instant access to their money at all times.

Accelerated Benefits

On November 11, 1998, the President signed legislation authorizing the payment of "Accelerated Benefits" in the SGLI and VGLI programs subject to the following:

- Terminally ill insureds will have access of up to 50% of the face amount of their coverage during their lifetime.
- This money will be available in increments of $5,000.
- An insured must have a medical prognosis of life expectancy of 9 months or less.

Insurance Options After Separation From Service

When released from active duty or the Reserve, members with full-time SGLI coverage can convert their coverage to Veterans Group Life Insurance **or** to an individual commercial life insurance policy with any one of 99 participating commercial insurance companies.

Filing Death Claims

A beneficiary may file a claim for VGLI proceeds by submitting *Form SGLV 8283, Claim For Death Benefits*, to:

Office of Servicemembers' Group Life Insurance
213 Washington Avenue
Newark, NJ 07102-2999

Taxation

SGLI proceeds that are payable at the death of the insured are excluded from gross income for tax purposes. (The value of the proceeds, however, may be included in determining the value of an estate, and that estate may ultimately be subject to tax.)

If SGLI proceeds are paid to a beneficiary in 36 equal installments, the interest portion included in these installments is also exempt from taxation. In addition, delayed settlement interest (interest accrued from the date of the insured's death to the date of settlement) is also exempt from taxation.

A beneficiary is not required to report to the Internal Revenue Service any installment interest or delayed settlement interest received in addition to the proceeds.

Customer Service

Any questions regarding SGLI should be directed to the office of Servicemembers' Group Life Insurance (OSGLI) at (800) 419-1473.

TRAUMATIC INJURY PROTECTION UNDER SERVICEMEMBERS' GROUP LIFE INSURANCE (TSGLI)

TSGLI is a program that provides automatic traumatic injury coverage to all servicemembers covered under the Servicemembers' Group Life Insurance (SGLI) program.

Every member who has SGLI also has TSGLI effective December 1, 2005. This coverage applies to active duty members, reservists, funeral honors duty and one-day muster duty. The premium for TSGLI is a flat rate of $1 per month for most service members.

This benefit is also provided retroactively for members who incur severe losses as a result of traumatic a injury between October 7, 2001 and December 1, 2005 if the loss was the direct result of injuries incurred in Operations Enduring Freedom or Iraqi Freedom. For the purposes of TSGLI only, "incurred in Operation Enduring Freedom or Operation Iraqi Freedom" means that the member must have been deployed outside the United States on orders in support of OEF or OIF or serving in a geographic location that qualified the service member for the Combat Zone Tax Exclusion under the Internal Revenue Service Code.

Effective December 1, 2005 every member who has SGLI also has TSGLI.

The service member is the beneficiary of TSGLI. The member cannot name someone other than himself or herself as the TSGLI beneficiary. If the member is incompetent, the benefit will be paid to his or her guardian or attorney-in-fact. If the service member is deceased, the TSGLI payment will be made to the beneficiary or beneficiaries of the member's basic SGLI.

TSGLI coverage will pay a benefit of between $25,000 and $100,000 depending on the loss directly resulting from the traumatic injury.

Effective November 26, 2008, VA has increased the number of traumatic injuries covered under TSGLI as well as liberalizing the criteria of other injuries. Changes to benefits are being made retroactive to October 7, 2001, the beginning of Operation Enduring Freedom, consistent with the original implementing legislation.

New injuries covered include the partial amputation of the foot and hands and the degree of injuries based on severe burns. Another important change to the TSGLI program is the payment of a $25,000 benefit to those injured members who are hospitalized for a period of 15 consecutive days as a result of a traumatic injury.

Expansion of Covered Losses

1) Loss of Sight
Loss of Sight lasting 120 days or more is considered as "permanent", qualifying the service member for the same payment rate as for permanent loss of sight ($100,000 for both eyes, $50,000 for one eye).

2) Uniplegia
Uniplegia (complete and total paralysis of one limb) has been added to the schedule of losses with payment at $50,000.

3) Amputation of the Hand
The definition of amputation of the hand has been expanded to include loss of four fingers (on the same hand) or loss of thumb, with payment remaining at $50,000 for one affected hand and $100,000 for both hands.

4) Amputation of the Foot
The definition of amputation of the foot has been expanded to include loss of all toes, with the payment remaining at $50,000 for one affected foot and $100,000 for both feet.

5) Loss of Four Toes
A new category has been created for loss of four toes (on the same foot and not including the big toe) with payment at $25,000 for one affected foot and $50,000 for both feet.

6) Loss of Big Toe
A new category has been created for the loss of the big toe, with payment at $25,000 for one affected foot and $50,000 for both feet.

7) Limb Salvage
Coverage has been expanded to include limb salvage (multiple surgeries intended to save a limb rather than amputate) with payment equivalent to amputation.

8) Burns
The burn standard, currently 3rd degree (full thickness) burns to at least 30% of face or body, has been expanded to include 2nd degree (partial thickness) burns to at least 20% of the face or body.

9) Hospitalization as a Proxy for ADL Loss
Continuous 15-day inpatient hospital care is deemed a proxy for the first ADL eligibility period for OTI (Other Traumatic Injury) and TBI (Traumatic Brain Injury) claims.

10) Facial Reconstruction
Facial Reconstruction, required as a result of traumatic avulsion of the face or jaw that causes discontinuity defects, has been added to the schedule of losses, with payment levels of $25,000 to $75,000, depending upon the severity of the injury.

SCHEDULE OF LOSSES

For losses listed in Part I, multiple injuries resulting from a single traumatic event may be combined with each other and treated as one loss for purposes of a single payment (except where noted otherwise), however, the total payment amount MAY NOT exceed $100,000.

For losses listed in Part II, payment amounts MAY NOT be combined with payment amounts in Part I - only the higher amount will be paid. The total payment amount MAY NOT exceed $100,000 for multiple injuries resulting from a single traumatic event.

Part I	
Loss	**Payment Amount**
1. **Sight:** Total and permanent loss of sight OR loss of sight that has lasted 120 days • For each eye	$50,000

2. **Hearing:** Total and permanent loss of hearing
    • For one ear
    • For both ears
	$25,000
	$100,000

3. **Speech**: Total and permanent loss of speech	$50,000
4. **Quadriplegia:** complete paralysis of all four limbs	$100,000
5. **Hemiplegia:** complete paralysis of the upper and lower limbs on one side of the body	$100,000
6. **Paraplegia:** complete paralysis of both lower limbs	$100,000
7. **Uniplegia:** complete paralysis of one limb* *Note: Payment for uniplegia of arm cannot be combined with loss 9, 10 or 14 for the same arm. Payment for uniplegia of leg cannot be combined with loss 11, 12, 13 or 15 for the same leg.*	$50,000
8. **Burns:** 2nd degree or worse burns to at least 20% of the body including the face OR, at least 20% of the face	$100,000
9. **Amputation of hand:** Amputation at or above the wrist • For each hand* *Note: Payment for loss 9 cannot be combined with payment for loss 10 for the same hand.*	$50,000
10. **Amputation of 4 fingers on 1 hand OR thumb alone:** Amputation at or above the metacarpophalangeal joint • For each hand	$50,000
11. **Amputation of foot:** Amputation at or above the ankle • For each foot* *Note: Payment for loss 11 cannot be combined with*	$50,000

	payments for losses 12 or 13 for the same foot.	
12.	**Amputation of all toes including the big toe on 1 foot:** Amputation at or above the metatarsophalangeal joint • For each foot *Note: Payment for loss 12 cannot be combined with payments for loss 13 for the same foot.*	$50,000
13.	**Amputation of big toe only, OR other 4 toes on 1 foot:** Amputation at or above the metatarsophalangeal joint • For each foot	$25,000
14.	**Limb salvage of arm:** Salvage of arm in place of amputation • For each arm* *Note: Payment for loss 14 cannot be combined with payments for losses 9 or 10 for the same arm.*	$50,000
15.	**Limb salvage of leg:** Salvage of leg in place of amputation • For each leg* *Note: Payment for loss 15 cannot be combined with payments for losses 11, 12 or 13 for the same leg.*	$50,000
16.	**Facial Reconstruction** – reconstructive surgery to correct traumatic avulsions of the face or jaw that cause discontinuity defects.	
	• **Jaw** – surgery to correct discontinuity loss of the upper or lower jaw	$75,000
	• **Nose** – surgery to correct discontinuity loss of 50% or more of the cartilaginous nose	$50,000

	• **Lips** – surgery to correct discontinuity loss of 50% or more of the upper or lower lip
	       ○ For one lip
	       ○ For both lips
		$50,000
		$75,000

	• **Eyes** – surgery to correct discontinuity loss of 30% or more of the periorbita For each eye	$25,000
	• **Facial Tissue** – surgery to correct discontinuity loss of the tissue in 50% or more of any of the following facial subunits: forehead, temple, zygomatic, mandibular, infraorbital or chin. For each facial subunit	$25,000
	Note 1: Injuries listed under facial reconstruction may be combined with each other, but the maximum benefit for facial reconstruction may not exceed $75,000.	

	Note 2: Any injury or combination of injuries under facial reconstruction may also be combined with other injuries listed in Part I and treated as one loss, provided that all injuries are the result of a single traumatic event. However, the total payment amount may not exceed $100,000.	
17.	**Coma from traumatic injury AND/OR Traumatic Brain Injury resulting in inability to perform at least 2 Activities of Daily Living (ADL)**	
	• at 15th consecutive day of coma or ADL loss	$25,000
	• at 30th consecutive day of coma or ADL loss	an additional $25,000
	• at 60th consecutive day of coma or ADL loss	an additional $25,000
	• at 90th consecutive day of coma or ADL loss	an additional $25,000
18.	**Hospitalization due to traumatic brain injury**	
	• at 15th consecutive day of hospitalization	$25,000
	Note 1: Payment for hospitalization replaces the first payment period in loss 17. Note 2: Duration of hospitalization includes dates on which member is transported from the injury site to a facility described in § 9.20(e)(6)(xiii), admitted to the facility, transferred between facilities, and discharged from the facility.	

Part II

	Loss	Payment Amount
19.	**Traumatic injury resulting in inability to perform at least 2 Activities of Daily Living (ADL)**	
	• at 30th consecutive day of ADL loss	$25,000
	• at 60th consecutive day of ADL loss	an additional $25,000
	• at 90th consecutive day of ADL loss	an additional $25,000
	• at 120th consecutive day of ADL loss	an additional $25,000
20.	**Hospitalization due to traumatic injury**	

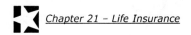

• at 15th consecutive day of hospitalization	$25,000
Note 1: Payment for hospitalization replaces the first payment period in loss 19. Note 2: Duration of hospitalization includes dates on which member is transported from the injury site to a facility described in § 9.20(e)(6)(xiii), admitted to the facility, transferred between facilities, and discharged from the facility.	

SERVICEMEMBERS' GROUP LIFE INSURANCE FAMILY COVERAGE

The Veterans' Opportunities Act of 2001 extended life insurance coverage to spouses and children of members insured under the SGLI program, **effective November 1, 2001.**

Amount of Coverage

Eligible individuals may purchase up to $100,000 of SGLI coverage for a spouse, in increments of $10,000. However, individuals may not purchase more SGLI coverage for a spouse than he or she has for him/herself.

Each dependent child of every active duty servicemember or reservist who is insured under SGLI is automatically insured for $10,000.

Eligibility

Family coverage is available for the spouses and children of:

- Active duty servicemembers; and
- Members of the Ready Reserve of a uniformed service.

Note: *Family coverage is available only for members insured under the SGLI program. Family coverage is not available for those insured under the VGLI program.*

Premiums

SGLI coverage for children is free. For monthly premiums for spouses, individuals should call (800) 419-1473.

Update
10/10/2009 - Dependent Child Coverage Extended to Include Stillborn Children

Public law 110-389 expanded the Servicemembers' Group life Insurance (SGLI) program to include a member's "stillborn child" as an insurable dependent. SGLI dependent coverage provides for a $10,000 payment to the insured service member upon the death of the member's dependent child. The law was enacted October 10, 2008, and on November 18, 2009, regulations implementing section 402 of the Veterans' Benefits Improvement Act of 2008, were published in the Federal Register, and immediately went into effect . This change applies only for stillbirths on or after October 10, 2008, the effective date of PL 110-389

Declining Coverage

If an individual does not want insurance coverage for a spouse, or wants a reduced amount of coverage, he or she must complete *form SGLV-82861, Family Coverage Election,* and submit it to his or her personnel officer.

Termination of Coverage

Coverage for a spouse ends 120 days after any of the following events:
* The date elected in writing to terminate a spouse's coverage;
* The date elected in writing to terminate the service member's own coverage;
* The date of the service member's death;
* The date the service member's coverage terminates;
* The date of divorce.

A spouse can covert his or her coverage to a policy with a commercial company within 120 days following one of the events listed above. He or she should contact the Office of Servicemembers' Group Life Insurance at (800) 419-1473.

Coverage for a service member's children ends 120 days after any of the following events:
* The date elected in writing to terminate the service member's own coverage;
* The date the service member separates from service;
* The date of the service member's death;
* The date the child is no longer the service member's dependent.

No conversion options are available to children.

Payment of Proceeds

The service member is paid the proceeds due to the death of a spouse or child. If the service member were to die before payment could be made, the proceeds of a spouse or child claim would be paid to the member's beneficiary, as designated by the member.

VETERANS' GROUP LIFE INSURANCE – VGLI (1974-PRESENT)

In 1974, the Veterans' Group Life Insurance (VGLI) program became available to veterans, providing term insurance protection after separation from service.

VGLI, like SGLI, is supervised by the Department of Veterans Affairs, but is administered by the Office of Servicemembers' Group Life Insurance (OSGLI). VGLI provides for the conversion of Servicemembers' Group Life Insurance to a five-year renewable term policy of insurance protection after a service member's separation from service.

Eligibility For VGLI

Full-time coverage is available for the following members:

- Full-time SGLI insureds that are released from active duty or the Reserves.

- Ready Reservists who have part-time SGLI coverage, and who, while performing active duty or inactive duty for training for a period of less than 31 days, incur a disability or aggravate a preexisting disability that makes them uninsurable at standard premium rates.

- Members of the Individual Ready Reserve (IRR) and Inactive National Guard (ING).

Coverage Amounts

> *Effective September 1, 2005, the maximum amount of SGLI and VGLI coverage increased from $250,000 to $400,000.*

VGLI is issued in multiples of $10,000 up to a maximum of $400,000, but not for more than the amount of SGLI coverage the member had in force at the time of separation from active duty or the reserves.

VGLI Renewal

Members may renew their VGLI coverage under the following conditions:

- Members who have separated from service may renew their VGLI coverage for life in 5-year term periods.

- Members of the IRR or ING may renew their VGLI for additional 5-year term periods, as long as they remain in the IRR or ING.

- Rather than renew, a member also has the right at any time to **convert** VGLI to an individual commercial life insurance policy with any one of 99 participating commercial insurance companies.

How To Apply For VGLI

VGLI applications are mailed to eligible members, generally within 60 days after separation, and again shortly before the end of the 16-month application period. Applications are mailed to the address shown on the member's DD-Form 214 or equivalent separation orders. *It is the member's responsibility, however, to apply within the time limits, even if they do not receive an application in the mail.*

Applications should be mailed to:

Office Of Servicemembers' Group Life Insurance
P.O. Box 5000
Millville, New Jersey 08332-9928.

Time Limits To Apply For VGLI

To be eligible, a member must apply for VGLI within the following time limits:

- Ordinarily, a member must submit an application to the OSGLI with the required premium within 120 days following separation from service.

- If a member is *totally disabled* at the time of separation from active duty *and* is granted extended free SGLI coverage, he or she may apply for VGLI anytime during the one-year period of extension.

- Individuals who are assigned to the IRR and ING have 120 days after assignment to apply, without evidence of good health, and one year after that with evidence of good health.

- If an application or the initial premium has not been submitted within the time limits above, VGLI may still be granted if an application, the initial premium and **evidence of insurability** (good health) are submitted to OSGLI within 1 year and 120 days following termination of SGLI. **Applications will not be accepted after one year and 120 days.**

- An application for an incompetent member may be made by a guardian, committee, conservator or curator. In the absence of a court appointed representative, the application may be submitted by a family member or anyone acting on the member's behalf.

VGLI Premiums Rates

VGLI premium rates are determined by age group and amount of insurance. To lessen the high cost of term insurance at the older ages, a Decreasing Term Option is available, starting at age group 60 to 64. Under this option an insured pays a level premium for life, while the insurance amount declines by 25% for three subsequent five-year renewals. At that point, coverage remains level at 25% of the original insurance amount.

Payment Of Premiums

Once the VGLI application is approved, the OSGLI will send the insured a certificate and a supply of monthly premium payment coupons.

Premiums may be paid:

- Monthly;
- Quarterly;
- Semiannually;
- Annually;
- By monthly allotment from military retirement pay;
- By monthly deduction from VA compensation payments .

If the insured does not pay the premium when it is due, or within a grace period of 60 days, the VGLI coverage will lapse. If VGLI lapsed due to failure to pay the premiums on time, the insured will receive a notification of the lapse and a reinstatement form. The insured may apply to reinstate coverage at any time within 5 years of the date of the unpaid premium. If the insured applies for reinstatement within 6 months from the date of lapse, the individual only needs to provide evidence that he or she is in the same state of health on the date of reinstatement as on the date of lapse. Otherwise, the individual may need to provide proof of good health.

Beneficiary Selection

Any beneficiary can be named. If none is selected, the insurance is distributed, by law, in the following order:

- Spouse, or

- Children, or

- Parents, or

- Executor of estate, or

- Other next of kin.

To name a beneficiary, the insured must submit *Form SGLV 8712, Beneficiary Designation-Veterans' Group Life Insurance.* The completed form should be sent to:

Office of Servicemembers' Group Life Insurance
213 Washington Avenue
Newark, NJ 07102-2999

When an insured converts SGLI to VGLI following separation from service, a new beneficiary designation form must be completed. If a new form is not filed, the SGLI beneficiary designation will be considered the VGLI designation for up to 60 days after the effective date of the VGLI. If a new beneficiary is not designated after this 60-day period, the proceeds would be paid "By Law" under the order of precedence in the law.

Options For Payment Of Policy Proceeds

Alliance Account

VGLI proceeds can be paid in a lump sum or over a 36-month period.
If the proceeds are to be paid in a lump sum then beneficiaries of SGLI and VGLI will receive the payment of their insurance proceeds via an *"Alliance Account"*.

Rather than the traditional single check for the full amount of insurance proceeds, the beneficiary receives a checkbook for an interest bearing account from which the beneficiary can write a check for any amount from $250 up to the full amount of the proceeds. The Alliance Account:

- Earns interest at a competitive rate;

- Is guaranteed by Prudential;

- Gives the beneficiary time to make important financial decisions while their funds are secure and earning interest;

- Gives them instant access to their money at all times.

Accelerated Benefits

On November 11, 1998, the President signed legislation authorizing the payment of _"Accelerated Benefits"_ in the SGLI and VGLI programs subject to the following:

- Terminally ill insureds will have access of up to 50 percent of the face amount of their coverage during their lifetime.

- This money will be available in increments of $5,000.

- An insured must have a medical prognosis of life expectancy of 9 months or less.

Filing Death Claims

A beneficiary may file a claim for VGLI proceeds by submitting _Form SGLV 8283, Claim For Death Benefits_, to:

> Office of Servicemembers' Group Life Insurance
> 213 Washington Avenue
> Newark, NJ 07102-2999

Taxation

VGLI proceeds are exempt from taxation. Any installment interest or delayed settlement interest that a beneficiary receives in addition to the proceed is also exempt from taxation, and does not need to be reported to the IRS.

Customer Service

Any questions regarding VGLI should be directed to the office of Servicemembers' Group Life Insurance (OSGLI) at (800) 419-1473.

VETERANS' MORTGAGE LIFE INSURANCE – VMLI (1971-PRESENT)

The Veterans' Mortgage Life Insurance (VMLI) program began in 1971, and is designed to provide financial protection to cover eligible veterans' home mortgages in the event of death. VMLI is issued to those severely disabled veterans, under age 70, who have received grants for Specially Adapted Housing from VA. (Refer to Chapter 4 of this book for information regarding Specially Adapted Housing.)

The maximum amount of VMLI allowed an eligible veteran is $90,000. (Effective October 1, 2011 the maximum will increase to $150,000. On January 1, 2012 it will increase to $200,000.) The insurance is payable if the veteran dies before the mortgage is paid off. VA will pay the amount of money still owed on the mortgage up to $90,000. **_The insurance is payable only to the mortgage_**

lender. The day-to-day operations of the program are handled by the Philadelphia VAROIC.

Coverage Amounts

VMLI coverage decreases as the insured's mortgage falls below $90,000. This reduced coverage cannot be reinstated. However, if the home is sold and a new home is purchased the veteran becomes eligible once again for the maximum amount of coverage.

Payment Of VMLI Proceeds

Certain conditions apply to the payment of VMLI benefits:

- The insurance is payable at the death of the veteran only to the mortgage holder.
- If the title of the property is shared with anyone other than the veteran's spouse, the insurance coverage is only for the percentage of the title that is in the veteran's name.
- No insurance is payable if the mortgage is paid off before the death of the insured or if it was paid off by other mortgage insurance before the VMLI payment is made.

The insurance will be canceled for any of the following conditions:

- The mortgage is paid in full.
- Termination of the veteran's ownership of the property securing the loan.
- The request of the veteran.
- Failure of the veteran to submit timely statements or other required information.

Premiums

Premiums are determined by the insurance age of the veteran, the outstanding balance of the mortgage at the time of application, and the remaining length of time the mortgage has to run. Veterans who desire insurance will be advised of the correct premium when it is determined.

Premiums **must** be paid by deduction from the veteran's monthly compensation or pension payments, if the veteran is receiving such payments. If such payments are not being received the veteran may make direct payments, on a monthly, quarterly, semiannual, or annual basis, to the VA Insurance Center in Philadelphia, Pennsylvania.

DIVIDEND OPTIONS

If a policyholder is eligible for a dividend, he or she may choose from several dividend options that are available:

- **Cash**, paid to policyholder by US Treasury check.

- **Credit**, held in account for the insured with interest. Can be used to prevent policy lapse. Will be refunded upon the insured's request, or will be included in the award to the beneficiary(ies) at the time of the insured's death.

- **Paid-Up Additions (PUA'S)**, used as a net single premium to purchase additional paid-up insurance. Available only on "V," "RS," "W," "J," "JR," and "JS" policies. PUA's will be whole life insurance if the basic insurance is an endowment policy.

- **Deposit**, held in account for insured with interest. Available only on permanent plan policies. Considered part of the policy's cash value for the purpose of purchasing reduced paid-up insurance, or if the policy lapses, extended insurance (except for "K" or "JS" policies). Will be refunded upon the insured's request. Will be included in the award to the beneficiary(ies) at the time of the insured's death.

- **Premium**, applied to pay premiums in advance.

- **Indebtedness**, applied toward a loan or lien on a policy.

- **Net Cash**, used to pay an annual premium with any remainder paid to the policyholder under the cash option.

- **Net PUA**, used to pan an annual premium with any remainder used to purchase paid-up additional insurance.

- **Net Loan-Lien**, used to pay an annual premium with any remainder used to reduce an outstanding loan or lien.

To change the method in which dividends are paid, individuals should speak with an Insurance Specialist at (800) 669-8477

MISCELLANEOUS INFORMATION ABOUT GOVERNMENT LIFE INSURANCE POLICIES

Power of Attorney is not acceptable for executing a change of beneficiary for government life insurance, even if certain state statutes allow it. Only a court appointed guardian that is recognized by state statutes can execute a beneficiary designation. If the state statute does not give the guardian broad powers to authorize a beneficiary change, a specific court order is needed to effectuate a change.

Assignment of government life insurance is not allowed, for any reason, nor can ownership of a policy be transferred. Only the insured can exercise the rights and privileges inherent in the ownership of the policy.

Policy Loans are available on permanent plans of insurance. The policyholder can take up to 94% of the reserve value of the policy, less any indebtedness. The policy cannot be lapsed, and premiums must be paid or waived at least one year before a policy has a loan value. Changes in interest rates are made on October 1 of each year, if warranted. Rate changes are tied to the "ten year constant maturities", U.S. Treasury securities index.

A policyholder can apply for a loan by filing *VA Form 29-1546, Application for Policy Loan.* The completed form can be faxed to (215) 381-3580, or mailed to:

Department of Veterans Affairs
Regional Office and Insurance Center
PO Box 7327
Philadelphia, PA 19101

An Annual Insurance Policy Statement is mailed to the insured on the policy anniversary date of each policy. The statement provides the insured with information about his or her VA insurance. The statement should be reviewed for accuracy each year, and the VA should be contacted immediately if there are any discrepancies.

Dividend Hoax - Rumors that Congress approved a "Special Dividend" for veterans who do or do not have Government life insurance have been spread for over 30 years. These rumors are false. The only dividends being paid by VA are on active Government life insurance policies. Dividends on active policies have been paid annually for many years and policyholders do not need to apply for them.

"Special Dividend" rumors are spread by well-meaning people who want to help veterans but fail to check out their sources before passing the information along to others. Notices have appeared in veterans' magazines, union newspapers, fraternal publications, newspapers and every other publication imaginable. The hoax has appeared in many forms and seems to change to fit the times. It started in the 1960's as a rumor about veterans with WW II insurance. More recently, it has been adapted to state that a dividend is being paid on Servicemembers' Group Life Insurance (SGLI) or Veterans' Group Life Insurance (VGLI) coverage.

Unfortunately, this misinformation unnecessarily raises the expectations of veterans and service personnel. There has been no recent legislation authorizing any "special" dividends.

If you have any questions regarding this issue, feel free to contact the VA Insurance Center at (800) 669-8477.

CHAPTER 22

HOME LOAN GUARANTIES

GENERAL INFORMATION

> *The VA does not actually lend the money to veterans. The VA guaranty means the lender is protected against loss if the veteran fails to repay the loan.*

The purpose of the VA loan guaranty program is to help veterans and active duty personnel finance the purchase of homes with competitive loan terms and interest rates. The VA does not actually lend the money to veterans. VA guaranteed loans are made by private lenders, such as banks, savings & loans, or mortgage companies. The VA guaranty means the lender is protected against loss if the veteran fails to repay the loan.

The VA Loan Guaranty Service is the organization within the VA that has the responsibility of administering the home loan program.

VA guaranteed loans offer the following important features:

- Equal opportunity for all qualified veterans to obtain a VA guaranteed loan.

- No downpayment (unless required by the lender or the purchase price is more than the reasonable value of the property).

- Buyer is informed of reasonable value.

- Buyer's interest rate is negotiable.

- Buyer has the ability to finance the VA funding fee (plus reduced funding fees with a downpayment of at least 5%, and exemption for veterans receiving VA compensation).

- Closing costs are comparable with other financing types (and may be lower).

- No mortgage insurance premiums are necessary.

- An assumable mortgage may be available.

- Buyer has the right to prepay without penalty.

VA guaranteed loans do not do the following:

- Guarantee that a home is free of defects (VA only guarantees the loan. It is the veteran's responsibility to assure that he or she is satisfied with the property being purchased. Veterans should seek expert advice as necessary, *before* legally committing to a purchase agreement.)

- If a veteran has a home built, VA cannot compel the builder to correct construction defects, although VA does have the authority to suspend a builder from further participation in the VA home loan program.

- VA cannot guarantee the veteran is making a good investment.

- VA cannot provide a veteran with legal service.

Uses For VA Loan Guaranties

> *Veterans must certify that they plan to live in the home they are buying or building in order to qualify for a VA loan guaranty.*

VA loan guaranties can be used for the following:

- To purchase, construct, or improve a home.

- To purchase and improve a home concurrently.

- To purchase a residential condominium or townhouse unit in a VA approved project. (If one veteran is purchasing the property, the total number of separate units cannot be more than 4.)

- To purchase a manufactured home or a manufactured home and manufactured home lot.

- To purchase and improve a manufactured home lot on which to place a manufactured home which the veteran already owns and occupies.

- To refinance an existing home loan.

- To refinance an existing VA loan to reduce the interest rate, and make energy-efficient improvements.

- To refinance an existing manufactured home loan in order to acquire a lot.

- To improve a home by installing a solar heating and/or cooling system, or other energy efficient improvements.

Veterans must certify that they plan to live in the home they are buying or building in order to qualify for a VA loan guaranty.

VA loan guaranties are available only for property located in the United States, its territories, or possessions (Puerto Rico, Guam, Virgin Islands, American Samoa, and Northern Mariana Islands).

VA loan guaranties are not available for farm loans, unless there is a home on the property, which will be personally occupied by the veteran. Non-realty loans for the purchase of equipment, livestock, machinery, etc. are not made. Other loan programs for farm financing may be available through the Farmers Home Administration, which gives preference to veteran applicants. (Interested veterans should refer to the local telephone directory for the phone number of a local office.)

Although business loans are not available through VA, the Small Business Administration (SBA) has a number of programs designed to help foster and encourage small business enterprises, including financial and management assistance. Each SBA office has a veteran's affairs officer available to speak with. (Interested veterans should refer to the local telephone directory for the phone number of a local SBA office, or call (800) 827-5722.)

ELIGIBILITY REQUIREMENTS

Individuals may qualify for VA home loan guaranties if their service falls within any of the following categories:

World War II Eligibility Requirements:

•

- Active duty on or after September 16, 1940 and prior to July 26, 1947; and

- Discharge or separation under other than dishonorable conditions; and

- At least 90 days of total service, unless discharged earlier for a service-connected disability.

- Unremarried widows of above-described eligible individuals who died as a result of service.

- Widows of above-described eligible individuals who died as a result of service **who remarried after age 57**. (This provision is effective January 1, 2004.)

Post World War II Eligibility Requirements:

•

- Active duty on or after July 26, 1947 and prior to June 27, 1950; and

- Discharge or separation under other than dishonorable conditions; and

- At least 181 days continuous service, unless discharged earlier for a service-connected disability.

- Unremarried widows of above-described eligible individuals who died as a result of service.

- Widows of above-described eligible individuals who died as a result of service **who remarried after age 57**. (This provision is effective January 1, 2004.)

Korean Conflict Eligibility Requirements:

•

- Active duty on or after June 27, 1950 and prior to February 1, 1955; and

- Discharge or separation under other than dishonorable conditions; and

- At least 90 days of total service, unless discharged earlier for a service-connected disability.

- Unremarried widows of above-described eligible individuals who died as a result of service.

- Widows of above-described eligible individuals who died as a result of service **who remarried after age 57**. (This provision is effective January 1, 2004.)

Post-Korean Conflict Eligibility Requirements:

•

- Active duty on or after February 1, 1955 and prior to August 5, 1964; and

- Discharge or separation under other than dishonorable conditions; and

- At least 181 days continuous service, unless discharged earlier for a service-connected disability.

- Unremarried widows of above-described eligible individuals who died as a result of service.

- Widows of above-described eligible individuals who died as a result of service **who remarried after age 57**. (This provision is effective January 1, 2004.)

Vietnam Eligibility Requirements:

•

- Active duty on or after August 5, 1964, and prior to May 8, 1975. (For those serving in the Republic of Vietnam, the beginning date is February 28, 1961.); and

- Discharge or separation under other than dishonorable conditions; and

- At least 90 days of total service, unless discharged earlier for a service-connected disability.

- Unremarried widows of above-described eligible individuals who died as a result of service.

- Widows of above-described eligible individuals who died as a result of service **who remarried after age 57**. (This provision is effective January 1, 2004.)

Post-Vietnam Eligibility Requirements for Veterans With Enlisted Service Between May 8, 1975 and September 7, 1980 (if enlisted) or October 16, 1981 (if officer):

-
  - At least 181 days of continuous service, all of which occurred on or after May 8, 1975, unless discharged earlier for a service-connected disability; and

  - Discharge or separation under other than dishonorable conditions.

  - Unremarried widows of above-described eligible individuals who died as a result of service.

  - Widows of above-described eligible individuals who died as a result of service *who remarried after age 57*. (This provision is effective January 1, 2004.)

Post-Vietnam Eligibility Requirements for Veterans Separated from Enlisted Service Between September 7, 1980 (October 17, 1981 for Officers) and August 1, 1990:

-
  - At least 24 months of continuous active duty, or the full period (at least 181 days) for which individual was called or ordered to active duty, and discharged or separated under other than dishonorable conditions; or

  - At least 181 days of continuous active duty, and discharged due to:

  - a hardship; or

  - a service-connected, compensable disability; or

  - a medical condition which preexisted service, and has not been determined to be service-connected; or

  - the convenience of the government as a result of a reduction in force; or

  - a physical or mental condition not characterized as a disability, and not the result of misconduct, but which did interfere with the performance of duty.

  - Early discharge for a service-connected disability.

  - Unremarried widows of above-described eligible persons who died as the result of service.

  - Widows of above-described eligible individuals who died as a result of service *who remarried after age 57*. (This provision is effective January 1, 2004.)

Persian Gulf War Eligibility Requirements:

-
- At least 24 months of continuous active duty on or after August 2, 1990, or the full period for which the individual was called or ordered to active duty, and discharged or separated under other than dishonorable conditions; or

- At least 90 days of continuous active duty, and discharged due to:

- A hardship; or

- A service-connected, compensable disability; or

- A medical condition which preexisted service, and has not been determined to be service-connected; or

- The convenience of the government as a result of a reduction in force; or

- A physical or mental condition not characterized as a disability, and not the result of misconduct, but which did interfere with the performance of duty.

- Early discharge for a service-connected disability.

- Unremarried widows of above-described eligible individuals who died as the result of service.

- Widows of above-described eligible individuals who died as a result of service *who remarried after age 57*. (This provision is effective January 1, 2004.)

(When law or Presidential Proclamation ends the Persian Gulf War, a minimum of 181 days of continuous active duty will be required for those who did not serve during wartime.)

Members of the Reserve and National Guard are eligible if activated after August 1, 1990, served at least 90 days, and discharged or separated under other than dishonorable conditions.)

Active Duty Personnel Eligibility Requirements:

Individuals who are now on regular duty (not active duty for training) are eligible after having served 181 days (90 days during the Gulf War), unless discharged or separated from a previous qualifying period of active duty service.

Eligibility Requirements for Members of the Selected Reserve:

- At least 6 years in the Reserves or National Guard, or discharged earlier due to a service-connected disability; and

- Discharged or separated under other than dishonorable conditions; or

- Placed on the retired list; or

- Transferred to an element of the Ready Reserve other than the Selected Reserve; or

- Continue to serve in the Selected Reserve.

- Unremarried widows of above-described eligible persons who died as the result of service.

- Widows of above-described eligible individuals who died as a result of service **who remarried after age 57**. (This provision is effective January 1, 2004.)

Eligibility Requirements for Other Types of Service:

- Certain U.S. citizens who served in the armed forces of a U.S. ally in World War II.

- Members of organizations with recognized contributions to the U.S. during World War II. (Questions about this type of service eligibility can be answered at any VA regional office.)

- Spouses of American servicemen who are listed as missing-in-action, or prisoners-of-war for a total of 90 days or more.

CERTIFICATE OF ELIGIBILITY

The Certificate of Eligibility is the medium by which VA certifies eligibility for A VA loan guaranty.

Individuals may request a Certificate of Eligibility by completing VA Form 26-1880, Request for a Certificate of Eligibility for VA Home Loan Benefits. The completed form should be submitted to a VA Eligibility Center along with acceptable proof of service.

Veterans separated after January 1, 1950 should submit DD Form 214, Certificate of Release or Discharge from active Duty.

Veterans separated after October 1, 1979 should submit copy 4 of DD Form 214.

Since there is no uniform document similar to the DD Form 214 for proof of service in the Selected Reserve a number of different forms may be accepted as documentation of service in the Selected Reserve:

- For those who served in the Army or Air National Guard and were discharged after at least 6 years of such service, NGB Form 22 may be sufficient.

- Those who served in the Army, Navy, Air Force, Marine Corps or Coast Guard Reserves may need to rely on a variety of forms that document at least 6 years of participation in paid training periods, or have paid active duty for training.

- Often it will be necessary to submit a combination of documents, such as an Honorable Discharge certificate together with a Retirement Points Statement. It is the reservist's responsibility to obtain and submit documentation of 6 years of honorable service.

In addition, if an individual is now on active duty, and has not been previously discharged from active duty service, he or she must submit a statement of service that includes the name of the issuing authority (base or command), and is signed by or at the direction of an appropriate official. The statement must identify the individual, include the social security number, provide the date of entry on active duty and the duration of any lost time.

The Certificate of Eligibility should be presented to the lender when completing the loan application. (However, if an individual does not have a Certificate, the lender may have the forms necessary to apply for the Certificate of Eligibility.)

PROCEDURES FOR OBTAINING LOANS

- Apply for a Certificate of Eligibility.

- Decide on a home the buyer wants to purchase, and sign a purchase agreement.

- Order an appraisal from VA. (Usually this is done by the lender.) Most VA regional offices offer a "speed-up" telephone appraisal system. Call the local VA office for details.

- Apply to a mortgage lender for the loan. While the appraisal is being done, the lender (mortgage company, savings and loan, bank, etc.) can be gathering credit and income information. If the lender is authorized by VA to do automatic processing, upon receipt of the VA or LAPP appraised value determination, the loan can be approved and closed without waiting for VA's review of the credit application. For loans that must first be approved by VA, the lender will send the application to the local VA office, which will notify the lender of its decision.

- Close the loan and the buyer moves in.

If a lender cannot be located, the local VA regional office can provide a list of lenders active in the VA program.

A VA loan guaranty does not guarantee approval of a loan. The veteran must still meet the financial institution's income and credit requirements. If a loan is approved, the VA guarantees the loan when it's closed.

VA Eligibility Centers

Regional Loan Center	Jurisdiction	Mailing Address	Telephone Number
Atlanta	Georgia North Carolina South Carolina Tennessee	Department of Veterans Affairs VA Regional Loan Center 1700 Clairmont Rd. Decatur, GA 30033-4032 (Mail: P.O. Box 100023, Decatur, GA 30031-7023)	1-888-768-2132
Cleveland	Delaware Indiana Michigan New Jersey Ohio Pennsylvania	Department of Veterans Affairs VA Regional Loan Center 1240 East Ninth Street Cleveland, OH 44199	1-800-729-5772
Denver	Alaska Colorado Idaho Montana Oregon Utah Washington Wyoming	Department of Veterans Affairs VA Regional Loan Center 155 Van Gordon Street Lakewood, CO 80228 (Mail: Box 25126, Denver, CO 80225)	1-888-349-7541
Honolulu	Hawaii Guam American Samoa Commonwealth of the Northern Marianas	Department of Veterans Affairs VA Regional Loan Center Loan Guaranty Division (26) 459 Patteson Rd. Honolulu, HI 96819 *Although not an RLC, this office is a fully functioning Loan Guaranty operation for Hawaii.	1-888-433-0481
Houston	Arkansas Louisiana Oklahoma Texas	Department of Veterans Affairs VA Regional Loan Center 6900 Almeda Road Houston, TX 77030-4200	1-888-232-2571

Manchester	Connecticut Massachusetts Maine New Hampshire New York Rhode Island Vermont	Department of Veterans Affairs VA Regional Loan Center 275 Chestnut Street Manchester, NH 03101	1-800-827-6311
Phoenix	Arizona California New Mexico Nevada	Department of Veterans Affairs VA Regional Loan Center 3333 N. Central Avenue Phoenix, AZ 85012-2402	1-888-869-0194
Roanoke	District of Columbia Kentucky Maryland Virginia West Virginia	Department of Veterans Affairs VA Regional Loan Center 210 Franklin Road, SW Roanoke, VA 24011	1-800-933-5499
St. Paul	Illinois Iowa Kansas Minnesota Missouri Nebraska North Dakota South Dakota Wisconsin	Department of Veterans Affairs VA Regional Loan Center 1 Federal Drive, Ft. Snelling St. Paul, MN 55111-4050	1-800-827-0611
St. Petersburg	Alabama Florida Mississippi Puerto Rico U.S. Virgin Islands	Department of Veterans Affairs VA Regional Loan Center 9500 Bay Pines Blvd. St. Petersburg, FL 33708 (Mail: P.O. Box 1437, St. Petersburg, FL 33731)	1-888-611-5916
Winston/ Salem		Department of Veterans Affairs Winston-Salem Eligibility Center P.O. Box 20729 Winston-Salem, NC 27120	1-888-244-6711

GUARANTY OR ENTITLEMENT AMOUNT

IMPORTANT UPDATE:

The Veterans Benefits Improvement Act of 2008 provides a temporary increase in the maximum guaranty amount for loans closed January 1, 2009 through December 31, 2011.

During this time period, the maximum VA home loan guarantee is 25% of the conforming VA home loan amount. The maximum VA lending limit for most states is $417,000 for a single family home - hence, the maximum VA home loan guarantee is $104,250 (25% of $417,000).

The states of HI and AK have higher conforming VA mortgage loan limit of $625,500. That is, the maximum VA home loan guarantee for Hawaii and Alaska is up to $156,375.

The maximum guaranty amounts set forth above will be adjusted annually. The first adjustment will affect loans closed on or after January 1, 2010.

HYBRID ADJUSTABLE RATE MORTGAGES

The Veterans Benefits Act of 2002 authorizes VA to carry out a demonstration project to guarantee Hybrid Adjustable Rate Mortgages (Hybrid ARMs or HARM loans). **(The Veterans Benefits Act of 2005 extends the VA's authority to guarantee hybrid ARM loans to September 30, 2008. The Veterans Benefits Improvement Act of 2008 further extended the authority through September 30, 2012.)**

DOWN PAYMENTS

The VA does not require a down payment be made, provided that:

- The loan is not for a manufactured home or lot (a 5% down payment is required for manufactured home or lot loans); and

- The purchase price or cost does not exceed the reasonable value of the property, as determined by VA; and

- The loan does not have graduated payment features. (Because with a graduated payment mortgage, the loan balance will be increasing during the first years of the loan, a down payment is required to keep the loan balance from going over the reasonable value or the purchase price.)

Even though the VA may not require a down payment, the lender may require one.

CLOSING COSTS AND FEES

The VA regulates the closing costs that a veteran may be charged in connection with closing a VA loan. The closing costs and origination fees must be paid in cash, and cannot be included in the loan itself, except in the case of refinancing loans.

Although some additional costs are unique to certain localities, the closing costs generally include:

- VA appraisal
- Credit report
- Survey
- Title evidence
- Recording fees
- A 1% loan origination fee
- Discount points

A veteran is charged the customary fees for title search, credit report, appraisal and transfer fees, etc., the same as any other borrower, but he is not required to pay commission or brokerage fees for obtaining the loan. In home loans, the lender may also charge a reasonable flat charge, called a funding fee, to cover the costs of originating the loan.

FUNDING FEES

A VA funding fee is payable at the time of loan closing. This fee may be included in the loan and paid from the loan proceeds. The funding fee does not have to be paid by veterans receiving VA compensation for service-connected disabilities, or who but for the receipt of retirement pay, would be entitled to receive compensation for service-connected disabilities, or surviving spouses of veterans who died in service or from a service-connected disability.

The funding fee rates are as follows (Unless otherwise specified, the following rates are effective January 1, 2004:

Loan Purpose	Percent Of Loan For Veterans	Percent Of Loan For Reservists
Purchase or construction loan with down payment of less than 5%; or Refinancing loan; or Home improvement loan	2.15% (10/1/04 – 9/30/2011)	2.4%
Purchase or construction loan with down payment between 5% and 10%	1.5	1.75
Purchase or construction loan with down payment of 10% or more	1.25	1.5
Manufactured home loan	1.0	1.0
Interest rate reduction loan	0.5	0.5
Assumption of VA guaranteed loan	0.5	0.5
Second or subsequent use without a down payment	3.3	3.3

FLOOD INSURANCE

If the dwelling is in an area identified by the Department of Housing and Urban Development as having special flood hazards, and the sale of flood insurance under the national program is available, such insurance is required on loans made since March 1, 1974. The amount of insurance must be equal to the outstanding loan balance, or the maximum limit of coverage available, whichever is less.

INTEREST RATES

The interest rate on VA loans varies due to changes in the prevailing rates in the mortgage market. One a loan is made, the interest rate set in the note remains the same for the life of the loan. However, if interest rates decrease, a veteran may apply for a new VA loan to refinance the previous loan at a lower interest rate.

REPAYMENT PERIOD

The maximum repayment period for VA home loans is 30 years and 32 days. However, the exact amortization period depends upon the contract between the lender and the borrower.

The VA will guarantee loans with the following repayment terms:

• Traditional Fixed Payment Mortgage

- (equal monthly payments for the life of the loan)

- Graduated Payment Mortgage – GPM

- (Smaller than normal monthly payments for the first few years – usually 5 years, which gradually increase each year, and then level off after the end of the "graduation period" to larger than normal payments for the remaining term of the loan. The reduction in the monthly payment in the early years of the loan is accomplished by delaying a portion of the interest due on the loan each month, and by adding that interest to the principal balance.)

- Buydown

- (The builder of a new home or seller of an existing home may "buy down" the veteran's mortgage payments by making a large lump sum payment up front at closing that will be used to supplement the monthly payments for a certain period, usually 1 to 3 years.)

- Growing Equity Mortgage (GEM)

- (Provides for a gradual annual increase in monthly payments, with all of the increase applied to the principal balance, resulting in early payoff of the loan.)

Prepayment of Loan

A veteran or serviceman may pay off his entire loan at any time without penalty or fee, or make advance payments equal to one monthly installment or $100, whichever is the lesser amount. Individuals should check with the mortgage holder for the proper procedure.

Loan Defaults

If a veteran fails to make payments as agreed, the lender may foreclose on the property.. If the lender takes a loss, the VA must pay the guaranty to the lender, and the individual must repay this amount to the VA. If the loan closed on or after January 1, 1990, the veteran will owe the VA in the event of default, only if there was fraud, misrepresentation, or bad faith on the veteran's part.

RELEASE OF LIABILITY

Any veteran who sells or has sold a home purchased with a VA loan guaranty may request release from liability to the VA. (If the VA loan closed prior to March 1, 1988, the application forms for a release of liability must be requested from the VA office that guaranteed the loan. If the VA loan closed on or after March 1, 1988, then the application forms must be requested from the lender to whom the payments are made.) The loan must be current, the purchaser must assume full liability for the loan, and the purchaser must sign an Assumption of Liability Agreement. The VA must approve the purchaser from a credit standpoint.

For loans closed on or after March 1, 1988, release of liability is not automatic. To approve the assumer and grant the veteran release from liability, the lender or VA must be notified, and release of liability must be requested.

If the loan was closed prior to March 1, 1988, the purchaser may assume the loan without approval from VA or the lender. However, the veteran is encouraged to request a release of liability from VA, regardless of the loan's closing date. If a veteran does not obtain a release of liability, and VA suffers a loss on account of a default by the assumer, or some future assumer, a debt may be established against the veteran. Also, strenuous collection efforts will be made against the veteran if a debt is established.

The release of a veteran from liability to the VA does not change the fact that the VA continues to be liable on the guaranty.

RESTORATION OF ENTITLEMENT

Veterans who have used all or part of their entitlement may restore their entitlement amount to purchase another home, provided:

- The property has been sold, and the loan has been paid in full; or

- A qualified veteran buyer has agreed to assume the outstanding balance on the loan, and agreed to substitute his entitlement for the same amount of entitlement the original veteran owner used to get the loan. (The veteran buyer must also meet the occupancy, income, and credit requirements of the VA and the lender.)

- If the veteran has repaid the VA loan in full, but has not disposed of the property securing that loan, the entitlement may be restored ONE TIME ONLY.

Restoration of entitlement does not occur automatically. The veteran must apply for restoration by completing Form 26, 1880. Completed forms may be returned to any VA regional office or center (A copy of the HUD-1, Closing Statement, or other appropriate evidence of payment in full should also be submitted with the completed Form 26, 1880.) Application forms for substitution of entitlement can be requested from the VA office that guaranteed the loan.

If the requirements for restoration of entitlement cannot be met, veterans who had a VA loan before may still have remaining entitlement to use for another VA loan. The current amount of entitlement available to eligible veterans has been increased over time by changes in the law.

For example, in 1974 the maximum guaranty entitlement was $12,500. Today the maximum guaranty entitlement is $36,000 (for most loans under $144,000). So, if a veteran used the $12,500 guaranty in 1974, even if that loan is not paid off, the veteran could use the $23,500 difference between the $12,500 entitlement originally used and the current maximum of $36,000 to buy another home with a VA loan guaranty.

DIRECT HOME LOANS

VA direct home loans are only available to:

- Native American veterans who plan to buy, build, or improve a home on Native American trust land; or

- Certain eligible veterans who have a permanent and total service-connected disability, for specially adapted homes.

Native American Veterans Living on Trust Lands

A VA direct loan can be used to purchase, construct, or improve a home on Native American trust land. These loans may also be used to simultaneously purchase and improve a home, or to refinance another VA direct loan made under this program in order to lower the interest rate. VA direct loans are generally limited to the cost of the home or $80,000, whichever is less.

UPDATE:

On June 15, 2006, the President signed P. L. 109233, the Veterans Housing Opportunity and Benefits Act of 2006. The Law affects VA direct loans to Native Americans Veterans living on Trust Lands in the following ways:

1. The $80,000 maximum loan amount is eliminated. Instead, the new limit is the same as the Federal Home Loan Mortgage Corporation (also known as "Freddie Mac") single-family conventional conforming loan limit.

2. The law extends eligibility for Native American Direct Loan to a veteran who is not a Native American, but who is married to a Native American nonveteran. To be eligible for such a loan, the qualified nonnative American veteran and the Native American spouse must reside on trust land, and both the veteran and spouse must have a meaningful interest in the dwelling or lot.

To qualify for a VA direct loan, the tribal organization or other appropriate Native American group must be participating in the VA direct loan program. The tribal organization must have signed a *Memorandum of Understanding* with the Secretary of Veterans Affairs that includes the conditions governing its participation in the program.

Veterans should contact their regional VA office for specific information regarding direct home loans.

RESALE OF REPOSSESSED VA HOMES

The VA sells homes that it acquires after foreclosure of a VA guaranteed loan. These home are available to veterans and non-veterans.

The properties are available for sale to the general public through the services of private sector real estate brokers. The VA cannot deal directly with purchasers. Real estate brokers receive the keys to the properties and assist prospective purchasers in finding, viewing, and offering to purchase them.

Participating brokers receive instructional material regarding the sales program, and are familiar with VA sales procedures. VA pays the sales commission.
Offers to purchase VA acquired properties must be submitted on VA forms. Offers cannot be submitted on offer forms generally used in the real estate industry.

VA financing is available for most, but not all, property sales. The downpayment requirements are usually very reasonable, the interest rate is established by VA based on market conditions. Any prospective purchaser who requests VA financing to purchase a VA-owned property must have sufficient income to meet the loan payments, maintain the property, and pay all other obligation. The purchaser must have acceptable credit, and must also have enough funds remaining for family support.

Anyone interested should consult a local real estate agent to find out about VA-acquired properties listed for sale in the area.

HUD / FHA LOANS

Veterans are not eligible for VA financing based on service in World War I, Active Duty for Training in the Reserves, or Active Duty for Training in the National Guard (unless "activated" under the authority of Title 10, U.S. Code). However, these veterans may qualify for a HUD / FHA veteran's loan.

The VA's only role in the HUD / FHA program is to determine the eligibility of the veteran, and issue a *Certificate of Veteran Status*, if qualified. Under this program, financing is available for veterans at terms slightly more favorable than those available to non-veterans.

A veteran may request a *Certificate of Veteran Status* by completing VA form 26-8261a. The completed form and required attachments should be submitted to the veteran's regional VA office for a determination of eligibility.

CHAPTER 23

OVERSEAS BENEFITS

MEDICAL BENEFITS

The Foreign Medical Program (FMP) is a healthcare benefits program for U.S. veterans with VA-rated service-connected conditions who are residing or traveling abroad (except Canada and the Philippines). Services provided in Canada and the Philippines are under separate jurisdictions, as indicated later in this chapter.

> *Under the FMP, VA assumes payment responsibility for certain necessary medical services associated with the treatment of service-connected conditions.*

Under the FMP, VA assumes payment responsibility for *certain necessary medical services* associated with the treatment of **service-connected conditions**.

The Foreign Medical Program Office in Denver, Colorado has jurisdiction over all foreign provided services, with the exception of medical services received in Canada and the Philippines. It is responsible for all aspects of the program, including application processing, verification of eligibility, authorization of benefits, and payments of claims.

Individuals who are traveling to or reside in one of the following countries should use the following number to contact the FMP Office in Denver, Colorado: (877) 345-8179

- Germany
- Panama
- Australia
- Italy
- England
- UK
- Japan
- Spain.

For individuals who are in Mexico or Costa Rica, first dial the U.S.A code and then (877) 345-8179. The number also works from the United States.

Generally, as long as the service is medically necessary for the treatment of a VA rated service-connected condition, it will be covered by the FMP. Additionally, the services must be accepted by VA and / or the U.S. Medical community (such as the American Medical Association and the U.S. Food and Drug Administration.)

Exclusions to Medical Benefits

The following services are not covered by the Foreign Medical Program:

- Procedures, treatments, drugs, or devices that are experimental or investigational;
- Family planning services and sterilization;
- Infertility services;
- Plastic surgery primarily for cosmetic purposes;
- Chiropractic services;
- Procedures, services, and supplies related to sex transformations;
- Non-acute institutional care such as long-term inpatient psychiatric care and nursing home care;
- Day care and day hospitalization;
- Non-medical home care (aid and attendance);
- Abortions, except when the life of the mother would be endangered if the fetus were carried to term;
- Travel, meals, and lodging (including transportation costs to return to the United States)

Prosthesis

If an individual residing in a foreign country requires a prosthesis for a VA rated service-connected condition, and the cost of the prosthetic appliance is less than $300 (U.S. currency), the individual may purchase the prosthetic appliance from a local healthcare provider, and send the invoice to the FMP Office for reimbursement, or the healthcare provider may bill the VA.

If the cost of the prosthetic appliance exceeds $300 (U.S. currency), the individual must obtain preauthorization for the VA Foreign Medical Program Office (see address below).

Application Process – Registration

Although pre-registration for eligible veterans is not necessary, veterans who are permanently relocating to a country under the FMP's jurisdiction are encouraged to notify the FMP once a permanent foreign address is established. At that time, FMP will provide detailed program material, such as benefit coverage, benefit limitations, selecting healthcare providers, and claim filing instructions.

Veterans who are simply traveling, and are not planning a permanent relocation do not need to notify the FMP of their travel plans. Program materials are available, however, upon request.

The FMP can be contacted at:

VA Health Administration Center
Foreign Medical Program (FMP)
P.O. Box 65021
Denver, CO 80206-9021
Phone: (303) 331-7590
Fax: (303) 331-7803

Medical Services in Canada

The VA Medical and Regional Office Center in White River Junction, Vermont, is responsible for determining eligibility of U.S. veterans for reimbursement of medical treatment while traveling or residing in Canada. The local offices of Veterans' Affairs-Canada assists veterans in obtaining authorizations for treatment, arranging for treatment (if necessary), and providing information about the medical treatment program.

The same exclusions listed earlier in this chapter also apply to medical services in Canada, and VA assumes payment responsibility only for *certain necessary medical services associated with the treatment of* **service-connected conditions.**

To receive reimbursed medical treatment, an authorization must be obtained from the White River Junction office **prior to treatment** (unless an emergency situation exists).

When required by the VA to support a claim for disability benefits, Veterans' Affairs-Canada will make arrangement for disability examinations for veterans residing in Canada. In some instances, arrangements will be made locally in Canada. In other instances, arrangements will be made at bordering VA medical facilities.

Information on how to obtain medical services in Canada, including procedures for filing claims, can be obtained by contacting the following office:

VAM & RO Center (136FC)
North Hartland Road
White River Junction, VT 05009-0001
Fax: (802) 296-5174

Or

Veterans Affairs-Canada
Foreign Countries Operations
Room 1055
264 Wellington Street
Ottawa, Ontario, Canada K1A 0P4
(613) 943-7461

Medical Services in the Philippines

The Republic of the Philippines is the only foreign country in which the VA operates a regional office and outpatient clinic.

The same exclusions listed earlier in this chapter also apply to medical services in the Philippines, and VA assumes payment responsibility only for *certain necessary medical services associated with the treatment of* **service-connected conditions.**

To receive reimbursed medical treatment, an authorization must be obtained **prior to treatment** (unless an emergency situation exists).

Information on how to obtain medical services in the Philippines, including procedures for filing claims, can be obtained by contacting the following office:

VA Outpatient Clinic (358/00)
2201 Roxas Boulevard
Pasay City 1300
Republic of the Philippines
011-632-838-4566 or (632) 833-4566

OTHER OVERSEAS BENEFITS

Virtually all VA monetary benefits, including compensation, pension, educational assistance, and burial allowances, are payable regardless of an individual's place of residence.

However, there are some program limitations in foreign jurisdictions, including:

- Home-loan guaranties are available only in the United States and selected territories and possessions.

- Educational benefits are limited to approved degree-granting programs in institutions of higher learning

Information and assistance are available to U.S. veterans worldwide at American embassies and consulates. In Canada, the local offices of Veterans Affairs-Canada provide information and assistance. Individuals may call toll-free within Canada, 1-888-996-2242.

In the Philippines, service is available at the VA Regional Office and Outpatient Clinic in Manila:

VA Regional Office
1131 Roxas Boulevard
Manila, Philippines
011-632-521-7521

Direct Deposit

The conventional method of direct deposit is not available outside of the U.S. However, there are foreign banks with branches in the United States, through which direct deposit can be established. Once the funds are received in the U.S. branch through electronic funds transfer, the U.S. branch transfers the money to the foreign branch.

While this process may take a few days longer than direct deposit within the United States, it is still quicker than having checks mailed overseas through the Department of State or International Priority Airmail.

CHAPTER 24

AGENT ORANGE, MUSTARD GAS, RADIATION AND PROJECT 112 / SHAD

AGENT ORANGE

Agent Orange was an herbicide used in Vietnam to defoliate trees and remove cover for the enemy. Agent Orange and other herbicides used in Vietnam were tested or stored elsewhere, including some military bases in the United States. The name "Agent Orange" came from the orange identifying stripe used on the 55-gallon drums in which it was stored.

The U.S. military herbicide program in South Vietnam took place between 1961 and 1975. Herbicides were sprayed in all 4 military zones of Vietnam. More than 19 million gallons of various herbicide combinations were used. Agent orange was the combination of herbicides the U.S. military used most often.

Heavily sprayed areas included:

- Inland forests near the demarcation zone;
- Inland forests at the junction of the borders of Cambodia, Laos, and South Vietnam;
- Inland forests north and northwest of Saigon;
- Mangrove forests on the southernmost peninsula of Vietnam;
- Mangrove forests along major shipping channels southeast of Saigon.

VA has offered special access to health services and studies since 1978, when it initiated a medical surveillance program for Vietnam veterans with health concerns. By 1981, VA offered priority medical care to Vietnam veterans with any health problems, which may have resulted from Agent Orange exposure. That program continues today.

Toll-Free Agent Orange Helpline

In the Spring of 2000, VA established a national toll-free helpline to answer questions about Agent Orange exposure, health care, and benefits.

The toll-free telephone number for the helpline is (800) 749-8387.

Callers can speak directly to VA representatives Monday through Friday from 8:00 a.m. to 4:00 p.m., Central Standard Time, or access a 24-hour automated system.

Eligibility for Veterans' Disability Compensation

Veterans may be eligible for disability compensation if they have a service-related disability and were discharged under conditions other than dishonorable.

Below are the different eligibility requirements for Veterans who were exposed to herbicides while serving inside or outside of Vietnam during the Vietnam War:

In-Vietnam Exposure to Agent Orange:

Veterans who served on land in Vietnam, went ashore when a ship docked to the shore of Vietnam, or served on the inland waterways of Vietnam anytime between January 9, 1962 and May 7, 1975 (including brief visits), and who have a disease that VA recognizes as associated with Agent Orange exposure are presumed to have been exposed to Agent Orange.

This includes:

> **"Brown Water Veterans"** who served aboard river patrol and swift boats that operated on inland waterways anytime between January 9, 1962 and May 7, 1975; and

> **"Blue Water Veterans"** who went ashore when a ship docked to the shore of Vietnam or served aboard ships that operated on the inland waterways of Vietnam anytime between January 9, 1962 and May 7, 1975.

2010 UPDATE:
VA Issues List of Ships with Agent Orange Exposure

In 2010, the Department of Veterans Affairs Compensation and Pension (C&P) Service initiated a program to collect data on Vietnam naval operations for the purpose of providing regional offices with information to assist with development of claims based on herbicide exposure from Navy Veterans.

To date, the Department of Veterans Affairs (VA) has received verification from various sources showing that a number of offshore "blue water naval vessels" conducted operations on the inland "brown water" rivers and delta areas of Vietnam. The VA also has identified certain vessel types that operated primarily or exclusively on the inland waterways.

If a Veteran's service aboard one of these ships can be confirmed through military records during the time frames specified, then exposure to herbicide agents can be presumed without further development:

- All vessels of Inshore Fire Support [IFS] Division 93 during their entire Vietnam tour
- USS Carronade (IFS 1)
- USS Clarion River (LSMR 409) [Landing Ship, Medium, Rocket]
- USS Francis River (LSMR 525)
- USS White River (LSMR 536)

- All vessels with the designation LST [Landing Ship, Tank] during their entire tour [WWII ships converted to transport supplies on rivers and serve as barracks for brown water Mobile Riverine Forces]
- All vessels with the designation LCVP [Landing Craft, Vehicle, Personnel] during their entire tour
- All vessels with the designation PCF [Patrol Craft, Fast] during their entire tour [Also called Swift Boats, operating for enemy interdiction on close coastal waters]
- All vessels with the designation PBR [Patrol Boat, River] during their entire tour [Also called River Patrol Boats as part of the Mobile Riverine Forces operating on inland waterways and featured in the Vietnam film "Apocalypse Now"]
- USS Ingersoll (DD-652) [Destroyer] [Operated on Saigon River, October 24-25, 1965]
- USS Mansfield (DD-728) [Destroyer] [Operated on Saigon River August 8-19, 1967 and December 21-24, 1968]
- USS Richard E. Kraus (DD-849) [Destroyer] [Operated on coastal inlet north of Da Nang, June 2-5, 1966, protecting Marines holding a bridge]
- USS Basilone (DD-824) [Destroyer] [Operated on Saigon River, May 24-25, 1966]
- USS Hamner (DD-718) [Destroyer] [Operated on Song Lon Tao and Long Song Tao Rivers, August 15-September 1, 1966]
- USS Conway (DD-507) [Destroyer] [Operated on Saigon River, early August 1966]
- USS Fiske (DD-842) [Destroyer] [Operated on Mekong River, June 16-21, 1966]
- USS Black (DD-666) [Destroyer] [Operated on Saigon River, July 13-19, 1966]
- USS Providence (CLG-6) [Cruiser, Light, Guided Missile] [Operated on Saigon River 3 days during January 1964]
- USS Mahan (DLG-11) [Guided Missile Frigate] [Operated on Saigon River October 24-28, 1964]
- USS Okanogan (APA-220) [Attack Transport] [Operated on Saigon River July 22-23, 29-30, 1968 and August 5-6, 1968]
- USS Niagara Falls (AFS-3) [Combat Stores Ship] [Unloaded supplies on Saigon River and Cam Rahn Bay, April 22-25, 1968]
- *All U.S. Coast Guard Cutters* with hull designation *WPB* [patrol boat] and *WHEC* [high endurance cutters]
- Barracks Barge (APL-26) [sleeping quarters]
- Barracks Barge (APL-30) Floating Base Platform (YRBM-17) [repair, berthing, and messing barge]
- Floating Base Platform (YRBM-18)
- Floating Base Platform (YRBM-20)
- *Winnemucca* (YTB-785) [harbor tug]
- *USS Mark* (AKL-12) [light cargo ship]
- *USS Brule* (AKL-28)
- *USS Patapsco* (AOG-1) [gasoline tanker]
- *USS Elkhorn* (AOG-7)
- *USS Genesee* (AOG-8)
- *USS Kishwaukee* (AOG-9)
- *USS Tombigbee* (AOG-11)

- *USS Noxubee* (AOG-56)
- *USS Okanogan* (APA-210) [attack transport]
- *USS Montrose* (APA-212)
- *USS Bexar* (APA-237)
- *USS Benewah* (APB-35) [self-propelled barracks ship]
- *USS Colleton* (APB-36)
- *USS Mercer* (APB-39)
- *USS Nueces* (APB-40)
- *USS Tutuila* (ARG-4) [repair ship]
- *USS Satyr* (ARL-23) [repair ship]
- *USS Sphinx* (ARL-24)
- *USS Askari* (ARL-30)
- *USS Indra* (ARL-37)
- *USS Krishna* (ARL-38)
- *USS Belle Grove* (LSD-2) [landing ship dock]
- *USS Comstock* (LSD-19)
- *USS Tortuga* (LSD-26)
- *USS Asheville* (PG-84) [patrol gunboat]
- *USS Gallop* (PG-85)
- *USS Antelope* (PG-86)
- *USS Ready* (PG-87)
- *USS Crockett* (PG-88)
- *USS Marathon* (PG-89)
- *USS Canon* (PG-90)
- *USS Card* (ACV-11) [escort carrier] mined, sunk, and salvaged in Saigon River Harbor during May 1964
- *USS Maury* (AGS-16) [mapping survey ship] conducted surveys of Mekong Delta and other coastal areas and rivers beginning November 1965 through 1969
- *USS Henrico* (APA-45) [amphibious attack transport] operated on Hue River during March 1965 and conducted numerous troop landings through March 1967
- *USS Montrose* (APA-212) operated on Song Hue River during December 1965; operated on Long Tau River during March 1967; and operated on Cua Viet River and at Dong Ha during May 1967
- *USS Talladega* (APA-208) operated on Saigon River during October 1967
- *USS Bolster* (ARS-38) [salvage ship] crew operated on land.
- *USS Canberra* (CAG-2) [guided missile cruiser] operated on Saigon River from March 31 through April 1, 1966; on Cua Viet River during December 15, 1966; and on Mekong Delta Ham Luong River during January 15, 1967
- *USS Sproston* (DD-577) [destroyer] operated on Mekong Delta and Ganh Rai Bay during January 1966
- *USS Picking* (DD-685) operated on Saigon River during November 16, 1965
- *USS Epperson* (DD-719) docked to Da Nang Pier on October 4, 1970
- *USS Southerland* (DD-743) operated on Song Nga Bay and Saigon River during July 1966
- *USS John W. Thomason* (DD-760) operated on Nga Be River during 1969
- *USS Buck* (DD-761) operated on Mekong River Delta and Saigon River during October 1966

- *USS Preston* (DD-795) operated on Mekong River Delta, Ganh Rai Bay, and Saigon River during September 28 - 29 and December 27 - 29, 1965
- *USS Warrington* (DD-843) operated on Mekong River Delta Rung Sat Special Zone, North of Vung Gahn Rai Bay during March 1967
- *USS Dyess* (DD-880) operated on Saigon River and Rung Sat Special Zone from June 19-July 1, 1966
- *USS Perkins* (DD-877) operated on Saigon River during June 1969
- *USS Orleck* (DD-886) operated on Mekong River Delta during July 1969
- *USS Joseph Strauss* (DDG-16) [guided missile destroyer] operated on Mekong River Delta and Ganh Rai Bay during November 7 and December 7, 1968
- *USS Waddell* (DDG-24) operated on Cua Viet River during March 1967
- *USS Newell* (DER-322) [radar destroyer escort] docked at port of Nha Trang during December 22-24, 1965
- *USS Duluth* (LPD-6) [amphibious transport dock] docked to pier at Da Nang during March and October 1971
- *USS Cleveland* (LPD-7) operated on Cua Viet River and at Dong Ha, as well as Hue River, from November 1967 through 1968 and Saigon River during September 1969
- *USS Dubuque* (LPD-8) docked at Da Nang on March 15, 1970
- *USS Boxer* (LPH-4) [amphibious assault ship] docked to pier at Cam Rahn Bay on September 9, 1965
- *USS Carter Hall* (LSD-3) [landing ship dock] operated on Cua Viet River and at Dong Ha during December 1967

Outside-Vietnam Exposure to Herbicides:

Veterans who did not serve inside Vietnam and were exposed elsewhere to Agent Orange or other herbicides may be eligible for service-connection on a "direct" basis. These veterans must show that their diseases are related to their military service in order to qualify for disability compensation.

Additionally, these veterans must show that they were exposed to Agent Orange or other herbicides during military service. This includes:

Blue Water Veterans who served on ships off the shore of Vietnam that did not dock to the shore of Vietnam or operate on the inland waterways of Vietnam; (Blue Water Veterans claiming non-Hodgkin's lymphoma as a disability may be granted service connection without showing inland waterway service or that they went ashore when their ships docked to the shore of Vietnam. This is because VA also recognizes non-Hodgkin's lymphoma as associated with service in Vietnam or the waters offshore of Vietnam during the Vietnam Era.)

Veterans who served in the Korea demilitarized zone in 1968 to 1969;

Veterans who served on or near the perimeters of military bases in Thailand during the Vietnam era;

Veterans who served where herbicides were tested or stored outside of Vietnam.

Determination of Service-Connected Diseases

Veterans who served in Vietnam anytime between January 9, 1962 and May 7, 1975, and who have a disease that VA recognizes as associated with Agent Orange exposure are presumed to have been exposed to Agent Orange. These veterans do not need to show that they were exposed to Agent Orange in order to get disability compensation.

The diseases referred to above are:

- **Acute and Subacute Peripheral Neuropathy**

    A nervous system condition that causes numbness, tingling, and motor weakness. Under VA's rating regulations, it must be at least 10% disabling within 1 year of exposure to Agent Orange and resolve within 2 years after the date it began.

- **AL Amyloidosis**

    A rare disease caused when an abnormal protein, amyloid, enters tissues or organs.

- **B Cell Leukemias**

    Cancers which affect B cells, such as hairy cell leukemia.

- **Chloracne (or Similar Acneform Disease)**

    A skin condition that occurs soon after dioxin exposure and looks like common forms of acne seen in teenagers. Under VA's rating regulations, chloracne (or other acneform disease similar to chloracne) must be at least 10% disabling within 1 year of exposure to Agent Orange.

- **Chronic Lymphocytic Leukemia**

    A disease that progresses slowly with increasing production of excessive numbers of white blood cells.

- **Diabetes Mellitus (Type 2)**

    A disease characterized by high blood sugar levels resulting from the body's inability to respond properly to the hormone insulin.

- **Hodgkin's Disease**

    A malignant lymphoma (cancer) characterized by progressive enlargement of the lymph nodes, liver, and spleen, and by progressive anemia.

- **Ischemic Heart Disease**

    A disease characterized by a reduced supply of blood to the heart.

- **Multiple Myeloma**

A cancer of specific bone marrow cells that is characterized by bone marrow tumors in various bones of the body.

- **Non-Hodgkin's Lymphoma**

  A group of cancers that affect the lymph glands and other lymphatic tissue.

- **Parkinson's Disease**

  A motor system condition with symptoms that include trembling of the limbs and face and impaired balance.

- **Porphyria Cutanea Tarda**

  A disorder characterized by liver dysfunction and by thinning and blistering of the skin in sun-exposed areas. Under VA's rating regulations, it must be at least 10% disabling within 1 year of exposure to Agent Orange.

- **Prostate Cancer**

  Cancer of the prostate; one of the most common cancers among men.

- **Respiratory Cancers**

  Cancers of the lung, larynx, trachea, and bronchus.

- **Soft Tissue Sarcoma (other than Osteosarcoma, Chondrosarcoma, Kaposi's sarcoma, or Mesothelioma)**

  A group of different types of cancers in body tissues such as muscle, fat, blood and lymph vessels, and connective tissues.

- Each additional disease (if any) that the Secretary of the VA determines warrants a presumption of service-connection by reason of having positive association with exposure to an herbicide agent, becomes manifest within the period (if any) prescribed in such regulations in a veteran who, during active military, naval, or air service, served in the Republic of Vietnam during the period beginning on January 9, 1962 and ending on May 7, 1975, and while so serving was exposed to that herbicide agent.

Veterans having a disease referred to above, shall be presumed to have been exposed during such service to an herbicide agent containing dioxin or 2,4-dichlorophenoxyacetic acid, and may be presumed to have been exposed during such service to any other chemical compound in an herbicide agent, unless there is affirmative evidence to establish that the veteran was not exposed to any such agent during that service.

If the Secretary of the VA later determines that a previously established presumption of service-connection for one of the above diseases is no longer warranted, all veterans currently awarded compensation on the basis of the presumption shall continue to be entitled to receive compensation. Additionally, all survivors of any such veterans who were awarded dependency and indemnity compensation shall continue to be entitled to receive dependency and indemnity compensation on that basis.

Rates of Disability Compensation

Rates of compensation depend upon the degree of disability, and follow a payment schedule that is adjusted annually and applies to all veterans. Please refer to the charts in Chapter 34 of this book.

Agent Orange Registry

VA developed the Agent Orange Registry Examination Program in 1978 to identify Vietnam veterans concerned about Agent Orange exposure. VA maintains a computerized registry of data from these examinations. Registrants receive periodic updates on Agent Orange studies and VA policy.

There is no cost for eligible veterans. Veterans receive a comprehensive examination, including exposure and medical histories, laboratory tests, and physical exams.

The Agent Orange Registry Exam is not a claim for VA benefits, nor is it required to receive VA benefits.

VA's Advisory Committees on Health-Related Effects of Herbicides & Environmental Hazards

The VA's Advisory Committee on Health-Related Effects Of Herbicides was established in 1979 to examine issues surrounding the possible health effects of herbicides on Vietnam veterans.

VA also established the Veterans' Advisory Committee on Environmental Hazards, consisting of non-VA experts in dioxin and radiation exposure as well as several lay members, to advise the Secretary on the results of Agent Orange-related research, and regulatory, administrative and legislative initiatives.

Since passage of a 1991 law (PL 102-4), which directs VA to request that the National Academy of Sciences (NAS) review diseases associated with herbicide exposure, the committee's work has been superseded by the NAS review.

National Academy of Sciences (NAS)

The NAS reviews and evaluates scientific literature about Agent Orange. NAS reviewed more than 6,000 abstracts of scientific or medical articles and analyzed 230 epidemiological studies before its initial July 1993 report, which led to the inclusion of additional diseases on the list for presumptive service-connection. The NAS review has been continuing, with acute and subacute peripheral neuropathy and prostate cancer added to VA's presumptive list after the NAS issued an updated report in March 1996. Also based on that report's findings of new "limited or suggestive evidence" of an association between herbicides and Spina Bifida in the children of Vietnam veterans, VA proposed legislation to aid children of Vietnam veterans who suffer from that disorder, and established a reproductive outcomes research center to investigate potential environmental hazards of military service.

A separate VA study led Secretary of Veterans Affairs Togo D. West Jr. to call for legislation to benefit children who suffer from birth defects that may have been caused by their mothers' Vietnam service, not necessarily by herbicide exposure. Secretary West also asked NAS to review a study by the National Institute of Occupational Safety and Health of dioxin-exposed production workers at two U.S. plants that revealed elevated rates of diabetes among workers. A decision whether to establish a presumption of service-connection for diabetes will be made once the additional review is completed.

MUSTARD GAS EXPOSURE AND LONG-TERM HEALTH EFFECTS

In 1991, the Department of Veterans Affairs (VA) relaxed requirements for evaluating mustard gas-related compensation claims because of the confidentiality of some of the World War II testing and a lack of military medical records and follow-up. At that time, a review of studies of the effects of mustard gas exposure led VA to publish regulations authorizing service-connection and disability compensation payments to veterans who were exposed to significant levels of mustard gas and who suffer from chronic forms of certain diseases.

An estimated 4,000 servicemen participated in tests using significant concentrations of mustard gas either in chambers or field exercises in contaminated areas during World War II. This secret testing was conducted in order to develop better protective clothing, masks and skin ointments. There is no central roster of World War II participants in either the laboratory or field tests. The Army conducted tests on Army personnel in the laboratory and in the field. The test sites included:

- Edgewood Arsenal, Maryland;
- Camp Sibert, Alabama;
- Bushnell, Florida;
- Dugway Proving Ground, Utah; and
- San Jose Island, Panama Canal Zone

Military personnel from the U.S. Navy Training Center, Bainbridge, Maryland., also were sent to the Naval Research Lab in Washington, D.C., to participate in tests. Gas testing facilities also were located at Great Lakes Naval Training Center in Illinois and Camp Lejeune, North Carolina.

Institute of Medicine Study

Also in 1991, VA contracted with the Institute of Medicine to conduct a study of medical and scientific literature worldwide to determine the long-term health effects of mustard gas and Lewisite. The $600,000 VA-funded study, entitled "Veterans at Risk: The Health Effects of Mustard Gas and Lewisite," was released Jan. 6, 1993. The study found a relationship between exposure and the subsequent development of certain diseases.

Veterans Who May Be Eligible for Compensation

VA policies generally authorize service-connection and compensation payments to veterans who were exposed to mustard gas and/or Lewisite and who suffer from a number of diseases or conditions, including:

- Full-body exposure to nitrogen or sulfur mustard together with the subsequent development of chronic conjunctivitis, keratitis, corneal opacities, scar formation, or the following cancers: nasopharyngeal; laryngeal; lung (except mesothelioma); or squamous cell carcinoma of the skin;

- Full-body exposure to nitrogen or sulfur mustard -- or exposure to Lewisite -- and the subsequent development of a chronic form of laryngitis, bronchitis, emphysema, asthma or chronic obstructive pulmonary disease;

- Full-body exposure to nitrogen mustard with the subsequent development of acute nonlymphocytic leukemia.

Service-connection is not allowed if the claimed condition is due to the veteran's own willful misconduct or if there is affirmative evidence that establishes some other nonservice-related condition or event as the cause of the claimed disability.

Veterans who were exposed to significant amounts of mustard gas and have health problems that may be compensable (or their survivors) may contact the nearest VA regional office at 1-800-827-1000 for more information about benefits.

VA PROGRAMS FOR VETERANS EXPOSED TO RADIATION

VA provides special priority for enrollment for health-care services to any veteran exposed to ionizing radiation in connection with:

- Onsite participation in a test involving the atmospheric detonation of a nuclear device (without regard to whether the nation conducting the test was the United States or another nation).

- The American occupation of Hiroshima and Nagasaki, Japan, during the period beginning August 6, 1945, and ending July 1, 1946.

- Internment as a prisoner of war in Japan (or service on active duty in Japan immediately following such internment) during World War II which (as determined by the Secretary of the VA) resulted in an opportunity for exposure to ionizing radiation comparable to that of veterans described above.

IMPORTANT UPDATE:

- The definition of radiation-risk activities was expanded in March 2002 to include service at Amchitka Island, Alaska, prior to January 1, 1974, if a veteran was exposed while performing duties related to certain underground nuclear tests.
- The new definition also includes service at gaseous diffusion plants located in Paducah, Ky., Portsmouth, Ohio and an area known as K25 at Oak Ridge, Tenn.

In addition, these veterans are eligible to participate in the VA ionizing radiation registry examination program. VA also pays compensation to veterans and their survivors if the veteran is determined to have a disability due to radiation exposure while in service.

Radiation Statistics

Some 195,000 service members have been identified as participants in the post-World War II occupation of Hiroshima and Nagasaki, Japan. In addition, approximately 210,000 mostly military members are confirmed as participants in U.S. atmospheric nuclear tests between 1945 and 1962 in the United States and the Pacific and Atlantic oceans prior to the 1963 Limited Test Ban Treaty. The Defense Threat Reduction Agency's Nuclear Test Personnel Review program since 1978 has maintained a database of participants in atmospheric nuclear test activities. About one-fourth of the participants received no measurable dose of ionizing radiation, with fewer than one per cent of the nuclear test participants identified as having a dose of 5 rem or higher. (The current federal guideline for U.S. workplace exposure is 5 rem per year.)

Determination of Service-Connected Diseases

VA may pay compensation for radiogenic diseases under two programs specific to radiation-exposed veterans and their survivors:

Statutory List

Veterans who participated in nuclear tests by the U.S. or its allies, who served with the U.S. occupation forces in Hiroshima or Nagasaki, Japan, between August 1945 and July 1946, or who were similarly exposed to ionizing radiation while a prisoner of war in Japan, are eligible for compensation for cancers specified in legislation.

The types of cancer covered by these laws are:

- All forms of leukemia except chronic lymphocytic leukemia;
- Cancer of the thyroid,
- Cancer of the breast,
- Cancer of the pharynx,
- Cancer of the esophagus,
- Cancer of the stomach,
- Cancer of the small intestine,
- Cancer of the pancreas,
- Cancer of the bile ducts,
- Cancer of the gall bladder,
- Cancer of the salivary gland
- Cancer of the urinary tract;
- Lymphomas (except Hodgkin's disease);
- Multiple myeloma;
- Primary liver cancer.

In March 2002, VA announced the addition of five new cancers to the list of diseases presumed to be connected to the exposure of veterans to radiation during their military service:

- Bone Cancer
- Brain Cancer
- Colon Cancer
- Lung Cancer

- Ovary Cancer

The new rules apply to those veterans who participated in "radiation-risk activities" while on active duty, during active duty for training or inactive duty training as a member of a reserve component.

Regulatory List

Disability compensation claims of veterans who were exposed to radiation in service and who develop a disease within specified time periods not specified in the statutory list are governed by regulation. Under the regulations, various additional factors must be considered in determining service-connection, including amount of radiation exposure, duration of exposure, and elapsed time between exposure and onset of the disease. VA regulations identify all cancers as potentially radiogenic, as well as certain other non-malignant conditions: posterior subcapsular cataracts; non-malignant thyroid nodular disease; parathyroid adenoma; and tumors of the brain and central nervous system.

A final rule that expanded the regulatory list from more than a dozen specific cancers to add "any other cancer" (any malignancy) was published Sept. 24, 1998. The rulemaking began following a 1995 review of the radiogenicity of cancer generally by the Veterans Advisory Committee on Environmental Hazards. It concluded that, on the basis of current scientific knowledge, exposure to ionizing radiation can be a contributing factor in the development of any malignancy. VA also will consider evidence that diseases other those specified in regulation may be caused by radiation exposure.

Rates of Disability Compensation

Rates of compensation depend upon the degree of disability and follow a payment schedule that is adjusted annually and applies to all veterans. Please refer to the charts in Chapter 3 of this book.

Ionizing Radiation Registry Program

In addition to special eligibility to enroll for VA healthcare for radiation-related conditions, atomic veterans are eligible to participate in VA's Ionizing Radiation Registry examination. Under the Ionizing Radiation Registry program, VA will perform a complete physical examination, including all necessary tests, for each veteran who requests it if the veteran was exposed to ionizing radiation while participating in the nuclear weapons testing program, or if he or she served with the U.S. occupation forces in Hiroshima or Nagasaki. Veterans need not be enrolled for general VA care to be eligible for the Ionizing Radiation Registry.

PROJECT 112 / PROJECT SHAD VETERANS

> *Veterans who believe their health may have been affected by these tests should contact the SHAD helpline at (800) 749-8387.*

Project SHAD, an acronym for Shipboard Hazard and Defense, was part of a larger effort called Project 112, which was a comprehensive program initiated in 1962 by the Department of Defense (DoD) to protect and defend against potential chemical and biological warfare threats. Project SHAD encompassed a series of tests by DoD to determine the vulnerability of U.S. warships to attacks with chemical and biological warfare agents, and the potential risk to American forces posed by these agents.

Project 112 tests involved similar tests conducted on land rather than aboard ships.

Project SHAD involved service members from the Navy and Army and may have involved a small number of personnel from the Marine Corps and Air Force. Service members were not test subjects, but rather were involved in conducting the tests. Animals were used in some, but not most, tests.

DoD continues to release declassified reports about sea- and land- based tests of chemical and biological materials known collectively as "Project 112." The Department of Veterans Affairs (VA) is working with DoD to obtain information as to the nature and availability of the tests, who participated, duration and agents used.

Veterans who believe their health may have been affected by these tests should contact the SHAD helpline at (800) 749-8387

Public Law 108-170, the Veterans Health Care, Capital Asset, and Business Improvement Act of 2003, enacted December 6, 2003, provides for veterans who participated in Project 112/SHAD to be enrolled in priority enrollment category 6 and as such, to be eligible for VA health care at no cost for any illness possibly related to their participation in that project.

Following is a table provided by the DoD regarding specific ships, tests, and current information available.

(FS = FACT SHEET   PR = PERSONNEL ROSTER)

#	Test Name	Date	Location	Agent/Stimulant	Investigation Status	Information at VA
1	63-1 Eager Belle I [SHAD]	Jan - Mar 1963	Pacific Ocean	BG	Fact Sheet Released 1/31/2002	FS, PR
	Eager Belle II [SHAD]	Jan, Mar, Jun 1963	Pacific Ocean	BG	Fact Sheet Released 1/31/2002	FS, PR
2	63-2 Autumn Gold [SHAD]	May 1963	Pacific Ocean	BG	Fact Sheet Released 9/13/2001	FS, PR
3	63-3 Whistle Down	Dec 1962 - Feb 1963	Ft. Greely, AK	GB, VX	Fact Sheet Released 10/09/2002	FS
4	63-4 Big Jack A	Feb - Mar 1963	Ft. Sherman, Panama Canal Zone	BG, FP	Fact Sheet Released 10/31/2002	FS
	Big Jack B	Feb - Mar 1963	Ft. Sherman, Panama Canal Zone	TOF	Fact Sheet Released 10/31/2002	FS
5	64-1 Errand Boy [SHAD]	September 1963	Oahu, HI	BG	Fact Sheet Released 6/30/2003	FS, PR
6	64-2 Flower Drum I [SHAD]	Feb - Apr 1964 Aug - Sep 1964	Pacific Ocean	GB, SO2, MAA	Fact Sheet Released 5/23/2002	FS, PR
	Flower Drum II [SHAD]	Nov - Dec 1964	Pacific Ocean	VX, P32, Bis	Fact Sheet Released 5/23/2002	FS
7	64-3 Little Mo [SHAD]	NA	NA	NA	Test Cancelled	NA
8	64-4 [Red Beva] Shady Grove [SHAD]	Jan - Apr 1965	Pacific Ocean	BG, OU, UL	Fact Sheet Released 9/13/2001	FS, PR
9	64-5 Night Train	Nov 1963 - Jan 1964	Ft. Greely, AK	BG, FP	Fact Sheet Released 10/09/2002	FS
10	64-6 Yellow Leaf	Feb 1964, Apr - May 1966	Ft. Sherman, Panama Canal Zone, Island of Hawaii	BG, Tiara	Fact Sheet Released 10/31/2002	FS
11	64-7 Big Thunder	NA	NA	NA	Test Cancelled	NA

#	Test Name	Date	Location	Agent/Stimulant	Investigation Status	Information at VA
12	64-8 Tall Timber	Apr - Jun 1966	Island of Hawaii	BZ	Fact Sheet Released 10/09/2002	FS
13	64-9 Big Piney	NA	NA	NA	Test Cancelled	NA
14	64-10 [65-18] Black Label	NA	NA	NA	Test Deferred/Renumbered	NA
15	64-11 [65-19] Laurel Grove	NA	NA	NA	Test Deferred/Renumbered	NA
16	65-1 Copper Head [SHAD]	Jan - Feb 1965	Atlantic Ocean off Newfoundland, Canada	BG, FP, Beta-propiolactone	Fact Sheet Released 9/13/2001	FS, PR
17	65-2 Chain Saw	NA	NA	NA	Test Cancelled	NA
18	65-3 West Side I	Jan - Feb 1965	Ft. Greely, AK	BG, FP	Fact Sheet Released 10/09/2002	FS
19	65-4 Magic Sword [SHAD]	May 1965	Baker Island	mosquitoes (Aedes aegypti)	Fact Sheet Released 10/09/2002	FS, PR
20	65-5 Iron Clad [SHAD]	NA	NA	NA	Test Cancelled	NA
21	65-6 Big Tom [SHAD]	May - Jun 1965	Pacific Ocean, off Oahu, HI & surrounding water & airspace	BG, FP	Updated Fact Sheet Released 6/30/2003	FS, PR
22	65-7 Great Sole [SHAD]	NA	NA	NA	Test Cancelled	NA
23	65-8 Lone Wolf [SHAD]	NA	NA	NA	Test Cancelled	NA
24	65-9 Silver Star	NA	NA	NA	Test Cancelled	NA
25	65-10 Little Egypt	NA	NA	NA	Test Cancelled	NA
26	65-11 [Bear River] Sun Down	Feb, Apr 1966	Ft. Greely, AK	GB, MAA, Tiara	Fact Sheet Released 10/09/2002	FS
27	65-12 Devil Hole I	Summer 1965	Ft. Greely, AK	GB, FP	Fact Sheet Released 10/09/2002	FS
28	65-13 High Low [SHAD]	Jan - Feb 1966	Pacific Ocean off San Diego, CA	MAA	Corrected Fact Sheet Released 12/31/2002	FS
29	65-14 Elk Hunt I	Jul - Aug 1964	Ft. Greely, AK	VX	Fact Sheet Released 10/09/2002	FS, PR
	Elk Hunt II	Jun - Jul 1965 Oct - Dec 1965	Ft. Greely, AK & Edgewood Arsenal, MD, & Canada	VX	Fact Sheet Released 10/09/2002	FS, PR
30	65-15 Little Corporal	NA	NA	NA	Test Cancelled	NA
31	65-16 Pine Ridge	May - Jun 1966	Island of Hawaii	GB, BZ	Fact Sheet Released 10/09/2002	FS
32	65-17 Fearless Johnny [SHAD]	Aug - Sep 1965	Pacific Ocean southwest of Oahu, HI	VX, Diethylphthlate	Fact Sheet Released 5/23/2002	FS, PR

#	Test Name	Date	Location	Agent/Stimulant	Investigation Status	Information at VA
33	65-18 [64-10] Black Label	NA	NA	NA	Test Cancelled	NA
34	65-19 [64-11] Laurel Grove	NA	NA	NA	Test Cancelled	NA
35	66-1 Devil Hole II	Jul - Aug 1966	Ft. Greely, AK	VX	Fact Sheet Released 10/09/2002	FS
36	66-2 Red Oak I	Apr - May 1967	Island of Hawaii, Ft. Sherman, Panama Canal Zone	GB	Fact Sheet Released 10/31/2002	FS
37	66-3 Swamp Oak I	Mar - Apr 1966	Ft. Greely, AK	GB	Fact Sheet Released 10/09/2002	FS
38	66-4 Green Mist	Mar - Apr 1967	Island of Hawaii	GB, MAA	Fact Sheet Released 10/09/2002	FS
39	66-5 Purple Sage [SHAD]	Jan - Feb 1966	Pacific Ocean off San Diego, CA	MAA	Fact Sheet Released 5/23/2002	FS, PR
40	66-6 Scarlet Sage [SHAD]	Feb - Mar 1966	Pacific Ocean off San Diego, CA	BG	Fact Sheet Released 1/31/2002	FS, PR
41	66-7 Clay Pigeon I	NA	NA	NA	Test Cancelled	NA
42	66-8 West Side II	Jan - Mar 1965	Southwestern Canada	BG, FP	Fact Sheet Released 10/09/2002	FS
43	66-9 Magic Sword II [SHAD]	NA	NA	NA	Test Cancelled	NA
44	66-10 Pin Point	1966	Unspecified	CS	Fact Sheet Released 10/31/2002	FS
45	66-11 Ebony Sun [SHAD]	NA	NA	NA	Test Cancelled	NA
46	66-12 [Bald Eagle I] Bold Captain [SHAD]	NA	NA	NA	Test Cancelled	NA
47	66-13 Half Note [SHAD]	Aug - Sep 1966	Pacific Ocean, off Hawaii	BG, E.coli, FP SM, calcaflour	Updated Fact Sheet Released 6/30/2003	FS, PR
48	66-14 Sandy Point [SHAD]	NA	NA	NA	Test Cancelled	NA
49	67-1 [68-15] Red Oak II	NA	NA	NA	Test Deferred/Renumbered	NA
50	67-2 Dew Point	Jun - Jul 1967	Ft. Greely, AK	GB	Fact Sheet Released 10/09/2002	FS
51	67-3 [68-11] [69-13] Tiny Doll	NA	NA	NA	Test Deferred/Renumbered	NA
52	67-4 Blue Note [SHAD]	NA	NA	NA	Test Cancelled	NA
53	67-5 Work Horse [SHAD]	NA	NA	NA	Test Cancelled	NA
54	67-6 Blue Tango	Jan - Feb 1967	Hawaii	BG, E.coli, SM	Fact Sheet Released 6/30/2003	FS, PR

#	Test Name	Date	Location	Agent/Stimulant	Investigation Status	Information at VA
55	67-7 [Coincidence] Red Cloud	Nov 1966 - Feb 1967	Ft. Greely, AK	BG, E.coli, SM, TT, ZZ	Fact Sheet Released 10/09/2002	FS
56	67-8 [Autobiography] Watch Dog	Summer 1967	Ft. Greely, AK	BG, E.coli, SM, TT, ZZ	Fact Sheet Released 10/09/2002	FS
57	67-9 [Key Fruit] Gray Fox [SHAD]	NA	NA	NA	Test Cancelled	NA
58	67-10 [Meddled] Night Fire [SHAD]	NA	NA	NA	Test Cancelled	NA
59	67-11 [Expunge] Slow Waltz [SHAD]	NA	NA	NA	Test Cancelled	NA
60	67-12 [68-72] [69-30] [69-70] [69-73] [Expulsion] Sharp Nail [SHAD]	NA	NA	NA	Test Deferred/Renumbered	NA
61	67-13 Steel Point	NA	NA	NA	Test Cancelled	NA
62	68-10 [68-2] Sharp Ravine	NA	NA	NA	Test Cancelled	NA
63	68-11 [67-3] [69-13] Tiny Doll	NA	NA	NA	Test Deferred/Renumbered	NA
64	68-12 [68-1] Narrow Trail	NA	NA	NA	Test Cancelled	NA
65	68-13 [68-4] Rapid Tan	Jul - Aug 1967 May - Jun 1968 Aug - Sep 1968	Phase I & III - Porton Down, England, Phase II - Ralston, Canada	GA, GB, GD, VX	Fact Sheet Released 10/09/2002	FS
66	68-14 [68-3] Channel Crab	NA	NA	NA	Test Cancelled	NA
67	68-15 [67-1] Red Oak II	NA	NA	NA	Test Cancelled	NA
68	68-30 [68-5] [69-74] Prairie Carpet	NA	NA	NA	Test Deferred/Renumbered	NA
69	68-31 [68-6] [69-33] Exit Line	NA	NA	NA	Test Deferred/Renumbered	NA
70	68-33 [68-7] Wicked Slice	NA	NA	NA	Test Cancelled	NA
71	68-50 [68-11] Speckled Start [SHAD]	Sep - Oct 1968	Eniwetok Atoll, Marshall Islands	BG, PG2, uranine dye	Fact Sheet Released 5/23/2002	FS, PR
72	68-51 [68-9] Strange Fruit	NA	NA	NA	Test Cancelled	NA

#	Test Name	Date	Location	Agent/Stimulant	Investigation Status	Information at VA
73	68-52 Cliff Rose	Sep 27, 1967 - Jan 18, 1968	Ft Stewart Georgia and Panama Canal Zone	CS	Fact Sheet Released 12/9/2002*	FS
74	68-53	Apr - Dec 1969	DPG, UT	CS	Fact Sheet Released 10/09/2002	FS
75	68-70 [68-12] Shining Pond	NA	NA	NA	Test Cancelled	NA
76	68-71 [68-13] Folded Arrow [SHAD]	Apr – May 1968	Oahu, HI and surrounding waters	BG	Fact Sheet Released 6/30/2003	FS, PR
77	68-72 [67-12] [69-70] Sharp Nail	NA	NA	NA	Test Deferred/Renumbered	NA
78	68-73 [68-8] [69-73] Leaning Shoe	NA	NA	NA	Test Deferred/Renumbered	NA
79	[68-10] Maple Board	NA	NA	NA	Test Cancelled	NA
80	69-10 [SHAD]	May 1969	Vieques, PR	TOF	Fact Sheet Released 10/09/2002	FS, PR
81	69-12	Spring 1969	Edgewood Arsenal, MD	GB, GD, GA, VX	Test Suspended Fact Sheet Released 10/09/2002	FS
82	69-13 [67-3] [68-11] Tiny Doll	NA	NA	NA	Test Cancelled	NA
83	69-14	Jul – Nov 1971	DPG, UT	DEHP	Fact Sheet Released 10/09/2002	FS
84	69-15 [SHAD]	NA	NA	NA	Test Cancelled	NA
85	69-16	NA	NA	NA	Test Cancelled	NA
86	69-30	NA	NA	NA	Test Cancelled	NA
87	69-31 [SHAD]	Aug - Sep 1968	Pacific Ocean off San Diego, CA	BG, MAA	Fact Sheet Released 10/09/2002	FS, PR
88	69-32 [SHAD]	Apr - Jun 1969	Pacific Ocean, southwest of Hawaii	BG, E.coli, SM, Calcaflour	Fact Sheet Released 5/23/2002	FS, PR
89	69-33 [68-6] [68-31] Exit Line [SHAD]	NA	NA	NA	Test Cancelled	NA
90	69-34	NA	NA	NA	Test Cancelled	NA
91	69-35	NA	NA	NA	Test Cancelled	NA
92	69-36 [SHAD]	NA	NA	NA	Test Cancelled	NA
93	69-37	NA	NA	NA	Test Cancelled	NA
94	69-70 [67-12] [68-72] Sharp Nail	NA	NA	NA	Test Cancelled	NA
95	69-71	NA	NA	NA	Test Cancelled	NA
96	69-72 [SHAD]	NA	NA	NA	Test Cancelled	NA

#	Test Name	Date	Location	Agent/Stimulant	Investigation Status	Information at VA
97	69-73 [68-73] [68-8] Leaning Shoe	NA	NA	NA	Test Cancelled	NA
98	69-74 [68-5] [68-30] Prairie Carpet	NA	NA	NA	Test Cancelled	NA
99	69-75	Oct - Dec 1968	Yeehaw Junction, FL	TX	Fact Sheet Released 10/09/2002	FS
100	70-A	NA	NA	NA	Test Cancelled	NA
101	70-B	NA	NA	NA	Test Cancelled	NA
102	70-C (SHAD)	Oct 1972, Feb – Mar 1973	Pacific Ocean, from San Diego CA to Babloa, Panama	NA	Fact Sheet Released 6/30/2003	FS
103	70-D	NA	NA	NA	Test Cancelled	NA
104	70-10	NA	NA	NA	Test Deferred	NA
105	70-11 Ph I, Subtest 3	June 1972 – Nov 1973	Dugway PG, UT	Bis, TOP, FP	Fact Sheet Released 6/30/2003	FS
	70-11 Ph I, Subtest 4	May 1974	Dugway PG, UT	Bis	Fact Sheet Released 6/30/2003	FS
106	70-12	NA	NA	NA	Test Cancelled	NA
107	70-30	NA	NA	NA	Test Deferred	NA
108	70-31	NA	NA	NA	Test Cancelled	NA
109	70-50	NA	NA	NA	Test Cancelled	NA
110	70-70 [SHAD]	NA	NA	NA	Test Cancelled	NA
111	70-71 [SHAD]	NA	NA	NA	Test Cancelled	NA
112	70-72	NA	NA	NA	Test Cancelled	NA
113	70-73	Jul - Dec 1970	DPG, UT	BG, FP	Fact Sheet Released 10/09/2002	FS
114	70-74	Au 1972 – Jan 1973	Dugway PG, UT	BG, SM	Fact Sheet Released 6/30/2003	FS
115	71-10	NA	NA	NA	Test Cancelled	NA
116	71-11	NA	NA	NA	Test Cancelled	NA
117	71-12	NA	NA	NA	Test Cancelled	NA
118	71-13	NA	NA	NA	Test Cancelled	NA
119	71-30	NA	NA	NA	Test Cancelled	NA
120	71-31	NA	NA	NA	Test Cancelled	NA
121	71-32	NA	NA	NA	Test Cancelled	NA
122	71-33	NA	NA	NA	Test Cancelled	NA
123	71-34	NA	NA	NA	Test Cancelled	NA
124	71-35	NA	NA	NA	Test Cancelled	NA
125	71-70	NA	NA	NA	Test Cancelled	NA
126	71-75	NA	NA	NA	Test Cancelled	NA
127	72-30 [SHAD]	NA	NA	NA	Test Cancelled	NA
128	72-70 [SHAD]	NA	NA	NA	Test Cancelled	NA

#	Test Name	Date	Location	Agent/Stimulant	Investigation Status	Information at VA
129	73-10	NA	NA	NA	Test Cancelled	NA
130	73-11	NA	NA	NA	Test Cancelled	NA
131	73-12	NA	NA	NA	Test Cancelled	NA
132	73-30	Jan – Feb 1973	Dugway PG, UT	BG, SM, P	Fact Sheet Released 6/30/2003	FS
133	74-10 PH I	Sep – Oct 1973	Dugway PG, UT	DMMP, Bis, Trichloropropane	Fact Sheet Released 6/30/2003	FS
	74-10 PH II	Apr – May 1974	Dugway PG, Ut	DMMP	Fact Sheet Released 6/30/2003	FS
134	74-030	NA	NA	NA	Test Cancelled	NA

CHAPTER 25

SPINA BIFIDA PROGRAM

Spina bifida is the most frequently occurring permanently disabling birth defect.

> *VA provides monetary benefits, vocational training, rehabilitation, and certain healthcare benefits to children of Vietnam veterans and certain veterans who served in Korea near the demilitarized zone for disabilities resulting from spina bifida.*

It affects approximately one of every 1,000 newborns in the United States. Neural tube defects (NTD) are birth defects that involve incomplete development of the brain, spinal cord, and/or protective coverings for these organs. Spina bifida, the most common NTD, results from the failure of the spine to close properly during the first month of pregnancy. (Anencephaly and encephalocele are less common types of NTDs). In severe cases, the spinal cord protrudes through the back of and may be covered by skin or a thin membrane.

Some Vietnam veterans, and certain other veterans have children with spina bifida. While Vietnam veterans and their mates are now moving out of the age category usually associated with childbirth, it is anticipated that some future births will occur and that some of these children may have birth defects, including spina bifida. Some research efforts have suggested that there may be a relationship between exposure by Vietnam veterans to Agent Orange and/or other herbicides used in Vietnam and the subsequent development of spina bifida in some of their children

Effective October 1, 1997, Public Law Number 104-204 authorized the VA to provide monetary benefits, vocational training, rehabilitation, and certain healthcare benefits to children of Vietnam veterans for disability resulting from spina bifida.

For the purpose of the Spina Bifida Program, the term *Vietnam Veteran* means an individual who performed active military, naval, or air service in the Republic of Vietnam during the period beginning on January 9, 1962, and ending May 7, 1975, without regard to the characterization of the individual's service. Service in the Republic of Vietnam includes service in the waters offshore and service in other locations if the conditions of service involved duty or visitation in the Republic of Vietnam.

UPDATE - Public Law 108-183, The Veterans Benefits Act of 2003, expanded benefit eligibility to children with spina bifida who were born to certain veterans who served in Korea near the demilitarized zone.

For purposes of this law, a veteran of covered service in Korea is any individual, without regard to the characterization of that individual's service, who:

- Served in the active military, naval, or air service in or near the Korean demilitarized zone (DMZ), during the period beginning on September 1, 1967, and ending on August 31, 1971; and

- Is determined by the VA to have been exposed to a herbicide agent during such service in or near the Korean demilitarized zone.

The term "herbicide agent" means a chemical in a herbicide used in support of United States and allied military operations in or near the Korean demilitarized zone, during the period beginning on September 1, 1967, and ending on August 31, 1971.

TOLL-FREE SPINA BIFIDA HOT LINE

In June 2001, VA opened a hot line for Vietnam veterans with questions about health care benefits for their children who have spina bifida.

The number for the hot line is (888) 820-1756.

Callers can speak to a benefits advisor Monday through Friday, from 10:00 a.m. to 1:30 p.m., and from 2:30 p.m. to 4:30 p.m., Eastern time. An after-hours phone message will allow callers to leave their names and telephone numbers for a return call the next business day.

The hot line is managed by VA's Health Administration Center in Denver, Colorado.

MONETARY BENEFITS

VA shall pay a monthly allowance based upon the level of disability to or for a child who is suffering from spina bifida, and who is a child of a Vietnam veteran. Receipt of this allowance shall not affect the right of the child, or the right of any individual based on the child's relationship to that individual, to receive any other benefit to which the child, or that individual, may be entitled under any law administered by VA. If a child suffering from spina bifida is the natural child of two Vietnam veterans, he or she is entitled to only one monthly allowance.

The monthly allowance is set at three levels, depending upon the degree of disability suffered by the child. VA shall determine the level of disability suffered by the child in accordance with the following criteria:

Level I

- The child is able to walk without braces or other external support (although gait may be impaired); and

- Has no sensory or motor impairment of upper extremities; and

- Has an IQ of 90 or higher; and

- Is continent of urine and feces.

Level II

Provided that none of the child's disabilities are severe enough to be evaluated at Level III, and the child is:
- Ambulatory, but only with braces or other external support; or

- Has sensory or motor impairment of upper extremities, but is able to grasp pen, feed self, and perform self care; or

- Has an IQ of at least 70 but less than 90; or

- Requires drugs or intermittent catheterization or other mechanical means to maintain proper urinary bladder function, or mechanisms for proper bowel function.

Level III

- The child is unable to ambulate; or

- Has sensory or motor impairment of upper extremities severe enough to prevent grasping a pen, feeding self, and performing self care; or

- Has an IQ of 69 or less; or

- Has complete urinary or fecal incontinence.

SPINA BIFIDA BENEFIT RATE TABLE (Effective 12-01-2008)	
Disability Level	Monthly Allowance
Level I	$286.00
Level II	$984.00
Level III	$1,678.00

VOCATIONAL TRAINING FOR CHILDREN WITH SPINA BIFIDA

To qualify for entitlement to a vocational training program an applicant must be a child:

- To whom VA has awarded a monthly allowance for spina bifida; and

- For whom VA has determined that achievement of a vocational goal is reasonably feasible.

A vocational training program may not begin before a child's 18th birthday, or the date of completion of secondary schooling, whichever comes first. Depending on the need, a child may be provided up to 24 months of full-time training.

HEALTHCARE BENEFITS

In addition to monetary allowances, vocational training and rehabilitation, the Department of Veterans Affairs (VA) also provides VA-financed healthcare benefits to Vietnam veterans' birth children diagnosed with spina bifida. For the purpose of this program, spina bifida is defined as all forms or manifestations of spina bifida (except spina bifida occulta), including complications or associated medical conditions related to spina bifida according to the scientific literature.

IMPORTANT UPDATE:

Effective October 10, 2008, there was a change to Public Law 110-387, Section 408, which outlines the benefits available under the Spina Bifida (SB) Program. As a result of this change, medical services and supplies for spina bifida beneficiaries are no longer limited to the spina bifida condition. This program now covers comprehensive health care considered medically necessary and appropriate.

Healthcare benefits available under this program are limited to those necessary for the treatment of spina bifida and related medical conditions. Beneficiaries should be aware that this program is not a comprehensive healthcare plan and does not cover care that is unrelated to spina bifida.

Administration of the program is centralized to VA's Health Administration Center (HAC) in Denver, Colorado. HAC is responsible for all aspects of the spina bifida healthcare program, including the authorization of benefits and the subsequent processing and payment of claims. All inquiries regarding healthcare benefits should be made directly to HAC.

Healthcare benefits may be claimed for services and supplies starting on the effective date specified in the VA regional office award letter.

Beneficiaries in receipt of a VA regional office spina bifida award will receive an identification card from the Health Administration Center.

There are no beneficiary co-payments or deductibles. VA is the exclusive payer for services provided to beneficiaries under this program, and billing should be sent directly to the Health Administration Center. The determined allowable amount for payment is considered payment in full, and the provider may not bill the beneficiary for the difference between the billed amount and the VA-determined allowed amount.

Covered Benefits

This program provides comprehensive health care for covered services and supplies that are considered medically necessary and appropriate.

General Exclusions

- Care as part of a grant study or research program
- Care considered experimental or investigational
- Care that is not medically necessary or appropriate

- Drugs not approved by the FDA for commercial marketing
- Services provided outside the scope of the provider's license or certification
- Services rendered by providers suspended or sanctioned by a federal agency
- Services, procedures or supplies for which the beneficiary has no legal obligation to pay, such as services obtained at a health fair
- Treatment for spina bifida occulta

Preauthorization Requirements

Although most health care services and supplies do not require approval in advance (preauthorization), some do.

Preauthorization is NOT required for routine health care services and supplies.

Preauthorization IS required for:

- Attendants
- Dental services
- Durable medical equipment (DME) with a total rental or purchase price in excess of $2,000
- Mental health services
- Hospice care
- Substance abuse treatment
- Training of family members
- Transplantation services
- Travel (other than mileage for privately owned automobiles for local travel)

Note: When in doubt, contact the HAC.

Selecting Healthcare Providers

Beneficiaries may select the provider of their choice, as long as the provider is an approved health care provider. The provider must be approved by the Centers for Medicare and Medicaid Services (CMS), Department of Defense TRICARE program, CHAMPVA, JCAHO or may be a health care provider approved for providing services pursuant to a state license or certificate. A provider is not required to contract with the HAC; the HAC does not maintain a list of providers.

CLAIMS

Claims are to be mailed directly to VA's Health Administration Center at the following address.

VA Health Administration Center
PO Box 469065
Denver CO 80246-9065

As a safeguard against claims getting lost in the mail, beneficiaries should keep copies of all claim documents submitted.

Filing Deadlines

Claims must be filed with the Health Administration Center no later than:

- One year after the date of service; or
- In the case of inpatient care, one year after the date of discharge; or
- In the case of a VA regional office award for retroactive eligibility, 180 days following beneficiary notification of the award.

Payments

Approved healthcare providers will be paid 100% of the VA-determined allowable charge for covered services. VA payment for covered services constitutes payment in full. Federal regulations prohibit providers from seeking any additional monies from beneficiaries and third party payers such as private insurers, for services paid by VA.

Note: If the beneficiary pays for care and subsequently files a claim for reimbursement, VA payment to the beneficiary will be limited to the VA-allowed amount. For this reason, beneficiaries are advised not to pay their providers- but instead, have the providers bill HAC directly.

Other Health Insurance

While VA assumes full responsibility for the cost of services related to the treatment of spina bifida and associated conditions, third-party insurers including Medicare and Medicaid, assume payment responsibility for services unrelated to the VA-covered conditions.

Explanation of Benefits

Upon completion of claim processing, an EOB will be mailed to the beneficiary. If a provider files the claim, an EOB will be mailed to them also. The EOB is a summarization of the action taken on the claim and contains, at a minimum, the following information.

- Beneficiary name;
- Description of services and/or supplies provided;

379

- Dates of service or supplies provided;
- Amount billed;
- VA-allowed amount;
- To whom payment, if any, was made;
- Reasons for denial (if applicable).

Reconsideration of Claims / Appeals

If a healthcare provider, beneficiary or beneficiary's representative disagrees with a claim determination, including the VA-allowed amount, a request for reconsideration of the disputed determination may be made. To do so, the request must:

- Be in writing;
- Be accompanied by a copy of the EOB in question; and
- State the specific issue that is being disputed, why the VA determination is considered to be in error, and include any new and relevant information not previously considered.

To meet the filing deadline, requests for reconsideration are to be mailed to the following address within one year of the date of the initial EOB:

VA Health Administration Center
Reconsideration/Appeals
PO Box 460948
Denver CO 80246-0948

Upon complete review of the request and all the relevant documentation and evidence, a written determination will be mailed to the claimant.

CHAPTER 26

BENEFITS FOR POST-TRAUMATIC STRESS DISORDER AND SEXUAL TRAUMA

POST-TRAUMATIC STRESS DISORDER (PTSD)

> *Studies show that PTSD affects 30 percent of war zone veterans, including those who saw combat in World War II, Korea, Vietnam, the Persian Gulf and Bosnia.*

PTSD is a condition resulting from exposure to direct or indirect threat of death, serious injury, or a physical threat. The events that can cause PTSD are called "stressors" and may include:

- Combat or war exposure;
- Sexual or physical abuse;
- Terrorist attacks;
- Serious accidents, such as a car wreck;
- Natural disasters such as a fire, tornado, hurricane, flood, or earthquake.

Symptoms of PTSD can include recurrent thoughts of the traumatic event, reduced involvement in work or outside interests, emotional numbing, hyper-alertness, anxiety and irritability. The disorder can be more severe and longer lasting when the stress is human initiated action (example: war, rape, terrorism).

There are many types of treatment for PTSD., including counseling and medicines known as SSRIs.

Disability Compensation

> *PTSD can be a service-connected disability.*

The process of applying for a VA disability for PTSD can take several months, and can be both complicated and quite stressful. The Veterans Service Organizations provide Service Officers at no cost to help veterans and family members pursue VA disability claims.

Service Officers are familiar with every step in the application and interview process, and can provide both technical guidance and moral support. In addition, some Service Officers particularly specialize in assisting veterans with PTSD disability claims. Even if a veteran has not been a member of a specific Veterans Service Organization, the veteran still can request the assistance of a Service Officer working for that organization. In order to get representation by a qualified and helpful Service Officer, you can directly contact the local office of any Veterans Service Organization -- or ask for recommendations from other veterans who have applied for VA disability, or from a PTSD specialist at a VA PTSD clinic or a Vet Center.

2010 UPDATE:
VA SIMPLIFIES ACCESS TO HEALTH CARE AND BENEFITS FOR VETERANS WITH PTSD

In July 2010, VA simplified the process for a veteran to claim service connection for PTSD. VA reduced the evidence needed if the trauma claimed by a veteran is related to "fear of hostile military or terrorist activity," and is consistent with the places, types, and circumstances of the veteran's service.

Previously, unless the veteran was a combat veteran, claims adjudicators were required to undertake extensive record development to corroborate whether a veteran actually experienced the claimed in-service stressor. This rule eliminates this time-consuming requirement where the claimed stressor is related to "fear of hostile military or terrorist activity," is consistent with the places, types and circumstances of their service, and a VA psychiatrist or psychologist, or contract psychiatrist or psychologist confirms that the claimed stressor is adequate to support a diagnosis of PTSD.

The new rule will apply to claims:

- Received by VA on or after July 13, 2010;
- Received before July 13, 2010 but not yet decided by a VA regional office;
- Appealed to the Board of Veterans' Appeals on or after July 13, 2010;
- Appealed to the Board before July 13, 2010, but not yet decided by the Board; and
- Pending before VA on or after July 13, 2010, because the Court of Appeals for Veterans Claims vacated a Board decision and remanded for re-adjudication.

Vet Centers

A nationwide system of community-based counseling centers, known as Vet Centers, provides counseling for psychological war trauma. Readjustment counseling features a non-medical setting, a mix of social services, community outreach activities, psychological counseling for war-related experiences, and family counseling. These services are designed to assist combat-affected and other veterans attain a well-adjusted post-war work and family life. Implemented by VA in 1979, Vet Centers were initially designed for Vietnam veterans. Current law has extended eligibility for the program to any veteran who has served in the military in combat operations during any period of armed hostility. VA operates more than 200 Vet Centers in all 50 states, Puerto Rico, the Virgin Islands, the District of Columbia and Guam. Interdisciplinary teams including psychologists, social workers, nurses and paraprofessionals staff the centers.

For a complete listing of Vet Centers, please refer to Chapter 15 of this book.

VA Medical Center Programs

While PTSD treatment is available through all of VA's 171 medical centers, a VA network of 124 facilities offers specialized inpatient and outpatient treatment. One notable program consists of PTSD clinical teams that provide outpatient treatment but also work closely with other VA treatment programs, including Vet Centers, to coordinate services and provide information on PTSD throughout the medical center and the community.

In addition to 83 PTSD clinical teams, VA operates 22 specialized inpatient units around the country, plus 13 brief-treatment units, 11 residential rehabilitation programs, and four PTSD day hospitals. There also are four outpatient Women's Stress Disorder and Treatment Teams and eight outpatient-based PTSD Teams Substance Use Disorder demonstration projects. A special focus in the program expansions has included underserved and minority populations, such as African Americans, Hispanics and Native Americans. A specialized PTSD inpatient treatment unit serves women veterans at the Palo Alto, Calif., VA Medical Center's Menlo Park Division.

National PTSD Center

In 1989, VA established the National Center for Post-Traumatic Stress Disorder -- a center for clinical research, training and information on PTSD. The center initially consisted of five divisions with distinct, but complementary responsibilities:

- Behavioral Science;
- Clinical Neurosciences;
- Education;
- Evaluation; and
- Executive and Resource Center Divisions.

Growing recognition of the dimensions of PTSD has brought new programs, such as the Women's Health Sciences Division, located at the Boston VA Medical Center, and the Pacific Islands Division in Honolulu.

SEXUAL TRAUMA

Some veterans (women and men) suffered personal assault and/or sexual trauma while serving on active military duty. They might still struggle with fear, anxiety, embarrassment, or profound anger as a result of these experiences.

VA defines sexual trauma as any lingering physical, emotional, or psychological symptoms resulting from a physical assault of a sexual nature, or battery of a sexual nature. Examples of this are:

- Rape;
- Physical assault;
- Domestic Battering; and
- Stalking.

Compensation for Disabilities

Disability Compensation is a monthly payment to a veteran disabled by an injury or a disease incurred or aggravated on active service. The veteran must have been discharged under other than dishonorable conditions to be eligible. The individual must currently be suffering from disabling symptoms to receive compensation. Refer to Chapter 3 of this book for information regarding Disability Compensation.

CHAPTER 27

BENEFITS FOR FORMER PRISONERS OF WAR (POWS)

Former American POWs are eligible for special veterans benefits from the VA, including medical care in VA hospitals and disability compensation for injuries and disease presumed to be caused by internment. Studies have shown that the physical deprivation and psychological stress endured as a captive have life-long effects on subsequent health, social adjustment, and vocational adjustment.

In 1981, Congress passed Public Law 97-37 entitled, "Former Prisoners of War Benefit Act." This law accomplished several things. It established an Advisory Committee on Former Prisoners of War and mandated medical and dental care. It also identified certain diagnoses as presumptive service-connected conditions for former POWs. Other public laws passed since then, and a policy decision by the Secretary of Veterans Affairs in 1993, have added additional diagnoses to the list of presumptive conditions.

On November 30, 1999, the President signed into law the Veterans Millennium Healthcare and Benefits Act, Pub. L. 106-117. Section 501, a provision of the law, authorizes VA to pay DIC under 38 U.S.C. 1318 to the survivors of former Prisoners of War who died after September 30, 1999, and who were rated totally disabled continuously for a period of not less than one year immediately preceding death for a service-connected disability. This provision is effective November 30, 1999.

A POW Coordinator has been designated at each VA regional office. The POW Coordinator can furnish former POWs with information about the benefits and services available to them.

HEALTHCARE

Former POWs are recognized as a special category of veterans, and will be placed on one of the top three Priority Groups established for VA healthcare by Congress.

Veterans who were POWs may receive complete dental care.

Former POWs are eligible for any prosthetic item, including eyeglasses and hearing aids. A VA physician must order the prosthetic items, when medically indicated, for eligible veterans.

Veterans may enroll in VA healthcare by completing VA Form 10-10, Application for Medical Benefits.

Update - Public Law 108-170, which became law December 6, 2003, eliminated **prescription drug co-payments** for former POWs.

DISABILITY COMPENSATION

Veterans are encouraged to apply for VA disability Compensation for any disabilities related to service, whether they were a POW or not. Some disabilities are *presumptive*, which means that if a veteran is diagnosed with certain conditions, and the veteran was a POW for at least 30 days (certain conditions do not include the 30-day requirement), the VA presumes the captivity caused the disability.

Presumptions Of Service-Connection Relating To Certain Diseases And Disabilities For Former Prisoners Of War

Public Law 108-183, The Veterans Benefits Act of 2003, eliminated the requirement that a veteran was a POW for at least 30 days for certain conditions. Therefore, there are now two categories of presumptive conditions – those that include the 30-day requirement, and those that do not.

On October 7, 2004 VA expanded benefits to all former POWs with strokes and common heart diseases. Affected veterans are automatically eligible for disability compensation for those common ailments, and their spouses and dependents are eligible for service-connected survivors' benefits if these diseases contribute to the death of a former POW.

In the case of any veteran who is a former prisoner of war, and **who was detained or interned for thirty days or more,** any of the following which became manifest to a degree of 10% or more after active military, naval or air service, shall be considered to have been incurred in or aggravated by such service, notwithstanding that there is no record of such disease during the period of service:

- Avitaminosis

- Beriberi (including beriberi heart disease, which includes Ischemic Heart Disease-coronary artery disease-for former POWs who suffered during captivity from edema-swelling of the legs or feet- also known as "wet" beriberi)

- Chronic dysentery

- Helminthiasis

- Malnutrition (including optic atrophy associated with malnutrition)

- Pellagra

- Any other nutritional deficiency
- Peripheral neuropathy, except where directly related to infectious causes
- Irritable bowel syndrome
- Peptic ulcer disease
- Cirrhosis of the liver (This condition was added as part of Public Law 108-183.)
- Atherosclerotic heart disease or hypertensive vascular disease (including hypertensive heart disease) and their complications (including myocardial infarction, congestive heart failure and arrhythmia) (These conditions were added as part of Public Law 109-233.)
- Stroke and its complications (This condition was added as part of Public Law 109-233.)

In the case of any veteran who is a former prisoner of war, and **who was detained or interned for any period of time,** any of the following which became manifest to a degree of 10% or more after active military, naval or air service, shall be considered to have been incurred in or aggravated by such service, notwithstanding that there is no record of such disease during the period of service:

- Psychosis
- Dysthymic disorder, or depressive neurosis
- Post-traumatic osteoarthritis
- Any of the Anxiety States
- Cold Injury
- Stroke and complications
- Heart Disease and complications

Update:

On October 7, 2004 VA expanded benefits to all former POWs with strokes and common heart diseases. Affected veterans are automatically eligible for disability compensation for those common ailments, and their spouses and dependents are eligible for service-connected survivors' benefits if these diseases contribute to the death of a former POW.

Former POWs should file a claim by completing VA Form 21-526, Application for Compensation or Pension. The VA also offers a POW protocol exam. This is a one-time exam available to all former POWs, and is conducted at a VA medical facility to help determine if any presumptive disabilities exist.

2008 UPDATE:

The Veterans Benefits Improvement Act of 2008, which became law 10/10/08, added osteoporosis to the list of disabilities presumed to be service-connected (and therefore compensable through VA disability compensation) in the case of veterans who are former prisoners of war, if the Secretary determines that such veteran has post-traumatic stress disorder (PTSD).

PRISONER OF WAR MEDAL

A Prisoner of War Medal is available to any member of the U.S. Armed Forces taken prisoner during any armed conflict dating from World War I. Please refer to Chapter 41 of this book for detailed information on how to obtain medals.

CHAPTER 28

BENEFITS FOR FILIPINO VETERANS

FOUR CATEGORIES

For purposes of VA benefits and services, the service of members of the Philippine armed forces can be categorized as service in one of four groups:

Regular Philippine Scouts (also called Old Philippine Scouts)

These veterans were members of a small, regular component of the U.S. Army that was considered to be in regular active service. Originally formed in 1901, long before any formal plan for Philippine independence, the Regular Philippine Scouts were part of the U.S. Army throughout their existence.

Special Philippine Scouts (also called New Philippine Scouts)

These individuals were Philippine citizens who served with the U.S. Armed Forces with the consent of the Philippine government, and served between October 6, 1945 and June 30, 1947, inclusive.

Commonwealth Army of the Philippines (also called the Philippine Commonwealth Army)

These individuals were called into the service of the United States Armed Forces of the Far East (USAFFE), its members serving between July 26, 1941 and June 30, 1946, inclusive.

Recognized Guerillas

People in this group served as guerrillas in USAFFE in resistance units recognized by, and cooperating with U.S. forces between April 20, 1942, through June 30, 1946, inclusive.

ELIGIBILITY FOR VA BENEFITS

Regular Philippine Scouts

Regular Philippine Scouts who served with U.S. forces before October 6, 1945, are entitled to all VA benefits, under the same criteria as veterans of the U.S. Armed Forces.

Monetary benefits are payable in Dollars, at the full rate authorized, and their dependents and survivors are entitled to benefits under the eligibility rules common to the survivors of all U.S. veterans.

Special Philippine Scouts (New Philippine Scouts)

These veterans and eligible dependents are entitled to:

- Disability Compensation;

- Clothing Allowance;

- Dependency & Indemnity Compensation (DIC);

- Health care benefits in the U.S. on the same basis as U.S. veterans, provided they reside in the United States, and are citizens or lawfully admitted for permanent residence;

- Burial benefits, at the full-dollar rate, if the veterans were lawfully living in the United States on the date of death, and were U. S. citizens or lawfully admitted permanent resident aliens. Eligibility applies to death on or after December 16, 2003, based on legislation enacted in 2003.

Note: Monetary benefits are payable at a rate of $.50 of each Dollar authorized. (Commissioned officers are paid at the full rate authorized.) However, those veterans who live in the United States receive full-dollar rate compensation payments if they are either U.S. citizens or lawfully admitted permanent resident aliens.

Benefit Programs Not Available:

- Non-service connected pension benefits for veterans and dependents;

- Death pension;

- Hospital care and outpatient treatment for service-connected or non-service-connected conditions, if the care is provided outside of the U.S., or at facilities outside of the U.S. over which the VA has no jurisdiction, or has not contracted;

- Dental care;

- VA loans such as home loan guarantees;

- Specially adapted homes;

390

- Automobile or other conveyances;
- Service-disabled veterans insurance (RH);
- Gravemarker or headstone;
- Burial flag;
- Burial in a national cemetery.

Commonwealth Army (Philippine Commonwealth Army):

These veterans and eligible dependents are entitled to:

- Disability Compensation;
- Clothing Allowance;
- Dependency & Indemnity Compensation (DIC);
- Health care benefits in the U.S. on the same basis as U.S. veterans, provided they reside in the United States, and are citizens or lawfully admitted for permanent residence;
- Burial benefits, at the full-dollar rate, if the veterans were lawfully living in the United States on the date of death, and were U. S. citizens or lawfully admitted permanent resident aliens. Eligibility applies to death on or after November 1, 2000, based on legislation enacted in 2000;
- Burial in national cemeteries (for deaths on or after November 1, 2000);
- Headstones and markers (for deaths on or after November 1, 2000);
- Burial Flag(for deaths on or after November 1, 2000).

Note: Monetary benefits are payable at a rate of $.50 of each Dollar authorized. (Commissioned officers are paid at the full rate authorized.) However, those veterans who live in the United States receive full-dollar rate compensation payments if they are either U.S. citizens or lawfully admitted permanent resident aliens.

Benefit Programs Not Available:

- Non-service connected pension benefits for veterans and dependents;
- Death pension;
- Dental care;
- VA loans such as home loan guarantees;
- Specially adapted homes;
- Automobile or other conveyances;
- Service-disabled veterans insurance (RH).

Recognized Guerillas

These veterans and eligible dependents are entitled to:

- Disability Compensation;

- Clothing Allowance;

- Dependency & Indemnity Compensation (DIC);

- Health care benefits in the U.S. on the same basis as U.S. veterans, provided they reside in the United States, and are citizens or lawfully admitted for permanent residence;

- Burial benefits, at the full-dollar rate, if the veterans were lawfully living in the United States on the date of death, and were U. S. citizens or lawfully admitted permanent resident aliens. Eligibility applies to death on or after November 1, 2000, based on legislation enacted in 2000;

- Burial in national cemeteries (for deaths on or after November 1, 2000);

- Headstones and markers (for deaths on or after November 1, 2000);

- Burial Flag (for deaths on or after November 1, 2000).

Note: Monetary benefits are payable at a rate of $.50 of each Dollar authorized. (Commissioned officers are paid at the full rate authorized.) However, those veterans who live in the United States receive full-dollar rate compensation payments if they are either U.S. citizens or lawfully admitted permanent resident aliens.

Benefit Programs Not Available:

- Non-service connected pension benefits for veterans and dependents;

- Death pension;

- Dental care;

- VA loans such as home loan guarantees;

- Specially adapted homes;

- Automobile or other conveyances;

- Service-disabled veterans insurance (RH).

Note: Veterans may be eligible for additional healthcare services at the Veteran's Memorial Medical Center, a facility in Manila operated by the Philippine government.

SPECIAL NOTE –
Stimulus Bill Provided $198 Million for Filipino Veterans

In February 2009, Secretary of Veterans Affairs Eric K. Shinseki announced a new benefit for Filipino Veterans who aided American troops in World War II -- a cash payment authorized through the American Recovery and Reinvestment Act.

Claims were accepted from Filipino Veterans eligible for one-time payments of $9,000 for non-U.S. citizens and $15,000 for Filipino Veterans with U.S. citizenship.

Claims must have been submitted by February 16, 2010, a year after the bill's signing.

The payments did not affect other benefits Veterans may be receiving.

CHAPTER 29

BENEFITS FOR ALLIED VETERANSAND CERTAIN NON-MILITARY GROUPS

ALLIED VETERANS

VA is authorized to provide medical care to certain veterans of nations allied or associated with the United States during World War I or World War II. Such treatment is available at any VA Medical Center if authorized and reimbursed by the foreign government. Necessary paperwork is obtained through the veteran's country in order to receive services for service connected conditions only.

MERCHANT MARINE SEAMEN

The Department of Defense announced January 19, 1988, that certain Merchant Marine seamen now qualify as veterans.

Merchant seamen who engaged in active, ocean-going service from December 7, 1941 to August 15, 1945 are eligible to apply for a certificate of release or discharge from the DoD. This certificate will then entitle the holder to apply for VA benefits currently available to World War II veterans. (Civil Service crewmembers aboard U.S. Army Transport Service and Naval Transportation vessels in ocean-going service or foreign waters were included in the DoD action.)

Generally, the newly designated veterans and their survivors are eligible to apply for the same benefits that are available to other World War II veterans. These benefits include:

- Medical care;

- Disability compensation;

- Disability pension;

- DIC;

- Dental treatment;

- GI Insurance;

- Vocational rehabilitation;

- VA-guaranteed home loans;

- Burial benefits (see following Special Note Regarding Burial Benefits).

These veterans are not eligible for VA-administered education programs, although in certain limited circumstances they may establish eligibility for vocational rehabilitation.

Special Note Regarding Burial Benefits:

The "Veterans Programs Enhancement Act of 1998", extended the ending qualifying date from August 15, 1945 to December 31, 1946 for eligibility for

- Burial flags;

- Headstones and markers;

- Internment in national cemeteries;

- Burial allowance for certain indigent wartime veterans;

- Markers in memorial areas of national cemeteries;

- Markers in memorial areas of Arlington National Cemetery; and

- Plot allowance payable to a State for burial in certain "state owned" cemeteries or cemetery sections.

Depending on the type of merchant marine service, certification of "qualified service" must come from the Department of Transportation or the Department of Defense. In general, benefits may be provided only for deaths occurring after November 11, 1998. However, in the case of an initial burial or columbarium placement in a national cemetery after November 11, 1998, benefits incident to burial and the provision of a headstone or marker are authorized regardless of the date of death.

Applying for Certificate of Release (Obtaining Veteran Status or Extension of Veteran Status)

Interested mariners or survivors should complete the following steps and mail to the proper address:

1. Compete Form DD2168 (available from all VA regional offices). Supply as much information as possible.

2. Include photocopies of discharges, identification, and any other supporting documents.

3. Survivors need to include a certified death certificate. (The Coast Guard will issue documents for a person listed as an official casualty list without a death certificate.)

4. Send to:

   The National Maritime Center (NMC-4A)

   4200 Wilson Blvd., Suite 630
   Arlington, VA 22203-1804
   (202) 493-1000

OTHER NON-MILITARY GROUPS

Through the years, a number of non-military groups have provided military-related service to the United States. Many of these groups have been formally recognized by the Department of Defense, and granted VA benefits.

Service in the following groups has been certified as active military service for benefits purposes:

- Women's Air Force Service Pilots (WASPs);

- Signal Corps Female Telephone Operators Unit of World I;

- Engineer Field Clerks;

- Women's Army Auxiliary Corps (WAAC);

- Quartermaster Corps female clerical employees serving with the American Expeditionary Forces in World War I;

- Civilian employees of Pacific naval air bases who actively participated in defense of Wake Island during World War II;

- Reconstruction aides and dietitians in World War I;

- Male civilian ferry pilots;

- Wake Island defenders from Guam;

- Civilian personnel assigned to OSS secret intelligence;

- Guam Combat Patrol;

- Quartermaster Corps members of the Keswick crew on Corregidor during World War II;

- U.S. civilians who participated in the defense of Bataan;

- U.S. merchant seamen who served on blockships in support of Operation Mulberry in the World War II invasion of Normandy;

- American merchant marines in oceangoing service during WW II;

- Civilian Navy IFF radar technicians who served in combat areas of the Pacific during World War II;

- U.S. civilians of the American Field Service who served overseas in World War I;

- U.S. civilians of the American Field Service who served overseas under U.S. armies and U.S. army groups in World War II;

- U.S. civilian employees of American Airlines who served overseas in a contract with the Air Transport Command between Dec. 14, 1941, and Aug. 14, 1945;

- Civilian crewmen of U.S. Coast and Geodetic Survey vessels who served in areas of immediate military hazard while conducting cooperative operations with and for the U.S. Armed Forces between Dec. 7, 1941, and Aug. 15, 1945;

- Members of the American Volunteer Group (Flying Tigers) serving between Dec. 7, 1941, and July 18, 1942;

- U.S. civilian flight crew and aviation ground support employees of United Air Lines who served overseas in a contract with Air Transport Command between Dec. 14, 1941, and Aug. 14, 1945;

- U.S. civilian flight crew and aviation ground support employees of Transcontinental and Western Air, Inc. (TWA), who served overseas in a contract with the Air Transport Command between Dec. 14, 1941, and Aug. 14, 1945;

- U.S. civilian flight crew and aviation ground support employees of Consolidated Vultee Aircraft Corp. (Consairway Division) who served overseas in a contract with Air Transport Command between Dec. 14, 1941, and Aug. 14, 1945;

- U.S. civilian flight crew and aviation ground support employees of Pan American World Airways and its subsidiaries and affiliates, who served overseas in a contract with the Air Transport Command and Naval Air Transport Service between Dec. 14, 1941, and Aug. 14, 1945;

- Honorably discharged members of the American Volunteer Guard, Eritrea Service Command, between June 21, 1942, and March 31, 1943;

- U.S. civilian flight crew and aviation ground support employees of Northwest Airlines who served overseas under the airline's contract with Air Transport Command from Dec. 14, 1941, through Aug. 14, 1945;

- U.S. civilian female employees of the U.S. Army Nurse Corps who served in the defense of Bataan and Corregidor during the period January 2, 1942 to February 3, 1945;

- U.S. Flight crew and aviation ground support employees of Northeast Airlines Atlantic Division, who served overseas as a result of Northeast Airlines' contract with the Air Transport Command during the period December 7, 1941 through August 14, 1945;

- U.S. civilian flight crew and aviation ground support employees of Braniff Airways, who served overseas in the North Atlantic or under the jurisdiction of the North Atlantic Wing, Air Transport Command, as a result of a contract with the Air Transport Command during the period February 26, 1942 through August 14, 1945.

For the service to qualify as military-related service, the Defense Secretary must certify that the group has provided active military service. Individual members must be issued a discharge by the Defense Secretary, which can then be used to qualify for VA benefits.

CHAPTER 30

NATURALIZATION PREFERENCE

On July 3, 2002, the president issued Executive Order 13269 providing naturalization for aliens and non-citizen nationals serving on active duty status in the U.S. armed forces from September 11, 2001, to a date not yet determined. In addition, if a person dies as a result of injury or disease incurred or aggravated by such service, their survivor(s) can apply for posthumous citizenship at any time within two years of the death of the alien or non-citizen national.

Aliens and non-citizen nationals with honorable service in the U.S. armed forces during specified periods of hostilities may be naturalized without having to comply with the general requirements for naturalization.

Veterans who served prior to September 11, 2001, are eligible to file for naturalization based on their U.S. military service. An applicant who served three years in the U.S. military and is a lawful permanent resident is excused from any specific period of required residence, period of residence in any specific place, or physical presence within the United States if the application for naturalization is filed while the applicant is still serving in the military or within six months of honorable discharge. Applicants who file for naturalization more than six months after termination of three years of U.S. military service may count any periods of honorable service as residence and physical presence in the United States.

Aliens and non-citizen nationals with honorable service in the U.S. armed forces during specified periods of hostilities may be naturalized without having to comply with the general requirements for naturalization. This is the only section of the Immigration and Nationality Act, as amended, which allows persons who have not been lawfully admitted for permanent residence to file an application for naturalization.

Any person who has served honorably during qualifying time may file an application at any time in his or her life if, at the time of enlistment, reenlistment, extension of enlistment or induction, such person shall have been in the United States, the Canal Zone, American Samoa or Swain's Island, or, on or after November 18, 1997, aboard a public vessel owned or operated by the United States for non-commercial service, whether or not lawful admittance to the United States for permanent residence has been granted.

Certain applicants who have served in the U.S. Armed Forces are eligible to file for naturalization based on current or prior U.S. military service. Such applicants should file the N-400 Military Naturalization Packet.

CHAPTER 31

HOMELESS VETERANS

Approximately one-third of the adult homeless population living on the streets or in shelters has served their country in the armed services. Many other veterans are considered at risk because of poverty, lack of support from family and friends and precarious living conditions in overcrowded or substandard housing.

VA has many benefits and services to assist homeless veterans, including:

Homeless Providers Grant and Per Diem Program

VA's Homeless Providers Grant and Per Diem Program is offered annually (as funding permits) by the Department of Veterans Affairs Health Care for Homeless Veterans (HCHV) Programs to fund community agencies providing services to homeless veterans. The purpose is to promote the development and provision of supportive housing and/or supportive services with the goal of helping homeless veterans achieve residential stability, increase their skill levels and/or income, and obtain greater self-determination.

2010 UPDATE – New Hotline for Homeless Veterans

In March 2010, VA announced a new hotline for homeless veterans – 1-877-4AID VET (1-877-424-2838).

Well trained expert responders will staff the hotline 24 hours a day, seven days a week. Responders can provide emergency support and resources to homeless veterans, as well as family members, community agencies and non-VA providers.

Loan Guarantee Program For Homeless Veterans Multifamily Housing

This initiative authorizes VA to guarantee no more than 15 loans with an aggregate value of $100 million within 5 years for construction, renovation of existing property, and refinancing of existing loans, facility furnishing or working capital. No more than 5 loans could be guaranteed under this program prior to November 11, 2001. The amount financed is a maximum of 90% of project costs. Legislation allows the Secretary to issue a loan guarantee for large-scale self-sustaining multifamily loans. Eligible transitional project are those that: 1) Provide supportive services including job counseling; 2) Require veteran to seek and maintain employment; 3) Require veteran to pay reasonable rent; 4)

Require sobriety as a condition of occupancy; and, 5) Serves other veterans in need of housing on a space available basis.

Stand Downs

Stand Downs are one part of the Department of Veterans Affairs' efforts to provide services to homeless veterans. Stand Downs are typically one to three day events providing services to homeless veterans such as food, shelter, clothing, health screenings, VA and Social Security benefits counseling, and referrals to a variety of other necessary services, such as housing, employment and substance abuse treatment. Stand Downs are collaborative events, coordinated between local VAs, other government agencies, and community agencies who serve the homeless.

For additional information on Stand Down dates and locations, please contact the Homeless Veterans Programs Office at (202) 273-5764.

Compensated Work Therapy/Transitional Residence (CWT/TR) Program

In VA's Compensated Work Therapy/Transitional Residence (CWT/TR) Program, disadvantaged, at-risk, and homeless veterans live in CWT/TR community-based supervised group homes while working for pay in VA's Compensated Work Therapy Program (also known as Veterans Industries). Veterans in the CWT/TR program work about 33 hours per week, with approximate earnings of $732 per month, and pay an average of $186 per month toward maintenance and up-keep of the residence. The average length of stay is about 174 days. VA contracts with private industry and the public sector for work done by these veterans, who learn new job skills, relearn successful work habits, and regain a sense of self-esteem and self-worth.

CHALENG

The Community Homelessness Assessment, Local Education, and Networking Groups (CHALENG) for veterans is a nationwide initiative in which VA medical center and regional office directors work with other federal, state, and local agencies and nonprofit organizations to assess the needs of homeless veterans, develop action plans to meet identified needs, and develop directories that contain local community resources to be used by homeless veterans.

More than 10,000 representatives from non-VA organizations have participated in Project CHALENG initiatives, which include holding conferences at VA medical centers to raise awareness of the needs of homeless veterans, creating new partnerships in the fight against homelessness, and developing new strategies for future action.

For more information, please contact CHALENG at (404) 327-4033.

DCHV

The Domiciliary Care for Homeless Veterans (DCHV) Program provides biopsychosocial treatment and rehabilitation to homeless veterans. The program provides residential treatment to approximately 5,000 homeless veterans with health problems each year and the average length of stay in the program is 4 months. The domiciliaries conduct outreach and referral; vocational counseling and rehabilitation; and post-discharge community support.

Drop-In Centers

These programs provide a daytime sanctuary where homeless veterans can clean up, wash their clothes, and participate in a variety of therapeutic and rehabilitative activities. Linkages with longer-term assistance are also available.

HUD-VASH

This joint Supported Housing Program with the Department of Housing and Urban Development provides permanent housing and ongoing treatment services to the harder-to-serve homeless mentally ill veterans and those suffering from substance abuse disorders. HUD's Section 8 Voucher Program has designated 1,780 vouchers worth $44.5 million for homeless chronically mentally ill veterans. VA staff at 35 sites provide outreach, clinical care and ongoing case management services. Rigorous evaluation of this program indicates that this approach significantly reduces days of homelessness for veterans plagued by serious mental illness and substance abuse disorders.

Supported Housing

Like the HUD-VASH program identified above, staff in VA's Supported Housing Program provides ongoing case management services to homeless veterans. Emphasis is placed on helping veterans find permanent housing and providing clinical support needed to keep veterans in permanent housing. Staff in these programs operate without benefit of the specially dedicated Section 8 housing vouchers available in the HUD-VASH program but are often successful in locating transitional or permanent housing through local means, especially by collaborating with Veterans Service Organizations.

Comprehensive Homeless Centers

VA's Comprehensive Homeless Centers (CHCs) place the full range of VA homeless efforts in a single medical center's catchment area and coordinate administration within a centralized framework. With extensive collaboration among non-VA service providers, VA's CHCs in Anchorage, AK; Brooklyn, NY; Cleveland, OH; Dallas, TX; Little Rock, AR; Pittsburgh, PA; San Francisco, CA; and West Los Angeles, CA, provide a comprehensive continuum of care that reaches out to homeless veterans and helps them escape homelessness.

VBA-VHA SPECIAL OUTREACH AND BENEFITS ASSISTANCE

VHA has provided specialized funding to support twelve Veterans Benefits Counselors as members of HCMI and Homeless Domiciliary Programs as authorized by Public Law 102-590. These specially funded staff provide dedicated outreach, benefits counseling, referral, and additional assistance to eligible veterans applying for VA benefits. This specially funded initiative complements VBA's ongoing efforts to target homeless veterans for special attention. To reach more homeless veterans, designated homeless veterans coordinators at VBA's 58 regional offices annually make over 4,700 visits to homeless facilities and over 9,000 contacts with non-VA agencies working with the homeless and provide over 24,000 homeless veterans with benefits counseling and referrals to other VA programs. These special outreach efforts are assumed as part of ongoing duties and responsibilities. VBA has also instituted new procedures to reduce the processing times for homeless veterans' benefits claims.

VBA'S ACQUIRED PROPERTY SALES FOR HOMELESS PROVIDERS

This program makes all the properties VA obtains through foreclosures on VA-insured mortgages available for sale to homeless provider organizations at a discount of 20 to 50 percent, depending on time of the market.

VA EXCESS PROPERTY FOR HOMELESS VETERANS INITIATIVE

This initiative provides for the distribution of federal excess personal property, such as hats, parkas, footwear, socks, sleeping bags, and other items to homeless veterans and homeless veteran programs. A Compensated Work Therapy Program employing formerly homeless veterans has been established at the Medical Center in Lyons, NJ to receive, warehouse, and ship these goods to VA homeless programs across the country.

PROGRAM MONITORING AND EVALUATION

VA has built program monitoring and evaluation into all of its homeless veterans' treatment initiatives and it serves as an integral component of each program. Designed, implemented, and maintained by the Northeast Program Evaluation Center (NEPEC) at VAMC West Haven, CT, these evaluation efforts provide important information about the veterans served and the therapeutic value and cost effectiveness of the specialized programs. Information from these evaluations also helps program managers determine new directions to pursue in order to expand and improve services to homeless veterans.

CHAPTER 32

BENEFITS FOR FEMALE VETERANS

Female veterans are entitled to all of the benefits available to male veterans, including:

- Disability Compensation For Service-Related Disabilities;

- Disability Pension For Non-Service Related Disabilities;

- Education Assistance Programs;

- Work-Study Allowance;

- Vocational Rehabilitation And Counseling;

- Insurance;

- Home Loan Benefits;

- Medical Inpatient And Outpatient Care;

- Substance Abuse Treatment And Counseling;

- Sexual Trauma And Assault Counseling;

- Nursing Home Care;

- Burial Benefits;

- Burial In A VA National Cemetery;

- Employment Assistance;

- Survivors' Benefit Programs.

VA has also designed services and programs to be responsive to the gender-specific needs of female veterans. VA offers comprehensive healthcare services for female veterans, including:

- Counseling for sexual trauma;

- Breast examinations;

- Pelvic examinations;

- Pap smears;

- General reproductive health care services;

- Contraceptive services;

- Menopause management;

- Mammography;
- General reproductive healthcare.

Referrals are made for services that VA is unable to provide. Women Veterans' Program Managers are available in a private setting at all VA facilities to assist women veterans seeking treatment and benefits.

VA has also established a division within the National Center for Post-Traumatic Stress Disorder, the Women's Health Science Division. The center is based at the Boston VA Medical Center, and conducts clinical research addressing trauma-related problems of female veterans. Veterans may contact the Center at:

VA Medical Center
Women's Health Sciences Division
150 South Huntington Avenue
Boston, MA 02130
(617) 232-9500

WOMEN VETERANS COMPREHENSIVE HEATH CENTERS

Eight Women Veterans Comprehensive Health Centers have been established to develop and enhance programs focusing on the gender-specific healthcare needs of female veterans. The locations are as follows:

Boston VA Medical Center
Boston, Massachusetts
(617) 232-9500, extension 4276

Chicago Area Network
(Hines, Lakeside, North Chicago, and West Side VA Medical Centers)
(312) 569-6168

Durham VA Medical Center
Durham, North Carolina
(919) 286-0411

Minneapolis VA Medical Center
Minneapolis, Minnesota
(612) 725-2030

Southeast Pennsylvania Network
(Coatesville, Lebanon, Philadelphia and Wilmington VA Medical Centers)
(215) 823-44496

San Francisco VA Medical Center
San Francisco, California
(415) 221-4810, extension 2174

Sepulveda / West Los Angeles VA Medical Centers
Sepulveda, California and Los Angeles, California
(415) 221-4810

Tampa VA Medical Center
Tampa, Florida
(813) 972-2000, extension 3678

STATE WOMEN VETERANS COORDINATORS

In addition to the Department of Veterans Affairs' Women Veterans Coordinators that are located at local regional offices and medical centers, there may be an *Office of State Veterans Affairs, or a State Commission for Veterans Coordinator* available within the State government veterans program. These State offices are part of the veteran-advocate community and their staff may assist female veterans in accessing State and Federal entitlements.   For specific information on availability in your state, contact your local VA office.

CHAPTER 33

BENEFITS FOR GULF WAR VETERANS

The first Gulf War, an offensive led by U.S. and coalition troops in January 1991, followed the August 1990 Iraqi invasion of Kuwait. The war was over on February 28, 1991, and an official cease-fire was signed in April 1991. The last U.S. troops who participated in the ground war returned home on June 13, 1991. In all, about 697,000 U.S. troops had been deployed to the Gulf region during the conflict.

Operation Iraqi Freedom, a military campaign which began on March 20, 2003, and Operation New Dawn, named for the reduced role of U.S. troops in Iraq, have created a new group of Gulf War veterans.

With variation in exposures and veterans' concerns ranging from oil well fire smoke to possible contamination from Iraqi chemical/biological agents, VA has initiated wide-ranging research projects evaluating illnesses as well as environmental risk factors.

> *VA operates a toll-free hotline at (800) 749-8387 to inform veterans of available programs.*

The Department of Veterans Affairs (VA) offers Gulf War veterans physical examinations and special eligibility for follow-up care, and it operates a toll-free hotline at (800) 749-8387 to inform these veterans of the program and their benefits. Operators are trained to help veterans with general questions about medical care and other benefits. It also provides recorded messages that enable callers to obtain information 24 hours a day.

GULF WAR SERVICE

Gulf War service is active duty in any of the following areas in Southwest Asia during the Gulf War, which began in 1990 and continues to the present:

- Iraq
- Kuwait
- Saudi Arabia
- The neutral zone (between Iraq and Saudi Arabia)
- Bahrain
- Qatar
- The United Arab Emirates
- Oman
- Gulf of Aden
- Gulf of Oman
- Waters of the Persian Gulf, the Arabian Sea, and the Red Sea

PERSIAN GULF REGISTRY PROGRAM

A free, complete physical examination with basic lab studies is offered to every Gulf War veteran, whether or not the veteran is ill. Veterans do not have to be enrolled in VA healthcare to participate in registry examinations. Results of the examinations, which include review of the veteran's military service and exposure history, are entered into special, computerized registries. The registries enable VA to update veterans on research findings or new compensation policies through periodic newsletters. The registries could also suggest areas to be explored in future scientific research. Registry participants are advised of the results of their examinations in personal consultations and by letters.

SPECIAL ACCESS TO FOLLOW-UP CARE

VA has designated a physician at every VA medical center to coordinate the special registry examination program and to receive updated educational materials and information as experience is gained nationally. Where an illness possibly related to military service in the Southwest Asia theater of operations during the Gulf War is detected during the examination, follow-up care is provided on a higher-eligibility basis than most non-service-connected care.

STANDARDIZED EXAM PROTOCOLS

VA has expanded its special registry examination protocol as more experience has been gained with the health of Gulf veterans. The protocol elicits information about symptoms and exposures, calls the clinician's attention to diseases common to the Gulf region, and directs baseline laboratory studies including chest X-ray (if one has not been done recently), blood count, urinalysis, and a set of blood chemistry and enzyme analyses that detect the "biochemical fingerprints" of certain diseases. In addition to this core laboratory work for every veteran undergoing the Gulf War program exam, physicians order additional tests and specialty consults as they would normally in following a diagnostic trail -- as symptoms dictate. If a diagnosis is not apparent, facilities follow the "comprehensive clinical evaluation protocol." The protocol suggests 22 additional baseline tests and additional specialty consultations, outlining dozens of further diagnostic procedures to be considered, depending on symptoms.

GULF WAR ILLNESS

Gulf War veterans have reported a variety of medically unexplained symptoms, such as fatigue, headache, joint pains, sleep disturbances and memory problems since serving in the Gulf. VA has recognized certain health problems as associated with Gulf War service or military service.

VA has recognized that certain health problems for Gulf War Veterans are associated with Gulf War service or military service. These Veterans may be eligible for disability compensation and health care for these illnesses. Surviving spouses, children and dependent parents of Gulf War Veterans who died as the result of illnesses associated with Gulf War service may be eligible for survivors' benefits.

For the purposes of these benefits, Gulf War Veterans are Veterans who served on active duty in the Southwest Asia theater of operations any time during the first Gulf War starting August 2, 1990 through the current conflict in Iraq. This includes Veterans who served in Operation Iraqi Freedom (2003-2010) and Operation New Dawn (2010 and continuing).

Illnesses that are associated with Gulf War service include:

- **Medically Unexplained Chronic Multi-symptom Illnesses**

  Gulf War Veterans have reported a variety of medically unexplained symptoms, such as fatigue, headache, joint pains, sleep disturbances and memory problems since serving in the Gulf. VA presumes certain medically unexplained symptoms existing for six months or more are associated with military service in the Gulf. The illnesses must have appeared during active duty in the Southwest Asia theater of operations or by December 31, 2011, and be at least 10 percent disabling.

  Illnesses include medically unexplained multi-symptom illnesses that have existed for six months or more, such as:

  - Chronic fatigue syndrome
  - Fibromyalgia
  - Irritable bowel syndrome
  - Undiagnosed illnesses with symptoms that may include but are not limited to: abnormal weight loss, cardiovascular symptoms, fatigues, gastrointestinal symptoms, headache, joint pain, menstrual disorders, muscle pain, neurologic symptoms, neuropsychological symptoms, skin conditions, upper and lower respiratory system symptoms, and sleep disturbances

  VA is revising the regulation for medically unexplained chronic multi-symptom illnesses to specify that **functional gastrointestinal disorders (FGIDs)** are covered in the presumption. Recent research has identified FGIDs, including irritable bowel syndrome and functional dyspepsia, as prevalent illnesses among Gulf War Veterans. Eligible Veterans may receive health care and disability compensation for these disorders when the proposed regulation* is final.

- **Infectious Diseases**

  In late 2010, VA established new presumptions of service connection for nine specific infectious diseases associated with military service in Southwest Asia during the first Gulf War starting August 2, 1990, through the conflict in Iraq and on or after September 19, 2001, in Afghanistan:

- Brucellosis
- Campylobacter jejuni
- Coxiella burnetii (Q fever)
- Malaria
- Mycobacterium tuberculosis
- Nontyphoid Salmonella
- Shigella
- Visceral leishmaniasis
- West Nile virus

A veterans now only has to show service in Southwest Asia or Afghanistan and that he or she had one of the nine diseases within a certain time after service, and has a current disability as a result of that disease, subject to certain time limits for seven of the diseases.

- **Amyotrophic Lateral Sclerosis (ALS)**

   VA does not presume that amyotrophic lateral sclerosis (ALS) is associated with hazardous exposures during the Gulf War. However, VA has recognized ALS diagnosed in Veterans with 90 days or more of continuously active service in the military was caused by their military service.

OBTAINING COPIES OF HOSPITAL RECORDS

A program is in place to help Gulf War veterans obtain copies of their in-patient hospital records from hospitals established during the Persian Gulf War.

Although these records were always located in the National Personnel Records Center in St. Louis, MO, they were stored only by the name of the hospital and the date of treatment.

An electronic database has been created to cross-reference patient names and social security numbers with their theater hospitals and admission dates.

Veterans may call (800) 497-6261 to find out if their inpatient record has been added to the database, and to obtain the paperwork necessary to request a copy.

VA-FUNDED EXAMINATION PROGRAM FOR THE SPOUSES AND CHILDREN OF GULF WAR VETERANS

In 1996, VA initiated a special program to fund health examinations for some spouses and children of Gulf War Veterans Registry participants. The results of these examinations, which are conducted under contract by non-VA physicians in non-VA medical facilities, are included in the Gulf War Registry. Funding for the program has been approved through December 31, 2003.

VA can provide examinations to any individual who:

- Is the spouse or child of a veterans, is listed in the Persian Gulf War Veterans Registry; and

- Is suffering from, or may have suffered from, an illness or disorder (including birth defect, miscarriage, or stillbirth) which cannot be disassociated from the veteran's service in the Southwest Asia theater of operations; and

- Has granted VA permission to include in the Registry relevant medical data from the evaluation.

Interested individuals should call the VA Persian Gulf Information Help line at (800) 749-8387.

Alternative Program

Eligible family members of Gulf War veterans may also have their medical information entered into the Persian Gulf War Registry by undergoing a physical examination from their private physician. The physician must complete a Registry code sheet, containing the protocol examination, and submit it to VA for entry into the database. The veteran or family member choosing this option must assume the cost of the examination and code sheet completion.

Interested individuals should contact the Persian Gulf Registry Coordinator at the nearest VA medical center for forms and information.

CONTINUING RESEARCH

A large number of studies are now in progress that will hopefully contribute to our understanding of Gulf War illnesses, including epidemiologic studies that will compare the types and frequency of illnesses in Gulf War veterans compared to veterans who did not serve in the Gulf War.

Additionally, more than 90 research studies are under way that will examine possible health consequences of exposure to a variety of factors present in the Persian Gulf, such as depleted uranium, pesticides, pyridostigmine bromide, and chemical warfare agents.

Any changes in benefits payable to Gulf War veterans as a result of this continuing research will be addressed in subsequent editions of this book, as well as in our monthly supplements.

CHAPTER 34

SERVICEMEMBERS' CIVIL RELIEF ACT

Congress and state legislatures have long recognized that military service can often place an economic and legal burden on servicemembers. The Soldiers' and Sailors' Civil Relief Act of 1918 was passed in order to protect the rights of service members while serving on active duty.

Service members were protected from such things as repossession of property, bankruptcy, foreclosure or other such actions while serving in the military. This Act remained in effect until shortly after World War I when it expired. The Soldiers' and Sailors' Civil Relief Act of 1940 (SSCRA) was passed in order to protect the rights of the millions of service members activated for World War II. The SSCRA has remained in effect until the present day and has been amended many times since 1940 to keep pace with the changing military.

> *The SCRA can provide many forms of relief to military members.*

In December 2003, Congress passed legislation renaming SSCRA as the Servicemembers' Civil Relief Act (SCRA). The SCRA updates and strengthens the civil protections enacted during World War II.

The SCRA is designed to protect active duty military members, reservists who are in active federal service, and National Guardsmen who are in active federal service. Some of the benefits under the SCRA extend to dependents of active duty military members as well.

Public Law 107-330 extended protections under the SSCRA to members of the National Guard who are called to active service authorized by the President or the Secretary of Defense, or a state governor for a period of more than 30 consecutive days, for purposes of responding to a national emergency declared by the President, and supported by Federal funds.

Under previous law, the SSCRA only applied to National Guard members if they were called to FEDERAL service. The protections did not apply to Guard members performing duty under authority of the State Governor. Following September 11, 2000, then-President Bush asked the state governors to activate members of the National Guard to perform "homeland security" duties, such as guarding airports and other facilities that were considered terrorist targets. Because these members were called by the STATE, and not the Federal government, SSCRA protections did not apply. The new provision extends SSCRA protection to National Guard members, anytime they are performing "homeland security" duties, even if under control of State government.

The SCRA can provide many forms of relief to military members. Below are some of the most common forms of relief.

PROTECTION FROM EVICTION

If a military member is leasing a house or apartment and his or her rent is below a certain amount, the SCRA can protect the individual from being evicted for a period of time, usually three months. The dwelling place must be occupied by either the active duty member or his or her dependents and the rent on the premises cannot exceed $2465.00 a month (rate as of 2004). This rent ceiling will be adjusted annually for consumer price index (CPI) changes. Additionally, the military member must show that military service materially affects his or her ability to pay rent. If a landlord continues to try to evict the military member or does actually evict the member, he or she is subject to criminal sanctions such as fines or even imprisonment.

TERMINATION OF PRE-SERVICE RESIDENTIAL LEASES

The SCRA also allows military members who are just entering active duty service to lawfully terminate a lease without repercussions. To do this, the service member needs to show that the lease was entered into prior to the commencement of active duty service, that the lease was signed by or on behalf of the service member, and that the service member is currently in military service or was called to active-duty service for a period of 180 days or more. Proper written notice with a copy of orders must be provided to the landlord.

TERMINATION OF RESIDENTIAL LEASES DURING MILITARY SERVICE

The SCRA allows military members who receive permanent change of station (PCS) orders or are deployed for a period of 90 days or more to terminate a lease by providing written notice to the landlord along with a copy of the military orders. The termination of a lease that provides for monthly payment of rent will occur 30 days after the first date on which the next rental payment is due and payable after the landlord receives proper written notice.

MORTGAGES

The SCRA can also provide military members temporary relief from paying their mortgage. To obtain relief, a military member must show that their mortgage was entered into prior to beginning active duty, that the property was owned prior to entry into military service, that the property is still owned by the military member, and that military service materially affects the member's ability to pay the mortgage.

MAXIMUM RATE OF INTEREST

Under the SCRA, a military member can cap the interest rate at 6% for all obligations entered into before beginning active duty if the military service materially affects his or her ability to meet the obligations. This can include interest rates on credit cards, mortgages, and even some student loans (except for Federal guaranteed student loans), to name a few. To qualify for the interest rate cap the military member has to show that he or she is now on active duty, that the obligation or debt was incurred prior to entry on active duty, and that military service materially affects the members' ability to pay. To begin the process, the military member needs to send a letter along with a copy of current military orders to the lender requesting relief under the SCRA. The interest rate cap lasts for the duration of active duty service. The interest rate cap will apply from the first date of active-duty service. The military member must provide written notice to the creditor and a copy of military orders not later than 180 days after the servicemember's termination or release from military service.

TERMINATION OF AUTOMOBILE LEASES DURING MILITARY SERVICE

The SCRA allows military members to terminate pre-service automobile leases if they are called up for military service of 180 days or longer. Members who sign automobile leases while on active-duty may be able to terminate an automobile lease if they are given orders for a permanent change of station outside the continental United States or to deploy with a military unit for a period of 180 days or longer.

STAY OF PROCEEDINGS

If a military member is served with a complaint indicating that they are being sued for some reason, they can obtain a "stay" or postponement of those proceedings if the military service materially affects their ability to proceed in the case. A stay can be used to stop the action altogether, or to hold up some phase of it. According to the SCRA, military members can request a "stay" during any stage of the proceedings. However, the burden is on the military member to show that their military service has materially affected their ability to appear in court. In general, individuals can request a stay of the proceedings for a reasonable period of time (30-60 days). For example, if they are being sued for divorce, they can put off the hearing for some period of time, but it is unlikely that a court will allow the proceedings to be put off indefinitely. The stay can be granted in administrative proceedings.

DEFAULT JUDGMENTS

A default judgment is entered against a party who has failed to defend against a claim that has been brought by another party. To obtain a default judgment, a plaintiff must file an affidavit (written declaration of fact) stating that the defendant is not in the military service and has not requested a stay. If someone is sued while on active duty, and fails to respond, and as a result a default judgment is obtained against them, they can reopen the default judgment by taking several steps. First, they must show that the judgment was entered during their military service or within 30 days after they've left the service. Second, they must write to the court requesting that the default judgment be reopened while they are still on active duty or within 90 days of leaving the service. Third, they must not have made any kind of appearance in court, through filing an answer or otherwise, prior to the default judgment being entered. Finally, they must indicate that their military service prejudiced their ability to defend their case and show that they had a valid defense to the action against them.

INSURANCE

Under SCRA, the U.S. Department of Veterans Affairs (VA) will protect, from default for nonpayment of premiums, up to **$250,000** of life insurance for servicemembers called to active duty. (This amount was previously $10,000.) The protection provided by this legislation applies during the insured's period of military service and for a period of two years thereafter. The following are conditions for eligibility for protection:

- The policy must be whole life, endowment, universal life or term insurance.
- The policy must have been in force on a premium-paying basis for at least six months at the time the servicemember applies for benefits.
- Benefits from the policy cannot be limited, reduced or excluded because of military service.
- Policies for which an additional amount of premium is charged due to military service are not eligible for protection under SCRA.

The servicemember must apply for protection of their life insurance by filing *VA Form 29-380 "Application For Protection Of Commercial Life Insurance Policy"* with his/her insurance company and forwarding a copy of the application to VA.

Benefits Of SCRA Life Insurance Protection

Once the servicemember has applied for protection of their life insurance policy and VA determines that the policy is eligible for protection under SCRA:

- The servicemember is still responsible for making premium payments. However, the policy will not lapse, terminate, or be forfeited because of the servicemember's failure to make premium payments or to pay any indebtedness or interest due during their period of military service or for a period of two years thereafter.
- The rights of the servicemember to change their beneficiary designation or select an optional settlement for a beneficiary are not affected by the provisions of this Act.

Limitations Of SCRA Life Insurance Protection

Once the servicemember has applied for protection of their life insurance policy and VA determines that the policy is eligible for protection under SCRA:

- Premium payments are deferred only, not waived. *During this period, the government does not pay the premiums on the policy but simply guarantees that the premiums will be paid at the end of the servicemember's period of active duty.*

- A servicemember cannot receive dividends, take out a loan, or surrender the policy for cash without the approval of VA. (Dividends or other monetary benefits shall be added to the value of the policy and will be used as a credit when final settlement is made with the insurer.)

- If the policy matures as a result of the insured's death, or any other means, during the protected period, the insurance company will deduct any unpaid premiums and interest due from the settlement amount.

Termination Of Period Under SCRA

The servicemember has up to two years after their military service terminates to repay the unpaid premiums and interest to the insurer. If the amount owed is not paid before the end of the two years, then:

- The insurer treats the unpaid premiums as a loan against the policy.
- The government will pay the insurer the difference between the amount due and the cash surrender value (if the cash surrender value of the policy is less than the amount owed.)
- The amount the United States government pays to the insurance company under the SCRA Act becomes a debt due the government by the insured.
- If the policy matures as a result of the insured's death, or any other means, during the protected period, the insurance company will deduct any unpaid premiums and interest due from the settlement amount.

TAXATION

A service member's state of legal residence may tax military pay and personal property. A member does not lose residence solely because of a transfer to another state pursuant to military orders.

For example, if an Illinois resident who is a member of Illinois Army National Guard is activated to federal military service and sent to California for duty, that person remains an Illinois resident while in California. The service member is not subject to California's authority to tax his/her military income. However, if the service member has a part-time civilian job in California, California will tax his/her non-military income earned in the state.

The Servicemembers Civil Relief Act also contains a provision preventing servicemembers from a form of double taxation that can occur when they have a spouse who works and is taxed in a state other than the state in which they maintain their permanent legal residence. The law prevents states from using the income earned by a servicemember in determining the spouse's tax rate when they do not maintain their permanent legal residence in that state.

IMPORTANT 2009 UPDATE FOR SPOUSES:

Public Law 111-98, which became law on November 11, 2009, provides that when a service member leaves his or her home state in accord with military or naval orders, the service member's spouse may retain residency in his or her home state for voting and tax purposes, after relocating from that state to accompany the service member.

RIGHT TO VOTE

In addition to the protections involving debt payments and civil litigation, the act guarantees service members the right to vote in the state of their home of record and protects them from paying taxes in two different states.

CAUTION

The SSCRA does not wipe out any of an individual's obligations. Rather, it temporarily suspends the right of creditors to use a court to compel an individual to pay, only if the court finds that the inability to pay is due to military service. The obligation to honor existing debts remains, and some day the individual must "pay up."

It is important to remember that the SSCRA affords no relief to persons in the Service against the collection of debts or other obligations contracted or assumed by them **after** entering such Service.

The Relief Act is highly technical. The above summary is intended only to give a general overview of the protection available. The specific nature of all the relief provided under the law is a matter about which an individual may need to contact an attorney. The Act is designed to deal fairly with military personnel and their creditors. While relief is very often available, individuals are expected and required to show good faith in repayment of all debts.

2010 UPDATE:

The Veterans' Benefits Act of 2010:

- Amends the Servicemembers Civil Relief Act (SCRA) to prohibit lessors from charging early termination fees with respect to residential, business, agricultural, or motor vehicle leases entered into by servicemembers who subsequently enter military service or receive orders for a permanent change of station or deployment in support of a military operation.

- Allows a servicemember to terminate a contract for cellular or home telephone service at any time after receiving military orders to deploy for at least 90 days to a location that does not support the contract. Requires the return of any advance payments made by a deploying servicemember under such a contract.

- Allows the Attorney General to bring a civil suit against any violator of the SCRA. Also gives servicemembers a "private right of action" to file their own lawsuits against those who violate their legal rights.

CHAPTER 35

APPEALS

Veterans and other claimants for VA benefits have the right to appeal decisions made by a VA regional office or medical center.

If a claimant wishes to appeal a VA decision, the appeal is first reviewed by the BOARD OF VETERANS APPEALS. If, after review by the Board of Veterans' Appeals, the claimant is still dissatisfied, he or she may appeal to the UNITED STATES COURT OF VETERANS APPEALS. Both entities, along with specific guidelines for the filing of appeals, are discussed in the remainder of this chapter.

BOARD OF VETERANS APPEALS

The Board of Veterans Appeals was established by law to decide appeals for benefits under laws administered by the Veterans Administration. The Board of Veterans' Appeals (BVA) is a part of the Department of Veterans Affairs, located in Washington, D.C. Decisions are made by the members of a section of the Board, appointed with the approval of the president. The Board members are attorneys experienced in veterans' law and in reviewing benefit claims. It is the mission of the Board to decide appeals with sympathetic understanding and as promptly as possible, in order to grant all benefits to which veterans and their dependents and beneficiaries are entitled. Decisions are based on a veteran's entire record.

General Information

Anyone who has filed a claim for benefits with VA and has received a determination from a local VA office is eligible to appeal to the Board of Veterans' Appeals. Some decisions, such as eligibility for medical treatment, issued by VA medical centers can also be appealed to the BVA. An appeal can be made based on a complete denial of a claim, or based on the level of benefit granted. For example, if a veteran files a claim for disability, and the local VA office awards a 10% disability, but the veteran feels he or she is more than 10% disabled, the veteran can appeal that determination to the Board of Veterans' Appeals.

> *An appeal must be filed within one year from the date the VA regional office or medical center mails its initial decision on a claim. If an appeal is not filed within the year, the original decision is considered final, and cannot be appealed unless the decision involves clear and unmistakable error by VA.*

Decisions concerning the need for medical care or the type of medical

418

treatment needed (such as a physician's decision to prescribe or not to prescribe a particular drug, or whether to order a specific type of treatment) are not within the BVA's jurisdiction.

UPDATE:

*   On December 22, 2006 then-President Bush signed Public Law 109-461, the Veterans' Benefits, Healthcare, and Information Technology Act of 2006. The law allows veterans to hire an agent or attorney to represent them after a Notice of Disagreement has been filed. (A Notice of Disagreement is the written statement submitted by the veteran stating he or she disagrees with the claim decision made by the VA regional office.) Veterans will still have the option of utilizing the representation services provided without charge by many veterans' organizations, but in addition they will have the option of hiring an attorney if they so choose. Until now, the United States Code has not allowed a veteran to hire an attorney until the veteran has received a final Board of Veterans' Appeals (BVA) decision – a process that often takes years from a veterans' initial application.

How to File an Appeal and Important Time Limits

No special form is required to begin the appeal process. All that is initially needed is a written statement that the veteran disagrees with a claim decision. This initial statement is known as the "Notice of Disagreement" (NOD). The NOD must include why the veteran disagrees with a regional office decision. (For example, perhaps the veteran feels that the office making the decision overlooked or misunderstood some evidence, or misinterpreted the law.)

The Notice of Disagreement should be filed at the VA regional office where the veteran's claims file is kept. Normally, this is the same VA regional office or medical facility that issued the decision being appealed. However, if a veteran moves after a filing a claim, his or her claims file is transferred to the appropriate VA regional office, and that is where the NOD should be sent.

After the local VA office reviews a Notice of Disagreement, it is possible that the local office will agree with the NOD, and will change its original decision. However, if the local VA office does not change its decision, it will prepare and mail the veteran a *Statement of the Case*, which includes a VA Form 9 - Substantive Appeal, which the veteran must complete and return. The Statement of Case will summarize the evidence and applicable laws and regulations, and provide a discussion of the reasons for arriving at the decision.

Within 60 days of the date the local VA office issue the Statement of Case, the veteran must submit a completed VA Form 9-Substantive Appeal. (Please note that if the one-year period from the date the VA regional office or medical center mailed its original decision is later than this 60-day period, the veteran has until that later one-year date to file the VA Form 9-Substantive Appeal.)

Completion of the VA Form 9-Substantive Appeal is very important. The form should include a clear statement of the benefit being sought, as well as any mistakes the veteran feels VA made when issuing its decision. VA Form 9-Substantive Appeal should also identify anything in the Statement of Case the veteran disagrees with. In addition to VA Form 9, any additional evidence, such as records from recent medical treatments or evaluations may be included as part of the appeal.

In most instances, a veteran can obtain civilian medical records and other non-government documents supporting his or her case by calling or writing directly to the office that keeps those records. VA regional office personnel and VSO representatives are experienced in locating many items that can support your case, such as service medical records, VA treatment records, and other government records. The VA does have a duty to assist veterans in the developing of their cases. However, individual veterans need to assist the VA in identifying the evidence that can prove the case.

If new information or evidence is included with VA Form 9, the regional office will prepare a Supplemental Statement of the Case (SSOC). The SSOC is similar to the Statement of the Case, but addresses the new information or evidence. If a veteran is not satisfied with the SSOC, a written statement must be mailed to the regional office within 60 days from the mailing date of the SSOC.

It is important to realize the importance of submitting the VA Form 9-Substantive Appeal on a timely basis, otherwise, the right to appeal may be lost. Remember, the VA Form 9 is due the later of:

1 year from Regional Office determination mailing date

or

60 days from Statement of Case (SOC) mailing date

(An extension of the 60-day period for filing VA Form 9-Substantive Appeal or the 60-day period following a Supplemental Statement of the Case **may** be approved if a written request is filed with the local VA office handling the appeal. An extension will only be approved if the veteran can show "good cause" (can offer a valid reason why the extra time is needed).

Docket

A veteran's VA Form 9-Substantive Appeal becomes part of his or her claims folder, and is the basis for adding the appeal to the Board's *docket*.

The Board's docket is the record of all appeals awaiting review by the Board, listed in the order that appeals (VA Form 9) are received.

When an appeal is placed on the Board's docket, it is assigned the next higher number than the one received before it. The Board reviews appeals in the order in which they were placed on the docket. Thus, the lower the docket number, the sooner the appeal will be reviewed.

Lawyers and Other Representatives

A veteran may represent himself or herself. However, over 90% of all people who appeal to the Board of Veterans' Appeals obtain representation. The majority choose to be represented by Veterans' Service Organizations (VSOs) or their state's veterans department.

A lawyer may also be hired for representation. There are strict guidelines about what a lawyer may charge for services, as well as restrictions on fees that a lawyer may charge for work performed prior to issuance of the Board's final decision.

In addition to VSOs and attorneys, some other agents are recognized by VA to represent appellants.

To authorize a VSO for representation, VA Form 21-22 must be completed. To authorize an attorney or recognized agent for representation, VA Form 22a must be completed. Both forms are available at all VA offices.

Length of Appeal Process

No one can determine exactly how long it will take form the time an appeal is filed until receipt of the Board's decision. However, veterans can expect an average of two years from the time an appeal is placed on the Board's docket until issuance of a BVA decision.

If a veteran believes his or her case should be decided sooner than others filed earlier, a *motion to advance on the docket* can be submitted. The motion should explain why the appeal should be moved ahead. Because most appeals involve some type of hardship, before a case can be advanced, there needs to be convincing proof of exceptional circumstances (i.e. terminal illness, danger of bankruptcy or foreclosure, or an error by VA that caused a significant delay in the docketing of an appeal. Veterans should be aware that, on average, fewer than 3 out of every 20 requests for advancement on the docket are granted.

Veterans can expect an average of two years from the time an appeal is placed on the Board's docket until issuance of a BVA decision.

To file a motion to advance on the docket, a written request should be sent to:

> Board of Veterans' Appeals (014)
> Department of Veterans Affairs
> 810 Vermont Avenue, NW
> Washington, DC 20420

Personal Hearings

A personal hearing is a meeting between the veteran (and his/her representative) and an official from VA who will decide the case. During the hearing, the veteran presents testimony and other evidence supporting the case. There are two types of personal hearings:

- Regional office hearings (also called RO hearing or local office hearings); and
- BVA hearings.

A regional office hearing is a meeting held at a local VA office with a "hearing officer" from the local office's staff. To arrange a regional office hearing, a veteran should contact the local VA office or appeal representative as early in the appeal process as possible.

In a BVA hearing, the veteran presents his or her case in person to a member of the Board. Appellants in most areas of the country can choose whether to hold the BVA hearing at the local VA regional office, called a "Travel Board Hearing," or at the BVA office in Washington, D.C. Some regional offices are also equipped to hold BVA hearings by videoconference. (Check with the regional office for availability.)

The VA cannot pay for any lodging or travel expenses incurred in connection with a hearing.

The VA Form 9-SubstantiveAppeal has a section for requesting a BVA hearing. VA Form 9 is not used, however, to request a local office hearing. Even if a BVA hearing is not requested on the VA Form 9, a request can still be requested by writing directly to the Board. If a BVA hearing is requested, the request must clearly state where the hearing is requested – at the VA regional office, or at the Board's office in Washington, D.C. A BVA hearing cannot be held in both places. (Travel Board hearings may not be available at regional offices located near Washington, D.C.)

The requested type and location of the hearing determines when it will be held. Generally, regional office hearings are held as soon as they can be scheduled on the hearing officer's calendar.

The scheduling of BVA hearings held at regional offices (Travel Board hearings) is more complicated, since Board members must travel from Washington, D.C. to the regional office. BVA videoconferenced hearings are less complicated to arrange, and can be scheduled more frequently than Travel Board hearings.

Hearings held at the Board's offices in Washington, D.C. will be scheduled for a time close to when BVA will consider the case – approximately three months before the case is reviewed by the BVA.

Location of Claims Folder

If a BVA hearing is not requested, the claims folder remains at the local VA office until shortly before the BVA begins its review, at which time it is transferred to the BVA.

If a Travel Board hearing is requested, the claims folder remains at the local VA office until the hearing is completed, at which time it is transferred to the BVA.

If a videoconferenced BVA hearing or a hearing held at the Board's office in Washington, D.C. is requested, the claims folder remains at the local VA office until shortly before the BVA hearing is held. It is transferred to the BVA in time for the hearing and the Board's review.

When a claims folder is transferred from the local VA office to Washington, D.C., the local VA office will send the claimant a letter advising that he or she has 90 days remaining (from the date of that letter) during which more evidence can be added to a file, a hearing can be requested, or a representative can be selected (or changed).

The BVA cannot accept items submitted after the 90-day period has expired, unless a written explanation (called a "motion") is also submit, explaining why the item is late and showing why the BVA should accept it (called "showing good cause"). A motion to accept items after the 90-day period will be reviewed by a Board member who will issue a ruling either allowing or denying the motion.

Checking on the Status of an Appeal

To check on the status of an appeal, veterans or their representatives should contact the office where the claims folder is located (see previous section).

If a claims file is at the Board, veterans or their representatives may call (202) 565-5436 to check on its status (be sure to have the claim number available).

The Board Review Process

When the VBA receives an appeal from a local VA office, the veteran and/or representative will be notified in writing. The Board will then examine the claims folder for completeness, and will provide an opportunity to submit additional written arguments . The case is then assigned to a Board member for review. If a BVA hearing was requested, the Board member assigned the case will conduct the hearing prior to reaching a decision.

When the docket number for an appeal is reached, the file will be reviewed by a Board member and a staff attorney, who will check for completeness, review all evidence and arguments, as well as the regional office's Statement of the Case (and Supplement Statement of the Case, if applicable), the transcript of the hearing (if applicable), the statement of any representative, and any other information included in the claims folder. The staff attorney, if directed to do so by the Board member, may also conduct additional research and prepare recommendations for the Board member's review.

When, in the judgment of the Board member, expert medical opinion, in addition to that available within the VA, is warranted by the medical complexity or controversy involved in an appeal, the Board may secure an advisory medical opinion from one or more independent medical experts who are not employees of the VA.

The VA shall make necessary arrangements with recognized medical schools, universities, or clinics to furnish such advisory medical opinions at the request of the Chairman of the Board. Any such arrangement shall provide that the actual selection of the expert or experts to give the advisory opinion in an individual case shall be made by an appropriate official of such institution.

The Board shall furnish a claimant with notice that an advisory medical opinion has been requested, and shall furnish the claimant with a copy of such opinion when it is received by the Board.

Prior to reaching a decision, the Board member must thoroughly review all materials and recommendations. The Board member will then issue a decision.

The Board member's decision will be mailed to the home address that the Board has on file, so it is extremely important that the VA be kept informed of any address changes.

The BVA must attempt to make its decisions as understandable as possible. However, due to the nature of legal documents, laws, court cases, and medical discussions, decisions can be confusing. If an appeal is denied , the Board will send a "Notice of Appellate Rights" that describes additional actions that can be taken.

The Board annually produces a CD-ROM with the text of its decisions. Most VA regional offices have these CD-ROMS available for review, or the CD-Rom may be purchased from the Government Printing Office. For further information, contact:

Department of Veterans Affairs
Board of Veterans' Appeals (01B)
Washington, D.C. 20420

Remands

Sometimes when reviewing a claims folder, the Board member determines additional development of the case is necessary. The appeal is then returned to the local VA office. This is called a "remand." After performing the additional work, the regional office may issue a new decision. If the claim is still denied, the case is returned to the Board for a final decision. (The case keeps its original place on the Board's docket, so it is reviewed soon after it is returned to the Board.)

Depending on the reason for the remand, the regional office may provide the veteran with a Supplement Statement of the Case (SSOC). The claimant then has 60 days from the date the local VA office mails the SSOC to comment on it.

APPEALING THE BOARD OF VETERANS' AFFAIRS DECISION

Motion for Reconsideration

If it can be demonstrated that the Board made an obvious error of fact or law in its decision, a written "motion to reconsider" can be filed. Any such motions should be sent directed to the Board, not to the local VA office. A motion to reconsider should not be submitted simply because of disagreement with the BVA's decision. The claimant must be able to show that the Board made a mistake, and that the Board's decision would have been different if the mistake had not been made. A motion to reconsider should be sent directly to the Board, not to the local VA office.

Reopening

If a claimant has "new and material evidence," he or she can request that the case be re-opened. To be considered "new and material," the evidence submitted must be information related to the case that was not included in the claims folder when the case was decided.

To re-open an appeal, the claimant must submit the new evidence directly to the local VA office that handled the claim.

CUE Motion

The law was amended in 1997 to provide one more way to challenge a Board decision. A Board decision can be reversed or revised if the claimant is able to show that the decision contained "clear and unmistakable error" (CUE).

The written request for the Board to review its decision for CUE is called a "motion." CUE motions should be filed directly with the Board, and not with the local VA office.

Because CUE is a very complicated area of law, most claimants seek help from a representative to file a CUE motion.

A motion for CUE review of a prior Board decision must meet some very specific requirements, described in the Board's *Rules of Practice*. If the motion is denied a claimant can't ask for another CUE review of the way the Board decided the issues raised in the first CUE motion, so it is very important that the motion be prepared properly the first time out.

Not many CUE motions are successful, because CUE is a very rare kind of error, the kind that compels a conclusion that the Board would have decided the claimant's case differently but for the error. A difference of opinion is not enough.

A motion to review a Board decision for CUE can be filed at any time, but if it is filed after filing a timely Notice of Appeal with the Court, the Board will not be able to rule on your CUE motion.

UNITED STATES COURT OF VETERANS' APPEALS

The United States Court of Veterans' Appeals was created under Public Law 100-687, on November 18, 1988. The Court has seven judges, appointed by the President and confirmed by the Senate. Judges are appointed for a 15-year term.

> *If a claimant is not satisfied with the Board of Veterans' Appeals decision, an appeal can be filed with the United States Court of Veterans Appeals.*

If a claimant is not satisfied with the Board of Veterans' Appeals decision, an appeal can be filed with the United States Court of Veterans Appeals (referred to as the "Court"). The Court is an independent court that is not part of the Department of Veterans Affairs. The Court does not hold trials, receive new evidence, or hear witnesses. It reviews the BVA decision, the written record, and the briefs of the parties. Claimants do not need to appear in Washington, D.C. for an appeal. (In approximately 1% of decided cases, the Court holds oral arguments in its Washington courtroom, or occasionally, by telephone conference call.)

A claimant may represent himself or herself, but may want to get advice from an attorney or from a service officer in a veterans organization or a state or county veterans' affairs office. The VA will be represented by its attorney, and a claimant's case may be better presented if he or she is represented.

The Court does not recommend or appoint attorneys to represent claimants. However, the Court does have a *Public List of Practitioners* which shows who is allowed to represent appellants in the Court, and have said that they are available. Most attorneys charge a fee.

To appeal a Board of Veterans' Appeals decision, a claimant must file a "Notice of Appeal" with the Court within 120 days from the date the Board's decision is mailed. (The first day of the 120 days a claimant has to file an appeal to the Court is the day the BVA's decision is postmarked, not the day the decision is signed.)

If a claimant filed a motion to reconsider with the Board of Veterans' Appeals within the 120 day time-frame, and that motion was denied, the claimant has an additional 120 days to file the "Notice of Appeal" with the Court. (This 120 day period begins on the date the Board mails a notification that it has denied the motion to reconsider.) If the Board denies the motion to reconsider, a "Notice of Appellate Rights" will be mailed to the claimant.

In addition to the above 120 day limit, in order for the Court to consider an appeal, a Notice of Disagreement must have been filed with the VA regional office handling the case on or after November 18, 1988.

An original "Notice of Appeal" must be filed directed with the Court at:

United States Court of Veterans Appeals
625 Indiana Avenue, NW, Suite 900
Washington, D.C. 20004
Fax: (202) 501-5848
(Appeals cannot be filed by e-mail)

The fee for an appeal is $50.00, and should be included with the "Notice of Appeal." If a claimant is unable to pay this fee, a "Motion to Waive Filing Fee" form must be completed and returned with the "Notice of Appeal."

If a claimant appeals to the Court, a copy of the "Notice of Appeal" must also be filed with the VA General Counsel at:

Office of the General Counsel (027)
Department of Veterans Affairs
810 Vermont Avenue, NW
Washington, D.C. 20420

Please note that the *original* "Notice of Appeal" that is filed with the Court is the only document that protects a claimants right to appeal a BVA decision. The copy sent to the VA General Counsel does not protect that right, or serve as an official filing.

If the Court accepts an appeal, it will send a printed copy of the rules of practice and procedure to the claimant and his/her representative, if applicable.

To obtain more specific information about the "Notice of Appeal," the methods for filing with the Court, Court filing fees, and other matters covered by the Court's rules, a claimant should contact the Court directly at:

United States Court of Veterans Appeals
625 Indiana Avenue, NW, Suite 900
Washington, D.C. 20004
(800) 869-8654

If either party disagrees with the Court's ruling, an appeal may be filed with the U.S. Court of Appeals for the Federal Circuit, and, thereafter, may seek review in the Supreme Court of the United States.

DEATH OF APPELLANT

According to the law, the death of an appellant generally ends the appellant's appeal, and the Board normally dismisses the appeal without issuing a decision. The rights of a deceased appellant's survivors are not affected by this action. Survivors may still file a claim at the regional office for any benefits to which they may be entitled.

GENERAL GUIDELINES FOR EFFICIENT PROCESSING OF CLAIMS

The following guidelines may help ensure that an appeal is not unnecessarily delayed:

- Consider having an appeal representative assist with the filing of the appeal.

- File the Notice of Disagreement and VA Form 9-Substantive Appeal as soon as possible

- Be as specific as possible when identifying the issues the Board should consider.

- Be as specific as possible when identifying sources of evidence for the VA to obtain. (For example, provide the full names and addresses of physicians, along with dates of treatment, and reasons for treatment.)

- Keep VA informed of current address, phone number, and number of dependents.

- When possible, provide clinical treatment records, rather than simply a statement from a physician.

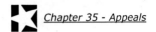

- Be clear on the VA Form 9 about whether or not a BVA hearing is requested, and where the hearing should take place, if applicable.

- Include the claim number on any correspondence with the VA.

- Do not submit material that is not pertinent to the claim. This will only delay the process.

- Do not use the VA Form 9 to raise new claims for the first time. (VA Form 9 is only to be used to appeal decisions on previously submitted claims.)

- Do not use the VA Form 9 to request a local office hearing.

- Do not raise additional issues for the Board's review late in the appeal process. This may cause the appeal to be sent back to the regional office for additional work, and may result in a longer delay.

- Do not submit evidence directly to the Board unless a written or typed statement is included, stating that consideration by the regional office is waived. The statement must clearly indicate that the Board is to review the evidence, even though the regional office has not seen it. If a waiver is not included with any additional evidence submitted directly to the Board, the case may be remanded to the regional office for review, and may result in further delays.

- Do not submit a last minute request for a hearing or a last minute change to the type or location of a hearing unless it is unavoidable. Such a request will likely result in a delay in reaching a final decision.

- Do not miss a scheduled VA examination or hearing.

CHAPTER 36

VA REGIONAL OFFICES & BENEFITS OFFICES

**Department of Veterans Affairs
Headquarters**
810 Vermont Avenue NW
Washington, DC 20420
(202) 273-5400

Alabama (SDN 5)
Montgomery Regional Office
345 Perry Hill Road
Montgomery, AL 36109

Alaska (SDN 8)
Anchorage Regional Office
2925 DeBarr Road
Anchorage, AK 99508-2989

Arizona (SDN 9)
Phoenix Regional Office
3225 North Central Avenue
Phoenix, AZ 85012

Arkansas (SDN 7)
North Little Rock Regional Office
2200 Fort Roots Drive
Building 65
North Little Rock, AR 72114

California (SDN 9)
Los Angeles Regional Office
Federal Building
11000 Wilshire Boulevard
Los Angeles, CA 90024

Oakland Regional Office
1301 Clay Street
Room 1300 North
Oakland, CA 94612

San Diego Regional Office
8810 Rio San Diego Drive
San Diego, CA 92108

Colorado (SDN 8)
Denver Regional Office
155 Van Gordon Street
Denver, CO 80228

Connecticut (SDN 1)
Hartford Regional Office
450 Main Street
Hartford, CT 06103

Delaware (SDN 3)
Wilmington Regional Office
1601 Kirkwood Highway
Wilmington, DE 19805

Florida (SDN 5)
St. Petersburg Regional Office
9500 Bay Pines Boulevard
Bay Pines, FL 33708

Georgia (SDN 4)
Atlanta Regional Office
1700 Clairmont Road
Decatur, GA 30033

Hawaii (SDN 9)
Honolulu Regional Office
459 Patterson Road
E-Wing
Honolulu, HI 96819-1522

Idaho (SDN 8)
Boise Regional Office
805 West Franklin Street
Boise, ID 83702

Illinois (SDN 6)
Chicago Regional Office
2122 West Taylor Street
Chicago, IL 60612

Indiana (SDN 2)
Indianapolis Regional Office
575 North Pennsylvania Street
Indianapolis, IN 46204

Iowa (SDN 6)
Des Moines Regional Office
210 Walnut Street
Des Moines, IA 50309

Kansas (SDN 6)
Wichita Regional Office
5500 East Kellogg
Wichita, KS 67211

Kentucky (SDN 3)
Louisville Regional Office
545 South 3rd Street
Louisville, KY 40202

Louisiana (SDN 7)
New Orleans Regional Office
701 Loyola Avenue
New Orleans, LA 70113

Maine (SDN 1)
Togus VA Med/Regional Office
1 VA Center
Togus, ME 04330

Maryland (SDN 3)
Baltimore Regional Office
31 Hopkins Plaza Federal Bldg
Baltimore, MD 21201

Massachusetts (SDN 1)
Boston VA Regional Office
JFK Federal Building
Government Center
Boston, MA 02114

Michigan (SDN 2)
Detroit Regional Office
Federal Building
477 Michigan Avenue
Detroit, MI 48226

Eastern Area Office
24 Frank Lloyd Wright Drive
Lobby B, 3rd Floor
Ann Arbor, MI 48106

Minnesota (SDN 6)
St. Paul Regional Office
1 Federal Drive
Fort Snelling
St. Paul, MN 55111-4050

Mississippi (SDN 5)
Jackson Regional Office
1600 East Woodrow Wilson Ave.
Jackson, MS 39216

Missouri (SDN 6)
St. Louis Regional Office
Federal Building
400 South, 18th Street
St. Louis, MO 63103

Montana (SDN 8)
Fort Harrison Regional Office
William Street
off Highway 12 West
Fort Harrison, MT 59636

Nebraska (SDN 6)
Lincoln Regional Office
5631 South 48th Street
Lincoln, NE 68516

New Hampshire (SDN 1)
Manchester Regional Office
Norris Cotton Federal Bldg
275 Chestnut Street
Manchester, NH 03101

New Jersey (SDN 2)
Newark Regional Office
20 Washington Place
Newark, NJ 07102

New Mexico (SDN 8)
Albuquerque Regional Office
Dennis Chavez Federal Building
500 Gold Avenue, S.W.
Albuquerque, NM 87102

Nevada (SDN 9)
Reno Regional Office
1201 Terminal Way
Reno, NV 89520

New York (SDN1)
Buffalo Regional Office
130 South Elmwood Avenue
Buffalo, NY 14202

New York Regional Office
245 West Houston Street
New York, NY 10014

North Carolina (SDN 4)
Winston-Salem Regional Office
Federal Building
251 North Main Street
Winston-Salem, NC 27155

North Dakota (SDN 6)
Fargo Regional Office
2101 North Elm Street
Fargo, ND 58102

Ohio (SDN 2)
Cleveland Regional Office
A.J. Celebrezze Federal Building
1240 East 9th Street
Cleveland, OH 44199

Oklahoma (SDN 7)
Muskogee Regional Office
125 South Main Street
Muskogee, OK 74401

Oregon (SDN 8)
Portland Regional Office
1220 SW 3rd Avenue
Portland, OR 97204

Pennsylvania (SDN 2)
Philadelphia Regional Office
5000 Wissahickon Avenue
Philadelphia, PA 19101

Pittsburgh Regional Office
1000 Liberty Avenue
Pittsburgh, PA 15222

Rhode Island (SDN 1)
Providence Regional Office
380 Westminster Mall
Providence, RI 02903

South Carolina (SDN 4)
Columbia Regional Office
1801 Assembly Street
Columbia, SC 29201

South Dakota (SDN 6)
Sioux Falls Regional Office
PO Box 5046
2501 West 22nd Street
Sioux Falls, SD 57117

Tennessee (SDN 4)
Nashville Regional Office
110 9th Avenue South
Nashville, TN 37203

Southern Area Office
3322 West End, Suite 408
Nashville, TN 37203

Texas (SDN 7)
Houston Regional Office
6900 Almeda Road
Houston, TX 77030

Waco Regional Office
1 Veterans Plaza
701 Clay Avenue
Waco, TX 76799

Utah (SDN 8)
Salt Lake City Regional Office
550 Foothill Drive
Salt Lake City, UT 84158

Vermont (SDN 1)
White River Junction
Regional Office
North Hartland Road
White River Junction, VT 05009

Virginia (SDN 3)
Roanoke Regional Office
210 Franklin Road SW
Roanoke, VA 24011

Washington (SDN 8)
Seattle Regional Office
Federal Building
915 2nd Avenue
Seattle, WA 98174

West Virginia (SDN 3)
Huntington Regional Office
640 Fourth Avenue
Huntington, WV 25701

Wisconsin (SDN 6)
Milwaukee Regional Office
5400 West National Avenue
Milwaukee, WI 53214

Wyoming (SDN 8)
Cheyenne Regional Office
2360 East Pershing Blvd.
Cheyenne, WY 82001

District of Columbia (SDN 3)
Washington DC Regional Office
1722 I Street N.W.
Washington, DC 20421

Puerto Rico (SDN 5)
San Juan Regional Office
150 Carlos Chardon Avenue
Hato Rey, Puerto Rico 00918

Philippines (SDN 9)
Manila Regional Office
1131 Roxas Boulevard, Ermita
0930 Manila, Philippines 96440

Note: SDN = Service Delivery Network

CHAPTER 37

STATE BENEFITS

Many states offer services and benefits to veterans in addition to those offered by the Department of Veterans' Affairs. To find out more about a particular state's programs, individuals should contact the following:

Alabama Department of Veterans' Affairs
P.O. Box 1509
770 Washington Ave, Suite 530
Montgomery, AL 36102-1509
(334) 242-5077

Alaska Department of Veterans' Affairs
P.O. Box 5800
Fort Richardson, AK 99505-5800
(907) 428-6031

Arizona Department of Veterans' Services
3839 North Third Street, Suite 200
Phoenix, AZ 85012
(602) 225-3373

Arkansas Department of Veterans' Affairs
2200 Fort Roots Drive
Room 119 – Bldg 65
North Little Rock, AR 72114
(501) 370-3820

California Department of Veterans' Affairs
1227 O Street, Suite 300
Sacramento, CA 95814
1-800-952-5626

Colorado Division of Veterans' Affairs
789 Sherman Street, Suite 260
Denver, CO 80203-1714
(303) 894-7474

Connecticut Department of Veterans' Affairs
287 West Street
Rocky Hill, CT 06067
(860) 529-2571

Delaware Commission of Veterans' Affairs
Robbins Building
802 Silverlake Blvd, Suite 100
Dover, DE 19904
(302) 739-2792
1-800-344-9900 (in state only)

Florida Department of Veterans' Affairs
Mary Grizzle Building, Room 311-K
11351 Ulmerton Road
Largo, FL 33778
(727) 518-3202

Georgia Department of Veterans' Affairs
Floyd Veterans Memorial Building
Suite E-970
Atlanta, GA 30334
(404) 656-2300

Hawaii Office of Veterans' Services
Mailing Address:
459 Patterson Road
E-Wing, Room 1-A103
Honolulu, HI 96819
Location:
Tripler Army Med Center (Ward Road)
VAMROC, E-Wing, Room 1-A103
Honolulu, HI 96819
(808) 433-0420

Idaho Division of Veterans' Affairs
320 Collins Road
Boise, ID 83702
(208) 334-3513

Illinois Department of Veterans' Affairs
P.O. Box 19432
833 South Spring Street
Springfield, IL 62794-9432
(217) 785-4114

Indiana Department of Veterans' Affairs
302 West Washington, Room E120
Indianapolis, IN 46204-2738
(317) 232-3910

Iowa Commission of Veterans' Affairs
7105 N.W. 70th Avenue
Camp Dodge - Building A6A
Johnston, IA 50131-1824
(515) 242-5331

Kansas Commission on Veterans' Affairs
Jayhawk Towers
Suite 701
700 S.W. Jackson Street
Topeka, KS 66603-3714
(785) 296-3976

Kentucky Department of Veterans' Affairs
1111 Louisville Road
NGAKY Building
Frankfort, KY 40601
(502) 564-9203

Louisiana Department of Veterans' Affairs
P.O. Box 94095
Capitol Station
1885 Wooddale Blvd.
10th Floor, Room 1013
Baton Rouge, LA 70806
(225) 922-0500

Maine Bureau of Veterans' Services
117 State House Station
Camp Keyes Building 7, Room 115
Augusta, ME 04333
(207) 626-4464

Maryland Department of Veterans' Affairs
Room 110, Federal Building
31 Hopkins Plaza
Baltimore, MD 21201
(800) 446-4926

Massachusetts Department of Veterans' Services
600 Washington Street, Suite 1100
Boston, MA 02111
(617) 210-5480

Michigan Department of Veterans' Affairs
7109 W. Saginaw
Lansing, MI 48913
(517) 335-6523

Minnesota Department of Veterans' Affairs
State Veterans Service Building
20 West 12th Street, 2nd Floor
St. Paul, MN 55155-2079
(651) 296-2562

Mississippi State Veterans' Affairs Board
3466 Highway 80 East
P.O. Box 5947
Pearl, MS 39288-5947
(601) 576-4850

Missouri Veterans' Commission
Mailing Address:
Post Drawer 147
Jefferson City, MO 65102-0147
Location:
1719 Southridge Drive
Jefferson City, MO 65109
(573) 751-3779

Montana Veterans' Affairs Division
P.O. Box 5715
1900 Williams Street
Helena, MT 59604
(406) 324-3740

Nebraska Department of Veterans' Affairs
State Office Building
301 Centennial Mall South
P.O. Box 95083
Lincoln, NE 68509-5083
(402) 471-2458

Nevada Commission for Veterans' Affairs
1201 Terminal Way, Room 215
Reno, NV 89502
(775) 688-1653

New Hampshire State Veterans' Council
275 Chestnut Street
Room 321
Manchester, NH 03101-2411
(603) 624-9230
1-800-622-9230 (in state only)

New Jersey Department of Veterans' Affairs
Eggert Crossing Road
PO Box 340
Trenton, NJ 08625-0508
(800) 624-0508

New Mexico Veterans' Service Commission
P. O. Box 2324
Santa Fe, NM 87504
(505) 827-6300

New York Division of Veterans' Affairs
5 Empire State Plaza
Suite 2836
Albany, NY 12223-1551
(518) 474-6114

North Carolina Division of Veterans' Affairs
Albemarle Building, Suite 1065
1315 Mail Service Center
325 North Salisbury Street
Raleigh, NC 27699-1315
(919) 733-3851

North Dakota Department of Veterans' Affairs
P.O. Box 9003
1411 32nd Street, South
Fargo, ND 58106-9003
(701) 239-7165

Ohio Governor's Office of Veterans' Affairs
77 South High Street
Columbus, OH 43215
(614) 644-0898

Oklahoma Department of Veterans' Affairs
2311 N. Central Avenue
Oklahoma City, OK 73105
(405) 521-3684

Oregon Department of Veterans' Affairs
700 Summer Street, NE
Salem, OR 97310-1285
(503) 373-2000

Pennsylvania Department of Veterans' Affairs
Fort Indiantown Gap
Building S-O-47
Annville, PA 17003-5002
(717) 861-2000

Rhode Island Division of Veterans' Affairs
480 Metacom Avenue
Bristol, RI 02809
(401) 462-0324

South Carolina Office of Veterans' Affairs
1205 Pendleton Street, Suite 369
Columbia, SC 29201
(803) 734-0200

South Dakota Division of Veterans' Affairs
425 East Capitol Avenue
c/o 500 East Capitol Avenue
Pierre, SD 57501
(605) 773-4981

Tennessee Department of Veterans' Affairs
215 Eighth Avenue North
Nashville, TN 37243-1010
(615) 741-6663

Texas Veterans' Commission
P.O. Box 12277
Austin, TX 78711
1-800-252-8387

Utah Division of Veterans' Affairs
550 Foothill Blvd, Room 206
Salt Lake City, UT 84108
(801) 326-2372

Vermont State Veterans' Affairs
118 State Street
Montpelier, VT 05620-4401
(802) 828-3379

Virginia Department of Veterans' Affairs
900 East Main Street
Richmond, VA 23219
(804) 786-0286

Washington Department of Veterans' Affairs
P.O. Box 41150
1011 Plum Street
Olympia, WA 98504-1150
1-800-562-0132

West Virginia Division of Veterans' Affairs
1321 Plaza East, Suite 101
Charleston, WV 25301-1400
(304) 558-3661

Wisconsin Department of Veterans' Affairs
30 West Mifflin Street
Madison, WI 53703
(608) 266-1311

Wyoming Veterans' Affairs Commission
Wyoming ANG Armory
5905 CY Avenue - Room 101
Casper, WY 82604
(307) 265-7372

American Samoa Veterans' Affairs
P. O. Box 8586
Pago Pago
American Samoa 96799
(001) 684-633-4206

Guam Veterans' Affairs Office
Mailing Address:
P.O. Box 3279
Agana, Guam 96932
(671) 475-4222
Location:
"M" Street
HSE #105
Tiyan, Guam

Puerto Rico Public Advocate for Veterans' Affairs
Mailing Address:
Apartado 11737
Fernandez Juncos Station
San Juan, PR 00910-1737
Location:
Mercantile Plaza Bldg,
Fourth Floor, Suite 4021
Hato Rey, PR 00918-1625
(787) 758-5760

Government of the Virgin Islands Division of Veterans' Affairs
1013 Estate Richmond
Christiansted, St. Croix VI 00820-4349
(340) 773-6663

CHAPTER 38

WHERE TO OBTAIN MILITARY PERSONNEL RECORDS

The U.S. Department of Veterans Affairs does not maintain veterans' military service records.

The personnel records of individuals currently in the military service, in the reserve forces, and those completely separated from military service are located in different offices. A nominal fee is charged for certain types of service. In most instances service fees cannot be determined in advance. If your request involves a service fee you will be notified as soon as that determination is made.

> *The personnel records of individuals currently in the military service, in the reserve forces, and those completely separated from military service are located in different offices.*

A veteran and spouse should be aware of the location of the veteran's discharge and separation papers. If a veteran cannot locate discharge and separation papers, duplicate copies may be obtained (further information regarding who to contact is included later in this chapter).

Use Standard Form 180, *Request Pertaining To Military Records*, which is available from VA offices and veterans organizations. Specify that a duplicate separation document or discharge is needed. The veteran's full name should be printed or typed so that it can be read clearly, but the request must also contain the signature of the veteran or the signature of the next of kin, if the veteran is deceased. Include branch of service, service number or Social Security number and exact or approximate date and years of service.

It is not necessary to request a duplicate copy of a veteran's discharge or separation papers solely for the purpose of filing a claim for VA benefits. If complete information about the veteran's service is furnished on the application, VA will obtain verification of service from the National Personnel Records Center or the service department concerned.

WHO TO CONTACT

The various categories of military personnel records are described in the tables below. Please read the following notes carefully, to make sure an inquiry is sent to the right address. Please note especially that the record is not sent to the National Personnel Records Center as long as the person retains any sort of reserve obligation, whether drilling or non-drilling.

Special Notes For Following Tables:

- **Records at the National Personnel Records Center:** Note that it takes at least 3 months, and often 6 or 7, for the file to reach the National Personnel Records Center after the military obligation has ended (such as by discharge). If only a short time has passed, please send the inquiry to the address shown for active or current reserve members. Also, if the person has only been released from active duty, but is still in a reserve status, the personnel record will stay at the location specified for reservists. A person can retain a reserve obligation for several years, even without attending meetings or receiving annual training.

- If there were two or more periods of service within the same branch, send your request (only one is necessary) to the office having the records for the LAST PERIOD OF SERVICE.)

LOCATION OF AIR FORCE MILITARY PERSONNEL & HEALTH RECORDS

Status of Service Member or Veteran	Location of Personnel Record	Location of Health Record
Discharged, deceased, or retired before 5/1/1994	National Personnel Records Center Military Personnel Records 9700 Page Avenue St. Louis, MO 63132-5100 (314) 801-0800	National Personnel Records Center Military Personnel Records 9700 Page Avenue St. Louis, MO 63132-5100 (314) 801-0800
Discharged, deceased, or retired on or after 5/1/1994	National Personnel Records Center Military Personnel Records 9700 Page Avenue St. Louis, MO 63132-5100 (314) 801-0800	Department of Veterans Affairs Records Management Center PO Box 5020 St Louis MO 63115 (314) 538-4500
Active (including National Guard on active duty in the Air Force), TDRL, or general officers retired with pay	Air Force Personnel Center HQ AFPC/DPSRP 550 C Street West Suite 19 Randolph AFB, TX 78150 (800) 616-3775	
Reserve, retired reserve in nonpay status, current National Guard officers not on active duty in the Air Force, or National Guard released from active duty in the Air Force	Air Reserve Personnel Center /DSMR HQ ARPC/DPSSA/B 6760 E. Irvington Place, Suite 4600 Denver, CO 80280-4600 (800) 525-0102	
Current Air National Guard enlisted not on active duty in the Air Force	Adjutant General of your state	

LOCATION OF ARMY MILITARY PERSONNEL & HEALTH RECORDS

Status of Service Member or Veteran	Location of Personnel Record	Location of Health Record
Discharged, deceased, or retired (Enlisted) before 11/1/1912	The National Archive's Old Military and Civil Records Branch (NWCTB-Military) Washington, DC 20408	
Discharged, deceased, or retired (Officer) before 7/1/1917	The National Archive's Old Military and Civil Records Branch (NWCTB-Military) Washington, DC 20408	
Discharged, deceased, or retired (Enlisted) 11/1/1912 – 10/15/1992	National Personnel Records Center Military Personnel Records 9700 Page Avenue St. Louis, MO 63132 (314) 801-0800	National Personnel Records Center Military Personnel Records 9700 Page Avenue St. Louis, MO 63132 (314) 801-0800
Discharged, deceased, or retired (Officer) 7/1/1917 – 10/15/1992	National Personnel Records Center Military Personnel Records 9700 Page Avenue St. Louis, MO 63132 (314) 801-0800	National Personnel Records Center Military Personnel Records 9700 Page Avenue St. Louis, MO 63132 (314) 801-0800
Discharged, deceased, or retired on or after 10/16/1992	National Personnel Records Center Military Personnel Records 9700 Page Avenue St. Louis, MO 63132 (314) 801-0800	Department of Veterans Affairs Records Management Center PO Box 5020 St Louis MO 63115-5020 314-538-4500
Reserve; or active duty records of current National Guard members who performed service in the U.S. Army before 7/1/1972	Commander U.S. Army Personnel Command ATTN: ARPC-ZCC-B 1 Reserve Way St. Louis, MO 62132-5200	
Active enlisted (including National Guard on active duty in the U.S. Army) or TDRL enlisted	Commander USAEREC ATTN: PCRE-F 8899 E. 56th St. Indianapolis, IN 46249	
Active officers (including National	U.S. Total Army Personnel Command	

Status of Service Member or Veteran	Location of Personnel Record	Location of Health Record
Guard on active duty in the U.S. Army) or TDRL officers	ATTN: TAPC-MSR-S 200 Stoval Street Alexandria, VA 22332	
Current National Guard enlisted not on active duty in Army (including records of Army active duty performed after 6/30/1972)	Adjutant General of your state	
Current National Guard officers not on active duty in Army (including records of Army active duty performed after 6/30/1972)	Army National Guard Readiness Center NGB-ARP 111 S. George Mason Dr. Arlington, VA 22204-1382	

LOCATION OF COAST GUARD MILITARY PERSONNEL & HEALTH RECORDS

Status of Service Member or Veteran	Location of Personnel Record	Location of Health Record
Discharged, deceased, or retired before 1/1/1898	The National Archive's Old Military and Civil Records Branch (NWCTB-Military) Washington, DC 20408	
Discharged, deceased, or retired: 1/1/1898 – 3/31/1998	National Personnel Records Center Military Personnel Records 9700 Page Avenue St. Louis, MO 63132-5100 (314) 801-0800	National Personnel Records Center Military Personnel Records 9700 Page Avenue St. Louis, MO 63132-5100 (314) 801-0800
Discharged, deceased, or retired on or after: 4/1/1998	National Personnel Records Center Military Personnel Records 9700 Page Avenue St. Louis, MO 63132-5100 (314) 801-0800	Department of Veterans Affairs Records Management Center PO Box 5020 St Louis MO 63115-5020 (314) 538-4500
Active, reserve, or TDRL	Commander, CGPC-adm-3 USCG Personnel Command	

Status of Service Member or Veteran	Location of Personnel Record	Location of Health Record
	4200 Wilson Blvd. Suite 1100 Arlington, VA 22203-1804	

LOCATION OF MARINE CORPS MILITARY PERSONNEL & HEALTH RECORDS

Status of Service Member or Veteran	Location of Personnel Record	Location of Health Record
Discharged, deceased, or retired before 1/1/1905	The National Archive's Old Military and Civil Records Branch (NWCTB-Military) Washington, DC 20408	
Discharged, deceased, or retired (Enlisted): 1906 – 9/8/1939	Archival Program Division National Personnel Records Center 9700 Page Avenue St. Louis, MO 63132-5100	National Personnel Records Center Military Personnel Records 9700 Page Avenue St. Louis, MO 63132-5100 (314) 801-0800
Discharged, deceased, or retired (Officer): 1/1/1905 – 4/30/1994	National Personnel Records Center Military Personnel Records 9700 Page Avenue St. Louis, MO 63132-5100 (314) 801-0800	National Personnel Records Center Military Personnel Records 9700 Page Avenue St. Louis, MO 63132-5100 (314) 801-0800
Discharged, deceased, or retired (Enlisted): 9/9/1939 – 4/30/1994	National Personnel Records Center Military Personnel Records 9700 Page Avenue St. Louis, MO 63132-5100 (314) 801-0800	National Personnel Records Center Military Personnel Records 9700 Page Avenue St. Louis, MO 63132-5100 (314) 801-0800
Discharged, deceased, or retired on or after: 5/1/1994	National Personnel Records Center Military Personnel Records 9700 Page Avenue St. Louis, MO 63132-5100 (314) 801-0800	Department of Veterans Affairs Records Management Center PO Box 5020 St Louis MO 63115-5020 (314) 538-4500
Active, Selected Marine Corps Reserve, TDRL	Headquarters U.S. Marine Corps Personnel Management Support Branch (MMSB) 2008 Elliot Road	

Status of Service Member or Veteran	Location of Personnel Record	Location of Health Record
	Quantico, VA 22134-5030 Phone: 800-268-3710	
Individual Ready Reserve or Fleet Marine Corps Reserve	Marine Corps Reserve Support Command (Code MMI) 15303 Andrews Road Kansas City, MO 64147 Phone: 800-255-5082	

LOCATION OF NAVY MILITARY PERSONNEL & HEALTH RECORDS

Status of Service Member or Veteran	Location of Personnel Record	Location of Health Record
Discharged, deceased, or retired (Enlisted) before 1/1/1885	The National Archive's Old Military and Civil Records Branch (NWCTB-Military) Washington, DC 20408	
Discharged, deceased, or retired (Officer) before 1/1/1903	The National Archive's Old Military and Civil Records Branch (NWCTB-Military) Washington, DC 20408	
Discharged, deceased, or retired (Enlisted): 1885 – 9/8/1939	The National Archive's Old Military and Civil Records Branch (NWCTB-Military) Washington, DC 20408	The National Archive's Old Military and Civil Records Branch (NWCTB-Military) Washington, DC 20408
Discharged, deceased, or retired (Enlisted) 9/9/1939 – 1/30/1994	National Personnel Records Center Military Personnel Records 9700 Page Avenue St. Louis, MO 63132-5100 (314) 801-0800	National Personnel Records Center Military Personnel Records 9700 Page Avenue St. Louis, MO 63132-5100 (314) 801-0800
Discharged, deceased, or retired (Officer) 1/1/1903 – 1/30/1994	National Personnel Records Center Military Personnel Records 9700 Page Avenue St. Louis, MO 63132-5100 (314) 801-0800	National Personnel Records Center Military Personnel Records 9700 Page Avenue St. Louis, MO 63132-5100 (314) 801-0800
Discharged, deceased, or retired	National Personnel Records Center	Department of Veterans Affairs

Status of Service Member or Veteran	Location of Personnel Record	Location of Health Record
1/31/1994 – 12/31/1994	Military Personnel Records 9700 Page Avenue St. Louis, MO 63132-5100 (314) 801-0800	Records Management Center PO Box 5020 St Louis MO 63115-5020 (314) 538-4500
Discharged, deceased, or retired on or after: 1/1/1995 (* see note on Navy Records from 1995 on)	Navy Personnel Command (PERS-313C1) 5720 Integrity Drive Millington, TN 38055 (901) 874-4885	Department of Veterans Affairs Records Management Center PO Box 5020 St Louis MO 63115-5020 (314) 538-4500
Active, reserve, or TDRL	Navy Personnel Command (PERS-313C1) 5720 Integrity Drive Millington, TN 38055 (901) 874-4885	
Naval Reserve members NOT currently on active duty, including those in the Ready Reserve (SELRES/IRR) and Standby Reserves (USNR-S1/USNR-S2)	Naval Reserve Personnel Command 4400 Dauphine Street New Orleans, LA 70149 (866)250-4778	

NOTE: Beginning in 1995, the United States Navy no longer retires military personnel records to the NPRC (MPR). For the conversion period between 1995 and 1997, either the NPRC or the Navy may hold the record, but it is recommended that all requests relating to Navy personnel discharged, deceased, or retired from 1995 to the present contact:

Navy Personnel Command
PERS-313C1, 5720 Integrity Drive
Millington, TN 38055-3130.

FACTS ABOUT THE 1973 ST. LOUIS FIRE AND LOST RECORDS

A fire at the NPRC in St. Louis on July 12, 1973, destroyed about 80 percent of the records for Army personnel discharged between November 1, 1912, and January 1, 1960. About 75 percent of the records for Air Force personnel with surnames from "Hubbard" through "Z" discharged between September 25, 1947, and January 1, 1964, were also destroyed.

What Was Lost

It is hard to determine exactly what was lost in the fire, because:
- There were no indices to the blocks of records involved. The records were merely filed in alphabetical order for the following groups:

- World War I: Army November 1, 1912 - September 7, 1939

- World War II: Army September 8, 1939 - December 31, 1946

- Post World War II: Army January 1, 1947 - December 31, 1959

- Air Force September 25, 1947 - December 31, 1963

- Millions of records, especially medical records, had been withdrawn from all three groups and loaned to the Department of Veterans Affairs (VA) before the fire. The fact that one's records are not in NPRC files at a particular time does not mean the records were destroyed in the fire.

Reconstruction of Lost Records

If veterans learn that their records may have been lost in the fire, they may send photocopies of any documents they possess -- especially separation documents -- to the NPRC at:

National Personnel Records Center
Military Personnel Records
9700 Page Blvd.
St. Louis, MO 63132-5100.

Alternate Sources of Military Service Data

When veterans don't have copies of their military records and their NPRC files may have been lost in the St. Louis fire, essential information about their military service may be available from a number of other sources, including:

- The Department of Veterans Affairs (VA) maintains records on veterans whose military records were affected by the fire if the veteran or a beneficiary filed a claim before July 1973.

- Service information may also be found in various kinds of "organizational" records such as unit morning reports, payrolls and military orders on file at the NPRC or other National Archives and Records Administration facilities.

- There also is a great deal of information available in records of the State Adjutants General, and other state "veterans services" offices.

By using alternate sources, NPRC often can reconstruct a veteran's beginning and ending dates of active service, the character of service, rank, time lost on active duty, and periods of hospitalization. NPRC can issue NA Form 13038, "Certification of Military Service," considered the equivalent of a Form DD-214, "Report of Separation From Active Duty," to use in establishing eligibility for veterans benefits.

Necessary Information for File Reconstruction

The key to reconstructing military data is to give the NPRC enough specific information so the staff can properly search the various sources. The following information is normally required:

- Full name used during military service;
- Place of entry into service;
- Branch of service;
- Last unit of assignment;
- Approximate dates of service;
- Place of discharge;
- Service number or Social Security number.

CHAPTER 39

CORRECTION OF RECORDS BY CORRECTION BOARDS

Retirees may feel that their records need correcting or amending for any number of reasons. Correction boards consider formal applications for corrections of military records.

Each service department has a permanent Board for Correction of Military (Naval) records, composed of civilians, to act on applications for correction of records.

In order to justify correction of a military record, the applicant must prove to a Corrections Board that the alleged entry or omission in the record was in error or unjust. This board considers all applications and makes recommendations to the appropriate branch Secretary.

An application for correction of record must be filed within three years after discovering the error or injustice. If filed after the three-year deadline, the applicant must include in the application reasons the board should find it in the interest of justice to accept the late application.

Evidence may include affidavits or signed testimony executed under oath, and a brief of arguments supporting the application. All evidence not already included in one's record must be submitted. The responsibility for securing new evidence rests with the applicant.

JURISDICTION

Correction boards are empowered to deal with all matters relating to error or injustice in official records. The boards cannot act until all other administrative avenues of relief have been exhausted. Discharges by sentence of Special Court-Martial and administrative discharges cannot be considered by correction boards unless:

- Application to the appropriate Discharge Review Board has been denied and rehearing is barred; or

- Application cannot be made to the Discharge review Board because the time limit has expired.

APPLICATION

DD Form 149, Application for Correction of Military or Naval record, must be used to apply for correction of military records. It should be submitted, along with supporting evidence, to one of the review boards listed below:

Army
Army Review Boards Agency (ARBA)
ATTN: Client Information and Quality Assurance
Arlington, VA 22202-4508
(703) 607-1600

Navy & Marine Corps
Board for Correction of Naval Records
2 Navy Annex, Room 2432
Washington, DC 20370-5100
(703) 614-1402

Coast Guard
Board for Correction of Military Records (C-60)
Room 4100
400 7th Street SW
Washington, DC 20590
(202) 366-9335

Air Force
Air Force Board for Correction of Military Records
1535 Command Drive
EE Wing 3rd Floor
Andrews AFB DC 20331-7002

DECISIONS

In the absence of new and material evidence the decision of a correction board, as approved or modified by the Secretary of the Service Department, is final. Adverse decisions are subject to judicial review in a U.S. District Court. Decisions of the Boards for Correction of Military or Naval Records must be made available for public inspection. Copies of the decisional documents will be provided on request.

CHAPTER 40

DISCHARGE REVIEW

DISCHARGE REVIEW BOARDS

Each branch of service has discharge review boards to review the discharge or dismissal of former service members. (The Navy Board considers Marine Corps cases.)

Authority

Discharge review boards can, based on the official records and such other evidence as may be presented, upgrade a discharge or change the reason and authority for discharge. Discharge review boards cannot grant disability retirement, revoke a discharge, reinstate any person in the service, recall any person to active duty, act on requests for re-enlistment code changes or review a discharge issued by sentence of a general court-martial. Discharge review boards have no authority to address medical discharges.

Application

DD Form 293, *Application for Review of Discharge or Dismissal from the Armed Forces of the United States*, is used to apply for review of discharge. (If more than 15 years have passed since discharge, DD Form 149 should be used.) The individual or, if legal proof of death is provided, the surviving spouse, next-of-kin, or legal representative can apply. If the individual is mentally incompetent, the spouse, next-of-kin, or legal representative can sign the application, but must provide legal proof of incompetence. The instruction for completing DD Form 293 must be read and complied with.

Time Limitation

Initial application to a discharge review board must be made within 15 years after the date of discharge.

Personal Appearance

A personal appearance before the Discharge Review Board is a legal right. A minimum 30-day notice of the scheduled hearing date is given unless the applicant waives the advance notice in writing. Reasonable postponements can be arranged if circumstances preclude appearance on the scheduled date. All expenses of appearing before the board must be paid by the applicant. If no postponement of a scheduled hearing date is requested and the applicant does not appear on the date scheduled, the right to a personal hearing is forfeited and the case will be considered on the evidence of record.

Hearings

Discharge review boards conduct hearings at various locations in the U.S. Information concerning hearing locations and availability of counsel can be obtained by writing to the appropriate board at the address shown on DD Form 293. Those addresses are listed at the end of this chapter.

Published Uniform Standards For Discharge Review

A review of discharge is conducted to determine if an individual was properly and equitably discharged. Each case is considered on its own merits.

- A discharge is considered to have been proper unless the discharge review determines:

- That there is an error of fact, law, procedures, or discretion which prejudiced the rights of the individual, or

- That there has been a change of policy which requires a change of discharge.

- A discharge is considered to have been equitable unless the discharge review determines:

- That the policies and procedures under which the individual was discharged are materially different from current policies and procedures and that the individual probably would have received a better discharge if the current policies and procedures had been in effect at the time of discharge; or

- That the discharge was inconsistent with the standards of discipline; or

- That the overall evidence before the review board warrants a change of discharge. In arriving at this determination, the discharge review board will consider the quality and the length of the service performed, the individual's physical and mental capability to serve satisfactorily, abuses of authority which may have contributed to the character of the discharge issued, and documented discriminatory acts against the individual.

Decisions

An authenticated decisional document is prepared and a copy provided to each applicant and council.

- A copy of each decisional document, with identifying details of the applicant and other persons deleted to protect personal privacy, must be made available for public inspection and copying. These are located in a reading room in the Pentagon, Washington, DC.

- To provide access to the documents by persons outside the Washington,. D.C. area, the documents have been indexed. The index includes case number of each case; the date, authority and reason for, and character if the discharge, and the issues addressed in the statement of findings, conclusions and reasons.

- Interested parties may contact the DVARO or the State veterans Agency for the location of an index. A copy of the index will be made available at the sites of traveling board hearings during the period the board is present.

- An individual can go through the index and identify cases in which the circumstances leading to discharge are similar to those in the individual's case. A copy of these case decisional documents can be requested by writing to:

DA Military Review Boards Agency
ATTN: SFBA (Reading Room)
Room 1E520
The Pentagon
Washington, D.C. 20310.

Examination of decisional documents may help to identify the kind of evidence that was used in the case, and may indicate why relief was granted or denied. Decisional documents do not set precedence - each case is considered on its own merits.

Reconsideration

An application that has been denied can be reopened if:

- The applicant submits newly discovered evidence that was not available at the time of the original consideration.

- The applicant did not request a personal hearing in the original application and now desires to appear before the board. If the applicant fails to appear at the hearings, the case will be closed with no further action.

- The applicant was not represented by counsel in the original consideration and now desires counsel and the application for reconsideration is submitted within 15 years following the date of discharge.

- Changes in policy, law or regulations have occurred or federal court orders have been issued which substantially enhance the rights of the applicant.

SERVICE DEPARTMENT DISCHARGE REVIEW BOARD ADDRESSES

Army

Army Discharge Review Board
Attention: SFMR-RBB
1901 South Bell Street, 2nd Floor
Arlington, VA 22202-4508

Navy & USMC

Navy Discharge Review Board
801 North Randolph Street
Suite 905
Arlington, VA 22203

Air Force

Air Force Military Personnel Center
Attention: DP-MDOA1
Randolph AFB, TX 78150-6001

Coast Guard

Coast Guard
Attention: GPE1
Washington, DC 20593

CHAPTER 41

PENAL AND FORFEITURE PROVISIONS

VA benefits are restricted if a veteran, surviving spouse, child, or dependent parent is convicted of a felony and imprisoned for more than 60 days.

The first section of this chapter outlines basic information for veterans with questions concerning the effect of incarceration on VA benefits. The later sections of this chapter provide detailed information regarding misappropriation by fiduciaries, fraudulent acceptance of payments, forfeiture for fraud, forfeiture for treason, and forfeiture for subversive activities.

BASIC INFORMATION

VA benefits are restricted if a veteran, surviving spouse, child, or dependent parent is convicted of a felony and imprisoned for more than 60 days. VA may still pay certain benefits, however, the amount paid depends on the type of benefit and reason for imprisonment. Following is information about the benefits most commonly affected by imprisonment.

Please note that overpayments due to failure to notify VA of a veteran's incarceration results in the loss of all financial benefits until the overpayment is recovered.

VA DISABILITY COMPENSATION

The disability compensation paid to a veteran incarcerated because of a felony is limited to the 10% disability rate, beginning with the 61st day of imprisonment. For a surviving spouse, child, dependent parent or veteran whose disability rating is 10%, the payment is at the 5% rate. (This means that if a veteran was receiving $188 or more prior to incarceration, the new payment amount will be $98. If a veteran was receiving $98 before incarceration, the new payment amount will be $49.)

If a veteran resides in a halfway house, participates in a work release program, or is on parole, compensation payments will not be reduced.

VA DISABILITY PENSION

VA will stop a veteran's pension payments beginning on the 61st day of imprisonment for conviction of either a felony or misdemeanor.

VA MEDICAL CARE

While incarcerated veterans do not forfeit their eligibility for medical care, current regulations restrict VA from providing hospital and outpatient care to an incarcerated veteran who is an inmate in an institution of another government agency when that agency has a duty to give the care or services.

However, VA may provide care once the veteran has been unconditionally released from the penal institution. Veterans interested in applying for enrollment into the VA health care system should contact the nearest VA health care facility upon their release.

EDUCATIONAL ASSISTANCE / SUBSISTENCE ALLOWANCE

A subsistence allowance may not be paid to an incarcerated veteran convicted of a felony, buy, under certain circumstances, all or part of the veteran's tuition and fees may be paid. Individuals should contact the VA to determine individual eligibility.

CLOTHING ALLOWANCE

In the case of a veteran who is incarcerated in a Federal, State, or local penal institution for a period in excess of 60 days and who is furnished clothing without charge by the institution, the amount of any annual clothing allowance payable to the veteran shall be reduced by an amount equal to 1/365 of the amount of the allowance otherwise payable under that section for each day on which the veteran was so incarcerated during the 12-month period preceding the date on which payment of the allowance would be due.

PAYMENT TO DEPENDENTS

VA may be able to take part of the amount that the incarcerated veteran is not receiving and pay it to his or her dependents, if they can show need. Interested dependents should contact the nearest VA regional office for details on how to apply. They will be asked to provide income information as part of the application process.

RESTORATION OF BENEFITS

When a veteran is released from prison, his or her compensation or pension benefits may be restored. Depending on the type of disability, the VA may schedule a medical examination to see if the veteran's disability has improved or worsened.

MISAPPROPRIATION BY FIDUCIARIES

Whoever, being a guardian, curator, conservator, committee, or person legally vested with the responsibility or care of a claimant or a claimant's estate, or any other person having charge and custody in a fiduciary capacity of money heretofore or hereafter paid under any of the laws administered by the VA for the benefit of any minor, incompetent, or other beneficiary, shall lend, borrow, pledge, hypothecate, use, or exchange for other funds or property, except as authorized by law, or embezzle or in any manner misappropriate any such money or property derived wherefrom in whole or in part, and coming into such fiduciary's control in any matter whatever in the execution of such fiduciary's trust, or under color of such fiduciary's office or service as such fiduciary, shall be fined in accordance with Title 18, or imprisoned not more than 5 ye4ars, or both.

Any willful neglect or refusal to make and file proper accountings or reports concerning such money or property as required by law shall be taken to be sufficient evidence prima facie of such embezzlement or misappropriation.

FRAUDULENT ACCEPTANCE OF PAYMENTS

Any person entitled to monetary benefits under any of the laws administered by the VA whose right to payment ceases upon the happening of any contingency, who thereafter fraudulently accepts any such payment, shall be fined in accordance with Title 18, or imprisoned not more than one year, or both.

Whoever obtains or receives any money or check under any of the laws administered by the VA without being entitled to it, and with intent to defraud the United States or any beneficiary of the United States, shall be fined in accordance with Title 18, or imprisoned not more than one year, or both.

FORFEITURE FOR FRAUD

Whoever knowingly makes or causes to be made or conspires, combines, aids, or assists in, agrees to, arranges for, or in any way procures the making or presentation of a false or fraudulent affidavit, declaration, certificate, statement, voucher, or paper, concerning any claim for benefits under any of the laws administered by the VA (except laws pertaining to insurance benefits) shall forfeit all rights, claims, and benefits under all laws administered by the VA (except laws pertaining to insurance benefits).

Whenever a veteran entitled to disability compensation has forfeited the right to such compensation under this chapter, the compensation payable but for the forfeiture shall thereafter be paid to the veteran's spouse, children, and parents. Payments made to a spouse, children, and parents under the preceding sentence shall not exceed the amounts payable to each if the veteran had died from service-connected disability. No spouse, child, or parent who participated in the fraud for which forfeiture was imposed shall receive any payment by reason of this subsection. Any apportionment award under this subsection may not be made in any case after September 1, 1959.

Forfeiture of benefits by a veteran shall not prohibit payment of the burial allowance, death compensation, dependency and indemnity compensation, or death pension in the event of the veteran's death.

After September 1, 1959, no forfeiture of benefits may be imposed under the rules outlined in this chapter upon any individual who was a resident of, or domiciled in, a State at the time the act or acts occurred on account of which benefits would, but not for this subsection, be forfeited unless such individual ceases to be a resident of, or domiciled in, a State before the expiration of the period during which criminal prosecution could be instituted. The paragraph shall not apply with respect to:

- Any forfeiture occurring before September 1, 1959; or

- An act or acts that occurred in the Philippine Islands before July 4, 1946.

The VA is authorized and directed to review all cases in which, because of a false or fraudulent affidavit, declaration, certificate, statement, voucher, or paper, a forfeiture of gratuitous benefits under laws administered by the VA was imposed, pursuant to this section or prior provisions of the law, on or before September 1, 1959. In any such case in which the VA determines that the forfeiture would not have been imposed under the provisions of this section in effect after September 1, 1959, the VA shall remit the forfeiture, effective June 30, 1972. Benefits to which the individual concerned becomes eligible by virtue of any such remission may be awarded, upon application for, and the effective date of any award of compensation, dependency and indemnity compensation, or pension made in such a case shall be fixed in accordance with the facts found, but shall not be earlier than the effective date of the Act or administrative issue. In no event shall such award or increase be retroactive for more than one year from the date of application, or the date of administrative determination of entitlement, whichever is earlier.

FORFEITURE FOR TREASON

Any person shown by evidence satisfactory to the VA to be guilty of mutiny, treason, sabotage, or rendering assistance to an enemy of the United States or its allies shall forfeit all accrued or future gratuitous benefits under laws administered by the VA.

The VA, in its discretion, may apportion and pay any part of benefits forfeited under the preceding paragraph to the dependents of the person forfeiting such benefits. No dependent of any person shall receive benefits by reason of this subsection in excess of the amount to which the dependent would be entitled if such person were dead.

In the case of any forfeiture under this chapter, there shall be no authority after September 1, 1959 to:

- Make an apportionment award pursuant to the preceding paragraph; or

- Make an award to any person of gratuitous benefits based on any period of military, naval, or air service commencing before the date of commission of the offense.

FORFEITURE FOR SUBVERSIVE ACTIVITIES

Any individual who is convicted after September 1, 1959, of any offense listed below shall, from and after the date of commission of such offense, have no right to gratuitous benefits (including the right to burial in a national cemetery) under laws administered by the VA based on periods of military, naval, or air service commencing before the date of commission of such offense, and no other person shall be entitled to such benefits on account of such individual. After receipt of notice of the return of an indictment for such an offense, the VA shall suspend payment of such gratuitous benefits pending disposition of the criminal proceedings. If any individual whose rights to benefits has been terminated pursuant to this section, is granted a pardon of the offense by the President of the United States, the right to such benefits shall be restored as of the date of such pardon.

The offenses referred to in the previous paragraph are:
- Sections 894, 904 and 906 of Title 10 (articles 94, 104, and 106 of the Uniform Code of Military Justice);

- Sections 792, 793, 794, 798, 2381, 2382, 2383, 2384, 2385, 2387, 2388, 2389, 2390, and chapter 105 of Title 18;

- Sections 222, 223, 224, 225 and 226 of the Atomic Energy Act of 1954 (42 U.S.C. 2272, 2273, 2274, 2275, and 2276);

- Section 4 of the Internal Security Act of 1950 (50 U.S.C. 783).

The Secretary of Defense, the Secretary of Transportation, or the Attorney General, as appropriate, shall notify the VA in each case in which an individual is convicted of an offense mentioned in this chapter.

INDEX

A

B

C

D

E

F

G

H

I

K

L

M

U

V

W

Y

Would You Like Additional Copies Of
What Every Veteran Should Know

Simply tear out this form, and:

Phone or Fax Orders: 309-757-7760

Mail To: VETERANS INFORMATION SERVICE
P.O. Box 111
East Moline, IL 61244-0111

ORDER ONLINE AT: www.vetsinfoservice.com

☐   Yes! Send me _____ copies of _"What Every Veteran Should Know"_, at
    $23.00 each (shipping & handling included). I request the _____
    (specify: <u>current already released 2011,</u> or <u>pre-reserve 2012</u>) edition.
    New annual books are published every March 1st.

☐   Yes! I would like to subscribe to _"What Every Veteran Should Know"_
    monthly supplement (an 8-page newsletter which keeps your book up-
    to-date), and receive _____ copies of all 12 monthly issues (1 year)
    for $32.00 per subscription (shipping & handling included).

☐   Yes! I want to save money, and receive both the book and the monthly
    supplement. I would like _____ sets, at $50 per set (shipping &
    handling included).

_____

Name

_____

Address

_____

City / State / Zip Code

_____

Telephone Number   E-mail Address

_____

Amount Enclosed   Daytime Phone # (including area code)

Method of Payment:

☐   Check   ☐   Visa   ☐   MasterCard   ☐   Money Order

_____

Credit Card #   Expiration Date (Month/Year)

_____

Signature

Thank you for your order!
If you have any questions, feel free to contact us at
(309) 757-7760
www.vetsinfoservice.com - Email: help@vetsinfoservice.com

Would You Like Additional Copies Of
What Every Veteran Should Know

Simply tear out this form, and:

Phone or Fax Orders: 309-757-7760

Mail To: VETERANS INFORMATION SERVICE
P.O. Box 111
East Moline, IL 61244-0111

ORDER ONLINE AT: www.vetsinfoservice.com

☐ Yes! Send me _____ copies of "*What Every Veteran Should Know*", at $23.00 each (shipping & handling included). I request the _____ (specify: <u>current already released 2011,</u> or <u>pre-reserve 2012</u>) edition. New annual books are published every March 1st.

☐ Yes! I would like to subscribe to "*What Every Veteran Should Know*" monthly supplement (an 8-page newsletter which keeps your book up-to-date), and receive _____ copies of all 12 monthly issues (1 year) for $32.00 per subscription (shipping & handling included).

☐ Yes! I want to save money, and receive both the book and the monthly supplement. I would like _____ sets, at $50 per set (shipping & handling included).

Name
_____

Address
_____

City / State / Zip Code
_____

Telephone Number   E-mail Address
_____

Amount Enclosed   Daytime Phone # (including area code)

Method of Payment:

☐ Check   ☐ Visa   ☐ MasterCard   ☐ Money Order

Credit Card #   Expiration Date (Month/Year)

Signature

Thank you for your order!
If you have any questions, feel free to contact us at
(309) 757-7760
www.vetsinfoservice.com - Email: help@vetsinfoservice.com

Would You Like Additional Copies Of
What Every Veteran Should Know

Simply tear out this form, and:

Phone or Fax Orders: 309-757-7760

Mail To: VETERANS INFORMATION SERVICE
P.O. Box 111
East Moline, IL 61244-0111

ORDER ONLINE AT: www.vetsinfoservice.com

☐ Yes! Send me _____ copies of "*What Every Veteran Should Know*", at $23.00 each (shipping & handling included). I request the _____ (specify: <u>current already released 2011,</u> or <u>pre-reserve 2012</u>) edition. New annual books are published every March 1st.

☐ Yes! I would like to subscribe to "*What Every Veteran Should Know*" monthly supplement (an 8-page newsletter which keeps your book up-to-date), and receive _____ copies of all 12 monthly issues (1 year) for $32.00 per subscription (shipping & handling included).

☐ Yes! I want to save money, and receive both the book and the monthly supplement. I would like _____ sets, at $50 per set (shipping & handling included).

_____

Name

_____

Address

_____

City / State / Zip Code

_____

Telephone Number   E-mail Address

_____

Amount Enclosed   Daytime Phone # (including area code)

Method of Payment:

☐ Check   ☐ Visa   ☐ MasterCard   ☐ Money Order

_____

Credit Card #   Expiration Date (Month/Year)

_____

Signature

Thank you for your order!
If you have any questions, feel free to contact us at
(309) 757-7760
www.vetsinfoservice.com - Email: help@vetsinfoservice.com